INTERNATIONAL LAW

SIXTH EDITION

By

REBECCA M.M. WALLACE, M.A., LL.B., Ph.D.

Director of U.H.I. Centre for Rural Childhood, Perth

and

OLGA MARTIN-ORTEGA, Ph.D.

Senior Research Fellow, Centre on Human Rights in Conflict, University of East London, London

SWEET & MAXWELL

THOMSON REUTERS

First Edition 1986
Second Impression 1990
Second Edition 1992
Second Impression 1994
Third Impression 1995
Third Edition 1997
Second Impression 1998
Fourth Edition 2002
Fifth Edition 2005
Sixth Edition 2009

Published in 2009 by
Thomson Reuters (Legal) Limited
(Registered in England & Wales, Company No 1679046.
Registered office and address for service: 100 Avenue Road, London, NW3 3PF)
trading as Sweet and Maxwell.
For further information on our products and services, visit
http://www.sweetandmaxwell.co.uk

Typeset by J&L Composition, Scarborough, North Yorkshire
Printed and bound in Great Britain by Athenaeum Press Ltd.

*A CIP catalogue record
for this book is available
from the British Library*

ISBN 978 1847036315

Thomson Reuters and the Thomson Reuters logo are
trademarks of Thomson Reuters.
Sweet and Maxwell is a registered trademark of
Thomson Reuters (Legal) Limited.
Crown Copyright material is reproduced with the permission of
the Controller of the HMSO and the Queen's printer for Scotland.

INTERNATIONAL LAW

Books are to be returned on or before
the last date below.

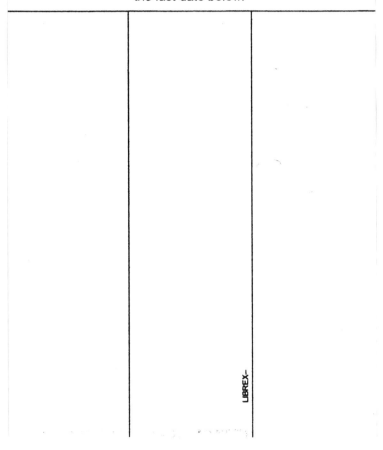

LIBREX—

To John P. Grant, with gratitude for igniting my interest in international law and his constant encouragement.

To the Memory of Pablo

FOREWORD

I am very happy, once again to write this Foreword for this, the sixth, edition of Rebecca Wallace's International Law, as I admire Rebecca, the name (we are not related) and the book. Olga Martin-Ortega has now joined Rebecca as co-author, a testament to the continued expansion of the scope of international law. As the authors point out in their Preface, the book has more than one use: it is a "narrative companion", in their words, to the many casebooks and specialized treatises now available; it is of course a general introductory text dealing with the basics of the rapidly expanding system, and, I would add, that it is a useful first place for a practitioner to come to for a quick orientation. I especially commend the authors for keeping the text so very up to date.

Writing as a professor, I give it very high marks as a "narrative companion" to any public international law casebook, even one with ample notes and text. I have used prior editions in that way. Students want and need such a companion. It is compact and its coverage complete. For professors, this is a boon; thus, in class they can work out the problems they wish, emphasize with cases the legal method they want, even the Socratic, and avoid the didactic lecturing on topics such as nature and sources of law which tends to leave many students cold.

I have also on occasion recommended the earlier editions to students who are not, *horrible dictu*, taking international law at all, but who wish a synoptic view of the field.

For the North American student or other reader, this book appears to have almost as much American material as British, citing U.S. cases, sources such as International Legal Materials and American (and Canadian) subjects. Thus, the discussion of such American doctrines as the Act of State, and the functioning of treaties, and executive agreements, in the American system is admirable.

The continued use of force, the controversies over the "war on terror", the hopes and difficulties surrounding the International Criminal Court, underline, if that is necessary, the abiding importance of law in the international system. As do the deep challenges of climate change, the rights of the child, a matter of particular salience to Rebecca Wallace, and so many other issues. The general reader may therefore find the book especially valuable and interesting. And in Rebecca's words to an earlier edition of the book, it is written "clearly and simply". The book also continues to serve the practitioner who wants an introduction in a nutshell to precise subjects of interest to him or her.

I welcome this sixth edition with enthusiasm.

June 4, 2009

Don Wallace Jr, Chairman,
International Law Institute; Professor of Law,
Georgetown University Law Center;
Of counsel, Morgan, Lewis and Bockius, Washington D.C.

PREFACE

Four years have lapsed since the publication of the fifth edition and throughout that period, international law has continued to expand. During these years the debate on torture, its definition and "rendition" has been constantly under the international spotlight, the controversy over Iraq and Afghanistan has continued, the so-called "war on terrorism" has been conducted and the spectre of Guantanamo Bay has continued to cast its shadow. The International Criminal Court is up and functioning and, in 2009, ventured into previously uncharted territory by issuing a warrant for the arrest of a serving Head of State, whereas Spain has sought to exercise universal jurisdiction on a number of occasions. This in turn underscores the tension between developing human rights law and traditional principles of immunity. Environmental issues, notably climate change, feature on the international agenda, as does the eradication of violence against women and the girl child, and poverty. These are only some of the issues which the international community seeks to grapple with in the context of globalisation and the global economic recession. There remains a continued need for the international legal system to be rooted in legal principle and for the international rule of law or the concept of legality to remain the linchpin on which the international legal system is founded. The increase in the scope and diversity of international law is reflected in the wide range of university programmes on offer which boast the adjective international. These include *inter alia* international trade law, international criminal law, international social justice, international human rights, international economic law, international banking, international arbitration and international dispute settlement. The list is seemingly endless. However, this growth of the international subject list makes it all the more imperative that students have a good grounding in the basic principles of international law.

On this basis the authors have made a determined effort throughout to provide a clear and comprehensive exposition of what is required for an understanding of the international legal process. This text remains a "taster", a reader, a narrative companion to the growing number of Cases and Material texts as well as the more specialised treatises.

The production of a book lies not just with the authors and accordingly, a number of "behind the scenes" persons must be thanked: Anne Holliday, Fraser Janeczko, and Karen Wylie for research assistance as well as their copious checking of references and proofs. However, any errors remain the responsibility of the authors.

The continued support and encouragement of Nicola Thurlow at Sweet and Maxwell, Thomson Reuters, is much appreciated.

The law is essentially that as of January 31, 2009.

Rebecca M.M. Wallace
Olga Martin-Ortega

April 2009

CONTENTS

ABBREVIATIONS

A.C.	Appeal Cases (U.K.) 1891–
A.D.	Appellate Division, New York Supreme Court
A.D. 2d	Appellate Division Reports, New York Supreme Court, Second Series
A.J.L.L.	American Journal of International Law
All E.R.	All England Reports, 1935–
A.S.I.L.	American Society of International Law
A.U.	African Union. (Replacing the Organisation of African States, see below)
B.F.S.P.	British and Foreign State Papers, 1812–
Burr.	Burrow's Reports (King's Bench, U.K.), 1757–71
B.Y.I.L.	British Yearbook of International Law
Cd., Cmnd., Cmnd.	U.K. Command Papers 1900–18, 1919–56, 1956–, respectively
Ch.	Chancery Reports (U.K.), 1891–
C.M.L.R.	Common Market Law Reports
Cranch.	United States Supreme Court Reports, 1801–15
C.W.I.L.J.	Californian Western International Law Journal
D.P.P.	Director of Public Prosecution
E.C.H.R.	European Court of Human Rights
E.C.J.	European Court of Justice
E.C.R.	European Court Reports, 1954–
E.E.Z.	Exclusive Economic Zone
E.H.R.R.	European Human Rights Reports
E.J.I.L.	European Journal of International Law
E.R.	English Reports
F (2d)	Federal Reporter, Second Series (US), 1924–
F (J)	Fraser, Justiciary Cases (Scotland), 1898–1906
F Supp	Federal Supplement (US), 1932–

G.A.	General Assembly (United Nations)
G.A.O.R.	General Assembly Official Records
Hague Recueil	Recueil des cours de l'Academie de droit international
Hudson	International Legislation
Hudson World Court Reports	(4 Vols, 1934–43)
I.C.C.	International Criminal Court
I.C.J.	International Court of Justice
I.C.J. Rep.	International Court of Justice Reports, 1947–
I.C.L.Q.	International and Comparative Law Quarterly
I.C.T.R.	International Criminal Tribunal for the Prosecution of Persons Responsible for Genocide and Other Serious Violations of International Humanitarian Law Committed in the Territory of Rwanda and Rwandan citizens reponsible for genocide and other such violations committed in the territory of neighbouring States, between January 1, 1994 and December 31, 1994
I.C.T.Y.	International Tribunal for the Prosecution of Persons Reponsible for Serious Violations of Humanitarian Law Committed in the Territory of the Former Yugoslavia since 1991
I.J.R.I.	International Journal of Refugee Law
I.L.C.	International Law Commission
I.L.M.	International Legal Materials, 1962–
I.L.R.	International Law Reports
I.M.F.	International Monetary Fund
I.T.L.O.S.	International Tribunal for the Law of the Sea
J.L.S.S.	Journal of the Law Society of Scotland
K.B.	King's Bench (U.K.), 1901–52
L.N.O.J.	League of Nations Official Journal
L.N.T.S.	League of Nations Treaty Series, 1920–45
L.Q. Rev.	Law Quarterly Review, 1885–
Moore Int. Arb.	International Arbitration, 5 Vols, 1898
N.A.T.O.	North Atlantic Treaty Organisation
N.E.	North Eastern Reporter, 1885–1936
N.Y.S.	New York Supplement Reporter, 1888
N.Y.S. 2d	New York Supplement, Second Series, 1937–

O.A.S.	Organisation of American States
O.A.U.	Organisation of African States. (Now known as the African Union, see above)
O.J.	Official Journal of the European Communities
Oppenheim	L. Oppenheim, International Law, Vols 1 and 2
P.	Court of Probate
P.C.	Privy Council
P.C.A.	Permanent Court of Arbitration
P.C.I.J.	Permanent Court of International Justice
P.C.I.J. Rep., ser. A.	Permanent Court of International Justice, Judgments and Orders, 1922–30
P.C.I.J. Rep., ser. A/B	Advisory Opinions, Judgements and Orders, 1931–40
P.C.I.J. Rep., ser. B	Advisory Opinions, 1922–30
P.D.	Probate Division Reports (U.K.), 1875–90
Pet.	Peter's United States Supreme Court Reports, 1828–42
Q.B.	Queen's Bench Reports (U.K.), 1891–1901, 1952–
Q.B.D.	Queen's Bench Division Reports (U.K.), 1875–80
R.I.A.A.	Reports of International Arbitral Awards, 1948–
S.C.	Security Council
S.C.O.R.	Security Council Official Records
S.C.R.	Supreme Court Reports (Canada), 1876–
S.L.T.	Scots Law Times
T.I.A.S.	Treaties and Other International Acts Series (US), 1950–30
T.L.R.	Times Law Reports (U.K.), 1841–1952
U.K.T.S.	United Kingdom Treaty Series
U.N.	United Nations
U.N.C.C.	United Nations Compensation Committee
U.N.H.C.R.	United Nations High Commission for Refugees
U.N.T.S.	United Nations Treaty Series, 1946–
U.S.	United States Supreme Court Reports, 1875–
U.S.C.	United States Code
U.S. Dept. State Bull.	United States Department of State Bulletin
U.S.T.	United States Treaties
U.S.T.S.	United States Treaty Series
Ves.	Vesey Juniors Chancery Reports (UK), 1789–1816

Whiteman	Digest of International Law, 14 Vols, 1936–73
W.H.O.	World Health Organisation
W.L.R.	Weekly Law Reports (UK), 1953–
W.T.O.	World Trade Organisation
Y.B.I.L.C.	Yearbook of the International Law Commission

TABLE OF CASES

TABLE OF PRINCIPAL
INTERNATIONAL CONVENTIONS

TABLE OF STATUTES

TABLE OF OTHER DOCUMENTS

1. INTRODUCTION

The focus of this text is international law, that is public international law. Public international law must be distinguished from private international law, or to use the correct term, conflict of laws. It also should be distinguished from foreign relations law.[1] The term international law as used throughout the text refers therefore to public international law.

---

[1] Private international law (conflict of laws) is a system of law, which is part of a State's domestic law and which is utilised to determine how conflicts of laws and jurisdiction are to be resolved. Foreign relations law "consists of rules of public international law which are binding upon [a State], and such parts of [a State's] law as are concerned with the means by which effect is given to the rules of public international law or which involve matters of concern to [a State] in the conduct of its relation with foreign States and governments or their nationals." (Restatement of the Law Third, The American Law Institute). The Foreign Relations Law of the United States, Vol.1, 1–488, May 14, 1986. Foreign relations law of the United States encompasses both international law, which embodies the rules that determine the rights and obligations of states and international organisations, and that part of the domestic law of the United States that involves matters of significant concern to the foreign relations of the United States.

DEFINITION

Contemporary international law[2] refers to those rules and norms that regulate the conduct of States and other entities which at any time are recognised as being endowed with international personality,[3] e.g. international organisations and, to a certain extent, individuals, in their relations with each other. Such a definition acknowledges the "youthfulness" of the international legal system and recognises actors other than States as participants on the international stage. States nevertheless remain the primary subjects of international law, but they are no longer its only subjects. International law was initially concerned exclusively with regulating interstate relations and then only in respect of diplomatic relations and the conduct of war. This is no longer true.

The subjects of international law have increased and its content has expanded. Major problems of international concern demand collective State action, this being more resource effective than individual State action. One consequence of collective action was a proliferation in the number of international organisations particularly in the post-second world war years since 1945.

Modern technology has brought States and their peoples into closer and more frequent contact with each other and, accordingly rules have had to evolve so that such contact is regulated. The subject matter of international law has also expanded, and the international legal system encompasses within its ambit subject matter which traditionally was regarded as being exclusively within a State's domestic jurisdiction, e.g. treatment of one's own nationals and the use of one's territory. This has had repercussions for individuals. Individuals are now recognised as possessing some, albeit limited, international personality. It has also led to some tension as State sovereignty has been eroded in favour of greater recognition of human rights.

The traditional definition of international law, namely a body of rules governing the relations of independent States in times of peace and war, is too rigid and outmoded. International law has had to be and must continue to be sufficiently flexible to accommodate developments in the international legal system such as those which took place in the twentieth century and which are continuing to be witnessed in the twenty-first. The international legal system must reflect the contemporary international commu-

---

[2] The term was first coined by Jeremy Bentham in *Introduction to the Principles and Morals and Legislation* (1789) but is something of a misnomer, as statehood and nationhood are not necessarily synonymous.

[3] International personality is dealt with in Ch.4.

nity. A more appropriate contemporary definition of international law is that it constitutes that body of rules which regulates the relations of States and also the relations of those other entities which are recognised as possessing international personality or at least a measure of international personality at any given time.

NATURE AND CHARACTERISTICS OF INTERNATIONAL LAW

Is international law, law?

This is not a question which the authors intend to explore. Any analysis as to whether international law is law presupposes a definition of law, and is one more aptly suited for consideration within a jurisprudence class than an international law class. Here, it is sufficient to say that international law is law. States acknowledge it as such. Some States make explicit reference to international law in their constitutions. It is also evident that States like to be seen acting in accordance with international law and legal advisers are employed to formulate, present and defend a State's position in international law. Others recognise international law but deny its effectiveness. However what many of those who are dismissive of international law fail to appreciate is that *their* expectations of international law may be unrealistic. Law cannot coerce States in matters which are primarily political. International law cannot of itself, and by itself, dictate the policies of States.

If force is used contrary to international law, international law is criticised for failing to maintain international peace yet international law cannot prevent its own violation any more than a municipal criminal law can prevent crimes being committed, or contract law can prevent contracts being broken. The violation of law does not in itself negate a legal system's law hallmark. Law is not a solution in itself, but is rather a means of handling a particular situation. The international legal system does not operate in a vacuum any more than any other legal system. International law is concerned with promoting international cooperation and achieving coexistence among States but its success depends on political will.

International law breaks down, that is undeniable, however the fault lies not with international law itself, but with those who operate within the international legal system. Of course international law receives a bad press, especially when it does break down. This is because invariably the issues involved are internationally, politically sensitive and therefore newsworthy. International law, however, functions very effectively on a day-to-day level. Today, pressing the "on" switch of the television allows events to be viewed "live" regardless of time and location. Communications such as postal, electronic and telecommunications allow people to converse and international travel is an everyday occurrence. All are taken for granted, but are only possible through the efficient functioning of international law. Nevertheless such "low-key" operations of international law are not newsworthy!

What are the characteristics of international law?

International law is not imposed on States—there is no international legislature. The international legal system is decentralised and founded essentially on consensus. International law is made primarily by one of two ways: through the practice of States (customary international law) and through agreements entered into by States (treaties).[4] International rules, once they are established, have an imperative character and cannot be unilaterally modified at will by States. The absence of strong enforcement machinery is highlighted by sceptics as a weakness of international law. Admittedly there is no international police force, nor is there an international court with compulsory jurisdiction to which States are required to submit. However, the creation of the Permanent International Criminal Court, as well as the creation of other judicial bodies and quasi-judicial bodies for the peaceful settlement of disputes, highlights an increasing commitment to the rule of law. This is further reflected in the increasing case load of the International Court of Justice (I.C.J.) to which States can refer their disputes for settlement. Such referral is, of course, not compulsory and States are not required to submit to the Court's jurisdiction, States must *agree* to submit to the Court's jurisdiction.

International law is not however ineffective. When international law is breached, international responsibility may be incurred. Sanctions are permissible in certain circumsances and these may be adopted and affect an "offending" State's conduct. If international law is violated, there are a number of self-help measures that the victim State may adopt, e.g. a treaty may be suspended or terminated, or the assets of an "offending" State may be frozen. The United Nations Security Council may authorise economic sanctions while the use of force may be authorised in specifically defined circumstances. Public opinion is also an effective sanction. States want to be seen to be adhering to international law: why otherwise do they go to considerable efforts to justify their particular position in international law?

---

[4] See Ch.2, "Sources".

The role of reciprocity in ensuring the observance of international law should not be minimised. It is in a State's self-interest to respect, for example, the territorial sovereignty of another State as that respect will be mutually reciprocated. The international legal system is intrinsically different from municipal law and to expect the international legal system to conform to the expectations of a domestic legal system is to invite disappointment. The principal participants of the international legal system, i.e. States, are equally sovereign.[5] The international community is composed not of a homogeneous grouping of States, but rather a heterogeneous group of some 192 States, which differ politically, economically, culturally and ideologically.

States need to coexist. This need led to the conception and birth of international law. International law was designed so as to promote international peace and security. A system which sought to characterise one State as "guilty" and another as "innocent" would not facilitate the realisation of international peace. International law must, because of its primary players and the environment in which it operates, seek to be conciliatory rather than adversarial.

The international legal system is a young legal system. It is constantly evolving and developing to accommodate contemporary needs and demands. It is not simply lawyers' black letter law, and the role of politics is an influential one.

THE DEVELOPMENT OF INTERNATIONAL LAW

International law as a system is of relatively recent origin.[6] Modern international law stems from the rise of the secular sovereign State in western Europe. As in any community, law was required to regulate the relations of States with each other. The rules of war and those on diplomatic immunity were the earliest expression of international law. The Age of Discovery in the sixteenth and seventeenth centuries necessitated the evolution of rules governing the acquisition of territory. At the same time, the principle of the freedom of the seas was articulated. International law grew out of necessity, the need for States to coexist.

International law sets the parameters of State action; these parameters established national competence within which States enjoyed freedom of action. International law continued to expand

---

[5] This is a legal fiction, as obviously some States carry more political weight than others in the international community.

[6] The embryo of international concepts was apparent within Greek City States, e.g. it was recognised that citizens of States in other territories had rights. There was, however, no concept of an international community as such.

as international engagement increased and by the nineteenth century had become, geographically at least, a universal system. It remained, however, rooted in western European traditions and values and its concept and content reflected this western European bias.

The twentieth century witnessed major changes with commensurate repercussions for the international legal system. The sovereign independent State was challenged; global war brought devastation twice and colonial territories attained independence. The twentieth century saw a greater emphasis on international cooperation, with States working together rather than individually. Matters once considered exclusively within domestic jurisdiction became susceptible to international review and regulation and the use of force has been limited except in strictly prescribed circumstances.

International law in the twenty-first century is no longer the preserve of some 50 States, but rather encompasses 192 States; nor is international law an exclusive "Western club".

International law now operates against the changing backcloth of globalisation. It has, for instance, to address the issue of non-State actors who make demands and of whom demands are made, e.g. transnational corporations and their liability for their alleged violation of human rights.

The existence of international law *per se* is not challenged, but the substantive content of its expression has been challenged and continues to be so. Human rights and the protection of the individual have assumed a high profile on the international agenda, as has sustainable development, with a particular emphasis on environmental issues such as climate change and biodiversity. The European bias of international law has been significantly reduced. Other political ideologies are now heard within the international fora. Modern technology has not only brought States into more frequent contact with each other, but has created new areas for international regulation, e.g. outer space, the deep seabed and the internet. International law has had to meet new challenges—challenges which demand an international response either at governmental level and/or by way of international regulation, as individual State action proves inadequate and deficient.

The twentieth century witnessed an unparalleled expansion of international law. Evidence points to that expansion continuing in the twenty-first century. The subject matter of this text is the contemporary international legal system.

2. SOURCES

Rules and norms of any legal system derive authority from their source.[1] The "sources" articulate what the law is and where it can be found. In a developed municipal legal system, sources may be readily identifiable in the form, for example, of Parliamentary legislation and judicial decisions. However, on the international plane there is neither an international legislature passing international legislation, nor is there an international Court to which all members of the international community are required to submit. Furthermore, the international legal system, unlike many municipal legal systems, does not possess a written constitution. There is no international constitution identifying the principal organs of government, investing them with authority, or defining the scope of their power and the procedures by which such power may be exercised. In the absence of such "law-giving" sources, how is the lawfulness of alleged rules of international law assessed?

Article 38 of the Statute of the International Court of Justice has provided an answer. This is a pragmatic response as art.38 does not mention "sources", but is rather a direction to the

---

[1] "Sources" may be interpreted in a variety of ways, e.g. the underlying reason why laws develop, but here its meaning is confined to that given in the text.

International Court of Justice on how disputes which come before it should be approached. Article 38 of the Statute provides:

> "1) The Court, whose function is to decide in accordance with international law such disputes as are submitted to it, shall apply:
>
> (a) international conventions, whether general or particular, establishing rules expressly recognized by the contesting states;
> (b) international custom, as evidence of a general practice accepted as law;
> (c) the general principles of law recognized by civilized nations;
> (d) subject to the provisions of Article 59, judicial decisions and the teachings of the most highly qualified publicists of the various nations, as subsidiary means for the determination of rules of law."

Sources of international law have traditionally been characterised as formal or material. Formal sources constitute what the law is, whereas material sources identify where the law is to be found. Hence, art.38 (1)(a)–(c) (treaties, custom and general principles) are formal sources, whereas art.38 (1)(d) (judicial decisions and juristic teachings) are material sources.

Article 38 (2) "recognizes the power of the Court to decide a case *ex aequo et bono*, if the parties agree thereto." Invoking this provision, States may request the Court to decide a case not just on the application of strict rules of law but by reference to such principles as fairness and equality.

Article 38, although primarily a direction to the International Court of Justice on how disputes coming before it should be tackled, is regarded as an authoritative statement on the sources of international law. Article 38 does not stipulate that it is establishing a hierarchy, but nonetheless it is self-evident that art.38 is establishing a hierarchy of procedure for the application of international law in the settlement of international disputes. Initially, existing relevant treaty provisions subsisting between the parties to the dispute must be applied. In the absence of a treaty provision, a custom, which is accepted as legally binding, is to be applied. If neither a treaty provision nor a custom can be identified then "general principles as recognized by civilized nations" may be invoked. In the absence of the foregoing, judicial decisions and judicial writings may be utilised as a means of determining the rules of international law.

Each "source" of law identified in art.38 will be considered. Custom, although cited second, historically preceded treaties and will be considered initially.

CUSTOM

In any society, rules of "acceptable" behaviour develop at an early stage and the international community was no exception. States in their relations with each other did, for whatever motives, what they wanted to do rather than what they agreed to do. However, with increasing contact between States, certain norms of behaviour crystallised into rules of customary international law. Custom, through the absence of an international executive and legislature, has exercised an influential role in the formation of international law. In a mature legal system, custom is considered cumbersome and relatively unimportant. In the international field custom, until at least recently, has been a dynamic source of law and its contribution is still witnessed in many treaties, as these mirror previously established rules of international customary law.

Definition of custom

What is meant by custom? Custom in international law is a practice followed by those concerned because they feel legally obliged to behave in such a way. Custom must be distinguished from mere usage, such as behaviour which may be done out of courtesy, friendship or convenience rather than out of legal obligation or a feeling that non-compliance would produce legal consequences, for example sanctions imposed by other members of the international community.

How is custom differentiated from behaviour that is motivated by reasons other than legal obligation? A rule of customary international law derives its law hallmark through the possession of two elements: (i) a material and; (ii) a psychological element.

The material element refers to the behaviour and practice of States, whereas the psychological element is the subjective conviction held by States that the behaviour in question is compulsory and not discretionary.

Accordingly, any alleged rule of customary international law must be assessed as to its: (i) material and; (ii) psychological elements.

Material element

The material element refers to the behaviour of States, but does that behaviour itself have to satisfy certain criteria? Has it to be practised for a certain length of time? Must it be indulged in frequently or is one act sufficient? Must the behaviour be consistently practised or may there be some divergences from the norm? Must the behaviour be universally practised by all States?

Finally, what, for the purposes of customary international law, constitutes State practice?

Duration of practice. There is no set time limit and no demand that the practice should be engaged in since "time immemorial". The fact that a practice has been engaged in only for a brief period of time will not in itself be a bar to the formation of a customary rule, provided that the other requirements of custom are met. The relative unimportance of time, if other criteria are satisfied, was highlighted by the International Court of Justice in the *North Sea Continental Shelf* cases,[2] in which it stated:

> "... Although the passage of only a short period of time is not necessarily, or of itself, a bar to the formation of a new rule of customary international law ... an indispensable requirement would be that within the period in question, short though it might be, State practice ... should have been both extensive and virtually uniform in the sense of the provision invoked—and should moreover have occurred in such a way as to show a general recognition that a rule of law or legal obligation is involved."[3]

The length of time required to establish a rule of customary international law will depend upon other factors pertinent to the alleged rule. If, for example, the rule is dealing with subject matter in which there are no previously established rules, then the duration of the practice will require to be less than if there is an existing rule to be amended. Time has also become less important as international communication has improved. It is now much easier to assess a State's response to an alleged rule than it was previously. Time thus may be of little importance in assessing a State's behaviour, and its importance in any given case depends on other factors peculiar to the activity concerned and these will be examined below.

Extent of State practice. The International Court of Justice in the *Asylum* case[4] held that before State practice could be acknowledged as law, it had to be in accordance with a "constant and uniform usage" practised by the States in question.[5] Of course, although a particular pattern of behaviour may be engaged in fre-

---

[2] I.C.J. Rep. 1969 at 3.
[3] *ibid*. at 43.
[4] I.C.J. Rep. 1950 at 266.
[5] *ibid*. at 277.

quently, it does not follow that the conduct is being practised out of any legal obligation. Similarly, an activity engaged in, albeit infrequently, may be practised because of a legal compulsion to act in such a way. The importance of frequency of practice will depend upon the circumstances surrounding each alleged rule. For instance, a State which is able to cite two examples of State practice to support its contention that the practice is law, will be in a better position than the State which can cite no such examples. However, a more significant factor than frequency is the consistency of practice. In other words, do those States engaging in the practice in question behave in a like manner, thus demonstrating conformity?

The Court's judgment in the *Asylum* case is again instructive on this point. In that case, the Court maintained that there was too much variance and discrepancy in both the practice, and the views expressed, regarding diplomatic asylum for a rule of customary international law to have been established. Consequently, the Court concluded that it was impossible to find "any constant and uniform usage accepted as law".[6] The existence of diverging practice proved to be the stumbling block in that particular practice's evolution into law.

Inconsistency of practice *per se*, however, is not sufficient to negate the crystallisation of a rule into customary international law. Any inconsistency must be analysed and assessed in the light of factors such as subject matter, the identity of the States practising the inconsistency, the number of States involved and whether or not there are existing established rules with which the alleged rule conflicts. Inconsistency of practice is explored in greater depth below, when the question of how customary international law may be amended or modified is discussed.

How many States must be involved in a particular activity before the practice is accepted as law? Universal practice is fortunately not necessary. Article 38(1)(b) speaks not of universal practice, but of a general practice. A practice can be general even if it is not universally followed by all States nor is there any precise formula indicating how widespread a behaviour must be for it to cross the customary law threshold.

What is more important than the number of States involved is the attitude of those States whose interests are actually affected. It is the stance of such States which is relevant and which has to be considered, as emphasised by the International Court of Justice in the *North Sea Continental Shelf* cases:

---

[6] Above n.4 at 266.

> ". . . an indispensable requirement would be that within the
> period in question, . . . State practice, including that of States
> whose interests are specially affected, should have been both
> extensive and virtually uniform in the sense of the provision
> invoked . . ."[7]

Thus the number of States is less consequential than is the identity
of the States involved. Each alleged rule must therefore be examined and assessed in context. In every activity certain States carry
more weight than others—their interest is greater than that of
other States and their attitude to an alleged rule is of importance.
If an alleged rule is to attain legitimacy, a favourable response
from "leading" States is a prerequisite. Hence, for example,
Britain's contribution in the nineteenth century to the law of the
sea and the role of both the United States and the Soviet Union in
developing the law of outer space. In any given area, the participation of certain States is required more than others if an alleged
rule is to be transformed into customary international law.

Numbers are more important when the custom is a local,
regional one, involving fewer States than general customary law.
A regional custom is of a more contractual nature than a general
one and therefore is required to be positively acknowledged and
supported by all the States involved. Hence, the International
Court's emphasis in the *Asylum* case on a "constant and uniform
usage".

Can a State choose not to be bound by a rule of customary
international law? If a State opposes a rule of customary international law and expresses opposition to that rule from the time of
the rule's inception, then the State will not be bound by the said
rule. Opposition, however, must be demonstrated from the outset. Only then can the State concerned not incur liability. In the
Anglo-Norwegian Fisheries case, the Court held that if the particular rule in question were one of international law, it would be
"inapplicable as against Norway inasmuch as she has always
opposed any attempt to apply it to the Norwegian coast".[8]

Dissent which is expressed only after the rule has become
established is too late to prevent the State from being bound and,
likewise, early opposition by a State to a rule, if abandoned, loses
its effectiveness. Dissension, of course, only prevents a rule from
becoming binding on the dissenter and does not affect the rule's
application *vis-à-vis* other States.

---

[7] Above, n.2 at 4.
[8] I.C.J. Rep. 1951 116 at 131. Arguably the opportunities for States to opt out of
customary international law are fewer today than previously, given the increase
in the use of treaties as a medium of international regulation.

Why is dissent important? Expression of dissent is vital as in reality attaining a State's consent is not practical. State consent is difficult to prove and thus consent is inferred and silence, although it may stem from indifference, will be regarded as acquiescence and will serve to reinforce the particular practice as law.

A State which becomes a member of the international legal system after a practice has ripened into an established rule is bound by it, regardless of whether it agrees with it or not. Such a State may seek, though, to amend or modify the rule in question.

How may this occur? Initially, it can be said that it is easier for custom to develop if there are no pre-existing conflicting rules, for example, in the exploration of outer space, rules of behaviour quickly evolved because not only were there no pre-existing norms regulating behaviour, there were only two States, the United States and the Soviet Union, actively engaged in exploration. The position is different and more complicated if established rules of behaviour exist. The "new" rule's future will depend on the number indulging in the behaviour contrary to the established rule relative to the number protesting against the creation of the new rule.

It is not to be expected that in the practice of States the application of the rules in question should have been perfect, in the sense that States should have refrained, with complete consistency, from behaviour contrary to the established rule. The Court does not maintain that for a rule to be considered as custom, the corresponding practice must be in absolute rigorous conformity with the rule. In order to deduce the existence of customary rules, the Court deems it sufficient that the conduct of States should, in general, be consistent with such rules, and that instances of State conduct inconsistent with a given rule should generally have been treated as breaches of that rule, not as indications of the recognition of a new rule.[9]

This begs the question as to how customary international law may be amended or modified if conflicting behaviour acts as a hindrance to the crystallisation of a practice into law. Contradictory behaviour has the effect of throwing uncertainty on the apparently established rule, which in turn produces ambiguity regarding the law of the subject matter, a fact which was highlighted in the *Fisheries Jurisdiction (United Kingdom v Iceland) Merits*,[10] which came before the International Court of Justice in

---

[9] *Military and Paramilitary Activities In and Against Nicaragua (Nicaragua v The United States) (Merits)* I.C.J. Rep. 1986 14 at 98.
[10] I.C.J. Rep. 1974 at 3.

1974, when, in a Joint Separate Opinion, Judges Forster, Bengzon, Arechaga, Singh and Rudha expressed the view:

> "If the law relating to fisheries constituted a subject on which there were clear indications of what precisely is the rule of international law in existence, it may then have been possible to disregard altogether the legal significance of certain proposals which advocate changes or improvements in a system of law which is considered to be unjust or inadequate. But this is not the situation. There is at the moment great uncertainty as to the existing customary law on account of the conflicting and discordant practice of States. Once the uncertainty of such a practice is admitted, the impact of the aforesaid official pronouncements, declarations and proposals have an unsettling effect on the crystallisation of a still evolving customary law on the subject."[11]

It is also possible, as is reflected in the above Opinion, that while States may behave in contradiction to an established rule, the conflicting behaviour may itself be inconsistently expressed. In such circumstances change, if it is to come about, will take longer than if the States demonstrate a consensus on the content of the emerging new law. If support is wide and consistent, then the practice's acceptance as law will be relatively smooth and rapid. Similarly, if there is substantial opposition to the "new rule", the established accepted practice will remain as law. However, if the members of the international community are evenly divided in their support for the established law and the alleged new law, then a period of ambiguity will, as a consequence, follow. Indeed, there may be a time when two rules of customary law may exist side by side. International customary law can accommodate change, but how quickly that change will occur is dependent upon the response of States to the proposed amendment of the law. There may well be a period in the change process when what is established and what is emerging exist simultaneously. In such circumstances, however, there is a fine line between the ending of the old law and the beginning of the new one.

This has the advantage, particularly if States are agreed upon the change they want, of providing flexibility, but the disadvantage of creating uncertainty as to what the law is at any given time.

---

[11] *ibid.* at 48.

State practice. Finally, what, for the purposes of establishing customary international law, constitutes evidence of State practice? Treaties, diplomatic correspondence, statements by national legal advisers in domestic and international fora are among the indicators of State practice. This was endorsed by Ammoun J. in his Separate Opinion delivered in the *Barcelona Traction, Light and Power Company* case,[12] when he stated:

> "to return to State practice as manifested within international organisations and conferences, it cannot be denied, with regard to the resolutions which emerge therefrom, or better, with regard to the votes expressed therein in the name of States, that these amount to precedents contributing to the formation of custom."[13]

Notwithstanding these indicators, overt State practice continues to be important, as was emphasised by the International Court of Justice in *Continental Shelf (Libya v Malta)*[14] when the Court stated:

> "It is of course axiomatic that the material of customary international law is to be looked for primarily in the actual practice and *opinio juris* of States even though multilateral conventions may have an important role to play in defining and recording rules, deriving from custom or indeed in developing them."[15]

The International Court has also highlighted that when considering the existence of a general custom, it is necessary to determine that from the practice of States as a whole. In other words the fact the States parties to the case have a common view of what the law is, is not sufficient.[16] However it should be noted that in the *Maritime Delimitation and Territorial Questions between Qatar and Bahrain* case[17] it was accepted that the parties to the case agreed that art.15 of the 1982 Law of the Sea Convention was part of customary law. The Court then proceeded to conclude art.15 was of a customary character.

---

[12] (Second Phase) I.C.J. Rep. 1970 at 3.
[13] *ibid.* at 303. As to the role of Resolutions in providing evidence of *opinio juris*, see statements in the *Nicaragua (Merits)* case above, n.9.
[14] I.C.J. Rep. 1985 at p.13.
[15] *ibid.* at 29–30. See, also the view of D'Amato, *The Concept of Custom in International Law* (Cornell University Press, 1971), p.88.
[16] Above, n.9, para.184.
[17] I.C.J. Rep. 2001 at p.40.

A State's response to a particular resolution adopted within an international organisation may be dictated by the occasion and circumstances pertaining at the time and this should be borne in mind when invoking resolutions and the like as evidence of the development of practice into law.[18]

This was acknowledged by the International Court of Justice in the *Nicaragua (Merits)* case[19] where documentary evidence before the Court included statements by "high-ranking official political figures, sometimes indeed of the highest rank" which could be "of particular probative value when they acknowledge facts or conduct unfavourable to the State represented by the person who made them".[20] Nevertheless, the Court stated it was natural that such statements should be treated with "caution".[21]

Practice in itself is not sufficient to establish custom. An alleged rule of customary international law has to manifest not only a material element, but also a psychological element, otherwise known as *opinio juris*.

Opinio juris sive necessitatis

States in their relations with each other engage in behaviour other than that which is required of them legally. If certain rules are to evolve into law, it is necessary to distinguish rules which are regarded as legally obligatory from those which are discretionary. State behaviour on the international plane may be prompted by reasons of mere courtesy, convenience or tradition rather than by legal obligation. Similarly, humanitarian considerations are insufficient in themselves to generate legal rights and obligations and the International Court of Justice, as "a Court of law", is competent to take account of moral principles only in so far as these are given a sufficient expression in legal form.[22]

Opinio juris was introduced as a legal formula in an attempt to distinguish legal rules from mere social usage, and refers to the subjective belief allegedly maintained by States that a particular practice is legally required of them. A practice which is generally followed but which States feel they are free to disregard at any time cannot be characterised as law. In the words of the International Court of Justice:

---

[18] See, e.g. J. Brierly, *The Law of Nations*, (1963), p.4.
[19] Above n.9, p.4.
[20] *ibid.* at p.41.
[21] Above n.9, p.41.
[22] *South West Africa (Second Phase)* I.C.J. Rep. 1966 6 at 34.

"... not only must the acts concerned 'amount to a settled practice', but they must also be accompanied by the *opinio juris sive necessitatis*. Either the States taking such action or other States in a position to react to it must have behaved so that their conduct is evidence of a belief that this practice is rendered obligatory by the existence of a rule of law requiring it. The need for such a belief, i.e. the existence of a subjective element, is implicit in the very notion of the *opinio juris sive necessitatis*."[23]

The Court highlighted in the *Nicaragua* case that *opinio juris* may, albeit with due caution, be deduced from, *inter alia*, the attitude of the parties and States towards General Assembly Resolutions (and in the instant case particularly Resolution 2625 (XXV) entitled "Declaration on Principles of International Law concerning Friendly Relations and Co-operation among States in accordance with the Charter of the United Nations"). It was emphasised that the effect of consent to the text of such Resolutions cannot be understood as merely that of "reiteration or elucidation" of the treaty commitment undertaken in the Charter. On the contrary, it may be understood as an acceptance of the validity of the rule or set of rules declared by the Resolutions.[24]

The problem with *opinio juris* is one of proof. It is frequently difficult to determine when the transformation into law has taken place. How can a State's conviction be proved to exist? Essentially, what must be established is the State's acceptance, recognition or acquiescence as to the binding character of the rule in question. The onus of proof is on the State relying upon the custom (it is the party alleging the existence of custom which must demonstrate that the custom is so established that it is binding on the other party). Insufficient evidence of *opinio juris* is fatal to the formation of customary international law, as for example in the *Lotus* case[25] and the *North Sea Continental Shelf* cases.

---

[23] Above n.9 pp.108–109.
[24] *ibid.* pp.99–100. The Court took US support of the 6th International Conference of American States Condemning Aggression; ratification of the Montevideo Convention on the Rights and Duties of States 1933; and the Declaration on the Principles Governing the Mutual Relations of States participating in the Conference on the Security and Co-operation in Europe as further evidence of an expression of *opinio juris*. The Court's stance that *opinio juris* could be deduced from the acceptance by States of GA Resolutions has been criticised, see, e.g. D'Amato, "Trashing Customary International Law" (1987) 81 *A.J.I.L.* 101.
[25] P.C.I.J.Rep. ser.A, no.10 (1927).

In the *Lotus* case, although France identified previous instances where in practice the victim's flag State had refrained from criminal prosecution, France, in the Court's view, failed to demonstrate that States refrained from prosecuting because they had been conscious of a legal obligation requiring them to do so.

Similarly, in the *North Sea Continental Shelf* cases, the International Court of Justice maintained that, although the principle of equidistance was employed in the delimitation of the continental shelf between adjacent States, there was no evidence:

> "... that they so acted because they felt legally compelled to draw them in this way by reason of a rule of customary law obliging them to do so—especially considering that they might have been motivated by other factors".[26]

Opinio juris and state practice are complementary in the creation of customary international law.

How may customary international law accommodate change if *opinio juris* demands behaviour in accordance with the law? How may new rules evolve if activity contrary to the established rules is prohibited?

If too rigid a view were to be taken of *opinio juris* then obviously the law would become stunted and in time deficient. States, however, do act contrary to established rules and do so in the belief that the new behaviour, if not already law, is about to become law. What will determine the future of such behaviour—whether it becomes law or withers—is the response of other States. Their reaction determines whether or not the new practice gains the necessary *opinio juris*.

Finally, mention must be made of another category of custom known by the somewhat anomalous term of "instant custom". The term is anomalous, being as it is self-contradictory, but what it is used to describe certainly defies classification as traditional custom. It refers not to behaviour, which is constant, uniform and frequently engaged in, but rather to spontaneous activity practised by a great number of States responding to particular circumstances. Instant custom is relatively rare. Two examples of "instant customary law" are the doctrine of the continental shelf, precipitated by President Truman's Proclamation in 1945, and the unilateral seaward extension throughout the 1970s by coastal States (Exclusive Economic Zone). The doctrine of the continental shelf became established as customary international law on the

---

[26] Above n.2, pp.44–45.

basis of assertions (that is, claims of exclusive rights and the denial of access to others) and general acquiescence.

The Truman Proclamation, which was quickly followed by similar declarations from other States, was prompted by a need to fill a void in international law as to the rights and duties of States given advancing technology, namely the possibility of mining the continental shelf. Although mining of the continental shelf was a possibility, it was neither technologically nor economically feasible at the time. The Exclusive Economic Zone (EEZ) became established customary international law in the 1970s. Coastal States particularly concerned with controlling the exploitation and conservation of fishery resources, rather than wait for agreement in UNCLOS III,[27] increasingly took unilateral action and extended their sovereign rights beyond their territorial sea to a maximum limit of 200 miles.[28]

"Instant custom" may appear an unsatisfactory term, but the activity it describes, while not fitting into the mould of traditional custom, still falls under the umbrella of custom, rather than under any "new" source of law. "Instant custom" is a response to new situations demanding a speedy response by way of international regulation. However "instant custom" is an exception to the norm.

Custom to be recognised as customary international law demands the presence of two elements, the material and the psychological. Although art.38 of the Statute of the International Court of Justice calls upon the Court to apply international custom, as evidence of a general practice "accepted as law" it is more accurate to define international custom as evidenced by general practice "accepted as law". This is because custom is the source to be applied and that custom is evidenced by practice accompanied by the belief that the practice is accepted as law.[29] The role of custom as a source of international law has diminished not least because of the substantial increase in the number of States participating on the international plane and the extension of the subject matter of international law beyond the traditional realm of diplomatic relations and the rules of warfare. These changes in the international community have meant that custom is no longer regarded as the most appropriate mechanism for the regulation of international discourse and behaviour. This, reinforced by the

[27] Third United Nations Conference on the Law of the Sea.
[28] See 1982 Convention on the Law of the Sea, arts 55 and 56. The GA Resolution on the Granting of Independence to Colonial Territories and Peoples (GA Res.1514) led to a significant number of African States being accorded political independence—another example of instant custom?
[29] See R. Higgins, *Problems and Process, International law and how we use it*, at p.18.

desire of States to be fully aware of any obligations undertaken, has led to the increasing use of treaties as the preferred means for the regulation of international relations.

TREATIES

Article 38(a) does not mention the term "treaties", but refers to "any international Conventions, whether general or particular, establishing rules expressly recognised by the contesting States". The effect of this direction to the Court is, if an existing treaty provision pertains between the parties to the dispute before the Court, then if relevant, the treaty provision must be applied.

A treaty, although it may be identified as comparable in some degree to a Parliamentary Statute within municipal law, differs from the latter, in that it only applies to those States which have agreed to its terms, and normally a treaty does not have universal application. In other words opting out, which is not available to individuals under national law, is available to the members of the international community.

Treaties are only examined here in so far as they constitute a source of law.[30] Treaties, as art.38(a) infers, may be between two States (bipartite) or between several States (multipartite).[31]

A distinction is sometimes drawn between law-making treaties ("*traite-lois*") and "treaty contracts" ("*traite-contracts*"). The essence of the distinction lies in the fact "treaty contracts", being agreements between relatively few parties, can only create particular law between the signatories, whereas treaties to which there are many signatories create law *per se*. However, all treaties involve a contractual obligation for the parties concerned, and consequently, create law for all parties agreeing to the terms of the treaty. In other words, a bipartite[32] treaty does not create a lesser law than the law created by a multipartite treaty. Multipartite treaties may admittedly have a wider effect, and as such, may be regarded as law-making, in that not only do they have a greater number of signatories, but the provisions of such a treaty may become customary international law, as the Netherlands and Denmark attempted to argue, albeit unsuccessfully, in the *North Sea Continental Shelf* cases. Multipartite treaties, although they may never have the truly legislative effect of municipal legislation, have a quasi-legislative effect, which is at least *prima facie*

---

[30] The technicalities of treaty law are examined in Ch.10.

[31] Participation in a treaty is not confined exclusively to States, but States are the only entities which have *locus standi* before the I.C.J. in contentious cases.

[32] Although the terms "bipartite" and "multipartite" are strictly correct, the terms "bilateral" and "multilateral" are more commonly used.

denied to bipartite treaties. The International Court acknowledged in *Territorial Dispute (Libya v Chad)*[33] that a principle first enunciated in a treaty (art.31 of the Vienna Convention) had achieved the status of customary international law. Conversely, a multipartite or bipartite treaty may merely spell out what has been accepted as customary international law, and a provision contained repeatedly in bipartite treaties may provide evidence that a particular rule of customary international law exists. Alternatively, it may be argued the very fact that States insert the rule in a bipartite treaty is evidence that such a rule does not have the status of customary international law.

Treaties represent the most tangible and most reliable method of identifying what has been agreed between States. Treaties regulate a diverse and extensive subject-matter including *inter alia* drug control, space exploration, the establishment of organisations, extradition and safety regulations in the air and at sea; the rights of the child; the elimination of discrimination against women; and the establishment of an International Criminal Court.

Customary law and law made by treaty have equal authority as international law, but, if a treaty and a customary rule exist simultaneously on the issue in dispute, then the treaty provisions take precedence, as is illustrated by the *Wimbledon* case.[34] In that case, the Permanent Court of International Justice, while recognising under customary international law it was prohibited to allow the passage of armaments through the territory of a neutral State to the territory of a belligerent State, upheld art.380 of the Treaty of Versailles, which provided the Kiel Canal was to be "free and open to the vessels of commerce and of war of all nations at peace with Germany on terms of entire equality". In stopping a vessel flying the flag of a State with which she was at peace, Germany was, the Court maintained, in breach of her treaty obligations under the Treaty of Versailles.

Therefore, unless the parties have expressed otherwise, a rule established by agreement supersedes, for them, a previous conflicting rule of customary international law. Generally in the event of inconsistency, the latter, be it custom or treaty, prevails as between the same parties. However, parties to a treaty may agree to adhere to the treaty obligations even in the light of subsequent general custom. Nevertheless, though modification of custom by treaty is common, there are few instances of customary law developing in conflict with earlier agreements. In such cases, the

---

[33] 6 I.C.J. Rep. 1994.
[34] P.C.I.J. Rep. ser.A, No.1 (1923).

principle, the latter in time prevails, will be applied on the presumption that the parties to the treaty have implied their consent.[35] However, where there exists customary international law comprising rules identical to those of treaty law "there are no grounds for holding . . . that the latter supervenes the former, so that the customary international law has no existence of its own".[36] Hence, the Court in the *Nicaragua (Merits)* case conceded although it was precluded from considering whether the United States had infringed UN art.2(4)'s prohibition on the use of force,[37] it was still competent to consider whether the existing customary international law on the use of force had been violated.

A presumption exists though against the replacement of customary rules by treaty and *vice versa*. Treaties are not intended to derogate from customary law, and a treaty which seemingly modifies or alters established custom should be construed so as to best conform to, rather than derogate from, accepted principles of international law. That is, unless the treaty in question is clearly intended to alter the existing rules of custom. A treaty will not however prevail over prior customary law if the latter is *jus cogens*.[38]

Whatever their legislative effect, treaties, unlike municipal legislation, do not generally have universal application. Nonetheless, this statement must be qualified. There are two types of treaties, which because of their purpose do produce consequences, which non-signatories cannot ignore. Namely, (i) those establishing a special international regime and (ii) those establishing an international organisation.

In 1920, a Committee of Jurists was appointed by the League of Nations to determine whether Finland, as successor State to Russia, was bound by the 1856 Convention under which Russia had agreed with France and Great Britain to the non-fortification of the Aaland Islands.[39] The Committee concluded the treaty extended beyond the three Contracting Parties. The islands enjoyed "a special international status", and until the 1856 Convention was replaced, every State interested had a right to insist upon it being complied with, while "any State in possession of the Islands must conform to the obligations binding upon it". Treaties of this type are, however, very unusual.

---

[35] One such example was the acceptance as law of the 200-mile EEZ in conflict with the 1958 Geneva Conventions on the Law of the Sea.

[36] Above, n.9, p.95.

[37] By virtue of the US reservation under art.36(2) of the I.C.J. Statute.

[38] See below, p.45 and Ch.10.

[39] League of Nations Official Journal (1920), Sp.Supp.No.3, p.3.

Constitutive treaties establishing international institutions, for example the United Nations, have created organisations which have subsequently been held to possess varying degrees of international personality[40]—a personality which has enabled such entities to operate on the international stage and which has, in certain instances, been enforced against non-Member States, e.g. in the *Reparations* case.[41]

"GENERAL PRINCIPLES OF LAW AS RECOGNISED BY CIVILISED NATIONS"

International law as a legal system would be undermined if the International Court of Justice, because of an apparent absence of relevant legal rules, was unable to give a decision based on law (such a situation is referred to as *non liquet*). In a municipal legal system, such a situation would be tackled by the deducing of relevant rules from already existing rules, or from basic legal principles such as justice and equity. A *"non liquet"* situation is, or at least was, more likely to arise in international law[42] than in a developed, mature legal system. Accordingly, "general principles of law ..." was inserted to "plug the gaps" and to avoid an undermining of international law, which an inability to render judgment through an insufficiency of law would undoubtedly incur.[43]

General principles were those as understood by "civilised nations". "Civilised nations" has for obvious reasons been dropped.

What then is understood by general principles? It is not clear whether general principles refers to those of the international legal system or those of municipal legal systems. Such ambiguity is advantageous, as it imposes no restraint on the principles which may be applied.

Rather than dwell on the conceptual arguments that have raged over the definition of general principles, it is more advantageous here to identify instances of when general principles have been employed. What has happened is that legal principles have been drawn from the developed municipal legal systems.

---

[40] International personality is covered in Ch.4.
[41] *Reparation for Injuries Suffered in the Service of the United Nations, Advisory Opinion*, I.C.J. Rep. 1949 at 185.
[42] It should always be borne in mind that the Statute of the I.C.J. is the direct successor of the Charter of the Permanent Court of International Justice, and that in the 1920s international law was certainly a less developed system than it is today.
[43] See however the *Legality of the Threat or use of Nuclear Weapons case, Advisory Opinion* (1997) 35 ILM 809 and 1343.

This does not mean judges have to have expertise in every legal system of the world. Legal systems can be divided into families and, consequently, common elements may be identified within legal systems. The general principles are therefore those, which are common to the major legal systems of the world, for example the civilian legal system, the common-law system and a hybrid system, e.g. Scottish legal system.

Most of the parallels drawn from municipal law have related to procedural, administrative or jurisdictional situations. The principles applied by international tribunals and the International Court and its predecessor, have been those of a State's responsibility for the acts of its agents;[44] the principle of *estoppel* (personal bar);[45] no one must be a judge of his own case;[46] and the principle of reparation.[47] However, not all claims to be a general principle are recognised, e.g. *actio popularis*.[48]

Analogies with municipal legal systems have been utilised in recent years in the new areas of international law, e.g. commercial and administrative law. In the *Barcelona Traction* case,[49] the International Court of Justice emphasised:

> "If the Court were to decide the case in disregard of the relevant institutions of municipal law it would, without justification, invite serious legal difficulties. It would lose touch with reality, for there are no corresponding institutions of international law to which the Court could resort. . . . It is to rules generally accepted by municipal legal systems . . . and not to the municipal law of a particular State, that international law refers".[50]

No precise definition either to the extent or scope of general principles has been universally agreed. The importance of general principles, however they may be defined, is that recourse to them has prevented a case from being shelved on the grounds that international law as it exists is lacking, or is inadequate for dealing with, the particular issue raised.[51]

---

[44] *Fabiani* case 10 R.I.A.A. 83 (1986).
[45] *Temple* case I.C.J. Rep. 1962 at 6.
[46] *Mosul Boundary* case, P.C.I.J.Rep. ser.B, No.12 (1925) at 32.
[47] *Chorzow Factory (Indemnity) (Merits)*, P.C.I.J.Rep. ser.A, No.17 (1928) at 29.
[48] *South West Africa case (Second Phase)* I.C.J. Rep. 1966 p6, see also *Seaco v Iran* 919920 28 Iran – USCTR 198 at 209.
[49] Above, n.12.
[50] *ibid.* at 37.
[51] Possible general fundamental principles of international law are considered under "*jus cogens*" below, p35.

Whether a particular general principle is eligible for absorption by international law will depend upon the development of international law at the time in question, for example the prohibition on the use of torture is now unquestionably part of international law based on the fact that the prohibition is at least *prima facie* common to all legal systems.

EQUITY[52]

"The Court has not been expressly authorised by its Statute to apply equity as distinguished from law. . . . Article 38 of the Statute expressly directs the application of 'general principles of law recognised by civilised nations,' and in more than one nation principles of equity have an established place in the legal system. . . . It must be concluded, therefore, that under Article 38 of the Statute, if not independently of that Article, the Court has some freedom to consider principles of equity as part of the international law which it must apply".[53]

In the *Rann of Kutch Arbitration*,[54] equity was identified as constituting part of international law, while the International Court of Justice in the *North Sea Continental Shelf* cases directed the parties involved to seek a solution by reference to "equitable principles".[55] Equitable principles are also referred to in multipartite treaties, e.g. the 1982 Convention on the Law of the Sea[56] and certain General Assembly Resolutions such as the preamble of the 1974 Charter of Economic Rights and Duties of States.[57]

Principles of equity in the sense of fairness, justice and reasonableness are akin to general principles, and this may beg the question why they are not always considered under the umbrella of general principles. However, equity differs from those general

---

[52] Equity is sometimes treated separately as a possible independent source of law.
[53] Separate Opinion of Hudson J. in *The Diversion of Water from the Meuse* case P.C.I.J.Rep. ser.A/B, no.70 (1937) at 76–77.
[54] 50 I.L.R. 2.
[55] Above, n.2, p.47; see also *Fisheries Jurisdiction (Merits)* I.C.J. Rep. 1974 3 at 33; *Continental Shelf (Tunisia v Libya)* case I.C.J. Rep. 1982 18 at 60; and *Gulf of Maine* case I.C.J. Rep. 1984 at 246, 314–315 and 325–330. A criticism levied against the utilisation of equity in maritime boundary cases is that it has introduced an "unduly subjective and uncertain element into international law". See also *Denmark v Norway: Maritime Boundary in the Area Between Greenland and Jan Mayen Island* (1993) I.C.J. 38, *ad passim*.
[56] arts 59, 74 and 83.
[57] GA Resolution 3281 (XXIX) 14 I.L.M. 251 (1975) which highlights the "need to establish a just and equitable economic and social order".

principles most frequently applied in that while the latter has related mainly to procedural techniques, equity as a concept reflects values, which though they may be hard to define, may profoundly affect the application of the law. Equity in itself cannot be a source of law in that it does not contribute to substantive law, however it can, nevertheless, affect the way substantive law is administered and applied.

Equity therefore plays a subsidiary role in supplementing existing rules. Equity, as understood above, must be distinguished from the International Court's power "to decide a case *ex aequo et bono*, if the parties agree thereto",[58] that is the Court may apply equity in precedence over all other rules. A judge can only exercise his power under art.38 (2) if he has been expressly authorised so to do.[59]

In the event of the International Court of Justice being unable to solve a dispute by reference to treaty law, custom or general principles, art.38 provides the subsidiary means of "judicial decisions and the teachings of the most highly qualified publicists of the various nations" may be employed. Judicial decisions and writings are subsidiary means of determining what the law is on a given issue and they constitute the material sources of international law, as distinct from the formal sources. They are not the law as such but rather are where the law may be found. However, the increasing growth of, in particular, treaty law has witnessed a decline in the employment of both judicial decisions and writings.

JUDICIAL DECISIONS

Judicial decisions may be applied "subject to the provisions of Article 59". Article 59 states ". . . the decision of the Court has no binding force except between the parties and in respect of that particular case". However, there is no rule of *stare decisis* in international law whereby the Court is obliged to follow its previous decisions. Nevertheless, in spite of the absence of *stare decisis* the International Court of Justice and international tribunals do examine previous decisions and may take them into account when seeking the solution to a subsequent dispute. This promotes judicial consistency. There is obviously value in judicial consistency—it provides some degree of certainty for those participating in the legal system as to what the law is on a particular issue. Although, strictly speaking, the International Court of Justice is only to apply the law and not to make law it has deliv-

---

[58] art.38 (2).

[59] art.38 (2) has never been invoked before the I.C.J. though some international arbitration awards have been decided *ex aequo et bono*.

ered a number of judgments and advisory opinions, which have influenced and contributed to the development of international law. Among the most notable are the *Reparations* case[60] (legal personality of the United Nations), *the Nottebohm* case[61] (genuine link between individual and claimant State), the *Anglo-Norwegian Fisheries* case[62] (baselines from which the territorial sea may be drawn) and the *Legality of the Use by a State of Nuclear Weapons in Armed Conflict.*[63]

Similarly, arbitration decisions have contributed to the growth of international law, for example the *Alabama Arbitration Awards*[64] (duties of a neutral State) and the *Island of Palmas Arbitration*[65] (evidence of territorial sovereignty). Caution, however, should be exercised when assessing the contribution of a particular decision, for example the Court may be equally divided and the casting vote of the President may be necessary for a decision as in the *Lotus* case.[66] Similarly, the importance of an arbitration decision will depend, for example on the subject matter involved and the parties concerned.

Before assessing the contribution of any arbitration decision to the development of international law, reference should be made to the contents of the *compromis;* namely, the agreement concluded between the parties to the arbitration, which may specify, for instance, the Tribunal's jurisdiction and the law to be applied. If parties wish law, other than international law or in addition to international law, to be employed by an arbitration tribunal the intention must be stipulated in the *compromis.*[67] In the *Trail Smelter Arbitration,*[68] the Tribunal was instructed to "apply the law and practice followed in dealing with cognate questions in the United States of America, as well as international law and practice". It is therefore necessary to remember an arbitration tribunal, in settling a dispute between two States, may not necessarily be applying international law or at least may not be applying it exclusively.

A judicial decision by the International Court of Justice may give the stamp of law to an alleged rule of custom. However, again caution must be exercised. For instance, the International Court of Justice in 1974 pronounced:

[60] Above, n.41.
[61] I.C.J. Rep. 1955 at 4.
[62] Above, n.8.
[63] 35 I.L.M. 809 (1996), I.C.J. Rep. 1996 at 226.
[64] Moore, 1 Int.Arb.495 (1872).
[65] 2 R.I.A.A. 829 (1928).
[66] Above n.25.
[67] In the absence of any stipulation, international law will be applied.
[68] 3 R.I.A.A. 1905 (1938/41).

"... Two concepts have crystallised as customary law in recent years arising out of the general consensus revealed at that Conference [1960 Law of the Sea Conference]. The first is the concept of the fishery zone ... The second is the concept of preferential rights of fishing in adjacent waters in favour of the coastal State in a situation of special dependency on its coastal fisheries. ..."[69]

The evidence produced by the Court in support of its contention was unconvincing. The Court took existing instances of preferential rights at face value and considered neither the reasons why preferential treatment was granted or whether the parties concerned felt any legal obligation to provide preferential treatment for coastal States. The evidence produced in court illustrated that relatively few States put preferential rights into practice (21) and that the practice was confined to a single geographical area (the North Atlantic). The Court did not attempt to demonstrate that States felt any legal obligation to act in the way they had done. Nor has State practice since the Court's judgment supported the view that the Court was giving "judgment *sub specie legis ferendae*" and was anticipating "the law before the legislator had laid it down".[70]

The Court also came in for criticism with respect to its assertion in the *Nicaragua (Merits)* case, that the necessary *opinio juris* could be deduced from the support of States for certain General Assembly Resolutions.[71]

DECISIONS OF NATIONAL COURTS

Article 38 does not limit the judicial decisions that may be applied to those of international tribunals. Thus, if a national Court's decision is relevant it may be applied. The weight attached to a decision of a national Court will depend upon the standing of the Court concerned.

The United States Supreme Court is held in high regard and in its decisions dealing with individual State boundaries it has not only applied but also played a role in developing the relevant principles of international law.

---

[69] Above, n.10 at 23.

[70] That this is what the Court may have been seeking to do is borne out by Ignacio-Pinto J.'s declaration (at 37) that the Court gave him the impression it was "anxious to indicate the principles on the basis of which it would be desirable that a general international regulation of rights of fishing should be adopted". However preferential fishing rights as articulated by the Court was not incorporated in the 1982 Convention on the Law of the Sea.

[71] See D'Amato, above, n.24.

Similarly, decisions of the English Prize Courts contributed to the growth of prize law—law relating to vessels captured at sea during war.

A national Court decision may also serve as evidence of a State's position on a particular issue. Nevertheless, it must always be borne in mind that although a national Court is apparently applying international law, it is more likely to be applying the rule in question because it is a rule of national law.

WRITERS

"Teachings of the most highly qualified publicists of various nations" may be referred to as a subsidiary means in an attempt to settle a dispute. Writers have played a considerable role in the development of international law. Their influence has been due, in part, to the absence of an executive and a legislative body and in part to the "youthfulness" of the international legal system. During the formative period of international law, writers, because of insufficient State practice, were able to help determine, mould and articulate the scope, content and basic principles of international law. However, as the substantive law of international law increased, *via* for example State practice and the growth of customary international law, the role of writers declined. Nevertheless, international law is still a relatively young system and its boundaries are constantly being extended. Writers may still make a contribution in identifying and highlighting areas where international regulation should be encouraged, e.g. environmental pollution and the right to development. Writers may also prompt an assessment of the aims and values of international law. Writings, though they have receded in importance, are utilised not as a source of law in themselves but as a means of ascertaining what the law actually is on a given subject.[72] They are a subsidiary means of determining what the law is on a certain issue at a particular point in time and have a continuing role to play given the absence of *stare decisis* in international law. Writings do not necessarily carry less weight than judicial decisions. Clearly, however, which publicists are "the most highly qualified" cannot be conclusively proved.

The contemporary international community is very different from the one which existed when art.38(1) and its predecessor

---

[72] See, for instance, reference by Lord Stephenson in *Trendtex Trading Corporation v Central Bank of Nigeria* [1977] 1 All E.R. 881 at 902. Note also the International Court's statement on the cognisance to be given to documentary evidence produced in the form of extracts from books namely that "even if they seem to meet high standards of objectivity", above, n.9 at 40.

were initiated. It is relevant, therefore, after having examined all of the possible "sources" identified by reference to art.38(1), to ask whether these are the only sources. Article 38(1) does not profess to be exhaustive and it is, especially because of the developing character of international law, quite legitimate to look beyond it.

OTHER POSSIBLE SOURCES OF INTERNATIONAL LAW

Acts of international organisations

The multiplication of international organisations is a phenomenon of the twentieth century. Of these the most notable, enjoying almost universal membership, is the United Nations. Every Member State of the United Nations (192 members) has one vote within the General Assembly. Voting on important questions requires a two-thirds majority, while on all other questions a simple majority will suffice. Only those Resolutions adopted by the Assembly on procedure and budgetary issues are legally binding on members. All other Resolutions are recommendations—statements on a given issue. However, certain General Assembly Resolutions, namely "Declarations of Principle", although they carry no legal obligation, do have considerable moral force, for example Resolution 1514 (XV), "Declaration on the Granting of Independence to Colonial Countries and Peoples"[73] and General Assembly "Declaration on Principles of International Law Concerning Friendly Relations and Co-Operation Amongst States in Accordance with the Charter of the United Nations" 1970.[74] Although such Resolutions may contribute to the development of international law, the status of customary international law was denied to General Assembly Resolution 3281 (XXIX) "Charter of Economic Rights and Duties of States" 1974[75] by the arbitrator in the *Texaco case*.[76]

General Assembly Resolutions cannot be dismissed out of hand as being of no significance, in the words of Lauterpacht J.:

> "It would be wholly inconsistent with sound principles of interpretation as well as with highest international interest, which can never be legally irrelevant, to reduce the value of the Resolutions of the General Assembly—one of the

---

[73] GA Resolution 1514 (XV) December 14, 1960; see *Advisory Opinion—Western Sahara*, I.C.J. Rep. 1975 12 at 31 *et seq*. For the effect of GA Resolutions in the evolution of the principle of self-determination.
[74] GA Resolution 2625 (XXV) October 24, 1970.
[75] 14 I.L.M. 251 (1975).
[76] 17 I.L.M. 1 (1978).

principal instrumentalities of the formation of the collective will and judgment of the community of nations represented by the United Nations—and to treat them . . . as nominal, insignificant and having no claim to influence the conduct of the Members. International interest demands that no judicial support, however indirect, be given to any such conception of the Resolution of the General Assembly as being of no consequence."[77]

General Assembly Resolutions however have no legal effect and before any law-making effect can be attributed to them a consistent approach requires to be adopted towards them. This is in contrast to the current selective approach where their impact is dependent upon such factors as the subject matter of the Resolution, how large a majority the Resolution commands and to what extent it receives the support of the principally affected States in the given field. Nevertheless, a vote in the General Assembly is cast by a State's representative and as such may reflect a particular State's position on a given issue and how a State votes may be the means of providing evidence of State practice. Thus, voting within an organisation may be a useful link in the international law-making process, that is, it may provide the evidence necessary for "law" to be attributed to usage. Therefore voting on General Assembly Resolutions may provide an indication of what the law is, or possibly what the law should be, or indeed what it may become on a particular topic at a given time.

General Assembly Resolutions are an example of what is known as "soft law".

Soft law

Soft law is the generic term used to describe non-legally binding international instruments. The term embraces treaties ("legal soft law") containing general obligations and non-binding or voluntary resolutions, statements of intent and codes of conduct produced by international and regional organisations and statements by individuals, for example groups of eminent international lawyers purporting to articulate international principles ("non-legal soft law").[78] A requisite of soft law is that it must be in written form. The number of instruments which fall within the category of soft law has spawned during the last 40 years, and the

---

[77] Separate Opinion in *Voting Procedure on Questions Relating to Reports and Petitions Concerning the Territory of South West Africa*, I.C.J. Rep. 1955 67 at 122.
[78] C. M. Chinkin, "The Challenge of Soft Law: Development and Change in International Law" (1989) 38 *I.C.L.Q.* 850.

subject matter of such instruments is becoming increasingly
diverse and includes *inter alia* economic measures and environmental instruments.

The Charter of Paris for a New Europe adopted by the
Conference on Security and Co-Operation in Europe[79] is a prime
example of soft law, as is the Rio Declaration on the Environment
and Development. An advantage of soft law is that it may be
employed to "overcome deadlock in relations between States pursuing conflicting ideological and/or economic aims",[80] whereas
an alleged disadvantage is that it may discourage States from
undertaking "hard law" obligations. Soft law is intended to
mould conduct on the international scene and may become hard
law. Subsequent State practice may be such to change the status
of soft law to hard law or a treaty with hard law obligations may
be concluded.[81]

The 1948 Universal Declaration of Human Rights is an example
of soft law. The Declaration was a statement of intent but led to
the promulgation of the 1966 International Covenant of Civil
and Political Rights,[82] and the 1966 International Covenant on
Economic, Social and Cultural Rights.[83]

Regional organisations

Regional organisations such as the Council of Europe, the
European Union, the Organisation of American States and the
African Union, can *via* their internal measures demonstrate what
they, representing a particular regional grouping of States, consider to be the law. Regional organisations enjoy varying degrees
of legal personality and if this should extend to a treaty-making
competence, the organisation in question may shape substantive
international law by participating in treaties.

The International Law Commission

A criticism of custom is it is diffuse and lacking in precision. In
the light of this, attempts have been made at codification—the

[79] 30 I.L.M. 190 (1991).
[80] Seidl-Hohenfeldern, 163 *Recueil des Coeurs* 169 (1979–11).
[81] H. Hartmut "A Fresh Look at Soft Law" (1999) no.10, no.3 *E.J.I.L.* 499, in which
   the author identifies "[E]ven if soft law is not a source of law in the sense of
   Art.38(1) ... it is a self-contained regime where the characteristics depend on
   the parties' intent—although soft law is not subject to international treaty law
   or the principle of *pacta sunt servanda*, it is not indifferent in legal terms and
   deserves the lawyer's attention. Such rules of behaviour must be ascertained on
   a case-by-case basis, depending upon the will of the parties".
[82] 999 U.N.T.S. 171, U.K.T.S. 6 (1977) Cmnd. 6702.
[83] 993 U.N.T.S. 3, U.K.T.S. 6 (1997) Cmnd. 6702.

Hague Conferences 1899 and 1907 produced Conventions on the law of war and neutrality and in 1930 the Hague Convention on Certain Questions Relating to the Conflict of Nationality Law was drawn up. Codification essentially involves a streamlining of all existing law on a particular subject and it is distinct from consolidation, which is simply a drawing together of all material on a particular subject.

In 1946, the International Law Commission was established and charged with the task of furthering the progressive development and codification of international law. "Progressive development" is defined in art.15 of the International Law Commission's Statute as:

> ". . . the preparation of draft conventions on subjects which have not yet been regulated by international law or in regard to which the law has not yet been sufficiently developed in the practice of States".

Codification however is defined as "the more precise formulation and systemisation of rules of international law in fields where there already has been extensive State practice, precedent and doctrine". All codification has, accordingly, since 1946 been effected *via* the International Law Commission. Nevertheless, the distinction between "progressive development" and "codification" is easier to maintain in theory than in practice, as was highlighted by *ad hoc* Sorenson J. (Dissenting Opinion) in the *North Sea Continental Shelf* case, stating:

> "It has come to be generally recognised, however, that this distinction between codification and progressive development may be difficult to apply rigorously to the facts of international legal relations. Although theoretically clear and distinguishable the two notions tend in practice to overlap or to leave between them an intermediate area in which it is not possible to indicate precisely where codification ends and progressive development begins. The very act of formulating or restating an existing customary rule may have the effect of defining its contents more precisely and removing such doubts as may have existed as to its exact scope or the modalities of its application."[84]

Notwithstanding the close relationship of progressive development and codification the International Law Commissions focus is now primarily on the former.

---

[84] Above, n.2 at 42–43.

The International Law Commission has 34 members,[85] who sit as individuals rather than as representatives of their governments[86] and it meets as authorised by the General Assembly for two sessions each year (amounting to two months in total). Initially the Commission met for 12 weeks in the year but this has been reduced since 2000 in an effort to make financial savings. The International Law Commission may be invited by the General Assembly to look at a particular field of law. However, this is rare and the International Law Commission as a rule normally initiates its own work programme. The International Law Commission has been responsible for undertaking the preparatory work on particular subjects and this has culminated in a number of Conventions being opened for signature. The Commission works by way of reports produced by a Special Rapporteur (appointed from the Commission's own body). Draft articles are prepared and subsequently submitted to Member States for their comments. A conference is convened, which will on the basis of the draft articles, produce a Convention, whereupon the Convention will eventually be opened for signature.[87] Topics covered by the International Law Commission include the law of the sea (1958 Geneva Conventions on the Law of the Sea); the law on diplomatic relations (1961 Vienna Convention on Diplomatic Relations); the law of Treaties (1969 Vienna Convention on the Law of Treaties); and the 1998 Statute of the International Criminal Court.

The International Law Commission has also been responsible for draft articles on a variety of topics including those on the Responsibility of States for Internationally Wrongful Acts 2001, and those on a Transboundary Aquifers Convention 2008. The International Law Commission has not been involved in all UN sponsored "legislative" activity, e.g. human rights, which has been the responsibility of the Commission on Human Rights. The value of the International Law Commission's work lies not only in that a multipartite treaty may be produced, but in its preparatory work where State practice can be identified and, as such, may assist the formation of customary international law. Again, the interrelation of treaty law and customary international law and *vice versa* is illustrated.

---

[85] Increased from 15 members to 21 in 1956, to 25 in 1961 and to 34 in 1981.

[86] Elections are by the General Assembly from lists of national groups and are elected with regard, e.g. to equitable geographical distribution. Sir Michael Wood is the current UK member of the Commission having been elected to fill the vacancy following the resignation of Professor Ian Brownlie who had served on the Commission from 1997–2008.

[87] Conferences may span a number of years.

Additional agencies other than the International Law Commission are engaged in attempts to clarify existing law on given subjects, e.g. the United Nations Commission on International Trade Law, the International Labour Organisation and independent bodies such as the International Law Association.

Mention, albeit brief, must be made of *jus cogens*.[88]

Jus cogens

Jus cogens is the technical term given to those norms of general international law which are of a peremptory force and from which, as a consequence, no derogation may be made except by another norm of equal weight. A treaty provision which conflicts with such a norm is void[89] and, should a new peremptory norm develop, any existing contrary treaty is rendered void and terminates.[90]

How does an international rule gain status as a peremptory norm? The only definitive definition is that contained in the Vienna Convention on the Law of Treaties in which a peremptory norm of general international law is defined as one "accepted and recognised by the international community of States as a whole . . .".[91] A peremptory norm may, it would appear, be derived from a custom or a treaty only and not from any other source.

Jus cogens is the label for what is essentially the "public policy" of the international legal system. There is, as might be anticipated, considerable uncertainty and indeed controversy as to the scope and extent of *jus cogens*. The prohibition on the use of force as expressed in the United Nations Charter was identified by the International Law Commission as a "conspicuous example of a rule in international law having the character of *jus cogens*"[92] and subsequently endorsed as such by the International Court of Justice in the *Nicaragua (Merits)* case.[93] Other examples of instances of norms warranting characterisation as *jus cogens* are the prohibitions on genocide and torture,[94] and on the denial of the realisation of self-determination.

---

[88] *Jus cogens* is examined more closely within the context of treaty law—Ch.10. See however Bianchi A Human Rights and the Magic of *Jus Cogens* E.J.I.L. 19(3) pp.491–508.

[89] Vienna Convention on the Law of Treaties, 1969, art.53.

[90] *ibid.*, art.64.

[91] For the purposes of the Convention.

[92] Commentary of the Commission to art.50 of Draft Articles on the Law of Treaties, *I.L.C. Yearbook*, 1966, II, p.247.

[93] Above, n.9 at 100.

[94] See, *Siderman de Blake v Republic of Argentina* 965 F.2d 699, 717 (9th Cr.1992) where the Court said, "the right to be free from official torture is fundamental and universal, a right deserving of the highest status under international law, a norm of *jus cogens*".

Of course, to go beyond the Vienna Convention on the Law of Treaties and argue for freestanding principles of *"jus cogens"*, demanding almost universal recognition and acceptance of certain basic principles as fundamental, is another issue altogether and out of the scope of this Chapter. Such a step would represent an advancement and refinement in the international legal system dependent not on the system itself but rather upon its principal participants—States.

3. INTERNATIONAL LAW AND MUNICIPAL LAW

International law today is not confined to regulating the relations between States. The scope of international law continues to extend and is no longer exclusively concerned with the rules of warfare and diplomatic relations. Today, matters of social concern such as health, education and economics fall within the ambit of international regulation. International law is more than ever aimed at individuals.

Can individuals invoke international law before national courts? Can individuals obtain rights under international law, which may be enforced within a municipal legal system?

The issue dealt with in this chapter is the extent to which national courts will give effect within the domestic system to rules of international law. The approach of a particular State's national courts to international law is determined by that State's attitude to and reception of international law—an attitude which may, and does, differ according to the type of international law in question—treaty law or customary international law. Strictly speaking, the reception of international law by a State and its internal effect is a matter of municipal law. There is no universal, uniform practice stipulating how States should incorporate international law into their domestic legal system and it is a State's perception of international law which determines the way in which international law becomes part of municipal law. In other words, States differ in the way their national courts are either required or allowed to give effect to international obligations.

Before looking at what happens in practice, mention, albeit brief, must be made of the theories which have evolved on the relationship of national law to international law. The theorists traditionally have been divided between two principal schools of thought—(i) the monistic school; and (ii) the dualistic school.

MONISTIC SCHOOL

Monists have a unitary concept of law and see all law, and consequently international law and municipal law, as an integral part of the same system. In the event of a conflict between international law and municipal law, most monists would contend that international law should unquestionably prevail.

DUALISTIC SCHOOL

Dualists see national law and international law as independent of each other. The two systems, it is maintained, regulate different subject matter. International law regulates the relations of sovereign States, while national law regulates affairs internal to the State, e.g. the relations of the executive *vis-à-vis* its citizens and the relations of individual citizens *vis-à-vis* each other. Accordingly, dualists hold, the two systems are mutually exclusive and can have no contact with, and no effect on, each other. If international law is applied within a State, it is only because it has been expressly incorporated into municipal law. The question of primacy is not one to which dualists address themselves. Dualism, as formulated, does not admit a conflict can arise between the international legal system and a municipal legal system.

Sir Gerald Fitzmaurice stepped into the debate between monists and dualists in the mid-1950s, when he articulated what has become popularly known as the "Fitzmaurice compromise".[1] Fitzmaurice acknowledged that international law and municipal law have, for the most part, separate fields of operation and each is supreme in its own domain. Nevertheless, on occasion they have a common field of application and, should a conflict arise, what is involved, Fitzmaurice concluded, is not a conflict of legal

---

[1] Fitzmaurice, "The General Principles of International Law Considered from the Standpoint of the Rule of Law" 92 *Hague Recueil* 5.

systems but rather a conflict of obligations. If a State is, by its national law, unable to act in the manner required by international law, it is not its internal law, which the national courts will uphold, which is called into question, but rather the State's liability on the international plane for the non-fulfilment of its international obligations.[2]

In practice, the differences between international law and a particular national system is minimised and every effort is made to achieve harmonisation between the two systems.

In the United Kingdom, there exists:

> "... a *prima facie* presumption that Parliament does not intend to act in breach of international law, including therein specific treaty obligations; and if one of the meanings which can reasonably be ascribed to the legislation is consonant with the treaty obligations and another or others are not, the meaning which is consonant is to be preferred".[3]

In the United States, such a presumption is an established principle of interpretation, so "an act of congress ought never to be construed to violate the law of nations, if any other possible construction remains . . .".[4]

What is meant, if it is said, that a country is monistic or dualistic in its approach to international law? Simply, it is monistic if it accepts international law automatically as part of its municipal law and does not demand an express act of the legislature, whereas if a State is dualistic, international law will only become part of its municipal law if it has been expressly adopted as such by way of a legislative act.

MUNICIPAL LAW IN INTERNATIONAL LAW

On the international scene, international law is unequivocally supreme, as is borne out by both arbitral and judicial decisions and international Conventions which reflect accepted international law.

In the *Alabama Claims Arbitration*,[5] the arbitration tribunal concluded that neither municipal legislative provisions nor the absence of them could be pleaded as a defence for non-compliance

---

[2] As illustrated in *Mortensen v Peters* (1906) 8 F. (J.) 93—see below, p.44.
[3] *Salomon v Commissioners of Customs and Excise* [1967] 2 Q.B. 116, CA—Lord Diplock at 143; also *Post Office v Estuary Radio Ltd* [1968] 2 Q.B. 740, CA.
[4] *Murray v Schooner Charming Betsy* 6 US (2 Cranch.) 64 at 118 (1804). Also *Lauritzen v Larsen* 345 US 571 at 578 (1953). For Canadian authority, see, e.g. *Bloxém v Favre* 8 P.C. 101 at 107 (1883, n.5).
[5] Moore, 1 Int.Arb. 495 (1872).

with international obligations, while the Permanent Court of International Justice in an advisory opinion expressed the view:

> ". . . a State which has contracted valid international obligations is bound to make in its legislation such modifications as may be necessary to ensure the fulfilment of the obligations undertaken."[6]

Article 13 of the Draft Declaration on Rights and Duties of States 1949 provides:

> "Each State has the duty to carry out in good faith its obligations arising from treaties and other sources of international law, and it may not invoke provisions in its constitution or its laws as an excuse for failure to perform this duty."[7]

Article 27 of the Vienna Convention on the Law of Treaties[8] stipulates that "a party may not invoke the provisions of internal law as justification for its failure to perform a treaty", nor may a State, under art.46 of the Vienna Convention,

> ". . . invoke the fact that its consent to be bound by a treaty has been expressed in violation of a provision of its internal law regarding competence to conclude treaties as invalidating its consent unless that violation was manifest and concerned a rule of its internal law of fundamental importance."[9]

The overriding conclusion to be extracted from the foregoing is that a State should not seek to evade fulfilling an international obligation because of either the presence or absence of an internal legislative provision. This must be the standpoint at the international level if international law is to succeed and maintain credibility.

---

6   *Exchange of Greek and Turkish Populations* case P.C.I.J.Rep., ser.B., No.10 (1925) at 20. See also, *Free Zones of Upper Savoy and Gex* P.C.I.J.Rep., ser.A/B, No.46 (1932). Note, however, that Libya sought to justify its refusal to extradite the alleged perpetrators of the Lockerbie bombing on the grounds that, *inter alia*, the Libyan Constitution prohibits the extradition of nationals.

7   This was prepared by the International Law Commission—*Y.B.I.L.C.*, 1949, pp.286, 288. See also *Applicability of the Obligation to Arbitrate under section 21 of the United Nations Headquarters Agreement of 26th June 1947*, I.C.J. Rep., 1988, 12.

8   U.K.T.S. 58 (1980) Cmnd.7964; 8 I.L.M. 679 (1969). See also Ch.10 below.

9   A violation is manifest if it shall be objectively evident to any State conducting itself on the matter in accordance with normal practice and in good faith (art.46(2)).

International tribunals may, of course, choose to look at national legislation. National legislation may be employed as evidence of a State's compliance or non-compliance with international obligations.[10] Consideration of national law may make it possible to ascertain what a State's stance is on a particular issue at a given time[11] and an international tribunal may, in the absence of relevant international law, be required to refer to national law. The latter was stressed by the International Court of Justice in the *Barcelona Traction, Light and Power Co* case.[12] The Court was confronted with issues pertaining to company law and held that "[I]n this field international law is called upon to recognise institutions of municipal law that have an important and extensive role in the international field . . .".[13]

Turning to the municipal scene, what is the position when municipal Courts and tribunals are confronted with international law? How do they apply it? What happens in the event of a conflict between international law and municipal legislation?[14]

INTERNATIONAL LAW BEFORE MUNICIPAL COURTS

United Kingdom practice

There is no written constitution defining the internal status within Britain of international law.[15]

Customary international law

Britain essentially adopts a monistic approach to customary international law. This is, however, an oversimplification. Although Lord Talbot maintained it in *Buvot v Barbuit*,[16] the true British

---

[10] For example the International Tribunal of the Law of the Sea, *M/V Saiga (No. 2)* case 1999, 120 I.L.R. 143.

[11] Highlighted by the Permanent Court of International Justice in *"Polish Upper Silesia"*, P.C.I.J.Rep., ser.A, no.7, (1926) at 22, Brazilian Loans case, P.C.I.J.Rep., ser.A, no.21, (1929), at 124–125.

[12] I.C.J. Rep. 1970 at 3.

[13] *ibid*. at 33.

[14] Of course international law may be invoked by national courts to interpret legislation, consistently, with international law. For instance the South African Constitution 1996 requires courts to consider international law when applying the South African Bill of Rights. See case *Mazibuko and the City of Johannesburg*, April 30, 2008.

[15] *cf*. FRG—art.25 German Constitution. "The general rules of public international law are an integral part of federal law. They shall take precedence over the laws and shall directly create rights and duties for the inhabitants of the federal territory."

[16] (1737) Cases t. Talbot 281, "That the law of nations, in its full extent was part of the law of England" and reaffirmed by Lord Mansfield in *Triquet v Bath* (1764)

view was best presented by Lord Alverstone in the *West Rand Central Gold Mining Co* case:[17]

> "It is quite true that whatever has received the common consent of civilised nations must have received the assent of our country, and that to which we have assented along with other nations in general may properly be called international law, and as such will be acknowledged and applied by our municipal tribunals when legitimate occasion arises for those tribunals to decide questions to which doctrines of international law may be relevant. But any doctrine so invoked must be one really accepted as binding between nations, and the international law sought to be applied must, like anything else, be proved by satisfactory evidence, which must shew either that the particular proposition put forward has been recognised and acted upon by our own country, or that it is of such a nature, and has been so widely and generally accepted, that it can hardly be supposed that any civilised State would repudiate it . . . that the law of nations forms part of the law of England, ought not to be construed so as to include as part of the law of England opinions of text-writers upon a question as to which there is no evidence that Great Britain has ever assented, and *a fortiori* if they are contrary to the principles of her laws as declared by her Courts."[18]

Lord Alverstone's emphasis was on assent and the need to demonstrate the existence and scope of any particular alleged rule of customary international law—an emphasis which has been reflected consistently in subsequent cases. In *The Cristina* case,[19] Lord Macmillan held that national Courts, before acknowledging customary international law as part of domestic law, should initially be satisfied it (that is, custom) had the hallmark of consent.[20] In *Chung Chi Cheung v The King*,[21] Lord Atkin said:

> "It must be always remembered that, so far, at any rate, as the courts of this Country are concerned, international law has no validity save in so far as its principles are accepted and

---

3 Burr. 1478. Court of King's Bench. See also Lord Lloyd in *R v Bow Street Magistrates Ex p. Pinochet* (Number 1) [2001] 1 A.C. 61 at 90.
[17] [1905] 2 K.B. at 391.
[18] *ibid.* at 406–408.
[19] [1938] A.C. 485.
[20] *ibid.* at 490. see also Lord Wright at 502.
[21] [1939] A.C. 160.

adopted by our own domestic law. There is no external power that imposes its rule upon our own code of substantive law or procedure. The courts acknowledge the existence of a body of rules which nations accept amongst themselves. On any judicial issue they seek to ascertain what the relevant rule is, and having found it, they will treat it as incorporated into the domestic law, so far as it is not inconsistent with rules enacted by Statutes or finally declared by their tribunals."[22]

Lord Denning in *Thakrar v Home Secretary*[23] said, "In my opinion, the rules of international law only become part of our law in so far as they are accepted and adopted by us."[24] However, three years later, in *Trendex Trading Corporation v Central Bank of Nigeria*,[25] in considering the two schools, incorporation or transformation, Lord Denning concluded that the doctrine of incorporation was correct. Nevertheless, that case dealing with sovereign immunity predated the 1978 Sovereign Immunity Act and therefore was governed by judicial decisions. The real question was whether the rules of precedent applying to rules of English law incorporating customary international law meant that any change in international law could only be recognised by the English Courts (in the absence of legislation) within the scope of the doctrine of *stare decisis*. Lord Denning concluded otherwise and held:

> "International law knows no rule of *stare decisis*. If this court today is satisfied that the rule of international law on a subject has changed from what it was 50 or 60 years ago, it can give effect to that change—and apply the change in our English law—without waiting for the House of Lords to do it."[26]

The decision in *Trendtex* would appear to allow an exception from an application of the principle of *stare decisis* in cases where international law has changed since the earlier decision was delivered. In the light of the *Trendtex* case, it seems that if international law has changed then the "new" international law may be applied in spite of the earlier municipal decision. Lord Denning's submissions in favour of the doctrine of "incorporation" received

---

[22] *ibid*. at 167–168. Lord Atkin's statement is self-contradictory.
[23] [1974] Q.B. 684.
[24] *ibid*. at 701.
[25] [1977] Q.B. 529.
[26] *ibid*. at 554.

judicial support in the *Tin Council* case.[27] In *R. v Jones*[28] the reception of customary international law was further discussed. In that case the House of Lords accepted that aggression consituted a crime under customary international law. However the Law Lords qualified the automatic incorporation of customary international law as part of domestic law. For example, Lord Bingham expressed the view that customary international law could only be assimilated into domestic criminal law where the constituiton allowed.

Rules of customary international law inconsistent with muncipal law

Any rule of customary international law which is inconsistent with a British statute will not be enforced in the British Courts. The domestic legislation will be upheld while the State will incur liability on the international scene, as in *Mortensen v Peters,*[29] when the Court quashed an appeal against a conviction made under a domestic legislative provision, which allegedly contravened customary international law. The Court, in dismissing the appeal, unanimously held, *inter alia*, that the relationship of municipal legislation and international law was one of construction and "of construction only" and it was not the function of the Court:

> ". . . to decide whether an Act of the Legislature is ultra vires as in contravention of generally acknowledged principles of international law. For us an Act of Parliament duly passed by Lords and Commons and assented to by the King, is supreme, and we are bound to give effect to its terms."[30]

The Court concluded that, while there was a presumption against Parliament violating international law:

> ". . . it is only a presumption, and as such it must always give way to the language used if it is clear, and also to all counter presumptions which may legitimately be held in view in determining, on ordinary principles, the true meaning and intent of the legislation. Express words will of course be conclusive, and so also will plain implication."[31]

[27] *Maclaine Watson v Dept of Trade and Industry* [1988] 3 W.L.R. 1033; 80 I.L.R. 49; [1989] 3 All E.R. 523; 81 I.L.R. 671.
[28] [2006] U.K.H.L. 16.
[29] (1906) 8 F.(J.) 93.
[30] *ibid.* at 100–101.
[31] *ibid.* at 103.

Customary international law will be treated as part of UK law, provided there is no contrary judicial decision of a higher Court, save possibly the exception admitted by the *Trendtex* case, or contrary statutory provision or now in the wake of *R. v Jones* a constitutional impediment to incorporation.[32]

Treaties

> "... as a matter of the constitutional law of the United Kingdom, the royal prerogative, whilst it embraces the making of treaties, does not extend to altering the law or conferring rights on individuals or depriving individuals of rights which they enjoy in domestic law without the intervention of Parliament. Treaties, as it is sometimes expressed, are not self-executing. Quite simply a treaty is not part of English law unless and until it has been incorporated into the law by legislation."[33]

A treaty does not become part of British domestic law unless and until it is specifically incorporated as such by a legislative measure—an Enabling Act. The United Kingdom adopts, therefore, a dualistic approach to treaty law.

Why is an Enabling Act required? Treaty-making power is an executive function coming within the royal prerogative. The legislature does not participate and its consent is not required before Britain can undertake international obligations. An Enabling Act is a safeguard against the possible abuse of executive authority, as it prevents the executive from using its treaty-making competence to introduce domestic legislation without going through the required parliamentary procedures. Treaties regulating the conduct of war and the cession of territory do not demand an Enabling Act.[34]

In practice, the Enabling Act giving internal effect to a treaty will be passed before the treaty is ratified and the opportunity will then be taken to make national law compatible with international law. There is also the practice known as the Ponsonby Rule, whereby a treaty, following signature, is laid for 21 days before

---

[32] The offence of aggression could not be automatically incorporated into domestic criminal law without statutory provision.

[33] Lord Oliver in *Maclaine Watson v Department of Trade*, above, n.27. See also Lord Bingham in *Al-Skeini v Secretary of State for Defence* [2007] U.K.H.L. 26.

[34] Treaties involving the cession of territory may be an exception to the principle that parliamentary consent is not required for a treaty. See McNair, *Treaties*, p.97: "it is unlikely that the Crown will agree to cede any territory without being sure that Parliament would approve, or, if in doubt, whether inserting a clause making the cession dependent upon Parliamentary approval."

both Houses of Parliament prior to ratification and publication in the United Kingdom Treaty Series.[35] Although expedient to provide this opportunity for discussion, it is not legally required.[36] The reason why an Enabling Act is required was spelt out by Sir Robert Phillimore in the *Parlement Belge* case,[37] when he concluded that to recognise the immunity granted by a Convention[38] to a vessel other than a public warship as being enforceable in the national Courts would be ". . . a use of the treaty-making prerogative of the Crown which I believe to be without precedent, and in principle contrary to the laws of the constitution."[39]

As from January 1, 1997, every international agreement laid before the UK Parliament under the Ponsonby Rule has been accompanied by an Explanatory Memorandum, identifying the main features of the Treaty. The aim of the Explanatory Memorandum is to assist Members of Parliament in understanding the substance of the Treaty without reference to the actual text. An Explanatory Memorandum is not required where a treaty enters into force on signature.[40]

In the event of a conflict between a national statute and a treaty, the national legislative measure will prevail. Such was the case with the European Convention for the Protection of Human Rights and Fundamental Freedoms, which was not part of British municipal law until 1998, when the Convention was incorporated by the Human Rights Act.[41] The position prior to 1998 continues to illustrate the stance taken *vis-à-vis* an international obligation which is not incorporated into UK domestic law.[42] In the event of

---

[35] *Hansard*, HC Deb., Vol.171, cols 2003–2004 (April 1, 1924).

[36] e.g. the Rule was not applied when the UK accepted the compulsory jurisdiction of the I.C.J. there being no requirement for ratification—*Hansard*, HC Deb., Vol.578, cols 1145–1146 (November 27, 1957).

[37] (1879) 4 P.D. 129. Probate, Divorce and Admiralty Division.

[38] Postal Convention Regulating Communications by Post (Belgium and Britain) 1876.

[39] Above, n.37 at 154. See also *Walker v Baird* [1892] A.C. 491; *The Republic of Italy v Hambros Bank Ltd* [1950] Ch. 314; *McWhirter v Att.-Gen.* [1972] C.M.L.R. 882, also illustrate the need for an Enabling Act.

[40] See the Guidelines published by the Foreign and Commonwealth Office, London on Explanatory Memoranda for Treaties and Text of a Parliamentary Statement made by Dr Liam Fox on December 16, 1996 in HC.

[41] The Act entered into force on October 2, 2000. However, see the Scotland Act 1998, see below p.47.

[42] *R. v Secretary of State for the Home Department and Another, Ex p. Bhajan Singh* [1976] Q.B. 198 at 207. See *R. v Chief Immigration Officer, Ex p. Bibi* [1976] 1 W.L.R. 979 at 984, CA; Lord Bridge in *Brind v Secretary of State* [1991] 1 All E.R. 722 at 722–723, HL. *Birdi v Secretary of State for Home Affairs*, unreported, 1975, but quoted in Singh at 207; *Kaur v Lord Advocate* 1981 S.L.T. 3222 at 329; *Moore v Secretary of State for Scotland* 1985 S.L.T. 38 ABD 41; *obiter dicta* of Lord Hope in *T. Petitioner* 1966 S.C.L.R. 897 at 910–911.

an Act of Parliament containing provisions contrary to an international Convention, that Act would prevail, although domestic legislation should always be construed as far as is possible to be in conformity with international obligations. There is a presumption in treaty interpretation that Parliament does not intend to violate the United Kingdom's international obligations.[43] The Human Rights Act also provides redress against public authorities which allegedly violate the Convention.[44]

The incorporation of the European Convention coincided with a major constitutional change within the United Kingdom, namely devolution and the establishment of a Scottish Executive, a legislative Parliament and a non-legislative Welsh Assembly. Under the Scotland Act 1998, all Acts of the Scottish Executive and Scottish Parliament must be compatible with the European Convention on Human Rights.[45] Acts of the Westminster Parliament cannot be struck out on human-rights grounds but merely declared "incompatible".[46] Notwithstanding the competence of Scottish Courts mentioned above, British Courts are concerned with the application of national law and, if their provisions cannot be reconciled with international law, that is a matter solely for the consideration of the legislature and not the judiciary.[47]

An issue which has been raised is that of unincorporated treaties and whether they can create legitimate expectations for individuals. The acceptance of the principle of legitimate expectations was made by Lord Woolf in *R. v Secretary of State for the*

---

[43] With respect to the European Convention, all new legislation must include a "compatibility" clause.

[44] Human Rights Act s.6.

[45] The Scottish Executive came into existence in May 1999, and the impact of the Convention was reflected primarily in the administration of justice, giving Scotland hands-on experience of incorporation some 18 months ahead of the rest of the UK.

[46] Human Rights Act s.4. For an instance of incompatibility see the House of Lords decision in *A and Others v Secretary of State for the Home Department; X and another v Secretary of State for the Home Department* [2004] UKHL 56, in particular the judgment of Baroness Hale of Richmond, paragraph 219–220, to the effect that s.23 of the Anti-terrorism, Crime and Security Act 2001 was incompatible with arts 5 and 14 of the European Convention of Human Rights. However, should the Scottish Parliament enact legislation incompatible with the Convention, that legislative measure may be deemed *"ultra vires"*. The Scottish Parliament only has competence in certain areas, namely devolved matters such as tax and education. Reserved matters such as foreign affairs and defence are retained by Westminster.

[47] See e.g. Lord Templeman in *Lord Advocate v Scotsman Publishers Ltd* 1989 S.L.T. 705 at 710.

Home Department Ex p. Ahmed and Patel,[48] when he made reference to the Australian case of *Teoh*.[49] However, the principle is of limited application and an individual can only anticipate that the Executive will honour the relevant treaty provisions. Other interpretive practices which bring international law into the national legal order are used, in particular the use of international law as persuasive or influential authority. In the Canadian case of *Baker v Canada (Minister of Citizenship and Immigration)*,[50] the Supreme Court considered whether an immigration officer had unreasonably exercised his discretion in ordering the deportation of a Jamaican woman, thereby separating her from her four Canadian-born children. The Supreme Court held that the children's interests were important considerations which should have governed the immigration officer's exercise of discretion.[51] The Supreme Court used the Convention on the Rights of the Child which, at the time of the case, had not been incorporated into Canadian law, as "an aid in interpreting domestic law",[52] and found on that basis that the immigration officer had unreasonably exercised his discretion.[53]

States may be required to give effect to UN sanctions. In the United Kingdom sanctions are implemented pursuant to the United Nations Act 1946 whereby the Crown is competent to adopt Orders in Council.[54]

Executive certificate

The executive certificate is a statement issued by the Foreign Office relating to "certain categories of questions of fact in the field of international affairs. In such cases the statement is conclusive even in the face of contrary evidence".[55] A certificate may stipulate, for instance, whether a particular foreign State or government is recognised by Britain,[56] whether a particular person is

---

[48] [1999] Imm. AR 22.

[49] *Minister for Immigration and Ethnic Affairs v Teoh*, 1995 C.L.R. 273.

[50] 1999 2 SCR 817, para.69–71.

[51] para.67.

[52] para.70.

[53] para.76. On the use of persuasive and influential authority see further Knop, "Here and There: International Law in Domestic Courts", (2000), 32 *NYU J Int'l L & Pol* 501.

[54] Orders in Council are a form of secondary legislation. Another instance of the 1946 UN Act being employed was the UK's cooperation with the International Criminal Tribunal for the Former Yugoslavia, The UN (International Tribunal) (Former Yugoslavia) Order 1996, SI 1996, No.716.

[55] L. Oppenheim, *International Law* (1967) Vol.I, para.357(a).

[56] s.21 of the 1978 State Immunity Act provides that the Secretary of State's certificate is conclusive evidence as to: (i) whether a country is a State within the meaning of the Act; (ii) who is the head of State; and (iii) who is the government.

entitled to diplomatic immunity or the existence and scope of British jurisdiction in a foreign country. An executive certificate is accepted as conclusive by the Courts, as was held in *The Fagernes,*[57] *Duff Development Co v Government of Kelantan*[58] and *Post Office v Estuary Radio Ltd*[59] and only reviewable in certain defined circumstances, see *R. v Secretary of State for Foreign and Commonwealth Affairs, Ex p. Trawnik.*[60]

An executive certificate is not conclusive in the interpretation of statutes or the construction of documents: *Re Al-Fin Corporation's Patent.*[61] The Courts still, however, determine what is the effect of such a factual situation, although they may not examine the basis on which the Foreign Office made its decision.

United States practice

American law, with its roots in the English legal system, adopts a similar attitude to international law as that adopted by Britain. Accordingly, with respect to customary international law, the United States is monistic in its approach and, in respect of treaties, dualistic.

Customary international law

Judicial decisions confirm that customary international law is part of United States law.

Marshall C.J., in *The Nercide,*[62] declared, in the absence of an Act of Congress, that the Court was bound by the law of nations, which was part of the law of the land, while Gray J. in 1900 pronounced:

> "International law is part of our law, and must be ascertained and administered by the courts of justice of appropriate jurisdiction, as often as questions of right depending upon it are duly presented for their determination."[63]

This acceptance of customary international law was, however, qualified:

> "[T]his rule of international law is one which prize courts, administering the law of nations, are bound to take judicial

---

[57] [1927] P. 311 at 324.
[58] [1924] A.C. 797, HL.
[59] [1968] 2 Q.B. 740.
[60] *The Times*, April 18, 1985, p.4. In this case a certificate issued pursuant to the State Immunity Act 1978 s.21 was held only reviewable if a nullity.
[61] [1971] Ch. 160.
[62] 9 Cr. 388 (US 1815).
[63] *The Paquete Habana* 175 US 677 at 700 (1900).

notice of, and to give effect to, in the absence of any treaty or other public act of their own government in relation to the matter"[64]

and so, in the case of *Garcia-Mir v Meese*,[65] the decision of the Attorney-General detaining illegal Cuban immigrants was held to be a "controlling executive act", although the length of the detention was such as to constitute a violation of customary international law.

The position today remains the same as demonstrated in the case of *United States v Fawaz Yunis*,[66] in which it was stated "our duty is to enforce the Constitution, laws, and treaties of the United States, not to conform the law of the land to norms of customary international law."

The Court proceeded to reiterate its previous judicial pronouncement by declaring:

> "Statutes inconsistent with principles of customary international law may well lead to international law violations. But within the domestic legal realm, that inconsistent statute simply modifies or supersedes customary international law to the extent of the inconsistency."[67]

Customary international law is accepted without any legislative measure as part of American law, provided there is neither a national judicial decision nor a national legislative measure to the contrary. In the event of a conflict between alleged international law and municipal legislation, the national Courts will uphold the municipal provisions:

> "International practice is law only in so far as we adopt it, and like our common law or statute law it bends to the will of Congress. . . . There is one ground only upon which a federal court may refuse to enforce an Act of Congress and that is when the Act is held to be unconstitutional. The act may contravene recognised principles of international law, but that affords no more basis for judicial disregard of it than it does for the executive disregard of it."[68]

---

[64] *ibid.* at 708.
[65] 688 F (2d) 1446 (1986).
[66] Heard by the US Court of Appeals (D.C.) 30 I.L.M. 403 (1991).
[67] *ibid.*
[68] *Schroeder v Bissell* 5 F (2d) 838 (1925) (US Dist. Ct D.Conn.).

However norms that have achieved *jus cogens* are part of US law. In *Filartiga v Pena-Irala*[69] the Court stated that torture perpetrated against an individual by a State Official was contrary to the law of nations.

What is the internal status of customary international law? Customary international law is accepted as federal law and its determination by the federal courts is binding on the State Courts.[70]

Treaty law

Under the American Constitution, the President has "Power by and with the advice and consent of the Senate, to make Treaties, provided two-thirds of the Senators present concur."[71]

Unlike Britain, the American legislature participates in the treaty-making process. The President, in the light of the Constitution, has the power to make a treaty, but he may only ratify a treaty after the Senate has given its advice and approval. "All treaties made or which shall be made under the authority of the US shall be the supreme law of the land."[72]

What is the status of a treaty within the United States? "Supreme" only places treaties on an equal footing with federal statutes.[73] In the event of a conflict between a treaty and a subsequent statute, the latter prevails. This was made quite clear by the Supreme Court in *Edye v Robertson*,[74] when it refuted the contention that an Act of Congress, which conflicted with an earlier United States treaty, should be declared invalid. The Court unanimously held that a treaty is a law of the land, as is an Act of Congress, that there was nothing which made a treaty "irrepealable or unchangeable" and the Constitution gave "it no superiority over an Act of Congress in this respect, which may be repealed or modified by an Act of a later date . . .". Congress, of course, does not enjoy the competence to act on the treaty itself and thus Congress cannot repeal a treaty. What Congress may do, however, is to enact legislation which will subsequently be determined as being inconsistent with the law as previously represented.

---

[69] 2nd Circ. 1980, 630 F.2d, 876. For further discussion of this case see Chs 2 and 9.
[70] Restatement of Foreign Relations Law (Third) of the US (Revised) § III Reporters' No.3. This is the prevailing view. It has not always been so. State and federal courts decided international issues for themselves and consequently issues of international law were determined differently by courts in different States and the federal courts.
[71] art.II(2).
[72] art.VI of the US Constitution.
[73] *Edye v Robertson* 112 US 580 at 599 (1884).
[74] *ibid.*

A treaty provision cannot "be rendered negatory in any part of the United States by municipal ordinances or state laws."[75] However, a later treaty provision will not be regarded as having repealed by implication an earlier statute unless "the two are absolutely incompatible and the Statute cannot be enforced without antagonising the treaty."[76] A treaty is not repealed or modified by a subsequent federal statute unless that is the clearly expressed intention of Congress.[77]

The presumption exists when interpreting domestic legislation that Congress does not intend to infringe international law, and Acts of Congress should be construed as conforming to international law. Courts strive to interpret Acts of Congress so that they do not conflict with earlier treaty provisions. Nevertheless, in *Diggs v Schultz*,[78] although recognising that the Byrd Amendment allowing imports contrary to the UN Security Council embargo on Rhodesian products was in blatant disregard of United States treaty obligations, the Court concluded under the American constitutional scheme that Congress could denounce treaties if it saw fit to do so and there was nothing other branches of government could do about it.

In the United States, a distinction is made between "self-executing treaties" and "non-self-executing treaties".

"Self-executing treaties" are automatically part of American domestic law, i.e. no implementing legislation is required—whereas "non-self-executing treaties" are not incorporated into domestic law until the necessary enabling legislation has been passed. Some provisions of an international agreement may be self-executing, while other provisions in the same agreement may be non-self-executing. The distinction was initially made in *Foster and Elam v Neilson*,[79] when Marshall C.J. submitted:

> "A treaty is in its nature a contract between two nations, not a legislative act. It does not generally effect of itself, the object to be accomplished, especially so far as its operation is intraterritorial but is carried into execution by the sovereign power of the respective parties to the instrument. In the United States a different principle is established. Our Constitution declares a treaty to be the law of the land. It is, consequently, to be regarded in courts of justice as equivalent

---

[75] *Asakura v City of Seattle* 265 US 332 at 341 (1924).
[76] *Johnson v Browne* 205 US 309 at 321 (1907).
[77] *Cooke v The United States* 288 US 102 at 119–120 (1933).
[78] 470 F (2d) 461 (1972).
[79] 27 US (2 Pet.) 253 at 314 (1829).

to an act of the legislature, whenever it operates of itself without the aid of any legislative provision. But when the terms of the stipulation import a contract, when either of the parties engages to perform a particular act, the treaty addresses itself to the political, not the judicial department; and the legislature must execute the contract before it can become a rule for the court."[80]

Similarly, in *Sei Fujii v California*,[81] it was said, in order to determine whether a treaty is self-executing, Courts must look to "the intent of the signatory parties as manifested by the language of the instrument, and, if the instrument is uncertain, recourse may be had to the circumstances surrounding its execution" and "for a treaty provision to be operative without further implementing legislation and have statutory effect and force, it must appear that the framers of the treaty intended to prescribe a rule that, standing alone, would be enforceable in the courts."

The determining factor as to whether a treaty provision will be self-executing within the United States is the intention of the treaty framers. If the agreement is silent and the intention of the United States is unclear, account must be taken of relevant circumstances surrounding its conclusion, such as any statement issued by the President or any views expressed by the Senate. A treaty provision, to be self-executing, must therefore be:

(a)   unambiguous,

(b)   certain, and

(c)   not forward-looking

(i.e. legally complete and not dependent on subsequent legislation for its implementation).[82]

---

[80] The treaty in *Foster v Neilson*, which Marshall C.J. held was not to be self-executing, was later held by him to be self-executing, after the Spanish text was placed before the Court. *United States v Percheman* 32 US (7 Pet.) 51 (1833). In the case of *Medellin v Texas*, 552 U.S.-(2008) the US Supreme Court held that the Optional Protocol to the 1963 Vienna Convention on Consular Relations, although binding as a matter of international law, was not of domestic binding effect because it was not self-executing and there was no incorporating legislative act.

[81] 242 P. (2d) 617 (1952); 19 I.L.R. 312 (1952) Supreme Ct of California.

[82] Hence in *Sei Fujii*, *ibid*. The provisions of the Preamble and arts 1, 55 and 56 of the UN were held not to be self-executing, as they lacked "the mandatory quality and definitions which would indicate an intent to create justiciable rights in private persons immediately upon ratification", but rather were "framed as a promise of future action by member nations."

Generally, agreements which can be readily given effect by executive or judicial bodies, federal or State, without further federal legislation, are deemed self-executing, unless a contrary intention is manifest. Treaties covering issues on which Congress has regulated extensively are more likely to be interpreted as non-self-executing.

Self-executing treaties are advantageous in that they prevent delay in the execution of obligations and they obviate the need: (i) to include the participation of the House of Representatives (excluded from the treaty-making process by the Constitution), and (ii) to further consult the Senate after having received its consent under the two-thirds majority rule.

Although there is no hard and fast rule as to what may and may not be the subject of a self-executing treaty, there nevertheless appears to be a generally assumed principle that "an international agreement cannot take effect as domestic law without implementation by Congress if the agreement would do what lies within the exclusive law-making power of Congress under the Constitution."[83]

Executive agreements[84]

Executive agreements are international agreements entered into by the President without the advice and consent of Senate. Executive agreements are nevertheless regarded as being of the same force as a treaty and thereby, under international law, can effectively bind the United States. The validity of an executive agreement was upheld in *US v Belmont*[85] and in *US v Pink*.[86] In the latter case, it was held "A treaty is a Law of the Land under the supremacy clause (art.VI, cl.2) of the Constitution. Such international compacts and agreements as the Litvinoff Agreement have a similar dignity."[87] Executive agreements may be superseded by subsequent federal legislation, but whether an executive agreement can supersede a prior treaty or Act of Congress is unclear.[88] The argument against such an effect is based essentially on the

---

[83] Restatement of Foreign Relations Law (Third) of the US (Revised) § III, Comment i; cf. *Missouri v Holland* 252 US 416 (1920). See below.

[84] For definition of "executive agreement", see letter of January 26, 1973 from C. Browne, Acting Legal Adviser to Carl Marcy, Chief of Staff of the Committee on Foreign Relations of the US Senate, Digest of US Practice in International Law (1973) p.187.

[85] 301 US 324 (1937).

[86] 315 US 203 (1942).

[87] *ibid.* at 230.

[88] See, e.g. *United States v Guy W. Capps Inc.* 204 F (2d) 655 (1953) (US CA, 4th Circuit).

view that it would be inconceivable that the act of a single person, the President, could repeal an Act of Congress. However, an executive agreement is federal law and there are not varying degrees of status for federal law. "All constitutional acts of power, whether in the executive or the judicial department, have as much legal validity and obligation as if they proceeded from the legislature."[89] If an executive agreement was held to supersede a statute, Congress could re-enact the statute and thereby supersede the intervening executive agreement as domestic law.[90]

Attempts have been made to subject executive agreements to greater congressional control, for example the abortive Bricker Amendment 1953–54, Department of State Circular 175, 1955 (as amended 1966)[91] and the Case Act 1972, as amended in 1977 and 1978. In the 1972 Case Act[92] it was required that "all international agreements other than treaties, hereafter entered into by the US, be transmitted to the Congress within 60 days after the execution thereof." The 1977 amendment required the procedure laid down in the Case Act to be applied to agreements made by any department or agency of the United States Government and, in 1978, this was extended to cover oral as well as written agreements.

Congressional executive agreements

A congressional executive agreement is an international agreement made by the President with the backing of a simple majority in both Houses of Congress. Such agreements have an advantage over the treaty as prescribed by the Constitution in that their use can simplify the legislative process. For example, a treaty goes to the Senate for consent and then subsequently often goes back to the Senate as well as to the House for implementation, whereas a congressional executive agreement can go to both Houses in the first instance, and thus "consent" and implementation are achieved simultaneously. The prevailing view is the Congressional executive agreement can be used as an alternative to the treaty method in every instance. Which procedure should be used is a political judgment, made in the first instance by the President, subject to the possibility that the Senate might refuse to consider a joint resolution of Congress to approve an agreement, insisting the President submit the agreement as a treaty.[93]

---

[89] The Federalist, No.64 (Jay) cited in *US v Pink*, above, n.86.
[90] Above, n.82, § 115 Reporters' N. 5. An executive agreement has been held to prevail over a subsequent inconsistent State law—*Territory of Hawaii v Ho 41 Hawaii 565* (1957); 26 I.L.R. 557.
[91] Foreign Affairs Manual, Vol.III.
[92] P.L. 92–403, 86 Stat. 619; 1 US CA 112b.
[93] Above, n.89, § 303 Comment e.

Examples of Congressional Executive Agreements are those enacting US participation in the North America Free Trade Agreement (NAFTA) and the World Trade Organisation (WTO), which have led to objections that under the Constitution significant international obligations should be submitted to the Senate and the prescribed procedure. However such a challenge against Congressional Executive Agreements has not been accepted by any court, see *Made in the USA Foundation v United States*.[94]

Problems peculiar to a federal State

In a unitary State, the authority to enter into international agreements and the competence (subject to legislative approval) to give internal effect to such legislation lies with the central government. This is not the case in a federal State, where legislative competence is divided between the federal government and the individual state governments. *Missouri v Holland*[95] illustrates how legislation may be introduced by the back door. A 1913 Act of Congress designed to protect migratory wild fowl was declared to be outside the legislative competence of the federal government, and within the residual power of the states' legislatures. In 1916, the United States concluded the Migratory Bird Act with Britain (acting on Canada's behalf) and the Act was given internal effect within the United States by the Migratory Bird Treaty Act 1918. Appeal was made to the Supreme Court following a district Court's dismissal of a suit brought by the state of Missouri attempting to prevent Holland, a game warden, from enforcing the Migratory Bird Act. The Supreme Court held the Act of Congress being challenged was valid, as:

> "[T]he power of the Federal Government to make and enforce treaties is not a limitation on the reserved powers of States, but is the existence of a power not reserved to the States under the 10th Amendment being both expressly granted to the United States and prohibited to the States."[96]

In other words, there was no limitation on what could be the subject matter of a treaty, and the enforcement of a treaty, regardless of subject matter, falls within the exclusive competence of the federal government.

---

[94] 56 F Supp. (2d) 1226 (N.D. Ala. 1999).
[95] 252 US 416 (1920).
[96] *ibid*. at 431.

Missouri v Holland may be contrasted with *Attorney General for Canada v Attorney General for Ontario.*[97] Canada, like the United States, is a federal State and in 1937, the Judicial Committee of the Privy Council was required to give its opinion on what was the position when the federal government did not have the competence to give internal effect to international obligations which it had undertaken.[98] The Committee advised:

> "there is no such thing as treaty legislation as such. The distribution is based on classes of subjects; and as a treaty deals with a particular class so will the legislative power of performing it be ascertained . . . the Dominion cannot, merely by making promises to foreign countries, clothe itself with legislative authority inconsistent with the Constitution."

And:

> ". . . In a unitary State whose legislature possesses unlimited powers the problem is simple. Parliament will either fulfil or not treaty obligations imposed upon the State by its executive. The nature of the obligations does not affect the complete authority of the Legislature to make them law if it so chooses . . . in a federal State where legislative authority is limited . . . or is divided up between different Legislatures . . . the problem is complex. . . . The question is not how is the obligation formed, that is the function of the executive; but how is the obligation to be performed . . .".[99]

It may also happen in a federal state that the federal government will undertake an international obligation which is inconsistent with the law of a particular constituent part of the federation. As far as possible, the "offending" legislation will be interpreted as being consistent with international law, but the general principle regarding such a conflict is that it is the central government and not the constituent state which will have to answer to the international community.

---

[97] [1937] A.C. 326.
[98] Legislation designed to give effect within Canada to draft conventions adopted by the International Labour Organisation and the League of Nations was claimed to be invalid, as the Dominion Parliament did not possess the competency to legislate on the subject matter concerned.
[99] Above, n.97 at 351, 352 and 347. The limited internal competence of the federal government was why Canada did not accede to the UN 1966 Covenants on Economic, Social and Cultural Rights and Civil and Political Rights until 1976.

A similar problem could arise within the United Kingdom in the wake of devolution. The United Kingdom remains responsible at the international level for (non) fulfilment of international obligations. However, the division in competence brought about by devolution might lead to a situation in which the Westminster Parliament does not have the internal competence to give effect to its international obligations.[100]

Suggestion

The State Department's "suggestion" is the American counterpart of the British executive certificate. However, the suggestion does not confine itself to merely giving the facts, but may include comments on the situation and indicate the executive's attitude. Although not regarded as conclusive, the suggestion will be accepted as persuasive by the courts.

Act of State doctrine[101]

What if a measure of a foreign State is contrary to international law? The act of State doctrine precludes a court from inquiring into the validity of the public acts of a recognised foreign sovereign power within its own territory: "the Judicial Branch will not examine the validity of a taking of property within its own territory by a foreign sovereign government."[102]

The essence of the act of State doctrine is that the act of one independent government cannot be successfully questioned by the courts of another: "Redress of grievances by reason of such acts must be obtained through the means open to be availed of by sovereign powers as between themselves."[103] In other words, the judiciary abstains from giving a decision in deference to the executive so as not to embarrass the conduct of the executive's foreign relations by questioning the acts of foreign States. The act of State doctrine is similar, but yet distinct from sovereign immunity[104] in that both are based on considerations of respect for the sovereign independence and equality of States, and on perceived limitations on the authority of domestic courts of one State to judge the

---

[100] See, however, the Scotland Act s.58(1); see also the *Tyrer* case (1978) 58 I.L.R. 339.
[101] Act of State has a different connotation in British constitutional law—an alien who is injured abroad by an act authorised or subsequently approved by the Crown has no remedy in English Courts.
[102] *Banco Nacional de Cuba v Sabbatino* 376 US 398 at 428 (1964).
[103] *Underhill v Hernandez* 168 US 250 at 252 (1897).
[104] Discussed below in Ch.6.

activities of another State. However, whereas sovereign immunity relates to activities carried out and provides jurisdictional defence to suit, the act of State doctrine operates so as to preclude judicial scrutiny of the activities of foreign States in their own territories. Strict adherence to the act of State doctrine was maintained by the United States Supreme Court in the *Sabbatino* case, even when the State Department had described the Cuban legislative measure as:

> "... manifestly in violation of those principles of international law which has long been accepted by the free countries of the West. It is in its essence discriminatory, arbitrary and confiscatory."[105]

The outcome of the *Sabbatino* case was the Court gave effect to the Cuban decree, in spite of its having been contrary to international law.

The act of State doctrine as understood in the *Sabbatino* case has its basis in the separation of powers and the raison d'être of the *Sabbatino* position was the need to avoid conflict between the judiciary and the executive on decisions regarding the legal nature of foreign actions.

The *Sabbatino* decision prompted a response from Congress in the form of the "Hickenlooper Amendments" to the Foreign Assistance Act, whereby:

> "... no court in the United States shall decline on the ground of the ... Act of State doctrine to make a determination on the merits giving effect to the principles of international law in a case in which a claim of title or other right to property is asserted by any party including a foreign State (or a party claiming through such State) based upon (or traced through) a confiscation or other taking ... by an act of that State in violation of the principles of international law."[106]

Accordingly, American Courts may review the acts of foreign governments which violate international law and which affect property owned by American citizens. The State Department can express in a "suggestion" that the act of State is to apply in a particular case.

---

[105] Above, n.102 at 403.
[106] s.620(e)(2) of the Foreign Assistance Act of 1965, Pub.L.No.89–171; 301(d)(2), 79 Stat. 653, 659, as amended.

Judicial determination of the legality of the foreign act of State will not necessarily interfere with the executive's conduct of foreign affairs.[107]

In *Alfred Dunhill v Republic of Cuba*,[108] the Legal Adviser to the State Department submitted a letter in which he stated that in the State Department's experience there was little support for the presumption "that adjudication of acts of foreign States in accordance with the relevant principles of international law would embarrass the conduct of foreign policy." Accordingly, he concluded it would not cause embarrassment to the conduct of United States foreign policy if the Court demanded to follow the holding in the *Sabbatino* case.[109] In *W.S. Kirkpatrick and Co v Environmental Tectonics Corp International*, the US Supreme Court declined to apply the act of State doctrine, stating:

> "The act of State doctrine does not establish an exception for cases and controversies that may embarrass foreign governments but merely requires that, in the process of deciding, the acts of foreign sovereigns taken within their own jurisdiction shall be deemed valid. That doctrine has no application to the present case because the validity of no foreign sovereign act is at issue".[110]

The act of State doctrine would not apply in respect of war crimes or offences over which there is universal jurisdiction. The act of State doctrine should be distinguished from the political question doctrine; namely, there are certain national issues so sensitive that they are non-justiciable.[111] Cases which raise the political question doctrine are dismissed by the courts, unlike those involving the act of State doctrine, which are adjudicated.

---

[107] See, *Banco Nacional de Cuba v First National City Bank* US Supreme Ct, 406 US 759 (1972); 92 S.L.T. 1808.

[108] 425 US 682 (1976).

[109] *ibid.* letter of Monroe Leigh, Legal Adviser, Department of State—printed as App.706, 709, 710–711.

[110] Scalia J. at 189, *ibid.*

[111] *US v Sisson* 294 F. Supp 515 (D.Mass. 1968), in which the Court concluded that a domestic tribunal was incapable of ascertaining facts pertaining during war and the defendant had submitted an issue of a political character not within the jurisdiction of the Court. The defendant had invoked as his defence to a charge of refusing to serve in the US armed forces that the US operations in Vietnam were contrary to international law. On non-justiciability of political questions, see also *Baker v Carr* 369 US 186 (1962) and *Greenham Women against Cruise Missiles v Reagan* 591 F. Supp 1332 (1984).

The act of State doctrine is one of American municipal law. There is no rule of international law which requires the application of the act of State doctrine.

In English law the position is as expressed in the *Butts Gas and Oil Company v Hammer (No.3)*[112] namely that "there exists in English law a general principle that the courts will not adjudicate upon the transactions of foreign sovereign states . . .".[113] However, notwithstanding the general rule the House of Lords refused to uphold an act of the Iraqi government in *Kuwait Airways Corporation v Iraqi Airways Company*.[114] What was at issue in that case was a violation of international law by one State against another.

---

[112] [1982] A.C. 888.
[113] *ibid.* at 931–932.
[114] [2002] U.K.H.L. 19.

4. INTERNATIONAL PERSONALITY

The possession of international personality means an entity is a subject of international law, is "capable of possessing international rights and duties, and has the capacity to maintain its rights by bringing international claims."[1]

A subject of international law owes responsibilities to the international community and enjoys rights, the benefits of which may be claimed, and which if denied may be enforced to the extent recognised by the international legal system, via legal procedures. That is, the entity will have procedural capacity.

Which entities possess international legal personality?

The concept of international personality is neither static nor uniform:

> "The subjects of law in any legal system are not necessarily identical in their nature or in the extent of their rights, and their nature depends upon the needs of the community. Throughout its history, the development of international life

---

[1] *Reparation for Injuries Suffered in the Service of the United Nations* I.C.J. Rep. 1949 at p.174.

... and the progressive increase in the collective activities of States has already given rise to instances of action upon the international plane by certain entities which are not States."[2]

As international law has developed and expanded in scope, so "new" entities have been admitted as "actors" on the international scene. The personality enjoyed by such actors varies considerably. States were once considered the exclusive subjects of international law:

> "Since the law of nations is based on the common consent of individual States, and not of individual human beings, States solely and exclusively are the subjects of international law."[3]

Today, however, although they remain the primary subjects, States are no longer the exclusive subjects of the international legal system. Throughout the twentieth century the scope of international legal personality widened considerably to take account of the proliferation of international organisations and the greater international awareness of human rights. However, while States possess full international legal personality as an inherent attribute of their Statehood, all other entities possessing personality do so only to the extent that States allow: that is, their personality is derived via States.

The personality of States thus may be characterised as *original* and that of other entities as *derivative*.

STATES

States are the principal persons of international law. International law is essentially the product of relations between States, be it through practice contributing to the formation of customary international law or through international agreements (treaties). Only States may be parties to contentious cases before the International Court of Justice.[4] States enjoy the exclusive discretion as to whether or not to espouse a claim on behalf of a national who has allegedly been aggrieved by another State; and once a State does take up a claim, the dispute is raised to the international level and becomes one between two States.[5] An individual cannot deny a State's right to espouse a claim on his behalf

---

[2] *ibid.* at 178.
[3] L. Oppenheim, *International Law* (2nd edn, 1912).
[4] art.34(1), Statute of the International Court of Justice.
[5] See, e.g. *Mavrommatis Palestine Concessions* case P.C.I.J.Rep., ser.A, No.2 (1924).

should it choose to do so[6] and a State does not act as the agent of its nationals when negotiating a treaty.[7]

What is a State?

A "State" under international law is an entity which has a defined territory, a permanent population, is under the control of a government and engages in, or has the capacity to engage in, formal relations with other entities.[8]

This definition reflects the indices of statehood enunciated in the 1933 Montevideo Convention on Rights and Duties of States.[9] The Convention, regarded as representing in general terms the requirements of statehood demanded by customary international law, was adopted by the Seventh International Conference of American States (15 Latin American and the United States) and provides:

> "The State as a person of international law should possess the following qualifications: (a) a permanent population, (b) a defined territory; (c) government; and (d) capacity to enter into relations with other states."[10]

Opinion Number 1 of the Arbitration Commission of the European Conference of Yugoslavia stated, "the State is commonly defined as a community which consists of a territory and a population subject to an organized political authority" and "such a state is characterised by sovereignty".[11]

Permanent population

States are aggregates of individuals and accordingly a permanent population is a prerequisite of statehood. However, no minimum population is required. Nauru, with a population of 12,000, is considered a State, as is Liechtenstein with a population of over 30,000 and Tuvalu with a population of 10,000.

[6] *North American Dredging Company* case 4 R.I.A.A. 26 at 29 *et seq.* (1926).
[7] See, e.g. *Rustomjee v R.* (1876) 1 Q.B.D. 487 at 492; *Civilian War Claimants' Association Ltd v The King* [1932] A.C. 14, HL at 26.
[8] The American Law Institute, Restatement of the Law Third, The Foreign Relations Law of the United States, Vol.1, § 201.
[9] 164 L.N.T.S. 19; U.S.T.S. 881; 28 A.J.I.L., Supp., 75 (1934).
[10] art.1, Montevideo Convention.
[11] 92 I.L.R., pp.162, 165.

Defined territory

States are territorial units and:

> "'territorial sovereignty' involves the exclusive right to display the activities of a State. This right has a corollary, a duty: the obligation to protect within the territory the rights of other States, in particular their right to integrity and inviolability in peace and in war, together with the rights which each State may claim for its nationals in foreign territory. Without manifesting its territorial sovereignty in a manner corresponding to circumstances, the State cannot fulfil this duty. Territorial sovereignty cannot limit itself to its negative side, i.e. to excluding the activities of other States, for it serves to divide between the nations the space upon which human activities are employed, in order to assure them at all points the minimum of protection of which international law is the guardian . . .".[12]

Article 9 of the Montevideo Convention provides that:

> "The jurisdiction of States within the limits of national territory applies to all the inhabitants. Nationals and foreigners are under the same protection of the law and the national authorities and the foreigners may not claim rights other or more extensive than those of the nationals."

However, while territory is necessary, there is no prescribed minimum geographical size. The requirement of territory may be satisfied even if the entity's territorial boundaries are not precisely defined or are to some extent in dispute, for example Israel in 1948 and Kuwait in 1963. This rule that indefinite boundaries need not defeat a claim to statehood was noted by the Court in the *North Sea Continental Shelf* cases:

> "The appurtenance of a given area, considered as an entity, in no way governs the precise determination of its boundaries, any more than uncertainty as to boundaries can affect territorial rights. There is for instance no rule that the land frontiers of a State must be fully delimited and defined, and often in various places and for long periods they are not . . .".[13]

---

[12] *Island of Palmas* case 2 R.I.A.A. 829, Huber J. at 839 (1928).
[13] I.C.J. Rep. 1969 3 at 32.

However, one of the reasons advanced by the British for the non-recognition of Bophuthatswana as an independent State is the fragmentation of its territory within South Africa.[14]

A government

Statehood must be evidenced by the establishment of an effective government, that is one independent of any other authority and one which enjoys legislative and administrative competence.[15] Non-dependence was stressed by the International Committee of Jurists in 1920 in its Report on the Status of Finland. The Committee highlighted the difficulty of ascertaining the actual date when Finland became, in the legal sense, a sovereign State, but concluded it certainly was not one:

> "... until a stable political organisation had been created, and until the public authorities had become strong enough to assert themselves throughout the territories of the State without the assistance of foreign troops. It would appear that it was in May 1918, that the civil war ended and that the foreign troops began to leave the country, so that from that time onwards it was possible to re-establish order and normal political and social life, little by little."[16]

An established State's statehood is not nullified if it is without an effective government for a period of time, for example during a civil war, e.g. Somalia. Somalia was ravaged by civil war from 1991 until 2004, but during that time continued to be recognised as a State and was a member of the United Nations. Somalia during the civil war may be characterised as a failed State in that in spite of possessing legal capacity it was unable to exercise it in the absence of an effective regime. Other such examples which may be cited include Afghanistan, Sierra Leone and the Democratic Republic of Congo, thereby highlighting that the absence of an effective regime does not negate statehood.

---

[14] Other reasons are the pattern of population, the economic dependency on South Africa and primarily the fact "the existence of Bophuthatswana is a consequence of apartheid ..." See, *Hansard*, HC, Vol.126, cols 760–761. (February 3, 1988); U.K.M.I.L. 1986; 57 B.Y.I.L. 507 (1986).

[15] Again note the British position *vis-à-vis* Bophuthatswana and the latter's economic dependence on South Africa. Bophuthatswana was re-incorporated into South Africa on April 27, 1994 and ceased to exist as a separate political entity. The flag is no longer in use.

[16] L.N.O.J., Special Supp. No.3 (1920) 3.

In 1992 Croatia[17] and Bosnia-Herzegovina[18] were accorded recognition as independent States by member States of the European Community, notwithstanding that large areas of their respective territories were controlled by non-governmental forces. Nor does military occupation terminate statehood, for example Germany's occupation of the European States during the Second World War. Contemporary international law is frequently confronted with secessionist movements and how to respond to calls for independence. The independence declaration of Kosovo in February 2008 has reignited the debate on state recognition and precipitated the request for an advisory opinion as to its status.[19]

Capacity to enter into international relations

This is an important indicator of statehood, but its realisation depends on the response of other actors on the international stage. The satisfaction of the first three criteria is essentially factual, but fulfillment of this criterion depends on recognition:

> "The political existence of the State is independent of recognition by the other States. Even before recognition the State has the right to defend its integrity and independence, to provide for its conservation and prosperity, and consequently to organise itself as it sees fit, to legislate upon its interests, administer its services, and to define the jurisdiction and competence of its Courts. The exercise of these rights has no other limitation than the exercise of the rights of other States according to international law."[20]

In other words, an entity may have the capacity to enter into foreign relations, but should other States decline to enter into relations with it, the entity in question is denied the opportunity to demonstrate this capacity in practice. For example, Southern Rhodesia, a British self-governing territory until it declared unilateral independence from Britain in November 1965, had a population, territory, a government and the capacity to enter into

---

[17] January 15, 1992, however note Croatia was deemed not to have met the requirements laid down in the Draft Convention on Yugoslavia on November 4, 1991 and in the Declaration on Yugoslavia and Guidelines on the Recognition of New States in Eastern Europe and in the Soviet Union, of December 16, 1991 (92 I.L.R., p.178).

[18] April 6, 1992. For reservations with respect to the independence of Bosnia and Herzegovina prior to holding a referendum, see Opinion Number 4 (92 I.L.R., p.173).

[19] The request to the I.C.J. in October 2008 was made pursuant to GA Resolution 63/3 (2008).

[20] art.3, Montevideo Convention, above n.9.

relations with other States. However, no other State was willing to enter into relations with Southern Rhodesia. Southern Rhodesia was therefore refused recognition as a State by the rest of the international community.[21] Similarly, governments consistently refused to enter into relations with the Transkei. The Transkei territory was declared by South Africa in 1976 to be a "sovereign and independent state", but the United Nations General Assembly subsequently adopted a resolution rejecting the "independence" as "invalid".[22] Similarly, the recognition of Bophuthatswana, Venda and Ciskei was denied by all members of the international community other than South Africa. The independence of Ciskei was refuted by the Security Council, which issued a statement calling upon "all Governments to deny any form of recognition to the so-called 'independent' Bantustans."[23]

An entity which possesses the ability to conduct foreign relations does not terminate its statehood if it voluntarily hands over all or part of the conduct of its foreign relations to another State, for example San Marino (Italy)[24] and Monaco (France). Another "mini" European State is Liechtenstein, which operates within the Swiss economic system and has delegated a number of sovereign powers to Switzerland but, nevertheless, is still recognised as a sovereign State.[25] Similarly, the personality of a protected State which existed before the conclusion of the agreement establishing its dependent status, is not extinguished. See, for example, *Nationality Decrees in Tunis and Morocco* case[26] and *Rights of Nationals of the United States in Morocco* case.[27] Such relationships were characteristic of the British and French Empires, and most

---

[21] See Security Council Resolution of November 12, 1965, Resolution 216 (1965) S.C.O.R., 20th year, Resolutions and Decisions, p.8 and Security Council Resolution of November 20, 1965, Resolution 217 (1965) S.C.O.R., 20th Year, Resolutions and Decisions, p.8 in which the Smith regime was characterised as illegal, the declaration of independence as of "no legal validity" and UN Members were called upon to refrain from assisting the "illegal racist minority regime". cf. the United Nations' response to PAIGC Declaration of Guinea-Bissau's independence in September 1973.

[22] GA Resolution, G.A.O.R., 31st Session, Supp.39, p.10.

[23] S.C.O.R., 36th Year, Resolutions and Decisions, p.1. The legislation relating to the homelands was repealed in 1993, and the four homelands have since been reabsorbed into South Africa.

[24] San Marino was admitted to the UN in March 1992.

[25] Although denied admission to the League of Nations on the grounds that she could not discharge all the international obligations which would be imposed upon her by the Covenant, Liechtenstein has been a party to a case before the I.C.J. (the *Nottebohm* case, I.C.J. Rep. (1955), p.4). Liechtenstein became a member of the UN on September 18, 1990.

[26] P.C.I.J.Rep., ser.B, No.4 (1923).

[27] I.C.J. Rep. 1952, 176.

were terminated during the decolonisation movement, which gathered momentum after the Second World War.

Membership of a regional organisation does not negate the statehood of individual members, for example the European Union, although admittedly, sovereignty in certain areas of competence may be restricted.

Existing States may refuse "statehood" to an entity, which has attained a characteristic of statehood in violation of international law, for example the acquisition of territory by the use of force contrary to art.2(4) of the United Nations Charter, or to the principle of non-intervention.[28] However, in most instances, whether or not there has been an unlawful threat or use of force will be disputed, and generally it is not an issue which will be authoritatively resolved, for example Indian intervention in Bangladesh was by many governments deemed to be illegal, while others argued to the contrary, justifying India's action as supporting the principle of self-determination. Territory acquired by the legitimate use of force, for example in self-defence, and then annexed from the aggressor, *may* (emphasis added) be an exception to the non-recognition-of-conquest rule.

Political self-determination, that is the principle whereby the political future of a colony or similar non-independent territory is determined in accordance with the wishes of its inhabitants, has, particularly since the 1960s, been taken into account in issues of Statehood. The principle, which some 30 years ago was articulated as "a formative principle of great potency . . .",[29] has now evolved into a rule of international law.[30] The Declaration on the Granting of Independence to Colonial Territories and Peoples[31] characterised the principle and para.2 reads:

[28] See G.A. Res.2625 (XXV), "Declaration on Principles of International Law Concerning Friendly Relations and Co-operation among States in Accordance with the Charter of the United Nations" G.A.O.R., 25th Session, Supp.28 (A/2028) 121 (1970), 65 A.J.I.L. 243 (1970), the Alma Ata Declaration which states "The Community and its Member States will not recognise entities which are the result of aggression", the Guidelines on the Recognition of New States in Eastern Europe and in the Soviet Union (1992) 31 I.L.M. 1486, the earlier Security Council Resolution (S.C. RES 541 18 November 1983) whereby all States were called upon not to recognize the Turkish Republic of Northern Cyprus, and the *Brcko International-Entity Boundary* case 36 I.L.M. 1997, 396.

[29] Schwarzenberger, *Manual of International Law* (6th edn, 1976), p.59.

[30] See decision of the Chamber of the International Court of Justice in the *Frontier Dispute (Burkino Faso/Mali)* I.C.J. Rep. 1986 554 at 566–567 in which the Chamber was required to consider the relationship between self-determination and *uti possidetis*. It has also been suggested that it constitutes a rule of *jus cogens*; see Espiell in UN Law/Fundamental Rights: Two Topics in International Law (Cassese edn, 1979) p.167.

[31] GA Resolution 1514 (XV), December 14, 1960, G.A.O.R., 15th Session, Supp.16, p.66.

"All peoples have a right to self-determination; by virtue of that right they freely determine their political status and freely pursue their economic, social and cultural development."

The aim of para.2 was identified in the *Western Sahara* case.[32] It was acknowledged therein "that the application of the right of self-determination requires a free and genuine expression of the will of the peoples concerned."[33] Dillard J., in a separate Opinion (though concurring in the Court's Opinion), stated:
"It seemed hardly necessary to make more explicit the cardinal restraint which the legal right of self-determination imposes. The restraint may be captured in a single sentence. It is for the people to determine the destiny of the territory and not the territory the destiny of the people . . ."[34]
However, Resolution 1514 did not negate a title to colonial and similar non-independent territory which does not reflect the wishes of its people, but rather emphasises that "immediate steps" should be taken to ensure independence is attained in accordance with self-determination. The emergence of self-determination, as a cardinal principle in shaping the political future of a colonial or similar non-independent territory, means that such territories can no longer be considered as mere adjuncts of the administering power. They have, according to the 1970 Declaration on Principles of International Law:

"a status separate and distinct from the territory of the State administering it; and such separate and distinct status under the Charter [i.e. UN Charter] shall exist until the people of the colony or non-self-governing territory have exercised their right of self-determination in accordance with the Charter, and particularly its purposes and principles."[35]

This separate identity of an administered people is further reflected in several legal statements relating to the status of South West Africa (Namibia).[36]
South West Africa was placed under a "C" Mandate at the conclusion of the First World War. Mandates were introduced as a novel type of administration for those territories taken from defeated powers and "inhabited by peoples not yet able to stand by themselves under the strenuous conditions of the modern

---

[32] Advisory Opinion I.C.J. Rep. 1975 12.
[33] *ibid.*, p.32.
[34] *ibid.* p.122.
[35] *ibid.* G.A. Res. 2625, above, n.27.
[36] South West Africa became the independent state of Namibia in November 1990.

world."[37] After the conclusion of the Second World War, the mandate system was replaced by that of trusteeship.[38] South Africa, however, refused to place South West Africa under that trusteeship system and this precipitated much political and legal argument on the status of South West Africa.[39] In the 1950 Opinion, McNair J. pronounced the system involved a:

> "new institution—a new relationship between territory and its inhabitants on the one hand and the government which represents them internationally on the other—a new species of international government, which does not fit into the old conception of sovereignty and which is alien to it."[40]

The sovereignty, McNair J. maintained, was held to be in abeyance until the inhabitants of the territory obtained recognition as an independent State. The issues before the Court concerned the responsibilities and duties of South Africa, but against the backcloth of the self-determination movement there was a move away from the traditional view that a mandated/trusteeship territory only achieved international recognition on attaining independence, to one according such an entity at least a degree of international status. This view was articulated by Ammoun J. when he concluded:

> "Namibia, even at the periods when it had been reduced to the status of a German colony or was subject to the South African Mandate, possessed a legal personality which was denied to it only by the law now obsolete ... It nevertheless constituted a subject of law ... possessing national sovereignty but lacking the exercise thereof ... Sovereignty, ... did not cease to belong to the people subject to mandate. It had simply, for a time, been rendered inarticulate and deprived of freedom of expression."[41]

Ammoun's J. view representing the Third World illustrates the change in international attitude, namely, non-self-governing

[37] Covenant of the League of Nations, art.22.
[38] The system applied only to 11 territories—10 former mandates and Somalia taken from Italy. No other territories were brought into the system as was envisaged by art.77(1) of the UN Charter.
[39] *International Status of South West Africa* case I.C.J. Rep. 1950, 128; *Legal Consequences for States of the Continued Presence of South Africa in Namibia (South West Africa) Notwithstanding Security Council Resolution 276 (1970)*. Advisory Opinion I.C.J. Rep. 1971, 16.
[40] *ibid.* p.150.
[41] Above, n.39, I.C.J. Rep. 1971 at p.68.

territories could no longer be dismissed as adjuncts of the administering power. They cannot, by definition, enjoy full sovereignty until independence has been attained, but they do apparently enjoy some status, be it one that falls short of full sovereignty.[42]

Self-determination is an issue which has generated considerable controversy. Contemporary international law does acknowledge self-determination as a legal right in the colonial context. However, a claim for self-determination outside the colonial context is one which still gives rise to considerable debate. Much of this controversy stems from an assumption that self-determination and its expression is premised on a granting of independence and thus the break-up of territorial units. The issue of self-determination beyond the traditional context of colonialism has highlighted that self-determination may have an internal aspect as well as an external aspect. In the Canadian Supreme Court decision in *Re Reference by the Governor in Council Concerning Certain Questions Relating to the Secession of Quebec from Canada*,[43] the Court dealt with whether the province of Quebec enjoyed the right to secede unilaterally from Canada.[44] The Court concluded in the negative, holding that any right of self-determination could only arise in strictly limited circumstances and international law does not support the "right" of entities within an existing State to secede unilaterally. The Court accordingly upheld the principle of territorial integrity of existing States. It was also noted that no right of external self-determination would be recognised when full participation in civil and political life is available, namely internal self-determination, which may be interpreted as the right of a minority people to pursue political, economic, social, and cultural development, within the framework of an existing State.[45]

The Arbitration Committee of the International Conference on Yugoslavia[46] (the Banditer Committee) stated: "That whatever

---

[42] e.g. Hong Kong, could not satisfy the criteria for statehood because it was subject to the legal authority of the UK. The Hong Kong Special Administrative Region (HKSAR) was established on July 1, 1997, under the legal authority of China (The PRC). The HKSAR has limited treaty-making competence and is able to conclude agreements independently of China in certain fields, e.g. shipping, trade, communications financial and monetary. Foreign and Commonwealth Office, Paper, London, Application after June 30, 1997 of Multilateral and Bilateral International Agreements, Hong Kong Department, April 1996.

[43] (1998) 161 D.L.R. (4th) 385.

[44] The Court was asked whether such a right existed under the Canadian Constitution or by way of existing international law.

[45] See Final Report and Recommendations of an International meeting of Experts on the Further Study of the Concept of the Right of People for UNESCO, February 22, 1990, SNS–89/CONF.602/7.

[46] Opinion No.2, 3 E.J.I.L. (1992) 183–184.

the circumstances, the right to self-determination must not involve changes to existing frontiers at the time of independence (*uti possidetis juris*) except where the State concerned agreed otherwise".[47]

Self-determination may be expressed legitimately without violating established international provisions protecting territorial integrity. However; the right of self-determination nevertheless has to be tempered otherwise: ". . . if every ethnic, religious or linguistic group claimed Statehood, there would be no limit to fragmentation, and peace, security, and economic well-being for all would be much more difficult to achieve."[48]

An additional consideration which has been introduced to State recognition has been that of compliance with human rights, and the rights of minorities. The Declaration on the Guidelines on the Recognition of new States in Eastern Europe and the Soviet Union[49] (The Alma Ata Declaration) issued by the Foreign Ministers of the European Economic Council in December 1991, demanded, *inter alia*, ". . . respect for the UN Charter, the Helsinki Final Act, and the Charter of Paris, 'especially with regard to the rule of law, democracy and human rights', . . . guarantees for the rights of ethnic and national groups and minorities."[50]

RECOGNITION OF STATES AND GOVERNMENTS

The international community is not static. New States are born while existing States may become extinct, for example the dissolution of the Socialist Federal Republic of Yugoslavia in 1991/92 and the creation of Bosnia-Herzegovina, Slovenia, Croatia and Macedonia as independent States.[51] Governments come to power and are removed from power. Recognition essentially denotes a willingness on the part of the recognising entity to enter into relations with the entity being recognised.

---

[47] The Banditer Committee was established by EU States and its mandate was to express its views on certain matters in relation to the peace process following the break up of Yugoslavia. In regards to self-determination, the Committee's opinion was sought on whether "The Serbian population in Croatia and Bosnia-Herzegovina, as one of the constituent peoples of Yugoslavia, have the right to self-determination."

[48] UN Secretary General Boutros Boutros Ghali, Agenda for Peace, reproduced in A. Roberts and B. Kingsbury, United Nations, Divided World (2nd edn, 1993).

[49] Above, n.28, p.62, Alma Ata Declaration.

[50] *E.J.I.L.* December 16, 1991, p.50. Similar conditions were demanded in respect of those entities claiming recognition as States following the break up of the former Yugoslavia.

[51] See, Marc Weller for an account of the "International Response to the Dissolution of the Socialist Federal Republic of Yugoslavia" (1992) 86 *A.J.I.L.* 569. Note that the two States of Serbia and Montenegro are now known as the Federal Republic of Yugoslavia, which was recognised by the UK in April 1996.

The recognition of a State is of importance as it is concerned with status, that is the status of the entity in question: (i) on the international scene; and (ii) within the domestic legal system of the recognising State.

Recognition is a complex issue. Factors other than legal considerations influence decisions to recognise any given entity. A State is accorded recognition in the majority of cases by the executive. It is a matter of policy in which the recognising State has discretion: an entity seeking recognition cannot however demand recognition as of right. An apt description of recognition is that it is a political act which produces legal consequences.

Recognition of States and governments distinguished

Recognition of a State is the formal acknowledgment by a State that the entity being recognised possesses the attributes of statehood and thus signifies a willingness to treat the latter as a State.

Recognition of a government is the formal acknowledgment by the recognising State that the regime in question is the effective government and accordingly signifies a willingness to treat that regime as such.

Recognition of a State is normally a one-off act—that is, once an entity has been recognised as a State, that recognition will not usually be retracted if the requirements of Statehood continue to be fulfilled. If these requirements cease to be fulfilled, the State may no longer exist but de-recognition will not be necessary. Two States, for example, may be consolidated into a single State, as in 1990, when the Yemen Arab Republic (North Yemen) and the People's Democratic Republic of Yemen (South Yemen) united to form the Republic of Yemen. However, the governmental regime of a State may not always be accorded recognition. Refusal to accord recognition to a particular governmental regime does not negate a State's Statehood. In normal circumstances, governments will be accorded recognition. The question of recognition is only raised when the regime in question has come to power by unconstitutional methods, e.g. by *coup d'état*. For example, in *Somalia (A Republic) v Woodhouse Drake & Carey (Suisse) SA*,[52] the Court held the plaintiff could not recover any money held by the Company as the plaintiff had not been recognised by the United Kingdom as the interim government in power at that time. The judge identified several criteria which should be considered by British Courts when determining whether a government is the sovereign government of a State, for example:

---

[52] [1993] 1 All E.R. 371.

(a)   whether the entity is the constitutional government of the State;

(b)   the degree, nature and stability of administrative control, if any, which are exercised over the territory of the State;

(c)   whether the British government has any dealings with that government, and, if so, the nature of those dealings; and

(d)   in marginal cases the extent of international recognition that has been accorded the government of that State.[53]

An entity may therefore be recognised as a State, but it is possible for its governmental regime not to be accorded recognition. It is evident from the foregoing case that the UK Courts are able to make an objective decision concerning the international legal personality of a government based on factors other than the official position of the UK government. The decision in *Sierra Leone Telecommunications v Barclays Bank Plc* [1998] 2 All E.R. 821, further reinforces that the courts enjoy a more central role than previously.

Before considering what happens in practice, the two principal schools of thought on recognition must be mentioned, albeit briefly.

Theories

The two principal theories on recognition are the constitutive school of thought and the declaratory school of thought.

(i) The constitutive theory. Supporters of the constitutive theory emphasise the act of recognition itself and maintain that it is the act of recognition which establishes (is constitutive of) the international personality of the entity in question. The act of recognition is a precondition of legal status, that is, it is the act of recognition which: (a) creates a State; and (b) determines the legal personality of a new governmental regime. The constituent theory immediately raises two questions: what is the position of unrecognised entities; are they free to behave as they choose on the international scene unfettered by obligations imposed by international law? What is the position of an entity recognised by some States and not by others?

(ii) Declaratory (or evidentiary) theory. Supporters of this theory minimise the importance of the act of recognition and regard

---

[53] *ibid.* at 372.

recognition as only a formal acknowledgement of already existing circumstances. Thus the act of recognition is not regarded as what creates the State. See response of the Arbitration Commission (Badinter Commission)[54] in reply to the question whether the dissolution of the Socialist Federal Republic of Yugoslavia was a new State calling for recognition. The Commission's view was that:

> "while recognition is not a prerequisite for the foundations of a State and is purely declaratory in its impact, it is nonetheless a discretionary act that other States may perform when they choose and in a manner of their own choosing . . ."[55]

Although the declaratory theory is more in line with State practice, it nevertheless remains too simple in that it denies some of the complexities which underline recognition. Recognition, when granted, has retroactive effect—that is, recognition is backdated. For example, Britain accorded recognition to the post-revolution regime in the Soviet Union in 1921, but the effect of that recognition was that the recognition was backdated to 1917.

Existing States do treat unrecognised entities as having obligations under international law. Such unrecognised entities are not free to behave as they choose on the international scene, for example, in 1949, Britain demanded compensation from the Jewish State in respect of British aircraft shot down by Jewish airmen over Egypt; in 1957, compensation was also demanded by the British from the unrecognised Taiwan Government for damage done by Taiwan forces to British vessels; and in 1968, the United States asserted that North Korea, which it did not recognise, had violated international law by attacking a United States vessel, *The Pueblo*.

Is there a duty to recognise?

The most notable exponent of the proposition that if an entity satisfies the formal factual requirements of a State or a government, then recognition should be awarded, was the late Sir Hersch Lauterpacht.[56] He did, however, acknowledge recognition should be withheld if the entity had come to power through a violation of international law, for example the use of force contrary to

---

[54] The Badinter Commission was established by the EC to help resolve the crisis in Yugoslavia. It dealt with the applications by Slovenia, Croatia, Macedonia and Bosnia-Herzegovina, requesting recognition. See *Weller*, p.576 for an account of the procedural rules of the Commission, above, n.51.

[55] See also Opinion Number 1.

[56] Lauterpacht, *Recognition in International Law* (1947), Chs 3 and 11.

art.2(4) of the UN Charter. Although States do look at the factual criteria which are manifested by an entity, the act of recognition is essentially governed by political expediency. A State is not required to enter into relations with another entity if it chooses not to do so. If there was a legal duty to recognise, recognition would not be discretionary but mandatory.

Criteria for recognition of states

The criteria of statehood have already been considered. States will generally accord recognition to an entity if the latter satisfies the requirements spelt out in the Montevideo Convention-defined territory, as well as other factors which may be employed:[57] permanent population; independent government; capacity to engage in relations with other international persons. If the governmental regime appears effective and stable, then recognition will be accorded. "Effective" refers to the physical control of the territory in question. Does the regime enjoy control over most of the territory, and is that control likely to continue? An affirmative answer will characterise the control as effective. "Stable", on the other hand, refers to the regime's likelihood of continuing in power (see below, especially distinction between recognition *de facto* and recognition *de jure*). The imposition of additional conditions upon Croatia, Slovenia and Bosnia-Herzegovina by the European Community in 1992 was clearly a political act[58] and is indicative of the constitutive theory.[59] Notwithstanding this, the decisions of the EC Arbitration Commission on Yugoslavia appear to favour the application of the declaratory theory to the dissolution of Yugoslavia.[60] If all the criteria are fulfilled, then when recognition is actually

---

[57] See above, pp.63 *et seq.*

[58] States applying for recognition were required to respect the rule of law, democracy and human rights, to reaffirm the inviolability of frontiers, to protect minorities and to adopt constitutional and political guarantees ensuring that the State has no territorial claim towards a neighbouring Community State. See the EC Guidelines on Recognition of New States in Eastern Europe and the Soviet Union and a Declaration on Yugoslavia, 1991 *B.Y.I.L.* 62, 559 at 560, particularly, and A. V. Lowe and Colin Warbrick, "Recognition of States Part 2" 42 *I.C.L.Q.* 433.

[59] It is important to acknowledge the unique set of circumstances that the European Community confronted when determining the applications for recognition. Recognition of Bosnia-Herzegovina would inevitably lead to inter-ethnic fighting between the Muslims and the Serbs, whereas a refusal to recognise would deny the Muslims the right to self-determination. The widely held view was that it would be easier to intervene to put an end to aggression when international boundaries had been violated as opposed to intervening in a civil war within the territory of one State.

[60] See (1993) 92 I.L.R. 162.

accorded is a matter for the recognising State—and usually the timing is with regard to the recognising State's own national interests, e.g. commercial.

In the case of Kosovo the international community has not provided a uniform response. States such as the France, Italy, Germany, UK and the USA were swift to accept Kosovo's declaration of independence and recognise it as a State. Others, for instance Spain, have been reluctant to follow suit in order to avoid precipitating further claims for secession.

Recognition of governments

The question of whether to recognise a government does not arise when the government comes to power by constitutional procedures. It only arises when the new governmental regime has assumed power by unconstitutional means.

British practice in the past has been not to look so much at how a government came to power, but to consider whether it displayed the criteria for recognition, namely effectiveness and stability. Recognition did not imply approval of the new regime. The British adopted an "acknowledgment of the facts" stance.

The United States, on the other hand, regarded recognition as a political weapon, not as something to be granted as a matter of international obligation. Its granting or refusal was discretionary and could be withheld to further national policy. However, Britain and the United States now adopt a similar stance in respect of the recognition of governments. Both countries have undertaken to de-emphasise recognition and do not formally recognise new regimes:

> "In recent years, U.S. practice has been to de-emphasise and avoid the use of recognition in cases of changes of governments and to concern ourselves with the question of whether we wish to have diplomatic relations with the new governments."[61]

In 1980, the then British Foreign Secretary, Lord Carrington, announced that the Government had concluded:

> ". . . there are practical advantages in following the policy of many other countries in not according recognition to governments. Like them, we shall continue to decide the nature of the dealings with regimes which came to power unconstitutionally in the light of our assessment of whether they are

---

[61] Digest of U.S. Practice in International Law (1977) 19–21.

able of themselves to exercise effective control of the territory of the State concerned, and seem likely to continue to do so."[62]

There is no formal acknowledgment of recognition, but the same test of effectiveness and likelihood of permanence still apply.[63]

The general rule is that a new governmental regime will be recognised if it has effective control over the territory it claims to represent and is likely to maintain its control.

De facto and *de jure* recognition

The practice of differentiating the recognition accorded to either a State or a government evolved in the nineteenth century. The practice was initiated by the British but was also employed by other countries such as Canada. The United States has generally accorded only *de jure* recognition. Such a distinction is of less significance given the decrease in importance of a formal act of recognition.

In reality, recognition is neither *de facto* or *de jure* and what is referred to by the use of these terms is rather the entity which is being recognised. If a government was recognised as the *de facto* government it implied that the government had effective control, the control appeared to be permanent and there was every likelihood the regime would be a permanent one. A government that was recognised as *de jure* was one which had effective control and was firmly established. An entity recognised as *de facto* was one which manifested most of the attributes of sovereignty, whereas a *de jure* entity displayed all the characteristics of sovereignty. *De facto* recognition was not a substitute for *de jure* recognition, nor was it a lesser alternative. *De facto* recognition in essence meant the recognising State had certain reservations regarding the entity concerned.

The distinction was one generally applied in respect of governments rather than States. The State of Israel, however, is an example of a State which was initially recognised *de facto* by some other States, e.g. Canada, while with respect to the Baltic States (Estonia, Latvia and Lithuania) Britain maintained *de facto* recognition in spite of the 1940 occupation of these territories by the USSR.

The benefit of the distinction was that it allowed the recognising entity to hold back and observe how a particular situation

---

[62] *Hansard*, HL Deb., Vol.408, cols 1121–1122 (April 28, 1980); Harris, p.156.
[63] The statement only refers to British practice in recognising governments which came to authority by unconstitutional means.

was going to develop. In particular, it prevented a State from according premature recognition. To afford, for example, recognition of insurgents while the existing government is attempting to quell the situation is an unquestionable breach of international law. The advantage of the distinction was that it enabled cognisance to be taken of factual circumstances while still acknowledging the *de jure* government—even if that government was not in physical control of every part of the State's territory,[64] or was in exile abroad.[65] In the event of competing authority within a territory, the general rule has been to recognise that the *de facto* regime is competent within the area in which it has physical control, whereas the *de jure* authority remains competent for matters arising outside that territory.

THE EFFECT OF RECOGNITION IN MUNICIPAL LAW

In practice the distinction between *de facto* and *de jure* is minimal, as is reflected in the consequences that recognition has within the UK domestic legal system.

United Kingdom practice

A recognised State or government, *de facto* and *de jure*:

    (a)   enjoys *locus standi* in the UK Courts and it can accordingly raise an action in the UK Courts;[66]

    (b)   enjoys immunity from suit[67] in the UK Courts and cannot be sued without its consent. In the *Arantzazu Mendi* case,[68] the House of Lords held that the British Government recognised Franco's Nationalist government, "a Government which at present exercises *de facto* administrative control over the larger portion of Spain",[69] and the Nationalist government enjoyed immunity. This case also illustrates the unfortunate consequences that may arise from recognising a *de facto* government and a *de jure* government in respect of the same territory simultaneously. The Republican government's action seeking repossession of the *Arantzazu*

---

[64] The UK, during the Spanish Civil War (1936–39), recognised *de facto* General Franco's forces as they extended their control throughout the country, but still recognised the Republican government as the *de jure* regime.

[65] e.g. the Polish government in exile in London during World War II was recognised as the *de jure* government, though it had no control over Polish territory.

[66] *The City of Berne v Bank of England*, 9 Ves.347 (1804); 32 E.R. 636 (Ch.).

[67] *Luther v Sagor* [1921] 3 K.B. 532, CA.

[68] [1939] A.C. 256, HL.

[69] *ibid.* at 258.

Mendi, which had been requisitioned under a decree by the Nationalist government, accordingly failed.[70] The case was initiated in the English Courts, as the *Arantzazu Mendi* was in London at the time the Republican government issued its writ of possession;

(c)   its legislative and administrative acts will be given effect to within the United Kingdom. In *Luther v Sagor*,[71] the Court of First Instance refused to give effect to a Soviet confiscation decree, as the Soviet regime had not been recognised by the British Government. However, by the time the case was heard on appeal, the British Government had accorded *de facto* recognition to the Soviet regime:

> "The Government of this country . . . recognised the Soviet Government as the Government in possession of the powers of sovereignty in Russia, the acts of that Government must be treated by the Courts of this country with all the respect due to the acts of a duly recognised foreign sovereign state."[72]

(d)   recognition once granted is retroactive. It is backdated to the establishment of the entity in question. It does not relate to the time recognition is accorded and in *Luther v Sagor*, Bankes J. concluded the Soviet government assumed the position of a sovereign government as of December 1917. British recognition of the Soviet government was therefore backdated to 1917 and all legislative and administrative acts of the Soviet Government after that date had to be recognised as valid. *Luther v Sagor* therefore demonstrates that a government, be it a *de facto* or a *de jure* government, is entitled to immunity before British Courts, that effect will be given to the legislative and administrative acts of a *de facto* and *de jure* regime, that recognition is retroactive and that generally the effects of *de facto* and *de jure* recognition are essentially the same.

---

[70] Franco's Nationalist forces were in control of the Basque region of the country. The Republican government issued a requisition decree in respect of all vessels registered in the Port of Bilbao. Some nine months later, the Nationalist government also issued a decree taking control of Bilbao vessels. The owners of the *Arantzazu Mendi* accepted the latter decree, but opposed that of the Republican government.

[71] Above, n.67.

[72] *ibid.*, at 543.

There are, however, two major differences between *de facto* and *de jure* recognition. *De jure* recognition alone implies full diplomatic relations and immunities and privileges for representatives.[73] Only a *de jure* government can recover a public debt or State asset. It was recognised in *Haile Selassie v Cable and Wireless Ltd (No.2)*[74] that only the ousted, but still *de jure* recognised, government of a State whose new government was only recognised *de facto*, was entitled to sue for a debt recoverable in England. However, when the *de facto* regime, in this case the Italian Government, was recognised *de jure*, because recognition is retroactive, it assumed the right as the *de jure* regime to pursue the claim, whereas the former *de jure* regime of Haile Selassie was divested of any such right.

The retroactivity of recognition can create problems. This can arise if two governments are simultaneously recognised as the *de jure* regime of the same State. In reality, this does not happen. One *de jure* government will be superseded by another *de jure* government. The effect, however, of backdating recognition of a new regime can be to place a State in the position of recognising measures of two *de jure* regimes simultaneously. The question of retroactivity and its *raison d'être* was considered in the *Gdynia Ameryka Linie Zeglugowe Spolka Akcyjna v Boguslawski* case.[75] Here, a new provisional government established itself as the *de facto* government of Poland on June 28, 1945 and, at midnight on July 5–6, the British Government accorded it *de jure* recognition. Prior to this, the British Government had recognised the government in exile in London as the *de jure* government of Poland. The issue which confronted the House of Lords was the effect of the *de jure* recognition of the provisional government on the validity of acts done by the government in London on July 3, 1945 with regard to Polish merchant marine personnel. The Lords emphasised English Courts were required to regard as valid not only acts done by the new government after recognition, but also acts done by it before its recognition in so far as those acts related to matters under its control at the time when the acts were performed. This did not, however, involve invalidating all measures of the old government prior to the withdrawal of recognition. It was, the Lords maintained: "not inconsistent to say that the recognition of the new government has certain retroactive effects, but that the recognition of the old government remains effective down to the

---

[73] *Fenton Textiles Assoc. v Krassin* [1922] 38 T.L.R. 259; see the Diplomatic Privileges Act 1964.
[74] [1939] Ch.182.
[75] [1953] A.C. 11.

date when it was in fact withdrawn."[76] What emerges from *Gdynia Ameryka Linie v Boguslawski* is that retroactivity relates specifically to matters within the effective control of the new government, and the *raison d'être* of the retroactivity of recognition is to give validity to the acts of a formerly unrecognised regime, but *not* (emphasis added) to invalidate the acts of the formerly recognised *de jure* authority.[77]

EFFECT OF NON-RECOGNITION

International law

At the international level, as already stated, non-recognition does not give an entity *carte blanche* to behave as it chooses. An unrecognised entity has responsibilities, which the international community requires it to discharge.

Municipal law

United Kingdom practice

As far as the United Kingdom is concerned,[78] the effect of non-recognition is the converse of the consequences of recognition.

An unrecognised State or government does not have *locus standi* in the British Courts; does not enjoy immunity from the jurisdiction of the British Courts and its legislative and administrative measures will be denied effect by British Courts, e.g. *Somalia (A Republic) v Woodhouse Drake & Carey (Suisse) SA.*[79]

The non-recognition of legislative and administrative measures, for example those of a private law nature, can produce severe repercussions for "innocent" persons. Britain withheld recognition from the Smith regime of Rhodesia, following the unilateral declaration of independence in 1965, and accordingly refused to recognise judicial decrees made by judges appointed by the Smith regime. For example, a divorce granted by a Rhodesian Court in 1970 was not recognised as valid under English law.[80] The Rhodesian situation was, of course, a unique one for the British Courts. They were confronted with a regime

---

[76] *ibid.* at 45.
[77] See also *Civil Air Transport Inc. v Central Air Transport Corp.* [1953] A.C. 70, Judicial Committee of the Privy Council.
[78] And also, for instance, Canada.
[79] Above, n.52.
[80] *Adams v Adams* [1971] P. 188. This decision prompted the introduction of an Order-in-Council to give effect to Rhodesian decrees which were concerned with personal status. See also the earlier *Madzimbamuito* case [1969] 1 A.C. 645, PC.

which was in rebellion to the British Crown—hence the strict enforcement of non-recognition.

The consequences of applying non-recognition to its logical conclusion were identified by Lord Reid in *Carl Zeiss Stiftung v Rayner and Keeler Ltd (No. 2)*,[81] where non-recognition of the measures adopted by the German Democratic Republic would mean:

> "... the incorporation of every company in East Germany under any new law made by the Democratic Republic or by the official act of any official appointed by its Government would have to be regarded as a nullity, so that any such company could neither sue nor be sued in this country. And any civil marriage under any such new law, or owing its validity to the act of any such official, would also have to be treated as a nullity, so that we should have to regard the children as illegitimate. And the same would apply to divorces and all manner of judicial decisions, whether in family or commercial questions. And that would affect not only status of persons formerly domiciled in East Germany but property in this country the devolution of which depended on East German law."[82]

The House of Lords in the above case employed a legal fiction and successfully sidestepped, for that particular case, the problem of non-recognition. The respondents argued that, as Britain did not recognise the German Democratic Republic, all its enactments should be considered nullities before the British Courts. The House of Lords, however, maintained that as Britain recognised the Soviet Government as the *de jure* authority in East Germany, the acts of the unrecognised East German regime could be recognised as those of a subordinate body acting under the authority of the Soviet Union, therefore the German Democratic Republic became irrelevant for the House of Lords. As far as the House of Lords were concerned the German Democratic Republic was merely a subordinate, dependent administrative body created by the *de jure* regime. The House of Lords adopted a pragmatic approach. This approach was endorsed by the Court of Appeal in *Gur Corporation v Trust Bank of Africa Ltd*,[83] when it was held the unrecognised Ciskei Government was acting as a subordinate body of the South African Government and accordingly enjoyed *locus standi* in the English Courts.[84]

---

[81] [1967] A.C. 853.
[82] [1967] A.C. 853, at 907.
[83] [1987] Q.B. 599.
[84] See also the HL finding in *Arab Monetary Fund v Hashim* (No.3) [1991] 1 All E.R. 871.

Mitigation of the strict non-recognition rule has been favoured where necessary by Lord Denning. He said, *obiter dicta*, in *Hesperides Hotels v Aegean Holidays Ltd*,[85] that effect should be given to laws of a body in effective control, even if not recognised by the British Government, which "regulate the day to day affairs of the people, such as their marriages, their divorces, their leases, their occupations and so forth."[86]

As seen, the 1980 Statement on Recognition has brought the judiciary into the arena of determining the status of the entity in question. Prior to 1980 recognition was exclusively an act of the executive which was binding on the courts. Now, recognition of governments which assume power by unconstitutional means is to be inferred through the dealings which the British government may have with the new regime. If the courts are in doubt as to the status of a particular regime they will have to assess the evidence available to them and exercise their judgment in deciding whether the regime is unrecognised or recognised. British Courts are no longer bound only by the official position of the government. The Court in the *Somalia (Republic)* case in 1993[87] did not depart from the official government position—the decision reflects the change in British practice regarding the recognition of governments. The courts may still obtain certificates from the Foreign Office, and accordingly a certificate may include, *inter alia*, confirmation of the dealings which the British Government has with the new regime, and, of course, an explicit statement of non-recognition.[88] The courts, when interpreting the terms "State" or "government" in a statute or another document (such as a commercial one) look, of course, to the intention of the draftsmen or those of the parties.[89]

United States practice

If the Executive unequivocally denies recognition, the courts must accept this as binding.[90] An unrecognised State or government cannot sue in the American Courts. An unrecognised government may be entitled to immunity from the jurisdiction of the American Courts, if the regime in question can be shown to

---

[85] [1978] Q.B. 205, CA.

[86] *ibid*. 218.

[87] Above, n.52.

[88] See Colin Warbrick, "Britain and the Recognition of Governments" 39 *I.C.L.Q.* 568 (1981). Recognition of States Part 1 (1992) 41 *I.C.L.Q.* 473; Recognition of States Part 2 (1993) 42 *I.C.L.Q.* 433.

[89] e.g. *Re Al-Fin Corporation's Patent* [1970] Ch.160; *Reel v Holder* [1981] 1 W.L.R. 1226, CA.

[90] e.g. as in *The Maret* 145 F.(d) 431 (1944).

exist.[91] The Executive may deny recognition, but may neverthe-less in its "suggestion" indicate to the courts that cognisance may be taken of the measures promulgated by the unrecognised regime. Thus, in *Salimoff v Standard Oil Co.*,[92] although the US Government's non-recognition of the Soviet regime was con-firmed in the State Department Certificate, it was nevertheless acknowledged that the Soviet regime was exercising control and power in the territory of the former Russian Empire, and such a fact could not be ignored. In the absence of either explicit or implied direction to the Court, the American Courts have shown a willingness to modify the legal consequences of non-recognition being carried to their logical conclusion. In other words, common sense and fairness may demand that legal cognisance be accorded.[93]

MODES OF ACCORDING RECOGNITION

Recognition may be expressed or implied. In the absence of an express formal declaration of recognition, the establishment of diplomatic relations between a State and the entity concerned will be taken to imply recognition. Similarly, the conclusion of a bipartite treaty on a general topic implies recognition. A bipartite treaty for a specific purpose does not imply recognition, nor does participation in a multipartite treaty such as the UN Charter. It is possible for parties to be signatories to a multipartite treaty, even though one party does not recognise the other party. Admission to the UN is an acknowledgment of statehood for the purposes of the Organisation. It does not constitute collective recognition by the international community, or recognition of the entity by indi-vidual Member States of the United Nations.[94] The most salient factor at all times remains intention—that is, the intention of the recognising State.

INTERNATIONAL ORGANISATIONS

States are the primary subjects of international law, but they are not the exclusive subjects. Other entities are afforded a degree of

---

[91] *Wulfsohn v R.S.F.S.R.* 138 N.E. 24 (1923); (1923–1924) 2 A.D. Case No.16.

[92] 186 N.E. 679 (1993); (1993–1934) A.D. Case No.8.

[93] See *Sokoloff v National City Bank* 145 N.E. 917 (1924); (1923–1924) 2 A.D. Case No.19; *Upright v Mercury Business Machines* 13 A.D. (2d) 36; 213 (N.Y.S.) (2d) 417 (1961).

[94] Admission of Members is effected by a two-thirds vote of the General Assembly. See, e.g. SC Res.777 (1992), December 19, 1992. Note also the UK regarded its affirmative vote on admission of Macedonia to the United Nations as constituting recognition that Macedonia was a State (223 H.C. Debs., Col. 241, Written Answer, 22 April 1993 and UKMIL, 64 B.Y.I.L., 1993, 601).

international legal personality. Of these entities, international organisations are undoubtedly the most important.

International organisations proliferated in number during the twentieth century. An international organisation, for the purposes of international law, is an entity established by agreement and which has States as its principal members.[95] Organisations vary considerably in their competencies, importance and membership. The United Nations, for example, is a global (or "open") organisation enjoying almost universal membership, while the Council of Europe is an example of a regional (or "closed") organisation as is the Organisation of American States.

Before an international organisation can make any impact on the international scene, it must be afforded some degree of international personality. The degree of international personality enjoyed by international organisations varies. An international organisation may enjoy certain rights but not others, and while all States enjoy the same degree of personality, that is not true of international organisations. In the words of the International Court of Justice "international organizations are subject to international law which do not, unlike States, possess a general competence. International organisations are governed by the 'principle of speciality', that is to say, they are invested by the States which create them with powers, the limits of which are a function of the common interests whose promotion those States entrust to them."[96]

Determination of personality

International organisations frequently resemble States regarding the personality they possess and their legal personality may, to some extent, parallel that of States. Organisations may have the capacity to own, acquire and transfer property and to enter into contractual agreements and international agreements with States and other international organisations. They may pursue legal remedies and may enjoy rights and duties under international law. International organisations are restricted though by their constituent charter, that is, the agreement establishing the organisation. Determination of an organisation's personality thus demands the constituent document be examined. The International Court of Justice has acknowledged that the object of constituent instruments "is to create new subjects of law endowed with a certain

---

[95] Inter-governmental organisations are distinct from non-governmental organisations established by individuals.

[96] *Legality of the Use by a State of Nuclear Weapons in Armed Conflict* I.C.J. Rep. 1996 p.66 at 78.

autonomy, to which the parties entrust the task of realizing common goals".[97]

The constituent document may expressly provide that an organisation is to have international legal personality.[98] As for example the Maastricht Treaty establishes that the European Community possesses legal personality allowing it to enter into juridical relations with States and other international organisations.[99]

Alternatively, and this is more usual, personality may only be implied from the constituent document and consolidated through the practice of the organisation.

The United Nations

The United Nations Charter is silent on the Organisation's international legal personality. Only two Charter articles deal explicitly with legal status, and then only with the United Nations' status within the municipal systems of Member States. Article 104 provides that the United Nations is to enjoy within Member States' territory "such legal capacity as may be necessary for the exercise of its functions and fulfilment of its purposes", while art.105 provides that the United Nations "shall enjoy in the territory of each of its Members such privileges and immunities as are necessary for the fulfilment of its purposes."

Articles 104 and 105 do not grant international legal personality to the United Nations. They have been supplemented by the Convention on the Privileges and Immunities of the United Nations drawn up by the General Assembly in 1946.[100] The agreement is in force between the United Nations and every Member of the Organisation and provides for functional privileges and immunities for the United Nations (see also the Convention on the Privileges and Immunities of the Specialised Agencies).[101] The United Nations has also entered into agreements with host States in which it operates, for example the UN/USA Headquarters Agreement.[102]

Headquarters agreements are necessary, as an organisation can only establish itself within a State's territory when it has that

[97] *ibid*, 75.
[98] Exceptionally, a Constituent Document may deny an organisation personality, e.g. art.4 of the Statute of the International Hydrographic Organisation.
[99] Article 281 EC.
[100] 1 U.N.T.S. 15; U.K.T.S. 10 (1950) Cmd.7891; 43 A.J.I.L. Supp.I.
[101] 33 U.N.T.S. 261; U.K.T.S. 69 (1959) Cmnd.855.
[102] 11 U.N.T.S. 11 (1947) Supplemented; 554 U.N.T.S. 308 (1966); 687 U.N.T.S. 408 (1969).

State's consent. Such agreements determine the status of the organisation's headquarters and its capacities, privileges and immunities.

The capacity of the United Nations to be a party to agreements with States helped the International Court to conclude that the Organisation indeed enjoyed international legal capacity. The Court held that the United Nations:

> "was intended to exercise and enjoy, and is in fact exercising and enjoying, functions and rights which can only be explained on the basis of the possession of a large measure of international personality and the capacity to operate on the international plane."[103]

The Court was presented with the opportunity to comment on the international personality of the United Nations when the General Assembly requested an Advisory Opinion as to whether the Organisation possessed the capacity to espouse an international claim in respect of injury sustained by a United Nations official while in the service of the United Nations. The Court, before delivering its Opinion, took the opportunity to discuss the international personality of the United Nations. The Court initially considered the objectives of the United Nations as an Organisation, namely the promotion of international peace and security, and concluded that such objectives could not be fulfilled if the United Nations did not possess international personality. In the words of the Court:

> "throughout its history, the development of international law has been influenced by the requirements of international life, and the progressive increase in the collective action of States has already given rise to instances of action upon the international plane by certain entities which are not States. This development culminated in the establishment in June 1945 of an international organization whose purposes and principles are specified in the Charter of the United Nations. But to achieve these ends the attribution of international personality is indispensable."[104]

---

[103] Above, n.1 at 179. The I.C.J. reaffirmed the independent legal personality of the UN, see *Advisory Opinion on the Applicability of Art.VI of the Convention on the Privileges and Immunities of the UN 1989* I.C.J. Rep. 177, 29 I.L.M. 98 (1990).

[104] *ibid.*, p.174.

The Court's Opinion was to the effect that:

> "the organization was intended to exercise and enjoy and is in fact exercising and enjoying functions and rights which can only be explained on the basis of the possession of a large measure of international personality and the capacity to operate on an international plane ... and it could not carry out the intentions of its founders if it was devoid of international personality. It must be acknowledged that its members, by entrusting certain functions to it, with the attendant duties and responsibilities, have clothed it with the competence required to enable those functions to be effectively discharged."[105]

As to whether the Organisation could initiate an international claim, the Court arrived at an affirmative conclusion.

The Court further confirmed that the United Nations could not only espouse a claim for the damage caused to the interests of the Organisation, that is its administrative machinery, its property and assets, but could initiate a claim for reparation in respect of damage caused to the UN official or agent, or to persons entitled through the UN official or agent. In reaching this conclusion, the Court again made reference to the purposes and functions of the United Nations and held that UN officials could only perform their duties satisfactorily if afforded adequate protection. Individual States could not be expected to and, indeed, were not able to offer such protection. The Court expressed the view that:

> "the functions of the organisation, are of such a character that they could not be effectively discharged if they involve the concurrent action, on the international plane, of 58 or more foreign offices, and the Court concludes that the Members have endowed the organization with capacity to bring international claims when necessitated by the discharge of its functions."[106]

The Court maintained in order:

> "to ensure the independence of the agent, and consequently, the independent action of the organisation itself, it is essential that in performing his duties he need not have to rely on

---

[105] *ibid.*
[106] *ibid.*

any other protection than that of the organisation . . . In particular, he should not have to rely on the protection of his own State. If he had to rely on that State his independence might well be compromised . . . and lastly, it is essential that . . . he should know that in the performance of his duties he is under the protection of the organisation."[107]

The Court endorsed the United Nations right of initiative against a non-Member State (in this case, Israel) because the Court maintained the United Nations possessed objective personality as opposed to subjective personality. Objective personality being such that it may be enforced *vis-à-vis* all members of the international community because of the stated purposes of the Organisation and its almost universal membership.

The Court's Opinion was a landmark one for not only the United Nations, but for international organisations generally. The Court emphasised that the rights and duties of an organisation (that is, any organisation) depend upon the purposes and functions of the organisation as specified or implied in its constituent document and developed in practice. Both the General Assembly and the Economic and Social Council enjoy the legal competence to request an advisory opinion from the International Court of Justice.[108] However, in respect of the World Health Organisation (WHO), the International Court of Justice, in the *Nuclear Weapons* case,[109] highlighted:

"international organisations do not, unlike States, possess a general competence, but are governed by the 'principle of speciality', that is to say, they are invested by the States which create them with powers, the limits of which are a function of the common interests whose promotion those States entrust to them. Besides, the World Health Organisation is an international organisation of a particular kind—a 'specialised agency' forming part of a system based in the Charter of the United Nations, which is designed to organise international co-operation in a coherent fashion by bringing the United Nations, invested with

---

[107] *ibid.*
[108] The General Assembly, for instance, asked the I.C.J. for an *Advisory Opinion concerning the Legality of the Use of Nuclear Weapons*, 35 I.L.M. 809, The Economic and Social Council asked for an Opinion concerning the Applicability of art.VI of the Convention on the Privileges and Immunities of the UN.
[109] Above n.96.

powers of general scope, into relationship with various autonomous and complementary organisations, invested with sectorial powers".

The Court therefore concluded:

"the responsibilities of the WHO are necessarily restricted to the sphere of public 'health' and cannot encroach on the responsibilities of other parts of the United Nations system. And that there is no doubt that questions concerning the use of force, the regulation of armaments and disarmament are within the competence of the United Nations and lie outside that of the special agencies."

The Court in that case concluded it did not have jurisdiction.

The administration of territories by the United Nations under the trusteeship system and the competence of the Organisation to intervene for the maintenance and restoration of international peace and security have also served to reinforce the United Nations' international personality. The United Nations has in recent years been responsible for the interim administration of geographical areas within existing States, e.g. Cambodia (UNTAC)[110] and East Timor (UNTAET),[111] and Kosovo, which was administered by the United Nations Interim Administration Mission in Kosovo (UNMIK)[112].

One word of caution: while a treaty-making power is evidence of international personality, a general treaty-making power should not be deduced from the possession of some degree of personality. In other words, entities having a treaty-making capacity possess some international personality, but not all international entities necessarily possess a general treaty-making capacity.

The overriding conclusion is that no generalisation should be made regarding the international personality of international organisations. Each organisation should be examined and its international legal status assessed in the light of its constituent document and the organisations own practice. The plethora of institutions on the international scene has resulted in the growth of law pertaining specifically to them.[113] The law of international

---

[110] UN Transitional Authority in Cambodia 1991.
[111] UN Transitional Authority in East Timor 2000.
[112] Set up in 1999 under the UN Charter Ch.VII, S.C. Resn. 1244 (1999).
[113] A good general text on international institutions is P. Sands and P. Klein, *Bowett: Law of International Institutions* (2001).

institutions is now a specialised subdivision of international law and can be treated as an autonomous subject.[114]

INDIVIDUALS

Individuals have limited international legal personality, although contemporary international law increasingly recognises that an individual may possess both international rights and duties. The increasing focus on human rights over the last 60 years has prompted the conclusion of international and regional instruments guaranteeing the protection of human rights for individuals.[115]

Simultaneously, it has been increasingly recognised individuals may be held responsible for certain conduct and the development of international individual criminal responsibility is a notable feature of international law today. Traditionally international law did not recognise individual responsibility except in the very limited case of piracy which under customary international law has long been recognised as an international crime. It is no longer believed that States are exclusively the perpetrators of conduct which breaches international law. The legal fiction that individuals do not participate on the international scene, and consequently may not be held responsible for their acts, was perceptibly dented in the latter half of the twentieth century. See, for example, the Statutes of the International Tribunals for the former Yugolslavia (the ICTY)[116] and Rwanda (ICTR)[117] and the Rome Statute establishing the International Criminal Court (ICC)[118]. Issues of individual international criminal responsibility are also increasingly being with in national courts, through the application of the universal jurisdiction principle such as the *Pinochet* case.[119]

---

[114] In a number of educational institutions, the law of international institutions is a separate course, independent of international law.

[115] See Ch.9.

[116] The International Tribunal for the Prosecution of Persons Responsible for Serious Violations of International Humanitarian Law Committed in the Territory of the Former Yugoslavia since 1991 (1993) established by Security Council Resolution 827 (1993).

[117] The International Criminal Tribunal for the Prosecution of Persons Responsible for Genocide and Other Serious Violations of International Humanitarian Law Committed in the Territory of Rwanda and Rwandan citizens responsible for genocide and other such violations committed in the territory of neighbouring states, between January 1, 1994 and December 31, 1994. Established under Security Council Resolution 955 (1994).

[118] Rome Statute, 2187 U.N.T.S. 90.

[119] *R. v Bartle & The Commissioner of Police for the Metropolis & Others, Ex p. Pinochet* 24 March 1999, [1991] 2 All E.R. 97. Universal Jurisdiction is dealt with in Ch.6.

Individual responsibility derives from international law and is independent of the law of any State. At Nuremberg the International Tribunal held:

"Crimes against international law are committed by men, not by abstract entities, and only by punishing individuals who commit such crimes can the provisions of international law be enforced."

Similarly, art.4 of the Convention on the Prevention and Punishment of the Crime of Genocide[120] provides that genocide is punishable as a crime irrespective of whether those committing it "are constitutionally responsible rulers, public officials or private individuals". The corollary of this acknowledgment that individuals may incur international responsibility is that they are under an obligation to refrain from such conduct.[121] Individuals, therefore, have limited rights and duties on the international scene. Other acts, which are now recognised as giving rise to individual responsibility at an international level, include, *inter alia*, hijacking, sabotage, terrorism, drug trafficking and acts upon diplomats.[122] A major handicap to individuals exercising international personality has been a lack of procedural capacity, denied to them because of the reluctance of States to grant them such capacity.

Procedural capacity of individuals

The Permanent Court of International Justice in the *Danzig Railway Officials* case[123] recognised, exceptionally, that treaties could create rights for individuals, and in certain circumstances these rights could be enforced in the domestic Courts:

"the very object of an international agreement, according to the intention of the Contracting Parties, may be the adoption by the Parties of some definite rules creating individual rights and obligations and enforceable by the national Courts."[124]

---

[120] Paris, December 9, 1948; T.S. 58 (1970) Cmnd.4421.
[121] The Statute of the ICTY affirms the principle of *ratione personae*, i.e. a person is not relieved of individual criminal responsibility for a crime because it was committed under superior orders (arts 6 and 7). This would only be considered as mitigating circumstances when passing sentence. See Ch.9 on Human Rights generally.
[122] See Chs 6 and 9.
[123] P.C.I.J.Rep., ser.B, No.15 (1928) 4–47; 4 A.D. 587; Hudson, World Court Reports, Vol.II (1927–32) 237.
[124] P.C.I.J.Rep., ser.B, No.15, (1928) 17; Hudson, p.247; cf. the concept of direct effect employed by European Community law, e.g. Case 26/62 *Van Gend en*

The Central American Court of Justice, established in 1908, was novel as it envisaged disputes between States and private individuals would come within the Court's jurisdiction. The Court's competence was to hear disputes between private individuals, nationals of any one of the five Contracting Parties and any of the other Contracting Governments. The Court's importance was the potential procedural capacity envisaged for individuals. The Court, however, ceased to function in 1918 after hearing only five cases—of which four were declared inadmissible and the fifth failed on the merits.

The Treaty of Versailles[125] provided for the espousal of claims by individuals against governments and nationals of the defeated States. However, as part and parcel of the peacekeeping treaty, this did not represent a major enhancement of the individual's position under general international law.

The Tribunal, established under the Upper Silesian Convention, was notable for its competence to hear cases brought by nationals of a State against their own State.[126]

Contemporary international law affords individuals a greater measure of procedural capacity. Under Arts 34 and 35 of the European Convention on Human Rights, individuals can initiate claims alleging breaches of the Convention by their national State.[127] The right of individual petition is similarly provided for in art.14 of the 1966 International Convention on the Elimination of All Forms of Racial Discrimination, while under the (First) Optional Protocol to the International Covenant[128] on Civil and Political Rights (1966) the Human Rights Committee is competent to receive and consider "communications from individuals claiming to be victims of violations of any of the rights set forth in the Covenant." Other instruments providing for individual petition include the Optional Protocol to the Convention on the Elimination of Discrimination against Women (1999), the Optional Protocol to the International Covenant on Economic, Social and Cultural Rights and the Optional Convention to the Convention on the Rights of Person with Disabilities. The International Convention for the Protection for all Persons from Enforced Disappearance (2006) includes an optional complaints

---

Loos v Nederlandse Tarief Commissie [1963] E.C.R. 1; C.M.L.R. 105, with respect to art.12 of the EC Treaty.

[125] U.K.T.S. 4 (1919) Cmd.153; 13 A.J.I.L.Supp.151; 16 A.J.I.L.Supp.207.

[126] See *Steiner and Gross v Polish State* 4 A.D. 291 (1928).

[127] Provided, that is, such a right has been recognised by the individual's State of nationality. The European Convention, as modified by Protocol No.11, which entered into force on November 1, 1998. N.B. the original Convention entered into force on September 3, 1953.

[128] U.K.T.S. 6 (1977) Cmnd. 6702; 6 ILM 383 (1967).

system for individuals to appeal to the Committee on Enforced Disappearance for assistance in locating disappeared persons. The American Convention on Human Rights provides for the initiation of a petition alleging a violation of the Convention by "any person or group of persons or non-governmental entity legally recognised in one or more Member States."[129]

In addition to the foregoing, individuals enjoy limited procedural capacity before the European Union Court of First Instance,[130] and the Convention on the Settlement of Investment Disputes between States and Nationals of Other States 1965 provides a mechanism for the settlement of disputes between contracting parties and companies of the nationality of a contracting party on the consent of both sides.[131] Individuals do not, however, enjoy *locus standi* before the International Court of Justice.

OTHER NON-STATE ACTORS

Non-state actors are not subjects of international law, however, they may enjoy certain rights, have special and limited capacities and *locus standi*. Some of these entities participate in international life actively and they influence the creation and development of international law.

Insurgents and rebel groups

Rebel groups are relevant to international law to the extent that they may have *de facto* control over certain territory. In such cases they may enter into international agreements which could be considered valid under international law. In the course of civil conflicts, rebel groups are also bound by international humanitarian law with regards to the conduction of hostilities. They do not, however, have *locus standi* in international law and therefore they could not be considered responsible as a group for its violations, notwithstanding the individual responsibility for international crimes that its members could bear. Similarly this could be said about terrorist groups such as Al-Qaeda.

National liberation movements

The most notable national liberation movement was arguably the Palestine Liberation Organisation (PLO).[132] The Palestinian

---

[129] art.44.
[130] art.230 Treaty of the European Union, Previously art.173 of the Treaty of Rome.
[131] 4 I.L.M. 532 (1965).
[132] The Palestinian Authority replaced the PLO in January 1996 and has been recognised by the Israeli Government. Another instance was the African National Congress (ANC), which is now the Majority Government of South Africa.

Authority enjoys permanent observer status at the United Nations—such recognition, however, does not impute recognition by the Member States of the Organisation. Nevertheless, note the Advisory Opinion of the International Court of Justice in 1988, concluding that the United States—as a party to the Agreement between the United Nations and the United States of America, regarding the Headquarters of the United Nations of June 26, 1947—was under "an obligation in accordance with section 21 of that Agreement, to enter into arbitration for the settlement of the dispute between itself and the United Nations."[133] An obligation was held to be incumbent on the United States towards the PLO, in spite of the former's non-recognition of the Organisation.

The Holy See

The Holy See is another notable example of an entity possessing limited international personality. The Holy See, of which the Pope is the head, has a population which is neither permanent nor indigenous, and its function is exclusively religious. However, it is a party to international treaties on such diverse subjects as arbitration, non-proliferation and monetary matters. The New Monetary Convention between the Holy See and Italy, signed on December 29, 2000, authorised the Euro as official currency within the Vatican City. The Holy See also replaced the Fundamental Law of the State of the Vatican (June 7, 1929) with one which entered into force on February 22, 2001. The latter draws a greater distinction between the legislative, executive and judicial powers and provides for a closer tie between the Governorate and the Secretary of State, for the maintenance of international relations.

The Holy See has permanent observer status at the United Nations and a presence at other international organisations, such as the Organisation for American States and the specialised agencies of the UN, e.g. the World Health Organisation and the International Labour Organisation. Some 174 States have diplomatic relations with the Holy See.

The Holy See is an anomaly on the international scene, enjoying and exercising international personality because other international actors are willing to enter into international relations with it. The same is true of the Sovereign Order of Malta, which performs functions of a charitable nature from its headquarters in Rome.[134]

---

[133] See *Applicability of Obligation in Arbitrate Under section 21 of the United Nations Headquarters Agreement of June 26*, 1947 I.C.J. Rep. 1988.
[134] *Nanni v Pace and the Sovereign Order of Malta* 8 A.D. 2 (1935–37) Italian Ct of Cassation.

Non-Governmental Organisations (NGOs)

The proliferation of NGOs and the active role of civil society in international life has been one of the main features of the international scenario since the last decade of the 20th century. These organisations seek to achieve very diverse aims, from the protection of specific human rights and humanitarian needs, the environment, animal rights, religious interests, etc. But their common characteristic is their non-lucrative nature. They are entities of municipal law, created under the law of a particular state, but many of them act in a global way, extending their activities transnationally, and considerably influencing public opinion. However, such social influence has not translated into international legal capacity. Some NGOs, though, enjoy consultative status before International Organisations, in particular, pursuant art.71 of the United Nations Charter, nearly 3,000 organisations are accredited with such status before the Economic and Social Council. The International Committee of the Red Cross has a particular hybrid nature, because while it is constituted under Swiss law, it has the capacity to conclude agreements with States and has been given specific competences granted by the 1949 Geneva Conventions.

Transnational Corporations

Multi-national corporations enjoy considerable power. These corporations negotiate with governments, some indeed enjoy economic power which may exceed that of States and the scope of their activities transcends national boundaries. A realisation as to the impact of such multi-national corporations has led to calls for corporate accountability and an expectation that this should be realised by way of the international legal system. It is not denied that many companies do subscribe voluntarily to corporate codes of conduct. However a criticism of such codes is that the authors are also the addressees of the codes, e.g. the companies themselves.[135] The problem which has to be addressed is how international law can be instrumental in affording protection to individuals who suffer or are at risk of suffering human rights violations through adverse corporate activity.

---

[135] On the international scene there have been a number of initiatives developed under the auspices, e.g. the OECD, the ILO, including an abortive attempt to define the human rights obligations of business: the Sub-commission on the Promotion and Protection of Human Rights Norms on the Responsibilities of Trans-National Corporations and Other Business Enterprises with Regard to Human Rights (Reso. 2003/16, 13 August).

CONCLUSION

There is no prototype international personality. States remain the primary subjects of international law and as such enjoy international personality as an inherent attribute of statehood and possess "the totality of international rights and duties recognised by international law."[136] However, given the development of international law States are no longer the exclusive subjects of the international legal system. Other entities, notably international organisations and individuals, have been accommodated and attributed with at least a measure of international personality and thereby acknowledged as an actor on the international stage.

---

[136] Above, n.1 at 180.

5. TERRITORY

"State territory is that defined portion of the surface of the globe which is subjected to the sovereignty of the State. A State without a territory is not possible, although the necessary territory may be very small. The importance of State territory lies in the fact that it is the space within which the State exercises its supreme authority."[1]

Territory is a tangible attribute of statehood within which a State enjoys and exercises sovereignty. Territorial sovereignty may be defined as the "right to exercise therein, to the exclusion of any other State, the functions of a State".[2] A State's territorial sovereignty extends over the designated landmass, subsoil, the water enclosed therein, the land under that water, the seacoast to a certain limit[3] and the airspace over the landmass and territorial

---

[1] L. F. L. Oppenheim, *International Law*, "Peace" (8th edn, 1955), Vol.1, pp.451–452.
[2] Arbitrator Max Huber in the *Island of Palmas* case, Permanent Court of Arbitration, 2 R.I.A.A. 829 at 838 (1928). For further discussion, see "State Jurisdiction", Ch.8, below.
[3] Twelve miles is the maximum allowed under the 1982 UN Convention on the Law of the Sea, art.3.

sea. The means whereby title to territory is established may appear to be only of academic interest—until, that is, a dispute arises and competing claims have to be assessed. Then the mode by which the parties claim to have established sovereignty over the territory will gain new relevance, e.g. in the *Case Concerning Land, Island and Maritime Frontier Dispute El Salvador v Honduras*, Nicaragua intervening[4] both parties agreed to refer the dispute concerning the boundaries between their respective territories to the International Court for resolution by reference to the principle *uti possidetis*.[5] The Court's decision had the effect of converting former colonial boundaries into accepted international frontiers.[6] It is also important to note the special status attributed to treaties establishing international boundaries. The boundary will continue to subsist even though the treaty falls.[7]

Historically, the need to demonstrate the existence of a valid title became imperative during the "Age of Discovery" when the European powers set sail in quest of new lands. Unfortunately, claims as to title to territory have been, and remain, a cause of conflict, e.g. the Falkland Islands dispute of 1982, the situation in the Middle East, Kashmir and the as yet unresolved dispute over Gibraltar. Turning to the means of establishing a valid title, discovery alone was not sufficient to establish a superior title. Occupation was also necessary.

OCCUPATION

Occupation gives a State original title to territory. It is the means of establishing title to territory, which is *terra nullius*, that is,

---

[4] I.C.J. Rep. (1992) 351.
[5] The principle whereby the territorial boundaries of former colonies remain the same on the granting of independence. The practice evolved in the early 19th century when various former Spanish/American colonies attained independence. The practice continued throughout the granting of independence to colonies in the African continent throughout the 1950s and 60s. For further discussion of this principle see the case *Concerning the Frontier Dispute (Burkina Faso/Republic of Mali)* I.C.J. Rep. (1986) 554 at 565–567.
[6] See Opinion No. 2 *Arbitration Commission on Yugoslavia* 92 I.L.R. (1993) that, except where otherwise agreed, "whatever the circumstances, the right to self determination must not involve changes to existing frontiers at the time of independence (*uti possidetis juris*) . . ." See also Opinion No.3 in which the Arbitration Commission, in dealing with the internal boundaries between Serbia and Croatia and Serbia and Bosnia Herzegovina, highlighted that unless otherwise agreed the previous boundaries were frontiers protected by international law. It was again maintained this arose from the principle of *uti possidetis*.
[7] See case *Concerning the Territorial Dispute between Libya Arab Jamahiriya/Chad* where the I.C.J. held "a boundary established by treaty thus achieves a permanence which the treaty itself does not necessarily enjoy." (1994) 33 I.L.M. 571 at 589; I.C.J. Rep. (1994) 6 at 37.

owned by no-one and therefore susceptible to acquisition.
Regarding occupation by the indigenous population this was of
no consequence, provided that the indigenous community was
not administratively so well organised that they could be said to
have a recognisable government. In the *Western Sahara* case State
practice of the late nineteenth century was such to indicate:

> "... that territories inhabited by tribes or peoples having a
> social and political organisation were not regarded as *terrae
> nullius*. It shows that in the case of such territories the acqui-
> sition of sovereignty was not generally considered as effected
> unilaterally through "occupation" of *terra nullius* by original
> title but through agreements concluded with local rulers.
> Such agreements with local rulers, whether or not considered
> as an actual "cession" of the territory, were regarded as
> derivative roots of title, and not original titles obtained by
> occupation of *terrae nullius*."[8]

Occupation is preceded by discovery. Discovery, *per se*, does not
establish a good title, giving only an inchoate and not a definite
title of sovereignty. An inchoate title must be completed within a
reasonable period by the effective occupation of the territory in
question.[9] Publication of discovery can of course intimate to the
international community a discovering State's prior interest, and
such a discovery is good against any subsequent title founded on
alleged discovery. An inchoate title does not prevail over the
continuous and peaceful display of authority by another State.

Effective occupation

Effective occupation applies to the actual exercise of sovereignty.
What will be regarded as sufficient to establish a good title will
vary in each particular instance:

> "Manifestations of territorial sovereignty assume ..., differ-
> ent forms, according to conditions of time and place.
> Although continuous in principle, sovereignty cannot be
> exercised in fact at every moment on every point of a terri-
> tory. The intermittence and discontinuity compatible with
> the maintenance of the right necessarily differ according as
> inhabited or uninhabited regions are involved, or regions
> enclosed within territories in which sovereignty is incon-

---

[8] *Western Sahara* case I.C.J. Rep. (1975) 12 at 39.
[9] *Island of Palmas* case, above, n.2 at 846.

testably displayed or again regions accessible from, for instance, the high seas."[10]

Max Huber was the sole arbitrator in a sovereignty dispute between the United States and the Netherlands relating to the Island of Palmas. The Island of Palmas, the United States alleged, was included in the cession of the Philippines to the United States by the Spanish at the conclusion of the Spanish–American War in 1898. The Dutch claimed the island on the basis of the exercise of sovereignty over a considerable length of time.

The display of sovereignty required to establish title by occupation, for example over territory inhospitable to habitation, may therefore be minimal and in certain circumstances may be little more than symbolic. Assessing the respective claims of Norway and Denmark to East Greenland, the Permanent Court of International Justice[11] highlighted the relative test to be utilised in establishing occupation and observed:

> "It is impossible to read the records of the decisions in cases as to territorial sovereignty without observing that in many cases the tribunal has been satisfied with very little in the way of the actual exercise of sovereign rights, provided that the other State could not make out a superior claim. This is particularly true in the case of claims to sovereignty over areas in thinly populated or unsettled countries."[12]

Minimal overt action may be sufficient to establish effective occupation over small, uninhabited territory.

An important and necessary condition of occupation is "the actual, and not the nominal, taking of possession".[13] The form of the actual taking is dependent on factors such as the geographical and geological terrain of the particular territory. In the *Clipperton Island Arbitration*,[14] a declaration of sovereignty made on behalf of France communicated to the French Consulate in Honolulu and transmitted to the Government of Hawaii along with publication (in English) of the French claim in the Honolulu journal, *The Polynesian*, was sufficient to establish a good title to the island for France.

---

[10] *ibid.* at 840.
[11] *Eastern Greenland* case (1933) P.C.I.J. Rep., ser.A/B, No.53, pp.22–147; Hudson, World Court Reports, Vol.III (1932–35), p.151.
[12] *Eastern Greenland* case, *ibid.*, p.46; Hudson, *ibid.*, p.171.
[13] *Clipperton Island Arbitration* (1932) 26 A.J.I.L. 390 at 393.
[14] The Arbitrator established that the Island at the date relevant to the dispute was "*territorium nullius* and, therefore, susceptible of occupation."

Discovery must be reinforced by an intention (*animus*) or will to act as sovereign. How that intention will be inferred depends on the facts in any particular case. Normally, the exercise of exclusive authority is evidenced when the State establishes an organisation capable of making its law respected; however, in respect of Clipperton Island, it was held that France had done sufficient and had made it apparent in a precise and clear manner and that the island was considered French territory. France had never had the *animus* of abandoning the island, and the fact she had not exercised authority in a positive manner did not imply the forfeiture of an acquisition already definitively perfected. The French title was further substantiated by the absence of any French intention to abandon the territory.

Characteristics of effective occupation

Max Huber's articulation of effective occupation is still regarded as the leading statement on the subject.

In the *Island of Palmas* case it was established that effective occupation must be open and public and involve the continuous, peaceful display of State authority extending over a long period of time. An inchoate title based on such a display of State authority would be regarded as superior to any other claim to title, whatever its basis.

Max Huber went to great lengths to attribute the acts of the Dutch East India Company to the Netherlands, thereby emphasising that occupation must be exercised on behalf of a State if it is to be effective. More recently, in *Eritrea v Yemen*,[15] it was stated:

> "The modern international law of the acquisition (or attribution) of territory generally requires that there be: an intentional display of power and authority over the territory, by the exercise of jurisdiction and State functions, on a continuous and peaceful basis. The latter two criteria are tempered to suit the nature of the territory and the size of its population, if any."[16]

Private individuals cannot legitimately purport to act on behalf of the State of which they are a national without that State's authorisation.[17] In international law:

---

[15] (1998) 114 I.L.R. p.1.
[16] *ibid.* p.69.
[17] See further "State Responsibility", Ch.8; see also *Sovereignty over Pulau Ligitan Pulau Sipadan*, I.C.J. December 17, 2002 General List Number 102.

"... the independent activity of private individuals is of little value unless it can be shown that they have acted in pursuance of a licence or some other authority received from their Governments or that in some other way their Governments have asserted jurisdiction through them."[18]

The exercise of State functions was similarly emphasised in the *Miniquiers and Ecrehos* case.[19]

The British claim to sovereignty over the Falkland Islands is: "derived from early settlement, reinforced by formal claims in the name of the Crown and completed by open, continuous, effective and peaceful possession, occupation and administration of the Island since 1833 . . ."[20]

Critical date

The critical date in a territorial claim is the date on which the attribution of territorial sovereignty is decisive, as the State, which can demonstrate an effective title in the period immediately preceding the critical date has the superior claim. For example the critical date in the *Island of Palmas* case was 1898, in the *Western Sahara* case, 1884 and in *El Salvador v Honduras*, 1821 (the date of independence of the former colonies of Latin America).[21] The responsibility of deciding when the critical date is lies with the adjudicating body charged with the task of deciding the territorial dispute. There is no general rule governing the selection of the critical date and selection, if indeed made, is made in the context of the relevant circumstances peculiar to each case. The consequences of establishing a critical date are that deeds undertaken subsequent to that date have no legal effect.

PRESCRIPTION

Claimants to title of territory based initially on discovery and occupation may invoke the principle of prescription to consolidate a claim.

---

[18] *Anglo-Norwegian Fisheries* case I.C.J.Rep. (1951) 116—Lord McNair at 184.
[19] I.C.J. Rep. (1953) at 47.
[20] British Government response to Report on the Falklands, Fifth Report of the Foreign Affairs Committee of the House of Commons, Session 1983–84, HC, Papers 268–261, Vol.1, pp.xiv–xvii; Misc.1 Cmnd.9447 (1985). The Report for its part concluded that the historical and legal evidence available demonstrated "such areas of uncertainty. . ." that it was "unable to reach a categorical conclusion on the legal validity of the historical claims of either country." para.22.
[21] Above, n4.

Prescription is the acquisition of title by a public, peaceful and continuous control of territory. Prescription involves a *de facto* exercise of sovereignty. It is distinct from occupation in that the latter can only arise in respect of virgin territory (*terra nullius*), while prescription can work to establish a title over any territory. Prescription can validate an initially doubtful title, provided the display of State authority is public. It must be public, as a title acquired via prescription implies the acquiescence of any other interested claimant. Protest from such a claimant or a dispossessed sovereign[22] can bar the establishment of title by prescription. What form must such protest take? Previously, force could legitimately be used. Today, diplomatic protests would have to be expressed and probably formally registered in the appropriate international fora.

As to the length of time required before prescription will give good title, there is no accepted prescribed period and much will depend on the circumstances of each particular case, such as the geographical nature of the territory and the existence or absence of any competing claims. There has to date been no decision of an international tribunal conclusively acknowledging title founded on prescription. The difficulty in establishing good title based on prescription is illustrated in the *Kasikili/Sedudu Island* case.[23] In this instance, Namibia was precluded from utilising prescription to establish title.

CONQUEST

Conquest is a mode of acquisition peculiar to the international community. It has no counterpart in municipal law. Conquest is taking possession of enemy territory by military force in time of war. To be effected there had to be not only the actual taking over (*factum*) but also an intention to take over (*animus*), e.g. the conqueror only acquired the territory if he intended to do so. Frequently the vanquished power would cede territory to the conqueror under treaty. In the absence of a treaty the territory could only be annexed if hostilities between the belligerent parties had ceased.

The observant reader will have noted the use of the past tense. Why has it been used? Simply because, although in earlier centuries there were no rules restricting a State's use of force, this is no longer true. The twentieth century witnessed the denunciation of war as legitimate, e.g. art.10 Covenant of the League of Nations, the 1928 Kellogg Briand Pact and art.11 of the 1949

---

[22] *Chamizal Arbitration* (1911) 5 *A.J.I.L.* 782.
[23] *Kasikili/Sedudu Island (Botswana v Namibia)* (2000) 49 *I.C.L.Q.* 964.

Draft Declaration on Rights and Duties of States, which imposes a duty on every State "to refrain from recognising any territorial acquisition by another State in violation of Article 9".[24]

The 1970 Declaration of Principles of International Law concerning Friendly Relations and Co-operation among States in accordance with the Charter of the United Nations, para.X, provides that:

"... The territory of a State shall not be the object of acquisition by another State resulting from the threat or use of force. No territorial acquisition resulting from the threat or use of force shall be recognised as legal."

This has been interpreted as meaning that territory cannot be acquired legitimately through the use of force, even if the use of that force is in accordance with the UN Charter (self-defence). The Security Council's denunciation of Israel's retention of territory taken during the 1967 War as unlawful is founded on the principle that force cannot give a good title;[25] accordingly, talks have centred on pre-1967 borders ever since.[26] Nevertheless, it must be acknowledged that *de jure* recognition by other States may validate titles based on conquest, for example Indian control over Goa, Danao and Diu (Portuguese territories on the Indian subcontinent invaded and taken by India in December 1961). The United States consistently refused to recognise the 1940 occupation of Estonia, Latvia and Lithuania by the Soviet Union. Britain accorded only *de facto* recognition.[27]

Conquest is, under contemporary international law, no longer recognised as a valid means of acquiring territory. Hence the international condemnation[28] precipitated by the Iraqi invasion of Kuwait and subsequent annexation of that territory in August

[24] i.e. prohibition on the use of war as an instrument of national policy and the use of force contrary to art.2(4) of the UN Charter. Ch.11 deals with the use of force in international law.
[25] e.g. Security Council Resolution on the Middle East, November 22, 1967—Security Council Resolution 242 (XXII), S.C.O.R., 22nd Yr., Resolutions and Decisions 1967, p.8.
[26] See the International Court of Justice's Advisory Opinion in the *Legal Consequences of the Construction of a Wall in the Occupied Palestine Territory*, I.C.J. Rep., 2004, 134. Where the International Court expressed the view the construction of the wall was contrary to international law.
[27] See Ch.4, above, recognition, pp.73 *et seq*. The three States now enjoy independent status and have been admitted to the UN.
[28] Note also the UN Security Council response to the Turkish Republic of Northern Cyrpus (SC Res. 541 (1983)); the only State which has recognised the TRNC is Turkey. The matter as yet remains unresolved following the rejection of the Greek Cypriots in 2004 of a proposed single federal State.

1990 culminating in UN Security Council Resolution 660,[29] calling for the immediate and unconditional withdrawal of all Iraqi forces from the territory of Kuwait,[30] declaring the Iraqi annexation as "null and void" having no legal validity "under any form and whatever pretext".

What of territories acquired by conquest when the use of force was accepted under international law? In accordance with the doctrine of intertemporal law, the law applicable when title was allegedly established will be applied. The essence of this doctrine is "a juridical fact should be appreciated in the light of the law contemporary with it, and not of the law in force at the time when the dispute in regard to it arises or falls to be settled."[31] To do otherwise and to require new doctrines to be of retroactive effect would be "highly disruptive" as "every State would constantly be under the necessity of examining its title to each portion of its territory in order to determine whether a change in the law had necessitated, as it were, a reacquisition."[32]

CESSION

This, the transfer of territory by one sovereign to another, is the most usual form of acquiring derivative title to land. Cession is always effected by treaty—most frequently in a peace treaty at the conclusion of a war as in the Treaty of Versailles, 1919, the Treaty of Peace with Japan, 1951,[33] the cession of Hong Kong by China to Great Britain after the Opium War[34] and that of Gibraltar to Britain pursuant to the Treaty of Utrecht 1714. To some extent the cession may be forced on the defeated power, in which case the latter's consent to the transfer of sovereignty will be recorded in the cession treaty. Cession requires that one party assumes sovereignty and another relinquishes it; one sovereign State is replaced by another. The acquiring sovereign cannot possess greater rights than those possessed by its predecessor. Should a third State have acknowledged rights in the territory, that is a right of passage,

[29] Adopted by 14–0, the Yemen abstaining.
[30] For text of Resolution see 29 I.L.M. 1323 (1990) and Resolution 662 of August 9, 1990, adopted by 15–0; for text, see 29 I.L.M. 1327.
[31] Parry and Grant, *Encyclopaedic Directory of International Law* (Oceana), 2004.
[32] P. C. Jessup, "The Palmas Island Arbitration" (1928) 22 A.J.I.L. 735 at 740.
[33] 112 B.F.S.P. 1; 136 U.N.T.S. 45.
[34] Hong Kong and the new Territories were leased to Britain under Treaty in 1898. Hong Kong was restored to China at a handover ceremony at midnight on June 30, 1997. The ceremony marked the return of Hong Kong to Chinese sovereignty and the establishment of a Hong Kong Special Administrative Region (HKSAR) as provided for by the Sino–British Joint Declaration on the Question of Hong Kong 1984. Under the terms of that Declaration, the British agreed to return the entire territory to China.

these must be respected. In the past, land has been ceded under an exchange agreement, for example in 1890 Britain and Germany exchanged Zanzibar and Heligoland, or purchased, as in the cases of Louisiana from France, and Alaska from the Soviet Union. The emergence of the principle of self-determination has made the cession of territory between States less likely.

ACCRETION AND AVULSION

Both accretion and avulsion refer to geographical processes. They refer to relatively rare occurrences and are of minor importance.

Accretion involves the gradual increase in territory through the operation of nature, for example the gradual shifting of a river's course leading to additional territory through the formation of alluvial deposits.

Avulsion refers to a violent change, such as a sudden alteration in a river's course, or the emergence by volcanic action of an island in territorial waters, i.e. the Island of Scutsey, which appeared in Icelandic territorial waters in 1963.

If accretion occurs on a boundary river (that is, between two States) then the international boundary changes, whereas with cases of avulsion the international boundary will remain where it was originally established. If the river is navigable the boundary will follow the *thalweg*, namely the centre of the navigable channel. If the river is not navigable the middle of the river stream will constitute the boundary.

NEW STATES

The attainment of independence, in accordance with the principle of self-determination (which may also be invoked to substantiate a claim of title to territory, e.g. with regard to the British claim over the Falkland Islands,[35] or the constitutional granting of independence to former colonial possession) involves the replacement of one sovereign by another and thus gives a derivative title to territory.

In October 2008, the General Assembly passed a resolution submitted by Serbia, requesting an Advisory Opinion from the ICJ on the legality of Kosovo's unilateral declaration of independence on February 17, 2008 (see above p.67).

Recognition of title to territory by an entity which comes to "statehood" by unconstitutional means, e.g. by revolt, will depend on recognition by the other members of the international

---

[35] See statement of the Foreign Secretary, "Our case rests on the facts, on prescription and on the principle of self-determination." (1983) 54 *B.Y.I.L.* 461.

community and title may finally only be established when an "acknowledgement of the facts" stance is adopted.[36]

POLAR REGIONS

The Arctic

The Arctic consists largely of ice rather than land. It is incapable of occupation in the accepted sense of the term but below the frozen masses navigation by submarines is possible. Sovereignty over such land, e.g. Eastern Greenland, can be established by minimum overt acts. Greenland belongs to Denmark while Norway exercises sovereign rights over Spitzbergen. The Russian Federation (previously the Soviet Union) and Canada, both anxious to eliminate any potential foreign, and possibly hostile, settlement, have also made claims in the area. Both have utilised a modification of the contiguity principle (principle whereby the occupying State may claim territory which is geographically pertinent to its area of lodgment) namely the sector principle. By this principle, all land falling within the triangle between the east–west extremities of a State contiguous to the Pole and the Pole itself should be the territory of that State, unless another State has a previously recognised established title. Both the Russian Federation and Canada have asserted sovereignty over extensive areas in the Arctic region and in September 1985 Canada declared its intention to establish straight baselines round the Arctic archipelago from latitude 60°E to the Beaufort Sea in the west and thereby all waters, including Hudson Bay and several routes of the North West Passage, within the baselines. These were designated Canadian as of January 1, 1986. Although the Canadian action did not meet with US approval, an agreement on Arctic Co-operation[37] was concluded between the two countries in 1988 and provides that Canadian permission will be sought before American icebreakers and other vessels navigate the North West Passage.[38] The United States and the other Arctic States have not utilised the sector principle. The major argument against claims in the Arctic is that what lies beneath the frozen wastes are high seas and not land and are not, therefore, capable of national appropriation. In August 2007 Russian explorers planted a Russian flag on the seabed, some 14,000 feet below the

---

[36] See, further, Ch.4 generally.
[37] 28 I.L.M. 141 (1989); A.J.I.L. (1989) at 63–64. Canada continues to conduct annual military exercises in the Arctic region.
[38] *ibid.*, art.4.

North Pole. This action arguably bolsters Russia's claim to the region.[39]

In 1991 the Arctic States[40] adopted the Arctic Environmental Protection Strategy (AEPS)[41] designed to promote regional environmental protection of the Arctic region. Eight Arctic States endorsed the AEPS and committed themselves to ensuring "the protection of the Arctic environment and its sustainable and equitable development, while protecting the cultures of indigenous peoples".[42] Environmental issues of particular concern to the Arctic and tackled in the AEPS are identified as persistent organic contaminants, oil pollution, heavy metals, noise, radioactivity and acidification. An Arctic Monitoring and Assessment Programme (AMAP) was established in 1991 to promote research and co-operation. Issues which have been addressed include the conservation of Arctic plant and animal life, e.g. the Conservation of Arctic Flora and Fauna (CAFF) working group has been in operation since 1992 and a working group on Protection of the Arctic Marine Environment (PAME) has been in operation since 1994. Following a ministerial review meeting of the AEPS in 1993, the Nuuk Declaration on the Environment and Development in the Arctic was adopted. The Declaration essentially reaffirms the principles established in the AEPS but highlights the need for additional co-operation to deal with Arctic marine pollution as well as effective domestic measures. The ATLA declaration on the Arctic Environmental Protection Strategy was adopted in 1997 and re-affirms the recognition of the Arctic States of the importance of co-operation. In 1997 the AEPS was subsumed by the Arctic Council, the Council is now charged with developing the work begun by the AEPS. It held its first ministerial meeting in Iqaluit, Canada in 1998, where it adopted a further declaration regarding the promotion of co-operation, co-ordination and interaction of the Arctic States, as well as involvement of Arctic indigenous communities on issues common to the area, such as sustainable development and environmental protection.

Antarctica

All of Antarctica has been the subject of territorial claims, though that made by Admiral Byrd on behalf of the United States has

[39] Russia, pursuant to art.76 of the 1982 United Nations Convention on the Law of the Sea, has extended its continental shelf beyond 200 nautical miles. See further Law of the Sea, Ch.7.
[40] Canada, Denmark, Finland, Iceland, Norway, Sweden, the US and the former USSR.
[41] 30 I.L.M. 1624 (1991).
[42] *ibid.* at 1629.

never been officially adopted. The United States favours an inter-nationalisation of the area and has not recognised any of the claims made by other States (Argentina, Australia, Chile, France, New Zealand, Norway and the United Kingdom). The sectors claimed by Argentina, Chile and the United Kingdom overlap to some extent.[43] The other States involved appear to have recog-nised each other's respective claims. However, in an attempt to avoid a "scramble for Antarctica", the Antarctic Treaty was drawn up in Washington in 1959,[44] and entered into force in 1961. The Treaty designates Antarctica exclusively for peaceful pur-poses and prohibits any measures of a "military nature".[45] The Treaty also provided for the regular meetings of the Consultative Parties[46] and these parties have been responsible for some the adoption of initiatives designed to afford comprehensive protec-tion of the Antarctic environment, such as Agreed Measures for the Conservation of the Antarctic Flora and Fauna 1964;[47] the 1972 Convention for the Conservation of Antarctic Seals;[48] and the 1980 Convention for the Conservation of Antarctic Marine Living Resources.[49] The *raison d'être* of the last, for example, is to curtail the use of resources by certain restrictive measures such as open and closed seasons.[50]

The most extensive agreement with respect to the Antarctic environment is the 1991 Madrid Protocol on Environmental Protection to the Antarctic Treaty and the four annexes, which form an integral part of the Protocol.[51] The key article is art.7, which prohibits "any activity relating to mineral resources other than scientific research". This prohibition will remain in force with no possibility of review until 50 years have lapsed following the entry into force of the Protocol. The Protocol entered into force 30 days after ratification by all States who were Antarctic Treaty

---

[43] The UK in 1955 initiated proceedings seeking a declaration from the I.C.J., but the latter struck the case from its list in 1956, as it had not received any response from either Argentina or Chile.

[44] Antarctic Treaty 1959, U.K.T.S. 97 (1961) Cmnd. 1535; 402 U.N.T.S. 71; (1960) A.J.I.L. 477. The Treaty suspends all territorial claims for the lifetime of the Treaty and does not provide for its own termination.

[45] *ibid.*, art.1.

[46] Namely ATCPs, of which there are 28.

[47] 17 U.S.T. 996.

[48] U.K.T.S. 45 (1978) Cmnd.7209; 1080 U.N.T.S. 176; 11 I.L.M. 251 (1978).

[49] U.K.T.S. 48 (1982) Cmnd.8714; 19 I.L.M. 841.

[50] For a synopsis of all measures recommended by Antarctic Treaty Consultative meeting and approved by Antarctic Treaty Consultative Parties, see 35 I.L.M. 1165 (1996).

[51] See 30 I.L.M. 1460 (1991). The annexes are: Environmental Impact Assessment; Conservation of Antarctic Fauna and Flora; Waste Disposal and Waste Management; Prevention of Marine Pollution.

Consultative States on the date when the Protocol was adopted.[52] Reservations are not permitted.[53] Article 19 provides a choice of dispute settlement, either by reference to the International Court of Justice or the Arbitral Tribunal, as established in accordance with the Schedule to the Protocol.

AIRSPACE

Every State enjoys exclusive sovereignty over the airspace above its territory to a height once thought to be indeterminable. In the wake of outer-space exploitation it is now recognised there is an upward limit to airspace, but what this limit is has yet to be established. State sovereignty over airspace quickly became customary international law in the early twentieth century, was crystallised in the 1919 Paris Convention on the Regulation of Aerial Navigation,[54] and art.1 of the 1944 Chicago Convention on International Civil Aviation.[55] International law does not give a right of innocent passage through airspace and entry into a State's airspace requires the permission of the host State.

The Chicago Convention, which entered into force in 1947, replaced the 1919 Paris Convention rules on aerial navigation. The Chicago Convention recognises the exclusive sovereignty of all States over their airspace that is regardless of whether or not they are Contracting Parties of the Convention. The Convention applies only to civil aircraft and not State aircraft, which, for the purposes of the Convention, are defined as "aircraft used in military, customs and police services".[56] Such aircraft require authorisation by special agreement.[57] The primary stipulation of the Convention is contained in art.6, namely that the scheduled international aircraft of a contracting State must, before flying into or over the territory of a contracting State, have that State's permission and comply with any conditions of the said authorisation. Thus, the regulation of airspace is effected via interstate agreement.

The failure of the Chicago Conference to reach agreement on the granting of reciprocal rights of overflight or of transportation of passengers and cargo led to the adoption of two supplementary agreements: (i) the International Air Services Transit Agreement (the "Two Freedoms" Agreement);[58] and (ii) the

---

[52] art.23.1. The Protocol entered into force on January 14, 1998.
[53] art.24.
[54] 11 L.N.T.S. 173; U.K.T.S. 2 (1922) Cmd.1609.
[55] U.K.T.S. 8 (1953) Cmd. 8742; 15 U.N.T.S. 295.
[56] Chicago Convention, above, art.3(b).
[57] *ibid*. art.3(c).
[58] U.K.T.S. 8 (1953) Cmd.8742; 84 U.N.T.S. 389.

International Air Transport Agreement (the "Five Freedoms" Agreement).[59] The "Two Freedoms" Agreement refers only to transit rights, namely each Contracting State must grant to all other Contracting States:

- (a) the privilege of flying across its territory without landing; and

- (b) the privilege of landing for non-traffic purposes (for example, refuelling or maintenance).

The "Two Freedoms" Agreement does not provide for commercial rights in the territory of the grantor State.

The "Five Freedoms" Agreement embraces the aforementioned freedoms plus three additional freedoms, which are traffic rights. These are:

- (c) the privilege of putting down passengers, mail and cargo taken on in the territory of the State whose nationality the aircraft possesses;

- (d) the privilege of taking on passengers, mail and cargo destined for the territory of the State whose nationality the aircraft possesses; and

- (e) the privilege of taking on passengers, mail and cargo destined for the territory of any other Contracting State and the privilege to put down passengers, mail and cargo coming from any such territory.

The practice, when granted, has been for the third and fourth freedoms to be granted in conjunction, while the fifth freedom, being more extensive, has not been so readily granted. However the Five Freedoms Agreement has not been widely adopted and the 1944 Chicago Convention, art.6 excludes scheduled flights and as such this has prompted the regulation of international scheduled flights through a network of bi- and multi-lateral agreements.

The State granting the freedoms may require: (i) transit flights to follow designated routes;[60] (ii) airlines of States granted the freedoms to provide reasonable services at the airports they use;[61] and (iii) payment for the use of airports.[62] A "host" State may

---

[59] 171 U.N.T.S. 387; 149 B.F.S.P. 1.
[60] Two Freedoms Agreement, art.1(4).
[61] *ibid.*, art.1(3).
[62] *ibid.*, art.1(4).

revoke permission granted "to an air transport enterprise of another State in any case when it is not satisfied that substantial ownership and effective control is vested in nationals of a Contracting State." Permission may also be revoked when an air enterprise fails to comply with the laws of the territorial State, or when it fails to perform its obligations under the agreement.[63]

Aircraft in distress

Aircraft possess the nationality of the State in which they are registered[64] and may only be validly registered in one State.[65] For jurisdiction purposes, it is the State of registration which is competent to exercise jurisdiction over offences and acts committed on board.[66] Contracting States, that is, to the Tokyo Convention, other than the State of registration, may exercise criminal jurisdiction in respect of, for instance, offences which have effect on their territory or have been committed by or against one of their nationals or permanent residents.[67] The increase in hijacking and terrorist activities in the 1960s and 1970s relating to aircraft prompted the adoption of the Hague Convention for the Suppression of Unlawful Seizure of Aircraft 1970,[68] the ICAO Montreal Convention for the Suppression of Unlawful Acts Against the Safety of Civil Aviation,[69] and the Protocol[70] whereby attacks against individuals in airports are brought within the ambit of the Convention. These Conventions (and the Protocol), which are all in force, require Contracting Parties to exercise jurisdiction[71] or to extradite the alleged offender. Following the 1988 Lockerbie aerial incident, Libya maintained that all obligations under the Montreal Convention had been fulfilled.[72]

Contracting Parties are required by art.25 of the Convention to render assistance to civil aircraft (of other Contracting Parties) that find themselves "in distress" in their airspace.

---

[63] *ibid.*, art.1(5).
[64] Chicago Convention, art.17.
[65] *ibid.*, art.18.
[66] Tokyo Convention on Offences and Acts Committed on Board Aircraft 1963, U.K.T.S. 126 (1969) Cmnd.4230.
[67] *ibid.*, art.4.
[68] U.K.T.S. 39 (1972) Cmnd.4956; 10 I.L.M. 133 (1971).
[69] U.K.T.S. 10 (1974) Cmnd.5524; 10 I.L.M. 1551 (1971).
[70] Protocol for the Suppression of Unlawful Acts of Violence at Airports Serving International Civil Aviation (1971).
[71] The Hague Convention requires the imposition of "severe penalties".
[72] See *Case Concerning Questions of Interpretation and Application of the 1971 Montreal Convention arising from the Aerial Incident at Lockerbie (Libyan Arab Jamahiriya v United States)* 31 I.L.M. 662 (1992).

There are no established rules of international law as to what response a "host" State should make on the appearance of an unauthorised civil aircraft in its airspace. Although arguably such an aircraft, not being "in distress", does not come within the ambit of art.25 it would be untenable to allege the "host" State enjoys discretion as to its response. If the host State is not a party to the Convention, there is still, on humanitarian grounds, no reason for a distinction to be made between its position and that of a party to the Convention. The international community will not accept death and injury to innocent air passengers. Unfortunately, the violation of air sovereignty has precipitated some States to shoot first and ask questions later, for example: the 1953 Aerial Incident in which an Israeli aircraft was shot down in Bulgarian airspace; the 1973 shooting down of a Libyan aircraft by Israel; the shooting down in 1983 of a South Korean aircraft by the Soviet Union; and the destruction by Indian Air Force planes of a Pakistani aircraft.[73] Such a response, in particular from a Contracting Party of the Convention is especially regrettable when, under art.4, Contracting States undertake that civil aviation is not to be used for any purpose inconsistent with the aims of the Convention. Owing to the regularity of such incidents and, in particular, the 1983 incident involving the South Korean aircraft, the Assembly of the International Civil Aviation Organisation (ICAO) adopted unanimously art.3 *bis* of the 1944 Convention.[74] Under this provision, the use of weapons against civil aircraft in flight is prohibited, save for the derogation allowed under art.51 of the UN Charter.[75] Article 3 *bis* recognised what has become an established rule of Customary International Law. This was endorsed by the Security Council Resolution 1067, which "condemns the use of weapons against civil aircraft in flight as being incompatible with elementary considerations of humanity, the rules of customary international law as codified in art.3 *bis* of the Chicago Convention and the standards and recommended practices set out in the annexes of the Convention".[76] This resolution was issued following the shooting down of two US civilian aircraft by Cuban military aircraft on February 24, 1996. Cuba claimed that it was acting in defence of its sovereign right to protect its borders and the US aircraft were suspected of forming part of a paramilitary terrorist organisation in war against the country. The United

[73] *Ariel Incident of August 10, 1999 (Pakistan v India).* Note the I.C.J. held it lacked the jurisdiction to judge the case, but held that India and Pakistan were obliged to resolve the dispute by peaceful means.
[74] 23 I.L.M. 705 (1984).
[75] See Ch.11.
[76] Security Council Resolution 1067 (1996), July 26, 1996, para.6.

States claimed the fundamental question was whether it was acceptable to shoot down two unarmed civilian aircraft.

The Convention does not identify any sanctions which are to be adopted against "offending" Contracting Parties, and States are left to take whatever measures they see fit in the circumstances. Thus, following the shooting down of the South Korean aircraft, a number of States refused, for a time, Soviet airlines landing rights and cancelled flights by their own aircraft to the then Soviet Union.

The Chicago Convention initiated the establishment of the International Civil Aviation Organisation (ICAO). ICAO is a specialised agency of the United Nations and is based in Montreal. Its functions are primarily to supervise the application of air law, report any breaches of the Convention and conduct research into matters of air transport and navigation which are of international importance.

OUTER SPACE

The launching of the first artificial satellite round the Earth by the Soviet Union in 1957 heralded the beginning of outer space exploration and the evolution of a legal regime regulating activities in outer space. Contrary to the position in respect of airspace, States have accepted that satellites may pass above their territory and no State has contended that such activity constitutes a violation of airspace sovereignty. The exploration of outer space has modified inevitably the view airspace extends upwards to an indefinite limit. It is now recognised that national sovereignty must cease at some point.

The United Nations Committee on the Peaceful Uses of Outer Space, established in 1958, has been responsible for the measures adopted regulating outer space activity and all such measures recognise outer space is: (i) to be used for peaceful means; and (ii) that it is the common heritage of all mankind.

The Treaty on Principles Governing the Activities of States in the Exploration and Use of Outer Space including the Moon and Other Celestial Bodies (commonly referred to as the Outer Space Treaty)[77] affirms:

" . . . exploration and use of outer space including the Moon and other celestial bodies, shall be carried out for the benefit and in the interests of all countries, irrespective of their

---

[77] U.K.T.S. 10 (1968) Cmnd.3519; 610 U.N.T.S. 205.

degree of economic or scientific development, and shall be the province of all mankind."[78]

No area of outer space is to be appropriated by any State[79] and the exploration is to be conducted "in accordance with international law, including the Charter of the United Nations . . ."[80] Article 4 is particularly important in that it prohibits the installation of nuclear weapons or any other weapons of mass destruction in outer space. Jurisdiction over an object once launched into space remains with the State of registration.[81] Article 9 requires States to conduct exploration so as to avoid the harmful contamination of outer space and "also adverse changes in the environment of the Earth resulting from the introduction of extra terrestrial matter . . ." Agreement was reached in 1988 between the representatives of the United States, Canada, Japan and nine Member States of the European Space Agency on the establishment of a permanently manned civil space station.[82] The primary purpose of creating such a station is to promote collaborative efforts in the field of, e.g. biomedical studies.

The 1967 Treaty has been revised and clarified by the 1979 Moon Agreement (Agreement Concerning the Activities of States on the Moon and Other Celestial Bodies).[83] In particular, the Moon Agreement provides the natural resources of the moon and other celestial bodies should be exploited as the common heritage of mankind in accordance with an international legal regime. This Treaty entered into force on July 11, 1984. The 1967 Treaty has been supplemented by two further agreements:

(a) the Agreement on the Rescue of Astronauts, the Return of Astronauts and the Return of Objects Launched into Outer Space, 1968;[84] and

(b) the Convention on International Liability for Damages Caused by Space Objects 1972.[85]

The Rescue and Return Agreement is essentially concerned with securing co-operation between Contracting Parties for the rescue

---

[78] *ibid.*, art.1.
[79] *ibid.*, art.2.
[80] *ibid.*, art.3.
[81] *ibid.*, art.8.
[82] Agreement on Co-operation on the Detailed Design Development Operation and Utilisation of the Permanently Manned Civil Space Station.
[83] 18 I.L.M. 1434 (1979).
[84] U.K.T.S. 56 (1969) Cmnd.3997; 63 A/J.I.L. 382 (1969).
[85] 10 I.L.M. 965 (1971); U.K.T.S. 16 (1974) Cmnd.5551.

and return of astronauts, while the 1972 Convention establishes the strict liability of a launching State "for damage caused by its space object on the surface of the earth or to aircraft in flight",[86] and fault liability "in the event of damage being caused elsewhere other than on the surface of the earth to a space object of one launching state or to persons or property on board such a space object . . .".[87]

Every launch and its intended purpose must be registered by the launching State on a public register maintained by the Secretary General of the United Nations. This is required by the 1975 Convention on the Registration of Objects Launched into Outer Space,[88] introduced when the voluntary registration system initially envisaged proved unsatisfactory.[89]

An important by-product of space exploration has been the development of telecommunications networks. The operation, co-ordination and monitoring of these telecommunications networks and services falls within the remit of the International Telecommunications Union (ITU), a specialised agency of the United Nations, based in Geneva. One of the primary roles of the ITU is to promote the working together of government and private industry.

CONCLUSION

As previously highlighted, States enjoy territorial sovereignty. However, that sovereignty is not unfettered. A State may, for instance, have to recognise that its territory has to be used for the benefit of another State, for example a right of passage, taking of water for irrigation purposes, or alternatively a State may have to refrain from taking certain action on its territory, e.g. the stationing of forces. Such rights (servitudes) attached to territory have to be recognised by successor States. Benefits may exist not for a single State, but for the international community, e.g. international waterways such as the Suez Canal.

The increasing awareness and concern for environmental issues has in recent years led to further restrictions being imposed on a State's territorial sovereignty.[90]

---

[86] Liability Convention, art.II. Article VI establishes joint and several liability in the event of a joint launch.
[87] *ibid*. art.III. See Also *COSMOS 954 Claim* (Canada v USSR) 18 I.L.M. 899 (1979).
[88] 14 I.L.M. 43 (1975).
[89] The Agreements on outer space are the product of the UN Committee on the Peaceful Uses of Outer Space established in 1958.
[90] Such restrictions are discussed more fully in Ch.8, State Responsibility, below.

6. JURISDICTION

Jurisdiction is an attribute of State sovereignty. A State's jurisdiction refers to the competence of the State to govern persons and property by its municipal law (criminal and civil). This competence embraces jurisdiction to prescribe (and proscribe), to adjudicate and to enforce the law. Jurisdiction is primarily exercised on a territorial basis, but there are exceptions, for example there will be persons within a State's territory who will be immune from that State's jurisdiction, while there will be occasions when the State may exercise jurisdiction beyond its territory. The exercise or the non-exercise of jurisdiction is governed by a State's municipal law.

In international law, jurisdiction relating to the allocation of competence between States is an ill-defined concept. International law confines itself to criminal rather than civil jurisdiction. The civil law is the concern of private international law or more correctly the conflict of laws, though in the last resort, civil jurisdiction may be backed by the sanctions of the criminal law. International law does not prescribe rules *requiring* the exercise of jurisdiction. International law concerns itself principally with the propriety of the exercises of State jurisdiction. The exercise of jurisdiction remains, for the most part, a discretionary matter for the State concerned.

BASES OF JURISDICTION

Bases on which jurisdiction may be exercised are:

(a)   territorial principle;

(b)   nationality principle;

(c)   protective (or security) principle;

(d)   universality principle; and

(e)   passive personality principle.

The first four principles, territorial principle, nationality principle, protective (or security) principle and universality principle, were accepted by the Harvard Research Draft Convention of 1935. The Convention, although not binding on any State and not in itself purporting to be State practice, remains of interest because of the extensive study of State practice which was undertaken at the time. The passive personality principle was not adopted by the Harvard Convention.

The bases of jurisdiction are not listed in any hierarchy. No State can claim precedence simply on the principle on which it exercises jurisdiction. A State may legitimately possess jurisdiction concurrently with another State and the State which will exercise jurisdiction will be decided by other factors, e.g. the physical presence of the alleged offender.

What contemporary international law demands is the existence of a tangible link between the alleged offender and/or the forum of the incident and the State exercising jurisdiction.[1]

Territorial principle

This is the favoured basis for the exercise of State jurisdiction. Events occurring within a State's territorial boundaries and persons within that territory, albeit their presence is temporary, are as a rule subject to the application of local law.

An offence may not, however, be committed entirely within the territory of one State. A crime may be initiated in one State and

---

[1]   *Lotus* case P.C.I.J. Rep., ser.A, No.10 (1927) at 25, in which the Court emphasised the need for a prohibition to be evident under international law for a State's jurisdiction to be instituted. Otherwise, the State enjoyed a wide measure of discretion in the exercise of its jurisdiction. See also the decision of the European Court of Human Rights *Bank of Bankovic v Belgium et al* No. 52207/99 (2001) 11 B.H.R.C. 435; and also Joint Separate Opinion of Judges Higgins, Kooijmans and Buergentahl *Case Concerning the Arrest Warrant of 11 April 2000* I.C.J. Rep. 2002 p.3.

consummated in another. If a person stands near to the border between two countries and fires a gun and thereby injures a person on the other side, which State has jurisdiction? The answer is both. The State from which the gun was fired has jurisdiction under the subjective territorial principle, while the State where the injury was sustained has jurisdiction under the objective territorial principle.

The subjective territorial principle allows the exercise of jurisdiction by the State in which a crime is commenced.

The objective territorial principle gives jurisdiction to the State in which the crime has been completed and has effect—the forum of injury.

Both States may claim jurisdiction and both may do so legitimately. The one which will actually exercise jurisdiction will most probably be the one which has custody of the alleged offender. There is no rule of international law which gives a State, where a crime is completed, exclusive jurisdiction. The State in which the crime was initiated is, in other words, not restricted from exercising jurisdiction. Such a State may bring preparatory criminal acts within the ambit of its criminal law. See for example, in the United Kingdom (UK), the Criminal Justice Act 1993. There is:

> "No rule of comity to prevent Parliament from prohibiting under pain of punishment persons who are present in the United Kingdom, and so owe local obedience to our law, from doing physical acts in England, notwithstanding that the consequences of those acts take effect outside the United Kingdom."[2]

Nor is there anything:

> "in precedent, comity or good sense that should inhibit the common law from regarding as justiciable in England inchoate crimes committed abroad which were intended to result in the commission of criminal offences in England; therefore conspiracies abroad to commit offences in England constituted offences in English law even though no overt acts pursuant thereto took place in England."[3]

---

[2] Lord Diplock in *Treacy v D.P.P.* [1971] A.C. 537, HL at 561. The case related to attempted blackmail by a letter mailed in England to a person in Germany. See also the case of *R v Markus* [1974] 3 All E.R. 705.

[3] *Somchai Liangsiriprasert v The Government of the United States of America and Another Privy Council* [1991] 1 A.C. 225, PC—reaffirmed in *R. v Sansom and Others*, [1991] 2 Q.B. 130, CA. See, however, the CA's decision in *R. v Governor of Belmarsh Prison, Ex p. Martin* [1995] 2 All E.R., where the Court declined to

A problem which has demanded a modification of the territorial principle has been the need to halt the growth of the so-called "child sex industry". Unfortunately the growth in this trade has been to meet the demand from countries such as Germany, America, Great Britain, Australia and France.[4] Certain countries, whose nationals rank as alleged principal offenders, have initiated legislative measures to extend the territorial application of the legislation. Australia led the way with the Australian Crimes (Child Sex Tourism Amendment) Act.[5] Other countries which have followed the Australian lead have been Sweden, Norway, France and Japan. The reluctance to extend UK legislation abroad is reflected in the UK's response—the Sexual Offences (Conspiracy and Incitement) Act 1996[6]—whereby it is an offence to conspire, within England and Wales, to commit abroad certain sexual acts against children. Incitement of such acts abroad is also an offence under the legislation. Under the 2007 UK Forced Marriage (Civil Protection) Act a protection order may be issued to assist individuals who have been coerced into legally binding partnerships against their will. In December 2008 the Act was invoked to assist a Bangladeshi national who, after having been resident in the UK for six years, was summoned home and subsequently detained by members of her immediate family. What is interesting here is that the UK Foreign Office issued a protection order, notwithstanding her non-British nationality, and that order was given cognisance by the Bangladeshi Court.[7]

More controversial has been the exercise of jurisdiction based on the effects principle so as to regulate the affairs of foreign nationals abroad, because such activities have an economic impact in the regulating State. The most frequent application of this principle, which is essentially an extension of the objective territorial principle, has been by the United States (US), e.g. anti-trust legislation, but certain European States have invoked the principle and the European Court of Justice (E.C.J.) affirmed what is relevant in the application of European competition rules is the place where the agreement is implemented.[8] The response of those critical of the principle[9] has resulted in the US Courts modifying their approach by introducing a "reasonableness" test and

---

apply a UK Act of Parliament extraterritorially in respect of certain acts occurring outside the relevant territory. The Court declined to do so.

[4] UNICEF, *The Progress of Nations* (1995).
[5] 1994, Pt III A.
[6] 1996 No.2262 (C.57).
[7] *The Guardian*, December 14, 2008.
[8] See, e.g. *Wood Pulp* case [1988] 4 C.M.L.R. 901.
[9] See, e.g. the United Kingdom's Protection of Trading Interests Act 1980, c.11.

a balancing of the national interests when considering the potential application of its jurisdiction.[10] The US practice to restrict investment in countries such as Libya and Cuba through imposing sanctions on foreign companies has been severely criticised as a "clear violation of the principle of extra-territoriality", including the Organisation of American States (OAS) declaring that the US Helms-Burton Act 1996 did not conform to the "applicable norms of international law in respect of the exercise of jurisdiction of States and its limits on such exercise."[11]

The trial of the two suspects in the Lockerbie bombing was a unique event in that it was the first occasion when a Court had sat as a national Court outside its own territory. Although the Court sat in the Netherlands (Camp Zeist), it was a Scottish Court applying Scots law in respect of an offence, which took place within Scottish territory. The venue of the Court was moved to the Netherlands to counter the fears that the suspects would not receive a fair trial in Scotland.[12]

The issue of jurisdiction has arisen in the context of the suspected terrorist detention centre at Guantanamo Bay. The USA has attempted to deny foreign held detainees the right to challenge their detention.[13]

Nationality principle

Jurisdiction exercised on this principle relates to the nationality of the offender. A State may exercise jurisdiction over any of its nationals wherever they may be and in respect of offences committed abroad. Although universally acknowledged as a basis of jurisdiction, it is utilised more extensively by civil-law countries than those with a common-law system. The latter restrict jurisdiction exercised on the nationality principle to more serious crimes, such as in the case of the UK, offences committed under

---

[10] See, however, *Hartford Fire Insurance Co. v California* US Supreme Court 113 S. Ct 2891 (1993) in which the Supreme Court declined to carry out a balancing exercise between US and UK interests and found in favour of the US Court, apparently on the basis there was no conflict with UK legislation. This was despite the fact that the acts of the UK insurance company were deemed to be lawful in the UK.

[11] 35 I.L.M. 1322 (1996) Organisation of American States: Inter-American Juridical Committee Opinion Examining the US Helms-Burton Act of August 27, 1996. The EU has also expressed opposition to the Helms-Burton Act, namely its validity under international law, its extraterritorial reach and its impact on trade interests in the EU. See, 35 I.L.M. 397 (1996).

[12] *Lockerbie* case, (1992) I.C.J. 3, 94 I.L.R. 478. One suspect was acquitted whilst the other was given a life sentence.

[13] See cases *Rasul v Bush* 542 U.S. 466 (2004); *Hamdan v Rumsfeld* 548 U.S. 557 (2006); and *Boumediene v Bush* 553 U.S. (2008).

the Official Secrets Act 1989 (s.15) and the Sexual Offences (Conspiracy and Incitement) Act 1996; the Sex Offenders Act 1997; murder; manslaughter; and bigamy.

The US has similarly restricted prosecutions on the grounds of nationality to such crimes as treason, drug trafficking and crimes by or against the armed forces.

The fact that jurisdiction may be claimed on the nationality principle does not preclude the State in which the offence was committed from exercising jurisdiction on the territorial principle.

Protective (security) principle

On the basis of this principle a State may exercise jurisdiction in respect of offences which, although occurring abroad and committed by non-nationals, are regarded as injurious to the State's security. Although acknowledged as a justification for the exercise of jurisdiction, it remains ill-defined. It is undoubtedly open to abuse if "security" or "vital interests" are given a broad interpretation. However, the justification lies in the need to protect a State from the prejudicial activities of a non-national when such activities are not, for instance, unlawful in the country in which they are being carried out.

Examples of when a State may claim jurisdiction on this principle would be in respect of plans to overthrow its government or counterfeit its currency. The protective principle was invoked by Israel along with the universality principle in the case against Adolph Eichmann (see below), while in the English Courts it has been said "no principle of comity demands that a State should ignore the crime of treason committed against it outside its territory."[14] "Lord Haw Haw" was found guilty of treason because of his pro-Nazi propaganda radio broadcasts from Germany to Britain during the war. His duty of allegiance was founded on his having acquired a British passport, albeit fraudulently.

Universality principle

The basis of jurisdiction on the universality principle is that there are particularly offensive acts which are contrary to international law and prohibited by the international community.

The idea of a universal crime over which all States could exercise jurisdiction, regardless of the alleged offender's nationality, evolved with piracy. Under customary international law, the crime of piracy has long been recognised as one over which all

---

[14] *Joyce v D.P.P.* [1946] A.C. 347, HL at 372.

States could exercise jurisdiction, provided that the alleged offender was apprehended either on the high seas or within the territory of the State exercising jurisdiction. The arresting State may also legitimately punish pirates. This rule of customary international law is reaffirmed in art.19 of the 1958 Geneva Convention on the High Seas and art.105 of the 1982 Convention on the Law of the Sea. Piracy in international law-piracy *jure gentium*—is strictly defined. This is in contrast to piracy in municipal law, where the term is used with less precision. Piracy, for the purposes of international law, is essentially any illegal act of violence or depredation which is committed for private ends on the high seas or without the territorial control of any State.[15] Only acts which satisfy this definition of piracy are susceptible to the exercise of jurisdiction on the universality principle. Attempts to commit acts of piracy, even though unsuccessful, will also constitute the offence of piracy. A 1971 UN Resolution (GA Resolution 2784 (XXVI)) characterised apartheid as a crime against humanity and two years later a Convention[16] was adopted, identifying apartheid as a crime subject to universal jurisdiction.[17] However the number of States which have signed and ratified this Convention remains low.

INTERNATIONAL CRIMES

War crimes are now also widely accepted as being susceptible to universal jurisdiction. No State has exercised jurisdiction exclusively on such a basis.[18] In the *Eichmann* case[19] Israel successfully (at least in Israeli Courts) claimed jurisdiction on two cumulative grounds:

---

[15] art.15 of the 1958 Convention on the High Seas; art.101 of the 1982 Convention on the Law of the Sea; see pp.171 below.

[16] International Convention on the Suppression and Punishment of the Crime of Apartheid, November 30, 1973 and entered into force July 18 1976.

[17] *ibid.* art.1; the Convention which entered into force in 1976 has been adopted by some 100 States. The UK and the US are not parties.

[18] Belgium attempted to turn the principle of universal jurisdiction into a reality when it amended its penal code in 1999 and provided for universal jurisdiction in respect of genocide and crimes against humanity without the need for a link between the suspect, victims or the incident and Belgium. On June 8, 2001, four defendants were convicted of international crimes arising from the Rwandan genocide. A.S.I.L., Linda Keller, May 2001. The 1999 law was amended in April 2003 as tension grew between the US and Belgium following attempts to have former members of the US Administration investigated. The amendment lists special criteria which must be met for jurisdiction to be exercised by Belgian courts.

[19] *Attorney-General of the Government of Israel v Eichmann* 36 I.L.R. 5 (1961).

"a universal source (pertaining to the whole of mankind), which vests the right to prosecute and punish crimes of this order in every state within the family of nations; and a specific or national source, which gives the victim nation the right to try any who assault its existence."[20]

The Charter of the Nuremberg Military Tribunal, in particular art.6, which referred to crimes against peace, violations of the laws and customs of war, and crimes against humanity and for which there was to be individual responsibility, and the judgments of the Tribunal are now accepted as international law.[21]

Genocide has been unanimously condemned by the UN General Assembly and the 1948 Convention on the Prevention and Punishment of the Crime of Genocide was one of the first human rights instruments. Prohibition of genocide is now recognised as a *jus cogens* norm.[22] The Genocide Convention provides for trial by either the territorial State or by an international penal tribunal, but a State which encourages, practises or fails to punish genocide would be acting contrary to customary international law of a fundamental nature. The International Law Commission's Draft Code of Crimes Against the Peace and Security of Mankind 1996 declares certain crimes, including genocide, as ones for which there is individual responsibility and thereby calls for an exercise of the "broadest possible jurisdiction" under the principle of universal jurisdiction.[23] However, both the Statutes of the International Criminal Tribunals for the Former Yugoslavia and Rwanda distinguish between war crimes, genocide and crimes

---

[20] For Genocide Convention, see U.K.T.S. 58 (1970) Cmnd.4421; 78 U.N.T.S. 277; 4 *A.J.I.L.* Supp.6 (1951).

[21] See Convention on the Non-applicability of Statutory Limitations to War Crimes and Crimes Against Humanity 1968. Note also the Geneva Red Cross Conventions 1949 contain provisions for universal jurisdiction in respect of grave breaches. Offences which fall within the charaterisation of grave beaches include torture or inhuman treatment and the taking of hostages. The 1977 Protocol I to the 1949 Conventions extended grave breaches to include attacking civilian populations.

[22] The *Case Concerning the Application Of The Convention On The Prevention And Punishment Of The Crime Of Genocide (Bosnia And Herzegovina v Yugoslavia (Serbia And Montenegro))* (Provisional Measures), Order Of September 13, 1993 and the *Case Concerning the Application of the Convention on the Prevention and Punishment of the Crime of Genocide (Bosnia and Herzegovina v Serbia and Montenegro,* I.C.J. February 26, 2007.

[23] The International Law Commission Draft Codes of Crimes Against the Peace and Security of Mankind 1996, art.8. Report (A/48/10). UN G.A.O.R., 49th Sess, Supp.No.10 UN Doc.A/49/10 (1997).

against humanity.[24] This distinction is retained in the Statute of the Permanent Court of the International Criminal Court.[25]

Significant steps were taken by the international community in the 1990s towards the creation of a permanent international criminal court with enforcement jurisdiction over individuals for a number of crimes against humanity. Simultaneous to these efforts was the establishment, in 1993 and 1994 by the United Nations (UN), of the aforementioned tribunals with jurisdiction to "prosecute persons responsible for serious violations of international humanitarian law".[26] Nevertheless these tribunals are limited in jurisdiction, both temporally and geographically, and are non-permanent.[27] The humanitarian crisis in former Yugoslavia precipitated a rekindling of efforts to establish an international criminal law regime. Televised reports of war camps, rape, genocide and the practice of ethnic cleansing shocked the international community, and led to the creation of the Tribunal under Ch.VII of the UN Charter to punish the alleged perpetrators of such crimes. This was the first occasion the Security Council had created an international tribunal using Ch.VII powers and can therefore be said to be a truly international entity.[28] UN Security Council Resolution 827 established the ICTY on May 23, 1993 for the sole purpose of:

> "prosecuting persons responsible for serious violations of international humanitarian law committed in the territory of the former Yugoslavia between 1st January, 1991 and a date to be determined by the Security Council upon the restoration of peace."[29]

Equally, the horrific genocide in Rwanda which culminated in the death of some 800,000 Tutsis and moderate Hutus, prompted the establishment of the ICTR, also by UN Security Council

---

[24] Statute of ICTY arts 3, 4 and 5 and Statute of ICTR arts 2 (genocide) and 3 (crimes against humanity).

[25] Rome Statute of the International Criminal Court art.5(1). Note art.5(2) states the Court shall have jurisdiction over the crime of aggression once the provision is adopted in accordance with arts 121 and 123 defining crime and setting out conditions under which the Court shall exercise jurisdiction with respect to this crime.

[26] U.N.Doc.S/Res/827/(1993).

[27] Nevertheless the Security Council acknowledged at the end of 2008 that in order to complete the work of both tribunals it would be necessary to provide for a new "small, temporary and efficient structure."

[28] The Nuremberg Tribunal was established in very different circumstances, when there was no government in power.

[29] S.C.Res 827, U.N. SCOR, 48th Year, 3217th mtg at 1, reprinted in 32 I.L.M. 1203 (1993).

Resolution 955 under Ch.VII of the UN Charter, to try those who participated in breaches of international humanitarian law in Rwanda. This Statute is based on that of the ICTY and has a similar institutional framework. The ICTR is located in Arusha (Tanzania).

Both the ICTY and ICTR were designed to establish a judicial process aimed at preventing the continuation of crimes against humanity and to contribute towards the restoration and maintenance of peace and security in the region. They differ from their predecessor (Nuremberg) in that they may also hear cases of crimes perpetrated in the course of inter-state war and internal strife. Nuremberg could only deal with crimes committed in international armed conflict.

The Statutes of the ICTY and ICTR embody rules and procedures reflecting international human rights and standards, particularly those enshrined in the International Covenant of Civil and Political Rights, for example dealing with the accused's right to be present at his trial, and providing the accused with a right to appeal. Both courts have now been functioning for over ten years and have produced a substantial body of jurisprudence which has significantly advanced international criminal law.

The experience of both the ICTY and the ICTR heightened calls for the creation of a permanent court and gave the impetus necessary for agreement to be reached. The international efforts towards the creation of the International Criminal Court (ICC) culminated in the opening for signature of the Rome Statute[30] in July 1999 and its entry into force on July 1, 2002. The International Criminal Court has jurisdiction over "... persons for the most serious crimes of international concern ..."[31] namely genocide (art.5(1)(a)), crimes against humanity (art.5(1)(b)), war crimes (art.5(1)(c)) and the crime of aggression (art.5(1)(d)). The crimes themselves are defined in arts 6, 7 and 8 respectively. However, aggression has not yet been defined. State Parties to the Statute have still to reach an agreement as to the definition of aggression and the conditions under which the ICC would exercise jurisdiction in respect of aggression. The ICC's jurisdiction is complimentary to national criminal jurisdictions (art.1). In other words, the ICC will only exercise its jurisdiction when a State is unable or unwilling to do so. The ICC is not designed to be a substitute for national Courts, the primary responsibility to prosecute those responsible for international crimes remains with States. The ICC

---

[30] Above, n.25.
[31] *ibid.*, art.1. The Pre Trial Chamber has initiated 12 arrest warrants and proceedings have been brought against 6 individuals as of early 2009.

may exercise its jurisdiction only if "one or more of the parties involved is a State Party; the accused is a national of a State Party; the crime is committed on the territory of a State Party; or a State not party to the Statute may decide to accept the ICC's jurisdiction over a specific crime that has been committed within its territory, or by its national."[32] The ICC will only have jurisdiction once a situation has been referred to the Prosecutor by a State Party (art.13 & 14), the Security Council refers a situation to the Prosecutor; or the Prosecutor initiates an investigation on his own authority (arts 13 and 15).

The ICC is based in The Hague in the Netherlands. The elections for the 18 Judges of the ICC took place in February 2003 and the Judges took their oath, in public, at the inaugural ceremony on March 11, 2003. The President of the ICC is Mr Philip Kirsch (Canada) and the two Vice-Presidents are Ms Akua Kuenyehia (Ghana), who was elected to a nine-year-term, and Mr René Blattmann (Bolivia) who was elected for a six-year term.

In April 2003 the Assembly of States elected Mr. Luis Moreno-Ocampo (Argentina) as the first Prosecutor of the ICC. The Office of the Prosecutor is an independent organ of the ICC and has its own budget.[33] The mandate of the Prosecutor's Office is to conduct investigations and prosecute crimes that fall within the ICC's jurisdiction as set out in its Statute.

The first situation referred in 2004 was concerning grave crimes allegedly committed on the territory of the Democratic Republic of Congo since July 1, 2002. The alleged crimes included mass murder, rape, torture, forced displacement and the illegal use of child soldiers. Other situations being investigated are Sudan, Uganda and the Central African Republic.[34]

In addition to the foregoing institutions a number of hybrid tribunals were established from 1997 to 2003. These include Sierra Leone, Cambodia, East Timor and Lebanon, as well as the so called War Crimes Chambers of Bosnia and the hybrid panels provided by UNMIK in Kosovo, on which international judges work alongside national judges and prosecutors to administer justice for past atrocities.

---

[32] art.12. However, these conditions do not apply when the Security Council, acting under Ch.VII of the Charter, refers a situation to the Prosecutor.

[33] In addition to the Office of the Prosecutor there are three other organs, *viz*, the Presidency, the Registry and Chambers. Chambers is made up of pre trial division, trial division and appeals division.

[34] The Security Council referred the situation in Darfur, Sudan to the Prosecutor of the ICC by way of Security Council Resolution 1593, 2005. The other situations were referred by State parties.

Efforts by domestic courts to exercise jurisdiction over international crimes. Some States have exercised universal jurisdiction over international crimes by prosecuting foreign nationals for crimes committed outside their borders. The Spanish jurisdictional provides that Spanish Courts can exercise universal jurisdiction over acts perpetrated by Spanish nationals or foreigners outside of the Spanish national territory when these acts can be qualified under Spanish law as genocide, terrorism, piracy and illegal appropriation of airplane, falsification of foreign currency, prostitution and corruption of minors or unfit individuals, illegal drug trafficking, illegal human trafficking, female genital mutilation (FGM) and any other crime which, according to international treaties, should be prosecuted by Spain. The only explicit limitation established by the Spanish procedural law to the principle of universal jurisdiction is that the alleged perpetrator had not been absolved, pardoned or condemned abroad, or in this last instance, that the sentence has not been served. The law does not even require that the acts are punishable in the forum of the alleged crime or that the alleged perpetrator is in Spanish territory to initiate the procedures, other than in the case of FGM. In 1986 a Spanish Court indicted several Argentinean and Chilean nationals, including General Augusto Pinochet, on a case relating to the "Condor Plan". Pinochet was not extradited to Spain by the UK and so did not stand trial there. However several Argentinean military leaders were tried such as Ricardo Miguel Cavallo, detained in 2000, and Adolfo Scilingo in 2001. These cases, and others such as the one brought in 1999 by the Nobel Peace Laureate, Rigoberta Menchu Tum, for crimes committed in Guatemala, have helped develop important jurisprudence in the country, which has contributed to the application of international criminal law and the development of universal jurisdiction practice. Even if severely criticised on occasions Spain continues to exercise universal jurisdiction for international crimes. Spanish Courts have issued an arrest warrant for high level members of the military and government of Rwanda in 2008 and have started considering the responsibility of Israeli military for the killing of 14 civilians in 2002 in the Gaza strip, as well as examining the alleged genocide in Tibet.

Belgium also has important legislation in relation to universal jurisdiction. In 1999 Belgium amended its penal code to provide for universal jurisdiction in respect of genocide and crimes against humanity, without the need for a link between the suspect, victims or incident and Belgium. On June 8, 2001, four defendants were convicted of international crimes arising from the Rwandan genocide.

Issues relating to alleged war crimes amounting to grave breaches of the 1949 Geneva Convention and Crimes Against Humanity were raised in the *Case Concerning the Arrest Warrant of 11 April 2000 (Congo v Belgium)*.[35] These were allegedly committed by a national of the Democratic Republic of Congo (DRC) who had made a speech in August 1998 inciting racial hatred, which led to violence. The international arrest warrant was made *in absentia* in pursuance of Belgium Penal Code 1993. No Belgian national was a victim of the alleged offences, nor was the accused in Belgium when the warrant was issued. The issue of Belgian jurisdiction was dealt with only in the joint Separate Opinion of Judges Higgins, Kooijmans and Buergenthal as the I.C.J. upheld the DRC's assertion that the individual in question enjoyed diplomatic immunity as a Minister for Foreign Affairs. In their Separate Opinion the Judges concluded in the affirmative that a State may claim jurisdiction over an alleged offender who is not on their territory and who has no other link with it, as such jurisdiction is not prohibited by international law. An opposing stance was adopted by President of the I.C.J., President Guillame, in a Separate Opinion in which he observed:

> "States primarily exercise a criminal jurisdiction on their own territory. In classic international law, they normally have jurisdiction in respect of an offence committed abroad only if the offender, or at least the victim, is of their nationality, or if the crime threatens their internal or external security. Additionally, they may exercise jurisdiction in cases of piracy and the situations of subsidiary universal jurisdiction provided for by various Conventions if the offender is present on their territory. But apart from these cases, international law does not accept universal jurisdiction; still less does it accept the universal jurisdiction in absentia."[36]

The 1999 law was amended however in April 2003 to limit the extent of the excercise of universal jurisdiction by Belgian courts, after tension developed between the US and Belgium following

---

[35] I.C.J. Report 2002 p.3.

[36] Subsidiary universal jurisdiction was used by President Guillame to cover the exercise of jurisdiction over alleged offenders arrested on national territory and not extradited. In the Joint Separate Opinion the term territorial jurisdiction was used. See also the I.C.J.'s decision in *Certain Criminal Proceedings in France* (Republic of the Congo v France) 2003 and the UK case of the Afghan Warlord against whom proceedings for the commission of alleged torture were initiated in the UK courts. In this case the alleged offender is not a British national, the crimes alleged took place exclusively outwith UK territory and no British national was a victim of the alleged crimes.

attempts to have former members of the US Administration investigated in relation to the 2003 invasion of Iraq.

Quasi-universal jurisdiction

Only international crimes "proper" are susceptible to universal jurisdiction under customary international law, that is, irrespective of whether a State is party to any international agreement. However, there is nothing to preclude offences currently regulated by way of Convention from crystallising into customary international law.

A growing number of crimes which are of international concern have been tackled by way of Conventions. These Conventions provide a quasi-universal jurisdiction by way of an obligation on Contracting Parties to either extradite the alleged offender to a State which has a link with the offence, or to exercise jurisdiction over the alleged offender. The types of offences which have been dealt with in this way include drug trafficking, slavery, terrorist activities and torture. The Hague Convention on the Suppression of Unlawful Seizure of Aircraft 1970[37] and the Montreal Convention for the Suppression of Unlawful Acts against the Safety of Civil Aviation 1971[38] were the response of the international community to hijacking a particular problem in the 1960s. Both Conventions have been adhered to by a large number of States and impose an obligation on Contracting States to punish offenders "by severe penalties" implemented by way of their domestic law (or alternatively extradite the alleged offender to a State which has a link with the offence). Similar provisions are contained in the Convention on the Prevention and Punishment of Crimes against Internationally Protected Persons including Diplomatic Agents,[39] the 1979 International Convention against the Taking of Hostages,[40] the 1984 UN Convention Against Torture and Other Cruel, Inhuman or Degrading Treatment or Punishment,[41] the 1988 Convention against Illicit Traffic in Narcotic Drugs[42] and the European Council Convention on Cybercrime.[43] The latter is the international response to the

---

[37] 860 U.N.T.S. 105; U.K.T.S. 39 (1972) Cmnd.4956; 10 I.L.M. 133 (1971).

[38] U.K.T.S. 10 (1974) Cmnd.5524; 10 I.L.M. 1151 (1971); see Ch.5, above.

[39] 13 I.L.M. 41 (1974); U.K.T.S. 3 (1980) Cmnd.7765.

[40] U.K.T.S. 81 (1983) Cmnd. 9100; 18 I.L.M. 1456 (1979).

[41] 23 I.L.M. 1027 (1984) and 24 I.L.M. 535 (1985). In *Filartiga v Pena-Irala* 630 F. 2d 876 (1980), a US tribunal held torture was a recognised crime under international law and every country could exercise jurisdiction over the alleged offenders of such an offence.

[42] 28 I.L.M. 493 (1989).

[43] Convention on Cybercrime, (ETS no.185) November 23, 2001.

tackling of crimes committed via the internet and other computer networks, particularly copyright, computer related fraud, child pornography and network-security violations.[44] Such agreements are effective only between Contracting Parties. States do not automatically possess competence under customary international law to apprehend and punish alleged offenders. As highlighted what the Conventions spell out are the particular situations in which States are required to exercise jurisdiction or alternatively initiate extradition proceedings.

Passive personality principle

The link between the State exercising jurisdiction and the offence is the nationality of the victim. A State may exercise jurisdiction over a non-national in respect of an act which has taken place outwith its boundaries. Historically it has not been widely accepted as a basis of jurisdiction—see Moore J.'s objection in the *Lotus* case[45]—but civilian legal systems recognise it more readily than common-law systems. The vigorous opposition of countries of the Anglo–American tradition was responsible for the principle not being adopted by the Harvard Draft Convention. Nevertheless, the passive personality principle is recognised in art.4(b) of the 1963 Tokyo Convention on Offences Aboard Aircraft,[46] art.5(1)(c) of the 1984 Convention Against Torture and Other Cruel, Inhuman or Degrading Treatment or Punishment[47] and, apparently, the current position of the US is although the principle is not generally accepted for ordinary torts or crimes, it is increasingly accepted as applied to terrorist and other organised attacks on a State's nationals by reason of their nationality, or to assassination of a State's diplomatic representatives or other officials.[48]

EXTRADITION

If an alleged offender is in a territory other than the State seeking to exercise jurisdiction, the lawful method of securing his return

---

[44] Although concluded under the auspices of the European Council, Japan, US, Canada and South Africa have ratified the Convention.

[45] P.C.I.J.Rep., ser.A, No.10, (1927), pp.141–148.

[46] U.K.T.S. 126 (1969) Cmnd.4230; 704 U.N.T.S. 219.

[47] Above, n.41.

[48] Third Restatement of the Law—The Foreign Relations Law of the United States—para.402g. The US passed the Public Law 107–40 authorising the use of united Armed Forces against those responsible for the attacks launched against the US (SJ 23 (September 18, 2001)). This authorised the US to exercise its right to self-defence and to protect US citizens both at home and abroad. The US also has the Omnibus Diplomatic Security and Anti-Terrorism Act of 1986. See above, n.35 at para.47 and separate opinion *ibid.* para.16.

to stand trial is to request his extradition. Extradition is the handing over of an alleged offender (or convicted criminal who has escaped before completing his prison term) by one State to another.

Extradition as a rule is effected by bipartite treaty.[49] There is no duty to extradite in the absence of a treaty.[50] Extradition treaties normally relate only to serious crimes and impose the same obligations on both the parties concerned, e.g. the offence must be designated a crime under the domestic laws of both countries. A country's own nationals may be protected from extradition, as may be persons who have committed offences of a "political" or "religious" character.[51] Many States do not allow their nationals to be extradited to another State.

ILLEGAL ARREST

A Tribunal does not normally concern itself with the means by which the accused is brought before it. If the alleged offender has been procured by illegal means, e.g. kidnap or in violation of an extradition treaty, this will not preclude the Tribunal from exercising jurisdiction. Unlawful arrest does not affect the Court's jurisdiction to hear a case. However, this established rule was modified to some extent in the *Toscanino* case,[52] in which it was stated a Court was divested of jurisdiction when the accused had been brought before it through the illegal conduct of the law enforcement authorities. Forcible abduction, involving brutality and like behaviour by a State's representatives, could impair a State's exercise of jurisdiction. The norm, however, is that a State will, in the absence of protest from other States, try alleged offenders brought before the courts by irregular means as in the

---

[49] See for example treaty of April 2004, between US and UK (Treaty No.108–23). The treaty replaces the 1972 Extradition Treaty and the 1985 Supplementary Treaty. See also Convention on Extradition between the Member States of the European Union 1996 and incorporated into UK law by the European Union Regulations 2002, pursuant to the Anti Terrorism, Crime and Security Act 2001.

[50] The I.L.C.'s Draft Code of Crimes, above, n.23 seeks to impose an obligation on a State to extradite an individual alleged to have committed crimes against humanity (art.6).

[51] See for example the European Convention on the Suppression of Terrorism 1977, art.1 listing those offences which may not be regarded as either political or inspired by political motives.

[52] *US v Toscanino* 500 F. 2d. 207 (1974) (US Ct of Appeals, 2nd Circuit). cf. *United States v Alvarez-Machain* 31 I.L.M. 902 (1992) where a Mexican national was forcibly removed from his country and brought before a US court. The Supreme Court held the Federal Court could exercise jurisdiction, despite the flagrant breach of international law, as this was a matter to be considered only by the Executive.

case of *Ex p. Elliott*[53] and *R. v Plymouth Magistrates Court, Ex p. Driver*.[54] In *R. v Horseferry Magistrates' Court, Ex p. Bennett*[55] the House of Lords held that where a defendant has been forcibly brought before a Court by an abuse of process, the UK Courts should refuse to exercise jurisdiction. Bennett had been taken from South Africa to the UK in a manner which appeared to contravene the Extradition Act 1989, and which was contrary to international law.[56] The US Courts have taken a somewhat different stance, as is illustrated in the *US v Alvarez-Machain*[57] and the Supreme Court's judgement in *Sosa v Alvarez-Machain et al*.[58]

The State whose sovereignty has been violated may initiate an international claim against the offending State. Argentina lodged a complaint with the UN Security Council in protest at the abduction of Adolph Eichmann to Israel, and called for his "immediate return". The claim was dropped, and in August 1960 Argentina and Israel announced in a joint decision that any violation of international law which had occurred had been "cured". States will only refrain from exercising jurisdiction over persons illegally brought before their Courts from another State if the latter protests.

DOUBLE JEOPARDY

What of the person who is susceptible to the jurisdiction of more than one country? Does conviction or acquittal in one country constitute a bar to a subsequent prosecution elsewhere?

International law does not provide an unequivocal answer, though art.13 of the Harvard Draft Convention does provide, at least in respect of exercising jurisdiction under the Draft Convention, that no State should prosecute or punish a non-national who "has been prosecuted in another State for a crime requiring proof of substantially the same acts or omissions and has been acquitted on the merits, or having been convicted, has been pardoned."

Article 13 refers only to non-nationals. Regarding the person who finds himself required to do in one State something which is prohibited in another, art.14 of the Draft Convention provides ". . . no State shall prosecute or punish an alien for an act which

---

[53] [1949] 1 All E.R. 373.
[54] [1986] Q.B. 95.
[55] [1993] 3 All E.R. 138.
[56] See in particular, opinions of Lords Griffiths and Bridge.
[57] (1992) 119 L.Ed. 2d 441.
[58] 542 US (2004).

was required of that alien by the law of the place where the alien was at the time of the act or omission." Article 14 applies only to non-nationals and not to nationals. Article 12 of the International Law Commission's Draft Code of Crimes Against the Peace and Security of Mankind (1996) upholds the principle of *non bis in idem* in relation to two scenarios, the second being subject to exceptions. The first situation is where an individual is tried for crimes by an international criminal court and is convicted or acquitted. In such instances the principle of *non bis in idem* applies fully. The second situation is where an individual may not be tried for a crime under the code arising from the same act or omission, as was the subject of the national trial unless one of these exceptions applies:

(a) if the individual was tried by a national court for an ordinary crime and not a more serious one (e.g. murder, not genocide); and

(b) if the proceedings in the national court were not impartial or independent.

IMMUNITY FROM JURISDICTION

Sovereign immunity and diplomatic immunity are the two principal exceptions to the exercise of territorial jurisdiction. Sovereign immunity refers to immunities enjoyed by foreign heads of State. Diplomatic immunity refers to the immunities enjoyed by their official representatives.

State immunity

"Par in parem non habat imperium"—one cannot exercise authority over an equal. All States are equal. No State may exercise jurisdiction over another State without its consent. Historically, a Sovereign and his State were regarded as synonymous. The ruler of a foreign State enjoys complete immunity—the principle that this extends to acts done in a private capacity was confirmed in *Mighell v Sultan of Johore*[59] and still applies today.

Traditionally a State was likewise immune from the jurisdiction of the courts of another State. States in the twentieth century, however, became increasingly involved in commercial activities until a point was reached when State enterprises enjoyed an immunity not enjoyed by non-State counterparts. Sovereign immunity placed State enterprises in a privileged position.

[59] [1894] 1 Q.B. 149.

Consequently, a number of States adopted a modified, absolute-immunity policy. A distinction was drawn between the public acts of a State (government acts) *jure imperii,* and private acts (trading and commercial acts) *jure gestionis.* Immunity was granted in respect of *jure imperii* acts, but not in respect of *jure gestionis.* Not all States abandoned the doctrine of absolute immunity, however, and as a result some States were affording complete immunity to the commercial activities of foreign States, whereas the same privileges were not being reciprocated.

The principle of absolute immunity was established in *The Parlement Belge* case,[60] in which it was held the *Parlement Belge,* a mail packet vessel belonging to the Belgian King, was entitled to complete immunity. The principle was confirmed in subsequent cases, e.g. *The Porto Alexandra,*[61] *The Cristina,*[62] *Krajina v Tass Agency*[63] and *Baccus SRL v Servicio Nacional del Trigo.*[64]

Moves towards the modified State immunity approach

Concerned at the privileged position enjoyed by foreign governments, the courts of a number of European States handed down judicial decisions curtailing the scope of immunity to government acts only (*jure imperii*), e.g. *Dralle v Republic of Czechoslovakia*[65] and the *Empire of Iran* case.[66] The so-called "Tate-letter" issued by the US State Department in 1952 intimated a similar change in American policy, that is ". . . the immunity of the sovereign is recognised with regard to sovereign or public acts (*jus imperii*) of a State, but not with respect to private acts (*jus gestionis*)."[67] A State acting in a manner similar to a private individual was no longer to be placed in the advantageous position of receiving immunity, and was to be liable in the same way and to the same extent as a private individual under similar circumstances. The American Foreign Sovereign Immunities Act of 1976[68] confirms restrictive immunity as American policy. The Act spells out the type of acts which are commercial and those which are private. A notable change of policy is provided for in the Act—the decision as to whether or not Sovereign immunity is to be accorded is

[60] (1879) 4 P.D. 129.
[61] [1920] P. 30.
[62] [1938] A.C. 485.
[63] [1949] 2 All E.R. 274.
[64] [1957] 1 Q.B. 438.
[65] (1950) 17 I.L.R. 155, Austrian S.C.
[66] (1963) 45 I.L.R. 57, Federal Constitution Court, German Federal Republic.
[67] 6 Whiteman, 569–571.
[68] 90 Stat. 2891; P.L. 94–583 (1976); 15 I.L.M. 1388 (1976).

now the responsibility of the Courts rather than the US State Department.

An increasing number of States followed the US and adopted a restrictive immunity policy. The number of States acceding to the 1926 Brussels Convention for the Unification of Certain Rules relating to the Immunity of State Owned Vessels,[69] under which government-owned vessels engaged in commercial purposes are subjected to the same legal regime as private vessels, also increased.

The UK and Commonwealth countries, however, maintained a strict adherence to absolute immunity—at least until the 1970s, when for example Britain adopted a restricted immunity policy. The common law was shaped by decisions of the courts—*The Philippine Admiral*,[70] *Trendtex Trading Corp. v Central Bank of Nigeria*,[71] and *I Congreso del Partido*.[72] The State Immunity Act was introduced in 1978 and entered into force on November 22 of that year. Sovereign immunity in Britain is now governed primarily by the statutory law which spells out the instances when, and in respect of what activities, a State will not be immune from proceedings in the British Courts.[73] Canada likewise adopted the restrictive doctrine in the State Immunity Act 1982. The State Immunity Act enabled the UK to become a party to both the 1926 Brussels Convention and the 1972 European Convention on State Immunity.[74]

The 1972 Convention was initiated in an attempt to obtain among States a uniform approach to the issue of sovereign immunity. The Convention specifies the circumstances in which sovereign immunity may and may not be claimed before the courts of

---

[69] U.K.T.S. 15 (1980) Cmnd.7800.

[70] [1977] A.C. 373, JC.

[71] [1977] Q.B. 529, CA.

[72] [1981] 3 W.L.R. 329, HL.

[73] See *Commissioners of Customs and Excise v Ministry of Industries and Military Manufacturing*, Republic of Iraq 43 I.C.L.Q. 194 (1994), where it was held a contract dealing with parts for an Iraqi super gun fell within s.3(3)(a) of the Act concerning commercial transactions and is therefore not immune from proceedings. cf. *Kuwait Airways Corporation v Iraqi Airways Company and Another* [1995] 1 W.L.R. 1147. See also *Sulaiman Al-Adsani v Government of Kuwait and Others* 100 I.L.R. p.465 and the subsequent decision of the European Court of Human Rights (ECHR) in *Al-Adsani v United Kingdom* (2001) 34 E.H.R.R. 273, concluding no violation of art.6 of the European Convention of Human Rights and Fundamental Freedoms (a right to fair trial) in which access to the English Courts had been denied by the defence of State immunity. See also *Jones v the Ministry of the Interior Al-Mamlaka Al-Arabiya as Saudiya (the Kingdom of Saudi Arabia) and Anor and Secretary of State for Constitutional Affairs* [2004] EWCA Civil 1394; and *Tachiona v United States* 386 F(3d) 205, 2004 US App. Lexus 20879 (2d Cir. October 6 2004) (Tachiona II).

[74] U.K.T.S. 74 (1979) Cmnd.7742; 66 *A.J.I.L.* 923; 11 I.L.M. 470 (1972).

Contracting States. Immunity may not be pleaded in proceedings in respect of contractual obligations to be carried out in the State exercising jurisdiction. States are also required, with certain exceptions, to give effect to judgments against them.

Today, most countries have adopted a restrictive immunity approach in respect of State trading enterprises.

At the international level, the International Law Commission has been addressing the issue of State immunity and a set of Draft Articles, following the model of the European Convention on State Immunity, was produced in 1986. These, after being referred to an ad-hoc committee, became the Draft UN Convention on Jurisdictional Immunities of States and Their Property 2004.[75] The Draft Convention, which represents an attempt to codify the international law of State immunity, expounds a general principle of immunity in art.5, subject, that is, "to the provisions of the present articles [and the relevant rules of general international law]" which is then further qualified in arts 10–17, which identify the proceedings in which State immunity cannot be invoked.

Diplomatic immunity

">. . . [T]he institution of diplomacy, with its concomitant privileges and immunities, has withstood the test of centuries and proved to be an instrument essential for effective cooperation in the international community, and for enabling States, irrespective of their differing constitutional and social systems, to achieve mutual understanding and to resolve their differences by peaceful means; . . . [w]hile no State is under any obligation to maintain diplomatic or consular relations with another, yet it cannot fail to recognise the imperative obligations inherent therein now codified in the Vienna Conventions of 1961 and 1963 . . . The rules of diplomatic law . . . constitute a self-contained regime which, on the one hand, lays down the receiving State's obligations regarding the facilities, privileges and immunities to be accorded to diplomatic missions and, on the other, foresees their possible abuse by members of the mission and specifies the means at the disposal of the receiving State to counter any such abuse."[76]

---

[75] The Convention on Jurisdictional Immunities of States and their Property to be open for signature from January 17, 2005.

[76] *Case Concerning US Diplomatic and Consular Staff in Tehran* (Provisional Measures) I.C.J.Rep. 1979 7 at 19–20 and (Judgment) I.C.J.Rep. 1980 3 at 40.

The second principal exception to territorial jurisdiction is diplomatic immunity—representatives of a foreign State are immune from the application of the host State's municipal law. Diplomatic law was the earliest expression of international relations, e.g. diplomatic immunity was enjoyed by representatives from Greek city States. Generally, the privileges and immunities accorded by customary international law have not been controversial and have been adopted and respected by States. The customary law was codified in the 1961 Vienna Convention on Diplomatic Relations (the 1961 Convention).[77]

The 1961 Convention, which came into force in 1964, deals with the immunities of foreign missions and foreign personnel in receiving host States and has been adhered to by the majority of independent States.

Diplomatic relations exist only through the mutual consent of States. Although all independent States enjoy the capacity to establish diplomatic relations, there is no right to diplomatic relations. The establishment of diplomatic relations implies unequivocally the recognition of an entity as a State by the recognising State. The cessation of diplomatic relations may be used as an expression of disapproval (an instance of a retorsion, e.g. the severance of relations between the UK and Argentina following the Falkland Islands dispute in 1982)[78] but will not negate recognition already accorded.

Diplomatic privileges and immunities have, as their *raison d'être*, a functional objective—the purpose of such privileges and immunities is not to benefit individuals, but to ensure the efficient performance of the functions of diplomatic missions as representing States.[79] The consent, *agrément*, of the host State must be obtained for the proposed head of the mission.[80] Reasons for refusal of *agrément* need not be given. The receiving State may, at any time and without providing reasons, notify the sending State that the head of the mission or any member of the diplomatic staff of the mission is *persona non grata*, or that any other member of the staff of the mission is unacceptable. The sending State is required to either recall the person concerned or terminate his functions at the mission.

Should the sending State refuse or fail to do this within a reasonable period, the receiving State may refuse to recognise the person concerned as a member of the mission.[81]

---

[77] U.K.T.S. 19 (1965) Cmnd.2565; 500 U.N.T.S. 95; 55 *A.J.I.L.* 1064 (1961).
[78] Relations were resumed in the summer of 1990.
[79] Preamble to the Vienna Convention.
[80] art.4 of the Vienna Convention.
[81] art.9.

Article 3 spells out the functions of a diplomatic mission as consisting of, *inter alia*:

> "(a) representing the sending State in the receiving State;
>
> (b) protecting in the receiving State the interests of the sending State and of its nationals within the limits permitted by international law;
>
> (c) negotiating with the government of the receiving State;
>
> (d) ascertaining by all lawful means conditions and developments in the receiving State, and reporting thereon to the government of the sending State;
>
> (e) promoting friendly relations between the sending State and the receiving State, and developing their economic, cultural and scientific relations."

Article 11 provides that, in the absence of specific agreement, the receiving State may require that the size of the mission be kept within reasonable limits.

The premises of a diplomatic mission are inviolable,[82] that is premises which are currently being used for the purposes of a mission—see *Westminster CC v Government of Iran*.[83] Agents of the receiving State may not enter there without the consent of the head of the mission and the receiving State must "take all appropriate steps to protect the premises of the mission against any intrusion or damage and to prevent any disturbance of the peace of the mission or impairment of its dignity."[84] Article 22 further provides that the premises of the mission, their furnishings and other property and the means of transport of the mission are immune from search, requisition, attachment or execution. The archives and documents of the mission are inviolable "at any time and wherever they may be."[85] The private residence of a diplomatic agent enjoys the same inviolability and protection as the premises of the mission.[86] Inviolability also embraces an agent's papers, correspondence[87] and his property.[88] The receiving State is accordingly under a duty to afford a high level of protection

---

[82] art.22(1).

[83] [1986] 1 W.L.R. 979, Ch D.

[84] art.22(2).

[85] art.24.

[86] art.30. Premises of the mission include only the private residence of the head of the mission and not the private residence of a diplomatic agent. For English authority see *Intro Properties Limited v Sauvel* [1983] Q.B. 1019, CA.

[87] Subject to the instances covered in art.31(1)(a)–(c).

[88] art.30(2).

(higher than that afforded to "ordinary" aliens) and must accord "full facilities for the performance of the functions of the mission."[89]

Respect for the inviolability of a foreign mission precluded the British police from entering the Libyan "People's Bureau" in April 1984. On April 17, 1984, a demonstration against the Gaddafi regime occurred outside the Libyan "People's Bureau" in St James's Square, London. Shots were fired from inside the Bureau and a police constable on duty outside the premises, WPC Yvonne Fletcher, was hit and died from the injuries sustained. The "People's Bureau"'s inviolability was respected by Britain[90] and continued to be respected for a limited period after the diplomats had left for Libya, even though the mission premises had been used to endanger the host State's nationals.[91] The diplomats left on April 27, but the diplomatic status of the premises did not cease until midnight on April 29, and at 6am on April 30, the British police legally entered the "People's Bureau". The sanction invoked by the UK against Libya was a severance of diplomatic relations with Libya and expulsion of the members of the mission. Inviolability is an absolute principle under the Vienna Convention and entry to mission premises is prohibited in all circumstances, save with the consent or invitation of the head of the mission.[92]

The 1979 Iranian hostages incident is an illustration of a receiving State's failure to afford due protection to a foreign embassy. On November 4, 1979, during a demonstration, several hundred armed individuals overran the US Embassy Compound in Tehran. Mission archives and documents were seized and 52 American nationals were taken as hostages. Iranian security personnel failed to counter the attack and in the subsequent case before the I.C.J., the lack of protection afforded to the mission was held to be directly attributable to the Iranian government, even though the initial seizure was "executed by militants not having an official character."[93]

---

[89] art.25. Note also the 1973 Convention on the Prevention and Punishment of Crimes Against Internationally Protected Persons, Including Diplomatic Agents, 13 I.L.M. 50 (1974).

[90] The exact legal nature/status of a People's Bureau nevertheless remains obscure.

[91] art.41(3) provides "the premises of the mission must not be used in any manner incompatible with the functions of the mission."

[92] This is not to deny that, although legally prohibited, there may be occasions where it might be argued entry might be justified because of, for example a threat to the host State or the Embassy in question is being used to store armaments, e.g. Pakistani raid on the Iraqi Embassy in 1973.

[93] Above, n. 76 p.30. Note also the seizure of the Japanese Embassy by rebels in the Peruvian capital of Lima in 1996.

The Iraqi order demanding the closure of diplomatic missions in Kuwait and the withdrawal of all privileges and immunities brought a response from the UN in the Security Council Resolutions 664 and 667. The former[94] called for an immediate rescission of the Iraqi order, while the latter[95] condemned the acts perpetrated by Iraq against diplomatic premises and personnel in Kuwait, and called for the immediate protection and well-being thereof and for the cessation of any action hindering the diplomatic and consular mission in the performance of their functions.

Inviolability does not mean extra-territorial jurisdiction. The premises are not an extension of the sending State's territory. Acts committed on mission premises are within the territorial jurisdiction of the receiving State. Only in exceptional cases, possibly for humanitarian reasons of a severe nature, will a State grant asylum to an individual within an embassy. To do otherwise would be regarded as a grave violation of another State's sovereignty.

Diplomatic staff enjoy free movement and travel within the territory of the host State, subject to laws regulating entry into certain areas for reasons of national security. The receiving State must also allow and protect free communication by the mission for all official purposes and the diplomatic bag, which must be clearly marked as such, must be neither opened nor detained.[96] The absence of "visible external marks" from the crate used in the attempted abduction from the UK of Mr Dikko, an ex-government minister of Nigeria, legitimised the opening by UK customs officials of the container in question and kept their actions within the bounds of the Convention.[97] The right of challenge in respect of the diplomatic bag was accepted practice before 1961. In the event of a bag being challenged the sending State could either agree to the bag being opened and inspected or being returned unopened to its original source. The right of challenge is not included in the Convention. The degree of scrutiny to which the diplomatic bag may be subject has remained controversial and is a sensitive issue, as the bag may be used to import illegally, *inter alia*, drugs and/or weapons. In an attempt to address the issue the International Law Commission has been considering the status of the diplomatic bag and in 1989 adopted Draft Articles on the Status of the Diplomatic Courier and the Diplomatic Bag Not Accompanied by the Diplomatic Courier. The 1989 Draft Articles

---

[94] Adopted August 18, 1990 by a vote of 15–0; 29 I.L.M. 1323 (1990).
[95] Adopted September 16, 1990 by a vote of 16–0, *ibid.*
[96] art.27(3).
[97] Mr. Dikko, a member of the overthrown Nigerian government, was kidnapped in London and drugged in the attempt to procure his return to Nigeria where he was wanted on criminal charges.

are designed to establish a comprehensive and essentially uniform regime applicable to all kinds of couriers and bags employed for official communications involved primarily in diplomatic and consular relations. The central provision is Draft Article 28 which enunciates the basic principle of inviolability. However, the competent authorities of the receiving State or the transit State may, if they have serious reason to believe the consular bag contains something other than correspondence, documents or articles intended exclusively for official use, request the opening of the bag in their presence by an authorised representative of the sending State. If this request is refused, the bag is to be returned to its place of origin.[98] The International Law Commission has proposed to the General Assembly that an international conference be convened with a view to the Draft Articles forming the basis of an international convention on the subject.

The person of a diplomatic agent is inviolable and is not liable to any form of arrest or detention; the receiving State must treat such a person with due respect and must take all appropriate steps to prevent any attack on his person, freedom or dignity.[99] A "diplomatic agent" is, for the purposes of the Convention, the head of the mission or a member of the diplomatic staff of the mission.[100]

A diplomatic agent enjoys absolute immunity from the criminal jurisdiction of the receiving State. Nevertheless, in 1987, the US took the first steps towards an indictment of an Ambassador prior to the termination of official accreditation. Following an accident involving two US nationals, one of whom was seriously injured, Ambassador Abisinito, Papua New Guinea's Extraordinary and Plenipotentiary to the US was charged by the District of Columbia police with "failing to pay full time and attention to driving". Ambassador Abisinito was recalled by his State on February 17, 1987 and his accreditation to the US ceased as of February 24. However, it was not until January 1988 that the US Attorney's Office informed Mr. Abisinito's criminal lawyers that prosecution was not "currently being contemplated".[101]

The diplomatic agent is also immune from the receiving State's civil and administrative jurisdiction, except in the case of:

---

[98] Draft art.28(2). N.B.: "consular" bag and not "diplomatic" bag.
[99] art.29.
[100] art.1(e).
[101] *Washington Post*, February 14–15, 1987; *Columbia Journal of Law*, 1988; *Legal Times*, May 4, 1987; *Diplomatic Note of the Embassy of Papua New Guinea*, February 24, 1987. cf. *Former Syrian Ambassador to the GDR* 121 I.L.R. 595.

> "(a) a real action relating to private immovable property sit-
>   uated in the territory of the receiving State, unless he
>   holds it on behalf of the sending State for the purposes
>   of the mission;
>
> (b)   an action relating to succession in which the diplomatic
>   agent is involved as executor, administrator, heir or
>   legatee as a private person and not on behalf of the
>   sending State;
>
> (c)   an action relating to any professional or commercial
>   activity exercised by the diplomatic agent in the
>   receiving State outside his official functions."[102]

In such instances, immunity from jurisdiction is not available. A
diplomatic agent is not obliged to give evidence as a witness.[103]
The immunity enjoyed by a diplomatic agent is extended to the
members of his family (normally spouse and children under the
age of 18) if they are not nationals of the host State.[104] The immunity of a national of the receiving State is limited to official acts
performed in the exercise of his functions.[105] Immunity is from
jurisdiction and not from liability. The sending State may waive
the right to immunity,[106] as did Thailand in the summer of 1991,
when one of its London embassy staff was apprehended by customs officials at Heathrow Airport for allegedly possessing and
attempting illegally to import heroin. In 1997, a diplomat from the
Republic of Georgia was held responsible for the death of a 16-
year-old American girl in a car accident. The President of Georgia
waived the immunity of the diplomat and stated in the American
press, "the moral principle of just punishment outweighs the
antiquated Cold War-era practice of diplomatic immunity".[107]
Waiver must be express.[108] If a diplomatic agent or other person
enjoying immunity initiates proceedings, they are then precluded
from claiming immunity from jurisdiction in respect of any
counter claim which is connected with the principal claim.[109]

---

[102] art.31(1).

[103] art.31(2).

[104] art.37. Other persons may be treated as a diplomat's family in certain
instances. It is British practice to treat certain persons, e.g. a person who fulfils
the social duties of hostess to the diplomatic agent—sister or adult daughter of
either an unmarried or widowed diplomat-as a member of the diplomat's
family.

[105] art.38.

[106] art.32(1). Waiver however is unusual.

[107] See, ASIL Newsletter, January–February 1997, Letters, p.4.

[108] art.32(2).

[109] art.32(3).

Waiver of immunity from jurisdiction in respect of civil or administrative proceedings does not imply waiver of immunity with regard to the execution of the judgment. A separate waiver is necessary.[110] A host State always reserves the right to declare a member of the diplomatic mission a *persona non grata*.[111]

Not all the staff of a foreign mission enjoy the same immunities. The Vienna Convention distinguishes between diplomatic agents, administrative and technical staff (e.g. archivists, clerical and secretarial staff) and service staff (e.g. kitchen staff). The administrative and technical staff, if non-nationals of the host State, enjoy complete immunity from criminal jurisdiction, but their immunity from civil and administrative jurisdiction extends only to acts performed in the fulfilment of their duties.[112] Non-national service staff likewise enjoy immunity only in respect of their official acts.[113] Distinguishing between mission staff and their respective immunities was an innovation in the 1961 Convention and represents a modification of the absolute immunity previously enjoyed under, e.g. English law—see *Empson v Smith*.[114]

A diplomat who is either recalled or who is declared by the sending State a *persona non grata* is allowed a period of grace during which his/her immunity continues. Thereafter, if the diplomat has not left the country the individual may be sued for private acts committed during his/her term of office. Immunity continues to subsist in respect of official acts.[115]

In addition to immunity from jurisdiction, diplomatic agents are, with certain exceptions such as purchase tax, exempt from taxes levied in the host State.[116] Mission premises are similarly exempt from local taxes except for those levied in respect of specific services rendered.[117] The right of immunity carries with it an obligation: it is the duty of all persons enjoying such privileges and immunities to respect the laws and the regulations of the receiving State. Such persons are also required not to interfere in the internal affairs of the receiving State,[118] e.g. in the political affairs of the host State.

---

[110] art.32(4).
[111] For example, in 1988 the Cuban Ambassador and his commercial attaché were expelled from the UK following a shooting incident in London. The UK government's decision to hold the Ambassador personally liable for the actions of one of his staff was unprecedented and earned the UK a reputation for taking tough action on abuses of diplomatic immunity.
[112] art.37(2).
[113] art.37(3).
[114] [1966] 1 Q.B. 426, CA.
[115] art.39(2).
[116] art.34.
[117] art.23.
[118] art.41.

The 1961 Convention was made part of UK law by the Diplomatic Privileges Act 1964 and part of US municipal law by the Diplomatic Relations Act 1978. The American legislation applies the 1961 Convention's provisions to all States and not just to those who have become parties to the 1961 Convention. The 1961 Convention does not preclude States either through practice or agreement, extending to each other more favourable treatment than that afforded by the 1961 Convention's provisions, art.47(b).

Heads of State

A number of questions were addressed in the case involving General Pinochet.[119] These can be identified as being:

(a)   Is the claim for immunity made by a serving or a former head of State?

(b)   Is the claim made in respect of the official government act or a private act?

(c)   Is the making of the claim consistent with international law?

The various facets of the *Pinochet* case illustrate an increasing tension between preserving the traditional absolute immunity approach and an evolving human rights culture. One of the issues in respect of General Pinochet was the extent to which a former head of State could enjoy immunity. It was held that a former head of State could only be immune for acts which fell within his functions as a head of State, although it remains unresolved as to which acts may be categorised as official and those which may be deemed personal. It was also held that an individual could not claim immunity, nor could a State, in respect of acts which are prohibited by international Convention and to which the State concerned is a Contracting Party of the said Convention. Accordingly, Chile could not claim immunity of liability after having signed and ratified the 1984 Convention on Torture.[120] General Pinochet, following his return to Chile, was initially

---

[119]   *R. v Bow Street Metropolitan Stipendiary Magistrate Ex p. Pinochet Ugarte (No.2)* [2001] 1 A.C. 119, *R. v Bow Street Stipendiary Magistrate Ex p. Pinochet Ugarte (No.3)* [2000] 1 A.C. 147; [1999] 2 W.L.R. 272, *R. v Bartle and the Commissioner of Police for the Metropolis Ex p. Pinochet*, March 24, 1999, [1991] 2 All E.R. 97, *R. v Evans and the Commissioner of the Police for the Metropolis Ex p. Pinochet*, March 24, 1999, House of Lords.

[120]   The Convention Against Torture and Other Cruel, Inhuman or Degrading Treatment or Punishment 1987, above n.41. Chile ratified the Convention on September 30, 1988.

found to be physically and mentally unfit to stand trial, however in May 2004 the Chilean Appeals Court ruled General Pinochet was medically fit to stand trial on new charges brought against him. This was initiated following an appearance by the General on Miami television. The legacy of the Pinochet jurisprudence has been to some extent to muddy the waters, at least as to the issue of immunity of heads of State particularly when acts of torture are alleged. The issue was raised in the *Al-Adsani* case, in which a more cautious position was adopted and the Kuwaiti government claim of State immunity was upheld, in civil proceedings initiated in the English Court for damages in respect of physical injuries and mental suffering, constituting torture, sustained in Kuwait. In the *Arrest Warrant* case the I.C.J. upheld the DRC immunity claim and recognised that the accused, a senior minister, had diplomatic immunity as a Minister for Foreign Affairs.[121]

In the US the Alien Tort Claims Act 1789 (ATCA)[122] has been utilised to seek redress for human rights violations. The Act provides the District Courts with jurisdiction in any civil action raised "by an alien for a tort only, committed in violation of the law of nations or a treaty of the United States." The Act was virtually unused until being employed as the basis of jurisdiction in the *Filartiga* case.[123] The Act was reinforced by the US 1991 Torture Victim Prevention Act, which extends to "any individual". The Act has been used in a number of cases and the extent of its use has become an issue, polarising human rights groups and corporate business organisations. Particularly significant have been the lawsuits instituted under ATCA against corporations for alleged violations of human rights committed abroad. One such landmark was the case initiated against Unocal corporation,[124]

---

[121] See above, n.35. Also there is criminal jurisdiction over individuals in respect of torture committed in the UK or elsewhere by way of the Criminal Justice Act 1988 s.134. Note also the case Against the Afghan Warlord. See also the decision of the Spanish Court convicting Adolfo Scilingo (Argentina) for crimes against humanity whilst serving as a member of the Military Junta. The decision is noteworthy, as it is the first successful prosecution for the Spanish Court in what it claims is its right under international law to try in Spain anyone accused of atrocities committed abroad, Time Magazine, May 2, 2005, p.18. See also decision of 11th US Circuit Court of Appeals 15 March 2005 upholding a US jury's decision, 2003, that Armando Fernandez Larios was guilty of crimes against humanity in Chile while serving as General Pinochet's bodyguard.

[122] 28 U.S.C. 1350 (1988).

[123] *Filartiga v Pena-Irala* 630 F (2d) 876; (1980) 19 I.L.M. 966. US Circuit of Appeals 2nd Circuit.

[124] The company made an undisclosed monetary settlement in 2005. There are a number of cases pending against ExxonMobile, Coca-Cola and Fresh DelMonte Produce Inc., however the outcome of any is undecided and the issues raised remain controversial.

alleging the company knew or should have known that the
Myanmar army committed human rights abuses while providing
security for the $1.2 billion pipeline project in Myanmar (Burma).

Consular relations

Consuls represent their State in another State, with the consent of
the latter. Consuls are concerned not with political affairs, but
rather with administrative issues, e.g. the issue of visas. They also
give various forms of assistance to nationals of the sending State
when they are in the territory of the receiving State. Consuls have
the right to access and communication of nationals who have
been detained in another country.[125] Failure to do so has resulted
in action being initiated before the I.C.J.[126] Consuls are posted in
provincial towns as well as in capital cities.

Consular relations, unlike diplomatic relations between States,
were largely governed by bipartite agreements. The Vienna
Convention on Consular Relations (the 1963 Convention)[127] was
adopted in 1963 to regulate, on a universal basis, the position and
functions of consuls. The 1963 Convention entered into force in
1967. If two States have a bipartite agreement and both are parties
to the 1963 Convention, the provisions which extend the greater
immunities prevail. Consular immunities, unlike diplomatic
immunities, may not be assumed, but must be shown to derive
from either the 1963 Convention, or from a bipartite agreement.
The immunities and privileges enjoyed by consuls and consular
premises resemble those accorded to diplomatic agents and
diplomatic missions; however, they are more limited in their
scope.

The principal difference is that, in the absence of special agreement, consuls are immune from arrest, detention and the criminal
process only in respect of acts and omissions in the performance
of their official functions. A consular officer must appear if summoned before the Courts and later plead and prove immunity by
virtue of the act or omission in question being in the performance
of his official functions. Some States have, by special agreement
and on a reciprocal basis, extended full immunity from criminal
jurisdiction to consular personnel, e.g. the American–Soviet

---

[125] The Vienna Convention on Consular Relations (1963), art.36.
[126] Germany and Paraguay both brought cases against the US. See *Paraguay v US*
(1998) I.C.J. 248 and *Germany v US (La Grand case)* 40 I.L.M. 1069 (2001) where
a judgment was passed on June 27, 2001. The I.C.J. in 2001 held that the US was
in breach of its obligations under art.36(1) of the Convention in that the US had
not informed the La Grand brothers of their rights under art.36(1) "without
delay". See also *Avena (Mexico v United States)* Decision of the I.C.J. General
List No.128 March 31, 2004.
[127] 596 U.N.T.S. 261; U.K.T.S. 14 (1973) Cmnd.5219.

Union Convention. A consular officer may only be arrested or detained in respect of a grave crime and pursuant to a decision by a competent judicial authority.[128] Proceedings against a consular officer should be conducted "with the respect due to him by reason of his official position" and save when charged with a grave crime, "in a manner which will hamper the exercise of consular functions as little as possible".[129] Members of a consul's family do not enjoy the same extensive jurisdictional immunities as the members of a diplomat's family, but they are exempt from such restrictions as immigration controls, customs duties and taxes, if they are not nationals of the receiving State.

Special missions

Special *ad hoc* missions sent by a State to fulfil a specific purpose in another State are a recent innovation. There are no rules of customary international law on the subject. A Convention Guaranteeing Immunities to Special Missions was drawn up in 1969 (the 1969 Convention).[130] The 1969 Convention, which entered into force on June 21, 1985, is based essentially on the 1961 Vienna Convention on Diplomatic Relations. Under art.8 of the 1969 Convention, the sending State must inform the host State of both the size and composition of the mission, while art.17 provides that the location of the mission must be mutually agreed by the States concerned, or must be in the Foreign Ministry of the receiving State.

International organisations

International organisations enjoy those privileges and immunities from the jurisdiction of a Member State as are necessary for the fulfilment of the organisation's purposes. Such immunities include immunity from legal process, financial controls, taxes and duties. The immunities and privileges to be enjoyed by the organisation and its personnel *vis-à-vis* Member States are provided for in the constituent charter of the organisation and supplementary agreements adhered to by members of the organisation, e.g. the General Convention on the Privileges and Immunities of the United Nations 1946.[131] The General Convention gives immunity from the legal process to, *inter alia*, the property and the assets of the UN, unless such immunity is waived, as well as immunity from criminal jurisdiction for its representatives.

---

[128] art.41(1).
[129] art.41(3).
[130] 9 I.L.M. 127 (1970).
[131] 1 U.N.T.S. 15; U.K.T.S. 10 (1950) Cmd.7891; 43 A.J.I.L. Supp.

7. THE LAW OF THE SEA

The law of the sea[1] is that law by which States, coastal, land-locked, and/or international organisations regulate their relations in respect of those areas subject to coastal State jurisdiction and in relation to those areas of the sea and the seabed beyond national jurisdiction. The rules governing the sea are drawn from both custom and treaty.

In the 1950s, the profusion of claims, the advance of technology and the need for a protection of conventional sea uses were responsible for the Geneva Conventions on the Law of the Sea. The Conventions were the outcome of the initial work undertaken by the International Law Commission. The four Conventions adopted by the 1958 Conference were the Convention on the Territorial Sea and Contiguous Zone,[2] the Convention on the High Seas,[3] the Convention on the Continental Shelf[4] and the Convention on Fishing and Conservation of Living Resources

---

[1] As distinct from Admiralty law or maritime law, which is essentially concerned principally with relations between private persons involved in the transport of passengers or goods.
[2] U.K.T.S. 3 (1965) Cmnd.2511; 516 U.N.T.S. 205; 52 A.J.I.L. 834 (1958).
[3] U.K.T.S. 5 (1963) Cmnd.1029; 45 U.N.T.S. 82; 52 A.J.I.L. 842 (1958).
[4] U.K.T.S. 39 (1964) Cmnd.2422; 499 U.N.T.S. 311; 52 A.J.I.L. 858 (1958).

of the High Seas.[5] The Conventions all entered into force, though by 1982, three-quarters of the States of the world were not a party to them. The Conventions, which codified certain existing State practices and also articulated rules of progressive development, proved inadequate, particularly with regard to the continental shelf and the ocean bed which, with advancing technology, came within the potential acquisition of certain States.

The need to preserve the seas as the common heritage of all mankind and the danger of a "scramble for the seas" precipitated the calling of the Third United Nations Conference on the Law of the Sea. The 1982 Convention on the Law of the Sea,[6] adopted on April 30, 1982, was the culmination of protracted negotiations over nine years. The Convention was opened for signature in December 1982 and was designed as a "complete package" with limited provision for reservation.[7] The Convention was the subject of considerable opposition, primarily from western nations who were concerned about the provisions regarding the exploitation of the deep seabed as contained in Part XI.[8] Attempts to resolve disagreement over Part XI were unsuccessful until 1994, when the General Assembly adopted a Resolution and Agreement Relating to the Implementation of Part XI of the UN Convention on the Law of the Sea.[9] The adoption of this Agreement was seen as the key to the implementation of the 1982 Convention and this is reflected in the preamble of the Resolution, which notes "the desire to achieve universal participation" in the Convention. Article 1 of the Agreement prescribes the fundamental obligation on States, namely that Part XI of the 1982 Convention should be implemented in accordance with the Agreement of which the Annex forms an integral part.[10] Articles 1 and 2 constitute the substantive provisions of the Agreement and the remaining eight deal, *inter alia*, with signature and ratification. The Agreement modifies the terms of Part XI in relation to the deep sea.[11] A State cannot become a party to the Agreement independently of the Convention.

5   U.K.T.S. 39 (1966) Cmnd.3208; 599 U.N.T.S. 285; 52 A.J.I.L. 851 (1958).
6   Misc.II (1983) Cmnd.8941; 21 I.L.M. 1261 (1982).
7   See art.309 of the 1982 Convention. For reservations and their effect, see Ch.10.
8   The US and the UK were particularly opposed to Part XI of the Convention. For the UK's objections as expressed in HC, see *Hansard*, Vol.69, col.642 (December 6, 1984).
9   On July 28, 1994. GA Res. 48/263, 121–0 in favour, seven abstentions, 35 I.L.M. 1309 (1994). The Agreement entered into force on July 28, 1996.
10 The Annex sets out the substance of the Agreement.
11 The Agreement has also phased out the Preparatory Commission. The Commission's role, *inter alia*, was to oversee the entry into force of the Convention. The Commission adopted its concluding report in August 1994 at its final meeting.

The Agreement sought to address the concerns of western nations regarding Part XI and reflects the significant changes in the economic and political climate since 1982. Specifically, it reallocates international and national responsibilities for the management of deep-sea mining.[12] The 1982 Convention came into force on November 16, 1994, and marked an important event in the progressive development and codification of the international law of the sea.[13] The Convention's entry into force confirmed the General Assembly's competence as the global forum for review of all developments relating to the law of the sea.[14]

Some of the provisions of the 1982 Convention simply restate provisions of the Geneva Convention—representing established customary international law. Others, notably those on the exclusive economic zone, mirror what is now customary international law-reflecting State practice before the 1982 Convention was finalised. Other provisions represent a departure from established law and indicate the way in which the law was developing. Any review of the laws of the sea must begin with the Geneva Conventions of 1958.

TERRITORIAL SEA

A coastal State enjoys sovereignty over "a belt of sea adjacent to its coast, described as the territorial sea"[15] which extends "to the air space over the territorial sea as well as its bed and subsoil".[16] The consequence of being a coastal State is that it possesses a territorial sea:

"To every State whose land territory is at any place washed by the sea, international law attaches a corresponding

---

[12] Certain provisions, which were the source of controversy, such as production limitation and technological transfer, are eliminated.

[13] For a detailed discussion of the 1994 Agreement, see, generally, J. Charney, "Law of the Sea Forum: The 1994 Agreement on Implementation of the Seabed Provisions of the Convention on the Law of the Sea" and D. Anderson, "Legal Implications of the Entry into Force of the UN Convention on the Law of the Sea" 44 I.C.L.Q. 313 (1995).

[14] There are currently 145 State Parties to the Law of the Sea Convention. Part XI has 117 ratifications (including the EC). The UK ratified Part XI on July 26, 1997. The US has yet to ratify it. The Agreement for the implementation of the provisions of the Convention Relating to the Conservation and Management of Straddling Fish Stocks and Highly Migratory Fish Stocks has 52 ratifications. That Agreement came into force on December 11, 2001.

[15] art.1 of the Geneva Convention on the Territorial Sea and the Contiguous Zone 1958; art.1 of the 1982 Convention on the Territorial Sea and the Contiguous Zone.

[16] art.2 of the 1958 Convention; art.2 of the 1982 Convention.

portion of maritime territory consisting of what the law calls territorial waters . . . International law does not say to a State: 'You are entitled to claim territorial waters if you want them.' No maritime States can refuse them. International law imposes upon a maritime State certain obligations and confers upon it certain rights arising out of the sovereignty, which it exercises over its maritime territory. The possession of this territory is not optional, not dependent upon the will of the State, but compulsory."[17]

Article 3 of the 1982 Convention establishes the breadth of the territorial sea at a limit "not exceeding 12 nautical miles".

Previously, agreement on the breadth of the territorial sea had eluded definition. State practice had been uncertain and varied. Some countries, for example the United Kingdom and the United States, rigidly maintained the traditional three-mile territorial sea, while certain Latin American countries made extensive claims to a maximum of 200 miles. The norm, however, was for States to claim a territorial sea of a width somewhere between three and 12 miles. The uncertainty of State practice was reflected in the 1958 and 1960 Geneva Conferences—neither Conference was successful in defining the breadth of the territorial sea. Various permutations were suggested, such as the United States formula of six-plus-six, (that is, a six-mile territorial sea with a six-mile fishing zone), an Asian/Latin American sponsored proposal calling for a 12-mile territorial sea and a Soviet proposal whereby every State would enjoy the discretion to declare the width of its territorial sea as a distance between three and 12 miles. None of the proposals were adopted. The 12-mile maximum, which has been widely reflected in State practice, including the United Kingdom and the United States,[18] is now accepted as customary international law—see the *Guinea/Guinea-Bissau Maritime Delimitation* case.[19] The advent and acceptance of a coastal State's exclusive economic zone (EEZ—see below) has enabled the territorial sea question to be settled independently.

In the 1950s and 1960s, increased fishing activity and advancing technology witnessed anxiety among coastal States in respect of fisheries. There was a need to control fishing, however at that time fisheries jurisdiction was very much an integral aspect of territorial jurisdiction. The failure of the 1958 and 1960 Conferences to reach agreement regarding the territorial sea and fishing zones

---

[17] McNair J. (dissenting opinion), *Anglo–Norwegian Fisheries* case I.C.J. Rep. (1951) 116 at 160.

[18] Territorial Sea Act 1987 (Commencement) Order 1987 (SI 1987/1270).

[19] 77 I.L.R. 636 at 638; 25 I.L.M. 251 (1988) at 272, para.43.

prompted States to take matters into their own hands and unilaterally extend their fisheries jurisdiction beyond the territorial sea.

Measurement of the territorial sea

As a general rule, the baseline employed to determine the breadth of the territorial sea is the low-tide water line, as marked on large-scale charts recognised by the coastal State.[20] The outer limit of the territorial sea is the line, every point of which is at a distance from the nearest point of the baseline equal to the breadth of the territorial sea.[21] Geography can present problems, and rules to resolve these problems have evolved.

In respect of deeply indented coastlines the 1958 and 1982 Conventions reflect the International Court of Justice's judgment in the *Anglo-Norwegian Fisheries* case.[22] This case came before the Court because Britain challenged the method employed by Norway to measure its territorial sea. Rather than use the low-water mark method, Norway used the baseline system. As a result, waters which would otherwise have been high seas were characterised as territorial sea. The Court affirmed the legality of the straight baseline method and thus acknowleged in delimiting Norway's territorial sea, cognisance had to be given to "geographical realities" and the drawing of the base-lines had to be adapted to the special conditions pertaining in different regions.[23]

Both the 1958 and 1982 Conventions acknowledge the derogation from the low-water mark allowed by the Court. Straight baselines joining appropriate points may be employed where a coastline is deeply indented,[24] provided that the lines do:

> "not depart to any appreciable extent from the general direction of the coast, and the seas lying within the lines must be sufficiently closely linked to the land domain to be subject to the regime of internal waters."[25]

They may not normally be drawn "to and from low-tide elevations" unless "lighthouses or similar installations which are permanently above sea level have been built on them"[26] or "where the drawing of baselines to and from such elevations has received

---

[20] art.3 of the 1958 Convention; art.5 of the 1982 Convention.
[21] art.6 of the 1958 Convention; art.4 of the 1982 Convention.
[22] Above, n.17.
[23] *ibid.* at 128.
[24] art.4(1) of the 1958 Convention; art.7(1) of the 1982 Convention.
[25] art.4(2) of the 1958 Convention; art.7(3) of the 1982 Convention.
[26] art.4(3) of the 1958 Convention.

general international recognition".[27] The International Court of
Justice has emphasised the use of State baselines "which is an
exception to the normal rules for the determination of baselines,
may only be applied if a number of conditions are met."[28]
However any such exception must be applied restrictively.

Both the 1958 and 1982 Conventions allow account to be taken
of a further possible consideration which may be employed in the
delimitation of the territorial sea.[29] This was acknowledged by the
International Court when it stated:

> "... one consideration not to be overlooked, the scope of
> which extends beyond purely geographical factors: that of
> certain economic interests peculiar to a region, the reality
> and importance of which are closely evidenced by a long
> usage."[30]

The Court recognised that the special economic interests of a
region could be taken into consideration. However, such a consideration is only supplementary (that is, special economic interests in themselves cannot be grounds justifying the application of
straight baselines) and is at all times optional rather than mandatory. Likewise, under the 1958 and 1982 Conventions, special economic interests may be invoked to support an application of the
straight baseline system, but only if their reality and importance
are clearly evidenced by long usage.[31]

States are prohibited from applying straight baselines in order
to cut off, from high seas or an EEZ, the territorial sea of another
State, and a State using the straight baseline system must publicise by way of charts the lines being employed. The 1982
Convention requires the coastal State to deposit copies of charts
and lists of geographical co-ordinates with the Secretary-General
of the United Nations.[32]

The 1982 Convention alone provides:

> "Where because of the presence of a delta and other natural
> conditions the coastline is highly unstable, the appropriate

---

[27] Added by art.7(4) of the 1982 Convention. See *also Nicaragua v Honduras* I.C.J.
Rep. (2007), p.1, at para.141, where the Court noted that "features which are not
permanently above water, and which lie outside of a State's territorial waters,
should be distinguished from islands."

[28] *Qatar v Bahrain* I.C.J. Rep.(2001), p.40, at 103.

[29] art.4(4) and art.7(5), respectively.

[30] *Anglo–Norwegian Fisheries* case, above, n.17 at 133.

[31] Both Conventions are silent on what constitutes real and important.

[32] art.4(5) and (6) of the 1958 Convention; art.7(6) and art.16 of the 1982
Convention.

points may be selected along the furthest seaward extent of
the low-water line and, notwithstanding subsequent regres-
sion of the low-water line, the straight baselines shall remain
effective until changed by the coastal State in accordance
with this Convention."[33]

Bays

A bay is defined under art.7(2) of the 1958 Convention as a:

"well-marked indentation whose penetration is in such proportion to the width of its mouth as to contain landlocked
waters and constitute more than a mere curvature of the
coast. An indentation shall not, however, be regarded as a
bay unless its area is as large as, or larger than, that of the
semi-circle whose diameter is a line drawn across the mouth
of that indentation."

Article 10(2) of the 1982 Convention reiterates this definition.

A special formula has been evolved in respect of bays which
belong to a single State and are more than mere curvatures of the
coast. The salient feature of the formula is that straight baselines
may be employed "If the distance between the low-water marks
of the natural entrance points of a bay does not exceed 24
miles . . ."[34] In the event of 24 miles being exceeded, a straight
baseline of 24 miles may be drawn within the bay in such a manner as to enclose the maximum area of water that is possible with
a line of that length.[35]

Neither Convention refers specifically to historic bays, namely
bays, the waters of which have been treated as internal waters by
the coastal State with the acceptance of other States, such as
Hudson Bay and the Gulf of Fonseca,[36] nor to bays bordered by
more than one State. The legal regime which will be applied in
both instances is dependent upon the response of affected States
but the position *vis-à-vis* the latter is one over which "there exists
a good deal of controversy . . ." The Gulf of Fonseca was dis-

---

[33] art.7(2).

[34] art.7(4) of the 1958 Convention; art.10(4) of the 1982 Convention.

[35] art.7(5) of the 1958 Convention; art.10(5) of the 1982 Convention.

[36] Previous to the 1958 Convention, it had been generally accepted under customary international law that straight baselines could be employed in respect of
bays, but there was uncertainty as to beyond what width the closing line could
not be employed. The I.C.J. in the *Anglo–Norwegian Fisheries* case, above, n.17,
rejected, because of inconsistent State practice, the ten-mile rule (which the UK
was claiming as the maximum width) and refuted that such a rule had ever
acquired the character of international law.

cussed by the International Court in the *Land, Island and Maritime Frontier Dispute (El Salvador/Honduras; Nicaragua intervening)*,[37] therein the Court, on the basis of particular historical circumstances and the consent of the relevant States, affirmed the Gulf beyond a three mile maritime belt for the coastal States was historical waters subject to the co-ownership or a condiminium of the three coastal States.[38]

Outermost permanent harbour works (which under the 1982 Convention do not include "offshore installations and artificial islands") forming an integral part of the harbour system are to be regarded as part of the coast for the purpose of delimiting the territorial sea.[39]

Islands

An island is defined in art.10 of the 1958 Convention "as a naturally-formed area of land, surrounded by water, which is above water at high tide". The territorial sea of an island is decided in the same way as the territorial sea of mainland territories. The 1982 Convention retains the same definition of an island, but introduces a "regime of islands".[40] This provides that "the territorial sea, the contiguous zone, the exclusive economic zone and the continental shelf of an island are to be determined in accordance with the provisions . . . applicable to other land territory". Rocks which cannot sustain human habitation or economic life of their own are denied both an EEZ and a continental shelf, though they may continue to have a territorial sea.[41] Low-tide elevations, on the other hand, do not have a territorial sea of their own, though the low-water mark on such an elevation, if it is within the territorial sea of a coastal State, may be utilised as a baseline,[42] and art.6 of the 1982 Convention provides:

---

[37] I.C.J. Rep.(1992), p.351.
[38] *Ibid.* p.601. See in contrast the response to Libya's claim that the Gulf of Sirte (Sidra) was a historical bay in 1973, Churchill, R. & Lowe, V., *Law of the Sea*, 3rd Edn, 1999, p.45.
[39] art.8 of the 1958 Convention; art.11 of the 1982 Convention.
[40] Pt VIII, art.121.
[41] art.121(3). This provision would deny an EEZ and continental shelf, e.g. to the area referred to as the Island of Rockall. In the *Jan Meyen Case (Denmark v Norway)* I.C.J. Rep. (1993) 38, Denmark asserted that the island in dispute could not sustain economic or human life but appeared to implicitly accept that it could have a continental shelf or fishery zone. The UK had, under the Fishery Limits Act 1976, proclaimed a 200-nautical-mile fishing zone around the Island of Rockall. However, the UK Government withdrew this claim in 1997 on accession to the Law of the Sea Convention.
[42] art.11 of the 1958 Convention; art.13 of the 1982 Convention.

"in the case of islands situated on atolls or islands having fringing reefs, the baseline for measuring the breadth of the territorial sea is the seaward low-water line of the reef, as shown by the appropriate symbol on charts officially recognised by the coastal State."

In the Court of Arbitration decision on maritime delimitation (*St Pierre and Miquelon*), the Court considered in some detail the role of islands in delimitation and declined to adjust the extent of the maritime rights of the islands by reference to either their political status or special geographical circumstances.[43]

Delimitation of territorial seas between opposite or adjacent States

The territorial sea between opposite or adjacent States is determined in one of three ways: by agreement between the States, e.g. the Anglo–French agreement relating to the Delimitation of the Territorial Sea in the Straits of Dover;[44] by the median line, every point of which is equidistant from the nearest points on the baselines from which the breadth of the territorial seas of each of the two States is measured;[45] or by another line required by historic title or other special circumstances.[46] The 1982 Convention envisages that a coastal State "may determine baselines . . . by any of the methods provided for . . . to suit different conditions".[47]

Archipelagic States

States such as Indonesia and the Philippines, which are made up of a number of islands, have, in the absence of international agreement, drawn straight baselines round the outer limits of their islands. The effect has been to turn what were formerly "high seas" into territorial waters.

International law traditionally sidestepped the problems raised by archipelagic States, and the Geneva Convention makes no pro-

---

[43] See Court of Arbitration for the *Delimitation of Maritime Areas between Canada and France: Decision in case Concerning Delimitation of Maritime Areas (St Pierre and Miquelon)*, in particular the dissenting opinion of Mr Prosper Weil interpreting the Court's decision 31 I.L.M. 1145 (1992) at 1216–1218. The issue of islands and delimitation was also considered in *Jan Meyen*, above, n.41, in which it was also held that art.121 mirrored "the present status of international law."

[44] Cmnd.557.

[45] *ibid.* Guinea and Guinea-Bissau submitted their dispute on the *Delimitation of the Maritime Boundary* to an Arbitration Tribunal, 25 I.L.M. 251 (1986).

[46] art.12 of the 1958 Convention; art.15 of the 1982 Convention.

[47] art.14 of the 1982 Convention.

vision for special treatment of mid-ocean archipelagos. The 1982 Convention, however, does deal separately with such States.[48] An archipelagic State is, for the purposes of the Convention, constituted wholly of one or more archipelagos and may include other islands ("archipelago" means a group of islands) including parts of islands, interconnecting waters and other natural features which are so closely interrelated that such islands, water and other natural features form an intrinsic geographical, economic and political entity, or which historically have been regarded as such.[49] The 1982 Convention recognises archipelago baselines joining the outermost points of the outermost islands. Such baselines may "not exceed 100 nautical miles, except that up to three per cent of the total number of baselines enclosing any archipelago may exceed that length, up to a maximum length of 125 nautical miles" and must "not depart to any appreciable extent from the general configuration of the archipelago".[50] The territorial sea, the contiguous zone, the EEZ and the continental shelf are drawn from the archipelagic baselines.[51] Archipelagic waters enclosed by the archipelago baselines fall within the territorial sovereignty of the archipelagic State,[52] subject to the right of all States to enjoy the right of innocent passage[53] similar to that enjoyed in territorial waters (see below). An archipelago State may designate archipelagic sea-lanes for passage and prescribe traffic separation schemes[54] comparable to the right of passage through straits.

The 1982 Convention does not address the issue of straight baselines by continental States with archipelagos. Nevertheless, Canada established baselines round the entire Arctic Archipelago from latitude 60°E to the Beaufort Sea in the west and designated all waters enclosed as Canadian.

Innocent passage

The definition of "passage" contained in art.18 of the 1982 Geneva Convention elaborates upon the accepted customary international law definition and that contained in art.14 of the Geneva Convention. Article 18 provides:[55]

---

[48] Pt IV, arts 46–54.
[49] art.46.
[50] art.47.
[51] art.48.
[52] art.49.
[53] art.52.
[54] art.53.
[55] *Nicaragua (Merits)* case I.C.J. Rep.(1986) p.14 at p.111.

"1. Passage means navigation through the territorial sea for
     the purpose of:

    (a) traversing that sea without entering internal
         waters or calling at a roadstead or port facility out-
         side internal waters; or
    (b) proceeding to or from internal waters or a call at
         such roadstead or port facility.

2.   Passage shall be continuous and expeditious. However,
     passage includes stopping and anchoring, but only in so
     far as the same are incidental to ordinary navigation or
     are rendered necessary by force majeure or distress or
     for the purpose of rendering assistance to persons, ships
     or aircraft in danger or distress."

The Geneva Convention recognises what had become established
under customary international law, namely, a coastal State's sovereignty over its territorial sea is subject to the obligation to allow
a right of innocent passage to all foreign ships.[56] Innocent passage
is defined in a very general way as that which "is not prejudicial
to the peace, good order or security of the coastal State".[57] Fishing
vessels are required to observe the laws and regulations of the
coastal State[58] and submarines are required to navigate on the
surface and to show their flag,[59] otherwise their passage will not
be regarded as innocent. The 1982 Convention is more specific in
its definition of "innocent" and enunciates a list of activities
which, if occurring in the coastal State's territorial waters, would
not be characterised as "innocent". Such activities include: any
threat or use of force against the sovereignty, territorial integrity
or political independence of the coastal State; any exercise or
practice with weapons of any kind, any act aimed at collecting
information to the prejudice of the defence or security of the
coastal State; any act of propaganda aimed at affecting the
defence or security of the coastal State; any fishing activities and
the carrying out of research or survey activities.[60] The coastal
State is under a duty not to hamper innocent passage.[61] The 1982

[56] art.5 of the 1958 Convention and art.8 of the 1982 Convention provide where
the straight baseline is employed, because of an indented coastline, and this has
led to territorial waters or high seas being designated internal waters, a right of
innocent passage shall exist in those waters.
[57] art.14(4).
[58] art.14(5).
[59] art.14(6).
[60] art.19 of the 1982 Convention.
[61] art.15 of the 1958 Convention.

Convention, again, is more precise and stipulates that the coastal State shall not:

> "(a) impose requirements on foreign ships which have the practical effect of denying or impairing the right of innocent passage; or
>
> (b) discriminate in form or in fact against the ships of any State or against ships carrying cargoes to, from or on behalf of any State."[62]

Under both Conventions, coastal States are required to give appropriate publicity of any dangers to navigation of which it has knowledge within its territorial sea.[63]

Article 17 of the 1958 Convention simply provides that foreign ships engaging in innocent passage must comply with the coastal State's laws and regulations. Once more, the 1982 Convention articulates to a greater extent the laws and regulations which a coastal State may adopt. These may, for instance, include measures on the safety of navigation and the regulation of maritime traffic, the protection of navigational aids and facilities and other facilities or installations, the protection of cables and pipelines, the conservation of the living resources of the sea, and the preservation of the environment of the coastal State and the prevention, reduction and control of pollution thereof.[64]

Two new provisions are included in the 1982 Convention. Article 22 provides a coastal State may require foreign ships to use such sea lanes and traffic separation schemes as it (that is, the coastal State) may designate or prescribe for vessels, in particular tankers, nuclear-powered ships and ships carrying nuclear or other inherently dangerous or noxious substances, or materials, engaged in innocent passage. Also art.23, which provides that foreign nuclear-powered ships and ships carrying nuclear or like material shall be required to carry documents and observe special precautionary measures established for such ships by international agreements.

A coastal State may take the steps necessary to prevent passage which is not innocent[65] and may, without discrimination among foreign ships, suspend innocent passage temporarily in specified areas of its territorial sea if that is required in the interest of the

---

[62] art.24.
[63] art.15(2) of the 1958 Convention; art.24(2) of the 1982 Convention.
[64] art.21.
[65] art.16 of the 1958 Convention; art.25 of the 1982 Convention.

coastal State's security.[66] If a vessel is proceeding to internal waters, the coastal State may take the steps necessary to prevent any breach of the conditions to which the admission of the ship to internal waters is subject.[67]

Foreign vessels engaged in innocent passage are only subject to the coastal State's criminal and civil jurisdiction in limited defined circumstances. A coastal State may only exercise jurisdiction:

(a)   if the consequences of the crime extend to the coastal State; or

(b)   if the crime is of a kind to disturb the peace of the country, the good order of the territorial sea; or

(c)   if the assistance of the local authorities has been requested by the captain of the ship, the consul of the country whose flag the ship flies; or

(d)   if it is necessary for the suppression of illicit traffic in narcotic drugs (or psychotropic substances—1982 Convention only).[68]

Civil jurisdiction may not be exercised against either the ship or against a person on board, save in respect of obligations and liabilities assumed by the ship itself in the course of, or for the purpose of, its voyage through the waters of the coastal State, or if the vessel is passing through the territorial sea, after having left internal waters.[69] Government vessels operated for commercial purposes also come within the ambit of the foregoing provisions. In respect of warships and government vessels operating for non-commercial purposes, the Convention does not affect the jurisdictional immunities from which they are entitled.

A foreign warship which does not comply with the coastal State's regulations may be required to leave the territorial sea ("immediately" has been added by the 1982 Convention).[70] Although mention is made of warships, neither the 1958 nor the 1982 Convention expressly grants or denies foreign warships a right of innocent passage. The 1982 Convention does provide, however, that the flag State of a vessel shall incur international liability for "any loss or damage to the coastal State resulting from the non-compliance by a warship or other government ship operated

---

[66] art.16(3) of the 1958 Convention; art.25(3) of the 1982 Convention.
[67] art.16(2) of the 1958 Convention; art.25(2) of the 1982 Convention.
[68] art.19 of the 1958 Convention; art.27 of the 1982 Convention.
[69] art.20 of the 1958 Convention; art.28 of the 1982 Convention.
[70] art.23 of the 1958 Convention; art.30 of the 1982 Convention.

for non-commercial purposes with the laws and regulations of the coastal State . . ."[71]

Passage through straits

What is a coastal State's jurisdiction in international straits bordering its coast?

Article 16(4) of the Geneva Convention on the Territorial Sea prohibits a coastal State from suspending innocent passage in territorial sea straits, which are used for international navigation between one part of the high seas and another part of the high seas, or the territorial sea of a foreign State.

The right of innocent passage similar to that provided by art.14 is retained by the 1982 Convention for straits which are formed by an island of a State bordering the strait and its mainland and where there exists seaward of the island a high seas route or an EEZ (see below),[72] and secondly, where the strait is between a part of the high seas or an EEZ and the territorial sea of a foreign State, namely where there is only territorial sea at one end of a strait.[73] The coastal State may not suspend such innocent passage.[74] However, for straits which are used for international navigation between one part of the high seas or an EEZ and another part of the high seas or an EEZ,[75] the 1982 Convention dispenses with the right of innocent passage and provides rather for a right of transit. In other words, the right of transit will only apply in straits which have high seas or an EEZ at both ends.

Article 38(2) defines transit passage as "the freedom of navigation and overflight solely for the purpose of continuous and expeditious transit of the strait". Ships and aircraft are charged with certain duties when travelling through and over the strait, for example proceeding without delay and refraining from any threat or use of force against the sovereignty, territorial integrity or political independence of States bordering the strait.[76] The strait State may, in the interest of safe passage, prescribe sea lanes and traffic separation schemes, but only after its proposals have been referred to and adopted by the "competent international organisation":[77] the authority of the strait State under the 1982 Convention is thus more restricted than under the 1958 Convention. The strait State may also adopt laws and regulations designed to prevent, reduce

[71] art.31.
[72] art.38.
[73] art.45(1)(b).
[74] art.45(2).
[75] art.37.
[76] art.39.
[77] art.41.

or control pollution. However, the strait State is under a duty not to hamper transit passage and is required "to give appropriate publicity to any danger to navigation or overflight within or over the strait of which they have knowledge".[78] There may be no suspension of transit passage.[79]

Why should international straits be subject to a special regime under the 1982 Convention?[80] The result of extended territorial seas has been to bring straits through which there were previously high seas exclusively within territorial waters. Consequently, maritime powers sought definite guarantees for shipping as a condition to their accepting a 12-mile territorial sea; the 1988 Anglo–French Agreement[81] relating to the Straits of Dover guarantees the right of "unimpeded transit passage for merchant vessels, State vessels and, in particular, warships following their normal mode of navigation . . .". The Geneva Convention is also deficient in that it fails to grant a right of passage to aircraft (under the 1982 Convention all aircraft will enjoy the right of transit) and submarines have to navigate on the surface and show their flag, whereas the 1982 Convention would appear, with respect to warships in time of peace, to support the International Court of Justice's pronouncement in the *Corfu Channel (Merits)* case[82] that it was generally accepted international custom:

> "that States in time of peace have a right to send their warships through straits used for international navigation between two parts of the high seas without the previous authorisation of a coastal State, provided that the passage is innocent."[83]

Contiguous zone

A coastal State, under the 1958 Geneva Convention, may claim a zone of the high seas, not exceeding 12 miles from the territorial sea baselines, contiguous to its territorial sea. A contiguous zone need not be claimed, as in the case of the United Kingdom, but if

[78] art.44.
[79] *ibid.*
[80] The regime does not apply to straits regulated by treaty, e.g. the 1936 Treaty of Montreux in respect of the Straits of the Bosphorus and Dardanelles.
[81] Cmnd.557.
[82] I.C.J. Rep. (1949) p.4.
[83] *ibid.* at 28. See also the "Joint Statement by the US and the USSR on Uniform Interpretation of Rules of International Law Governing innocent Passage 1989" (1989) 28 I.L.M. 1444.

it is it must be done so specifically. Although the status of the contiguous zone remains that of high seas, the coastal State may exercise control to prevent or punish infringement of its customs, fiscal, immigration or sanitary regulations within its territory or territorial sea (emphasis added). The 1982 Convention extends the maximum breadth of the contiguous zone to 24 miles from the territorial baselines.[84]

The equality of States, including those without a sea-coast (some 40 States), on the high seas is enshrined in art.3 of the Geneva Convention, which provides "States having no sea-coast should have access to the sea". The right of access of land-locked States to and from the sea and freedom of transit is exclusively elaborated upon in arts 124 and 132 of the 1982 Convention.[85]

HIGH SEAS

The high seas constitute "all parts of the sea that are not included in the territorial sea or in the internal waters of a State".[86] This definition has had to be modified with the advent of the EEZ and the recognition of archipelagic waters. Waters not included in the EEZ, the archipelagic waters of an archipelagic State, the territorial waters or internal waters of a State, constitute the high seas.[87]

According to classical doctrine, the high seas are free and may not be apportioned by any one nation. The freedom of the high seas, with qualified jurisdiction over adjacent waters by the coastal State, was articulated by Hugo Grotius in *Mare Liberum* (1609). The freedom principle was initially articulated in an effort to break the monopoly of the Spanish and Portuguese over the seas and was accepted subsequently by the major maritime States, including the United Kingdom, the United States, the Netherlands and Japan, which all sought to keep the territorial waters narrow and the high seas as broad as possible.

The freedoms of the high seas, which may be exercised by both coastal and non-coastal States, are the freedom of navigation, the freedom of fishing, the freedom to lay submarine cables and pipelines and the freedom of overflight.[88] These freedoms are not exhaustive and others which are recognised by the general principles of international law and which may be "exercised by all

---

[84] art.33.
[85] See also the 1965 Convention on Transit Trade of Land-locked States, 597 U.N.T.S. 3; 4 I.L.M. 957 (1965).
[86] art.1 of the Geneva Convention on the High Seas.
[87] art.86 of the 1982 Convention.
[88] art.2 of the 1958 Geneva Convention; art.33 1982 Convention.

States with reasonable regard to the interests of other States in their exercise of their freedom of the high seas"[89] may also exist.[90]

The 1982 Convention reaffirms the four freedoms[91] (though the freedom of fishing is now subject to the rules governing the EEZ) and acknowledges two additional freedoms: the freedom to construct artificial islands and other installations permitted by international law and the freedom to undertake scientific research. As under the 1958 Convention, consideration must be given to the rights of other States on the high seas and must be treated "with respect to activities in the area"[92] (that is, the area of the deep seabed and ocean floor and subsoil—see below).

Nuclear testing

The testing of conventional weapons and nuclear weapons may limit other States from exercising the freedom of navigation. The International Court of Justice in the *Nuclear Test* cases,[93] brought by Australia and New Zealand against France, did not address itself to the legality under international law of nuclear testing.[94] Petren J.,[95] however, highlighted the fact that, in spite of the 1963 Nuclear Test Ban Treaty,[96] the prohibition on nuclear testing had not evolved into a rule of customary international law. He asserted that the signatories to the 1963 Treaty, (France was not a party to that Treaty) by mutually banning themselves from carrying out further atmospheric nuclear tests, had shown "they were still of the opinion that customary international law did not pro-

---

[89] *ibid.*, art.87 of the 1982 Convention.
[90] Spain instituted proceedings against Canada in the I.C.J. on March 28, 1995 with respect to a dispute which had arisen relating to the Canadian Coastal Fisheries Protection Act 1985 and various other measures which had been taken on the basis of that legislation, in particular, the boarding on the high seas of a Spanish ship by Canadian officials. Spain contended that these measures seriously affected the principle of the freedom of the high seas and infringed the sovereign rights of Spain. The Court, in December 1998, declared it had no jurisdiction to hear the case by virtue of the reservation contained in para.2(d) of the Canadian Declaration, May 10, 1994.
[91] Above, n.89.
[92] art.87(2) of the 1982 Convention.
[93] I.C.J. Rep. (1974) at 253 *(Australia v France)*; I.C.J.Rep. (1974) at 457 *(New Zealand v France)*.
[94] The cases were withdrawn following assurances by France in a number of statements that the tests would cease.
[95] I.C.J.Rep. (1985) at 305.
[96] 480 U.N.T.S. 43; U.K.T.S. 3 (1964) Cmnd.2245; 14 U.S.T. 1313. For a case dealing with a situation not dealt with under the Convention see Land and Maritime Boundary between Cameroon and Nigeria I.C.J. October 10, 2002, General List No.94.

hibit atmospheric nuclear tests". In an Advisory Opinion in 1996, the I.C.J. confirmed that the threat or use of nuclear testing is now considered contrary to contemporary international law. France renewed its nuclear testing activities in the South Pacific in 1996, despite the prohibition.[97]

Article 88 of the 1982 Convention designates the high seas as an area reserved for peaceful purposes. There are also a number of regional agreements which prohibit nuclear weapons, e.g. Treaty on the South East Asia Nuclear Weapon Free Zone 1995 and the African Nuclear Weapon Free Treaty 1996.

Nationality of ships

Ships must fly the flag of a State; their nationality is that of the State whose flag they fly. A State may establish its own conditions for the granting of nationality to a ship, but there:

> "must exist a genuine link between the State and the ship; in particular, the State must effectively exercise its jurisdiction and control in administrative, technical and social matters over ships flying its flag."[98]

A ship may sail under the flag of one State only, and a ship:

> "which sails under the flags of two or more States, using them according to convenience, may not claim any of the nationalities in question with respect to any other State, and may be assimilated to a ship without nationality."[99]

A ship is not prohibited from sailing without a flag, but if it does it cannot invoke diplomatic protection for any international wrong it may have allegedly suffered: *Naim Molvan v Attorney-General for Palestine.*[100] A ship may not normally change its flag during a voyage.

---

[97] 35 I.L.M. 809 (1996). See also Ch.11. In response to the actions of France, New Zealand submitted a request to the I.C.J. on August 21, 1995, for an examination of the situation arising from the proposed nuclear testing in accordance with para.63 of the I.C.J.'s judgment in the *Nuclear Tests* case in 1974. New Zealand argued that renewed nuclear testing action would affect the judgment in that case. The I.C.J. dismissed the request on the grounds that the basis of its original judgment was not affected by the proposed course of action. (Order of the Court I.C.J. Rep. (1995) at 288).

[98] art.5 of the 1958 Convention; art.91 of the 1982 Convention.

[99] art.6 of the 1958 Convention; art.92 of the 1982 Convention.

[100] [1948] A.C. 351; see 369–370.

The introduction of the genuine link requirement was prompted by the increase in the use of "flags of convenience" i.e., where ship owners register in a particular State because of less onerous municipal taxation and labour laws. The United Nations addressed the issue, which culminated in the 1986 UN Convention on Conditions for Registration of Ships.[101] The *raison d'être* of the Convention is to introduce improved standards of responsibility and accountability, thereby reinforcing the "genuine" link requirement.[102] Obligations incumbent on the flag State under the 1958 and 1982 Conventions include, *inter alia*: the maintenance of a register of all ships flying its flag; the exercise of effective authority and control over the ships in administrative, technical and social matters; to take those measures necessary to ensure safety at sea, to prevent collisions and to prevent, reduce and control pollution of the marine environment and adopt laws and regulations and to take such steps as are required to achieve conformity with generally accepted standards, regulations, procedures and practices, and to serve their implementation and observance.[103]

It is not always for economic benefits that a ship may seek to fly the flag of a State other than that of its State of nationality. During the Iran–Iraq conflict, Kuwaiti vessels seeking the military protection of British and American naval vessels patrolling the Gulf re-registered under the UK and the US flags.[104]

Jurisdiction on the high seas

Jurisdiction over ships on the high seas lies with the flag State. The flag State is, for instance, responsible for the manning of ships and the labour conditions of the crew.[105] The 1982 Convention's counterpart Article—art.94[106]—sets out in greater detail the measures

---

[101] 26 I.L.M. 1236 (1987).

[102] The Convention requires the ratification of 40 countries before it shall enter into force. The I.C.J. in the *IMCO* case, I.C.J. Rep. (1960), p.150, considered the term 'largest ship owning nations' and held the term referred only to registered tonnage. The issue arose in the context of the eligibility of Liberia and Panama to be elected to the Committee of the Inter-Governmental Maritime Consultative Organisation. The I.C.J. did not consider in-depth the notion of genuine link.

[103] Relevant arts in the 1958 Convention are 5(1), 10, 11, 24 and 25; in the 1982 Convention, 94, 192, 211 and 219.

[104] See *M/V Saiga* (No.2) 120 I.L.R., p.143, wherein the Tribunal for the Law of the Sea held that a ships nationality is a factual question to be established on the basis of evidence provided by the parties concerned, (at p.175–176).

[105] art.10 of the 1958 Convention.

[106] art.94. Also Pursuant to the provisions of its Statute, the Tribunal has formed the following Chambers: the Chamber of Summary Procedure, the Chamber for

which a flag State is required to take to ensure safety at sea. In respect of a collision on the high seas, neither penal nor disciplinary proceedings may be initiated against either the master or a crewmember, except before the judicial or administrative authorities of the flag State or the State of which such person is a national. The ship itself may only be arrested or detained, even for investigation purposes, by the authority of the flag State.[107] Warships and government ships used for other than commercial purposes are accorded sovereign immunity and are subject only to the jurisdiction of their flag State.

Exceptions to the freedom of navigation—interference on the high seas

The most important limitation to the freedom of navigation is:

> "every State may seize a pirate ship or aircraft, or a ship taken by piracy and under the control of pirates, and arrest the persons and seize the property on board."[108]

Piracy is strictly defined in international law as:

> "(a) any illegal acts of violence, detention or any act of depredation committed for private ends by the crew or the passengers of a private ship or a private aircraft, and directed:
>
> (i) on the high seas, against another ship or aircraft, or against persons or property on board such ship or aircraft;
>
> (ii) against a ship, aircraft, persons, or property in a place outside the jurisdiction of any State;
>
> (b) any act of voluntary participation in the operation of a ship or of an aircraft with knowledge of facts making it a pirate ship or aircraft;

Fisheries Disputes and the Chamber for Marine Environment Disputes. At the request of Chile and the European Community, the Tribunal has also formed a special chamber to deal with the case Concerning the Conservation and Sustainable Exploitation of Swordfish Stocks in the South-Eastern Pacific Ocean (Chile/European Community).

[107] Hence, the EU's condemnation of Canada's actions directed at Spanish trawlers as "international piracy" in March 1995. art.11 of the 1958 Convention; art.97 of the 1982 Convention; *cf.* decision in the *Lotus* case P.C.I.J. Rep., ser.A, No.10 (1927).

[108] art.19 of the 1958 Convention; art.105 of the 1982 Convention.

(c)   any act of inciting or of intentionally facilitating an act described in sub-paragraph 1 or sub-paragraph 2 of this article."[109]

What is necessary in international law for an act to be characterised as piracy is that it be committed for private ends.

The courts of the seizing State are competent to decide the penalties which may be imposed.[110] If the suspicion for the seizure proves groundless, the State making the seizure is liable for any loss or damage it has caused as a consequence.[111] Only warships, military aircraft or other authorised vessels may carry out such a seizure.

Unless provided for by treaty a foreign merchant ship may only be boarded by the crew of a warship if there is reasonable ground for suspecting:

"(a)   that the ship is engaged in piracy; or

(b)   that the ship is engaged in the slave trade; or

(c)   that, though flying a foreign flag or refusing to show its flag, the ship is, in reality, of the same nationality as the warship."[112]

Again, if the suspicions prove unfounded, the boarded ship shall be entitled to receive compensation. In 2005 the 1982 Convention principles were reflected in the Regional Co-operation Agreement on Combating Piracy and Armed Robbery against Ships in Asia. The Agreement proposes an information sharing center being established in Singapore and extends the regulation of piracy to include internal waters; territorial seas; and archipelagic waters.[113]

---

[109] art.15 of the 1958 Convention; art.101 of the 1982 Convention. The hijacking of the Italian liner *Achille Lauro* by four Palestinians in October 1985 did not constitute an act of piracy under international law. On October 7, 2008 the Security Council acting under Ch.VII passed Resolution 1838, characterising the attacks perpetrated against vessels off the coast of Somalia as acts of piracy.

[110] *ibid.* Canada's Criminal Code, e.g. states that it is an offence, punishable by life imprisonment to do "any act that, by the law of nations, is piracy" (s.75). The Code also makes it an offence to carry out "piratical acts", which include stealing a Canadian ship or its cargo, starting a mutiny or inciting others to do so (s.76).

[111] art.20 of the 1958 Convention; art.106 of the 1982 Convention.

[112] art.22 of the 1958 Convention; art.110 of the 1982 Convention—the latter also includes the right of visit in respect of ships suspected of engaging in unauthorised broadcasting—see below.

[113] 44 I.L.M. 2005, p.829.

The 1982 Convention requires States to co-operate in the suppression of illicit traffic in narcotic drugs and psychotropic substances engaged in by ships on the high seas contrary to international conventions, and provides that a State:

> "which has reasonable grounds for believing that a ship flying its flag is engaged in illicit traffic in narcotic drugs or psychotropic substances may request the co-operation of other States to suppress such traffic."[114]

The *Achille Lauro* incident and fears of escalating maritime terrorism prompted the International Maritime Organisation to produce a Convention for the Suppression of Unlawful Acts against the Safety of Maritime Navigation[115] and a Protocol for the Suppression of Unlawful Acts against the Safety of Fixed Platforms Located on the Continental Shelf.[116]

Article 3 of the above Convention articulates what constitutes an offence for the purposes of the Convention and includes, *inter alia*, the seizure or exercising of control over a ship by force or threat thereof or any form of intimidation.[117] Contracting Parties are required to take such measures as may be necessary to establish its jurisdiction over the offences identified by the Convention when the offence is committed:

(a) against or on board a ship flying its flag at the time when the offence is committed; or

(b) in its territory, including territorial sea; or

(c) by one of its nationals.[118]

Jurisdiction *may* be exercised by a Contracting Party in the event of the offence:

(a) being committed by a Stateless person who is habitually resident in its territory; or

(b) resulting in one of its nationals being threatened, injured or killed; or

---

[114] art.108.
[115] The Convention entered into force on March 1, 1992.
[116] The Protocol entered into force on March 1, 1992.
[117] art.3.1.(a). Note the Convention does not apply to warships, State vessels being used as a naval auxiliary or for customs or police purposes; art.2.
[118] art.6.1.

(c)   being committed in an attempt to compel that State to do or abstain from doing any act.[119]

The Convention requires Contracting Parties to make the relevant offences punishable by penalties appropriate to the gravity of the offences[120] and obliges them to either institute proceedings through the national courts or extradite the offender or alleged offender.[121]

The 1982 Convention also tackles the problem of high seas broadcasting (pirate radio), particularly in art.109(3), which provides that a person:

> "engaged in unauthorised broadcasting may be prosecuted before the Court of:
>
> (a)   the flag State of the ship;
> (b)   the State of registry of the installations;
> (c)   the State of which the person is a national;
> (d)   any State where the transmissions can be received; or
> (e)   any State where authorised radio communication is suffering interference."

Article 109(4) confirms the right of visit to ships suspected of engaging in unauthorised broadcasting and provides that any person or ship engaged in unauthorised broadcasting may be arrested and the broadcasting apparatus seized by any State which has jurisdiction under art.109(3).

Fishing activities on the high seas

The 1982 Convention[122] provides for a management and conservation scheme for the living resources of the high seas. These provisions, which consolidate and elaborate on those imposed upon States by the 1958 Geneva Convention on the Fishing and Conservation of Living Resources, are, of course, independent of those provisions in respect of the coastal States' rights in the EEZ.

Hot pursuit

The warships, law enforcement vessels or aircraft (the 1982 Convention requires that such vessels and aircraft should be

---

[119] art.6.2.
[120] art.5.
[121] art.10.
[122] arts 116–120.

clearly marked) of a coastal State may pursue a vessel leaving its territorial waters when it suspects it of having violated its laws and regulations.[123] Pursuit must be continuous and must cease immediately when the pursued vessel reaches the territorial waters of another State, be it the vessel's own State or a third State. If pursuit is initiated in contiguous waters it must only be because of a violation of the rights for which the contiguous zone was established (see above). Pursuit may only be initiated after the offending vessel has received a visual or auditory signal to stop.

Failure to stop may lead to the use of "necessary and reasonable force for the purpose of effecting the object of boarding, searching, seizing and bringing into port the suspected vessel."[124] The right of hot pursuit has evolved and is now accepted as an established rule of customary international law.

Protection of marine environment

The 1958 Geneva Convention on the High Seas requires every State to draw up regulations to prevent pollution of the seas by the discharge of oil from ships or pipelines or resulting from the exploitation and exploration of the seabed and its subsoil, taking account of existing treaty provisions on the subject.[125]

Notwithstanding growing concern regarding the dangers of oil pollution on the marine environment, it was 1954 before an international Convention was agreed upon, namely the International Convention for the Prevention of the Pollution of the Sea by Oil (OILPOL).[126] Essentially the 1954 Convention prohibited the discharge of oil or any oily mixture by vessels and made any such violation subject to the jurisdiction of the State of registration. The 1954 Convention, as amended in 1962, 1969 and 1971, has been replaced for parties to both Conventions by the 1973 Convention for the Prevention of Pollution from Ships (MARPOL),[127] which covers not only oil discharges from ships, but discharges such

---

[123] art.23 of the 1958 Convention; art.111 of the 1982 Convention.
[124] The *I'm Alone* case 3 R.I.A.A. 1607 at 1615; 29 *A.J.I.L.* 326 (1935)—where, in fact, the sinking of the vessel concerned was held to be excessive action which "could not be justified by any principle of international law". See also *M/V Saiga* n.4 above, at p.194, confirming that lawful hot pursuit demands the fulfillment of each of art.111 conditions.
[125] art.24.
[126] 327 U.N.T.S. 3; U.K.T.S. 56 (1958) Cmnd.595; 12 U.S.T. 2989.
[127] Misc.26 (1974) Cmnd.5748; 12 I.L.M. 1319 (1973). As of February 18, 2002, Annex I/II has 120 Contracting States (95.90 per cent world tonnage); Annex III has 101 Contracting States (81.4 per cent world tonnage); Annex IV has 85 Contracting States (46.34 per cent world tonnage); Annex V has 106 Contracting States (87.88 per cent world tonnage); Annex VI has 4 Contracting States (14.05 per cent world tonnage).

as sewage, garbage and other noxious harmful substances.[128] The Marpol Convention is the most important international Convention dealing with pollution from ships. An international Convention on Liability and Compensation for Damage in Connection with the Carriage of Hazardous and Noxious Substances by Sea was adopted on May 3, 1996, under the auspices of the International Maritime Organisation (IMO). The Convention imposes strict liability upon ship owners for *inter alia* loss of life or personal injury, loss of or damage to property outside the ship and loss or damage by contamination of the environment. The Convention also introduces a system of compulsory insurance.[129]

The *Torrey Canyon* incident of 1967, when the United Kingdom bombed a Liberian tanker stranded off the Cornish coast so as to avoid further damage to the coastline through the spillage of oil, precipitated the 1969 International Convention Relating to Intervention on the High Seas in Cases of Oil Pollution Casualties.[130] The Convention allows parties to:

"take such measures on the high seas as may be necessary to prevent, mitigate or eliminate grave and imminent danger to their coastline or related interests from pollution or threat of pollution of the sea by oil, following upon a maritime casualty or acts related to such a casualty, which may reasonably be expected to result in major harmful consequences."[131]

[128]Technical difficulties in respect of the provisions dealing with noxious liquid substances acted as an obstacle to the ratification of the 1973 Convention. A Protocol was adopted in 1978 (Misc.26 (1974) Cmnd.5748) to facilitate the entry into force of the regulations pertaining to oil discharge. A number of amendments to the MARPOL Convention were adopted by the IMO Assembly and entered into force on March 3, 1996. The amendments were designed to improve the application of the Convention and apply to four of the Convention's five technical annexes. Ships can now be inspected in the ports of other Contracting Parties so as to ensure that the crews are competent to perform important procedures relating to the prevention of marine pollution.
[129]The Convention will come into force 18 months after the fulfilment of two conditions. First, that there is acceptance by 12 States of the Convention, four of which have not less than two million units of gross tonnage and secondly, that the persons in those States who are required to contribute to a general fund established under the Convention have received at least 40 million tonnes of contributing cargo in the preceding year. There are complex arrangements for calculating contributions to the Fund. At present, the Liability Convention has two Contracting Parties, accounting for 1.89 per cent world tonnage, and has not yet entered into force.
[130]U.K.T.S. 77 (1975) Cmnd.6056; 26 U.S.T. 765; 9 I.L.M. 25 (1969). The International Convention on Civil Liability for Bunker Oil Pollution Damage (2001) was adopted on March 23, 2001. It will enter into force 12 months after 18 States have signed it without reservation as to ratification or have ratified it.
[131]art.1.

The measures taken must be "reasonably necessary" and proportionate to the damage, actual or threatened.[132]

A 1973 Protocol to the Convention[133] authorises intervention with respect to threats of pollution from substances other than oil. The Intervention Convention is supplemented by the Convention on Civil Liability for Oil Pollution Damage.[134] The Convention imposes a regime of strict liability (save in certain circumstances) on the owners of vessels and provides for the payment of compensation in respect of damage caused by oil spillage. The Liability Convention is supplemented by the 1971 Convention on the Establishment of an International Fund of Compensation for Oil Pollution Damage,[135] which establishes a fund for the payment of compensation in circumstances where the Liability Convention proves deficient. Tanker owners have also established their own compensation schemes, namely the Tanker Owners' Voluntary Agreement concerning Liability for Oil Pollution 1969 (TOVALOP);[136] and the Contract Regarding an Interim Supplement to Tanker Liability for Oil Pollution 1971 (CRISTAL).[137] Protocols to the 1969 Civil Liability Convention and the 1971 International Fund Convention provide higher limits of compensation and have a wider scope of application than the Conventions originally envisaged.[138] Both Protocols apply to the EEZ.

Article 25 of the Geneva Convention on the High Seas requires States to take measures to prevent pollution by the dumping of radioactive waste as well as co-operating with competent international organisations. Article 5(7) of the Convention on the Continental Shelf requires coastal States "to undertake, in the safety zones all appropriate measures for the protection of the living resources of the sea from harmful agents." These provisions have been reinforced by international Conventions on dumping and pollution from land-based sources, such as the Oslo

---

[132] art.5.

[133] U.K.T.S. 27 (1983) Cmnd.8924; 13 I.L.M. 605 (1974).

[134] U.K.T.S. 106 (1975) Cmnd.6183; 9 I.L.M. 45 (1970). Amending Protocol 1976, U.K.T.S. 26 (1981) Cmnd.8238; 16 I.L.M. 617 (1977). Replaced by the 1992 IMO Convention on Civil Liability for Oil Pollution Damage, and Protocol (see below, n.136).

[135] U.K.T.S. 95 (1978) Cmnd.7383; 11 I.L.M. 284 (1972). Amending Protocol Misc.27 (177) Cmnd.7029; 16 I.L.M. 621 (1977). Replaced by the 1992 IMO Convention on the Establishment of an International Fund of Compensation for Oil Pollution Damage and Protocol (see below, n.138).

[136] 8 I.L.M. 497 (1969).

[137] 10 I.L.M. 137 (1971).

[138] The Protocols entered into force on May 30, 1995 and superseded earlier Protocols adopted in 1984.

Convention for the Prevention of Marine Pollution by Dumping from Ships and Aircraft 1972,[139] the London Convention on the Prevention of Marine Pollution by Dumping of Wastes and Other Material 1972,[140] the Paris Convention for the Prevention of Marine Pollution from Land-based Sources 1974,[141] and regional arrangements such as the Barcelona Convention for the Protection of the Mediterranean against Pollution 1976.[142] The UN Environment Programme (UNEP) operates a Regional Seas Programme.

The International Maritime Organisation (IMO) is the principal international organisation concerned with vessel pollution issues. The IMO is responsible for convening conferences and drafting and revising Conventions. The IMO, although one of the smaller UN agencies, has, through its work, achieved considerable success in reducing oil pollution and improving safety at sea. There are 164 Member States.[143]

The 1982 Convention envisages a comprehensive regime (provided for in 46 Articles)[144] for the protection and preservation of the marine environment. Article 192 places States under a general obligation to protect and preserve the marine environment, and further to this parties are required to adopt national and international measures. The 1982 Convention further provides, inter alia, for global and regional co-operation, contingency plans against pollution, studies, research programmes, exchange of information and data, and scientific and technical assistance to developing States. States are required to adopt laws and regulations with regard to pollution from land-based sources, seabed activities, dumping, pollution from vessels and pollution from or through the atmosphere. Enforcement is envisaged by flag States, port States and coastal States. Non-fulfilment of international obligations by a party will give rise to international responsibility. The UN Conference on the Environment and Development held in

---

[139]U.K.T.S. 119 (1975) Cmnd.6228; 11 I.L.M. 262 (1972).
[140]U.K.T.S. 43 (1976) Cmnd.6486; 26 U.S.T. 2403; 11 I.L.M. 1291 (1972). A Protocol to the London Convention was adopted at an IMO Conference on November 7, 1996. The Protocol introduces a radical new approach to the regulation of the use of the sea as a depositary for waste materials (see art.3—"the polluter pays" principle). It will enter into force 30 days after ratification by 26 countries, 15 of whom must be Contracting Parties to the 1972 Convention (art.25) 36 I.L.M. 1 (1997). To date, there have been 16 ratifications.
[141]U.K.T.S. 64 (1978) Cmnd.7251; 13 I.L.M. 352 (1974).
[142]15 I.L.M. 290 (1976).
[143]IMO was established in 1958 and was primarily charged with the task of improving maritime safety. The increase in oil transportation by sea and a number of serious spills in the 1960s led to IMO's involvement in pollution prevention.
[144]arts 192–238.

Rio de Janerio in 1992 endorsed the environmental provisions of the 1982 Convention, and the link between UNCLOS and Ch.17 of Agenda 21 emphasised the need for international co-operation in this area.

EXCLUSIVE ECONOMIC ZONE (EEZ)

The 1982 Convention acknowledges the EEZ as "an area beyond and adjacent to the territorial sea . . ."[145] which "shall not extend beyond 200 nautical miles from the baselines from which the breadth of the territorial sea is measured."[146] UNCLOS III recognised the right to claim an EEZ as one existing under customary law. Subsequent judicial endorsement for the exercise of this right is found in the *Continental Shelf (Tunisia v Libya)* case.[147]

The concept of the EEZ evolved with the realisation that fishery resources are not inexhaustible and consequently it was imperative to adopt conservation measures.

It was only with the failure of both the 1958 and 1960 Conferences to establish the width of the territorial sea and fisheries zone that the two jurisdictional areas became independent of each other. Fisheries jurisdiction, until then, was an integral part of territorial waters jurisdiction. The failure to reach international agreement saw State practice developing the law of fisheries independently. Iceland, for example, did not wait for the 1960 Conference but in 1958 extended its exclusive fishery zone to 12 miles by employing the straight baseline method recognised by the International Court of Justice in the *Anglo-Norwegian Fisheries* case, see above.

Throughout the 1960s, the trend both within and outside Europe was towards recognition of a 12-mile exclusive fishery zone (with, as a general rule, recognition being given to the rights of foreign vessels which had traditionally fished within these waters).[148] By the end of the 1960s, a coastal State's territorial waters and fisheries jurisdiction were no longer synonymous and judicial recognition was accorded to a 12-mile exclusive fisheries zone by the International Court of Justice in 1974, when it concluded in the *Fisheries Jurisdiction (Merits)* case *(United Kingdom v Iceland)*[149] that the 12-mile fishery zone had in the years subsequent

---

[145] art.55.
[146] art.57.
[147] I.C.J. Rep. 1982, p.18 at 74; *Gulf of Maine* case I.C.J. Rep. 1984 246 at 294–295; *Continental Shelf (Libya v Malta)* case I.C.J. Rep. 1985 13 at 33; *Guinea/Guinea Bissau Delimitation of the Maritime Boundary* 25 I.L.M. 251 (1986) at 272, para.42.
[148] See e.g. 1964 European Fisheries Convention 581 U.N.T.S. 57; US legislation Public Law 89–658, 5 I.L.M. 1103 (1966).
[149] I.C.J. Rep. 1974 at p.3.

to the 1960 Conference "crystallised as customary international law".[150] Nevertheless, the Court failed to answer explicitly the question addressed to it, that is whether Iceland's claim to a 50-mile exclusive fishing zone was compatible with international law,[151] but rather characterised Iceland's unilateral extension as "an infringement of the principles enshrined in Art.2 of the 1958 Geneva Convention on the High Seas. . . ."[152] The door was left open for expansion by coastal States and such expansion occurred throughout the 1970s. The impact of such claims is reflected in the 1982 Convention and in State practice.

The right to claim an EEZ is discretionary, not mandatory, e.g. the United Kingdom does not claim an EEZ, as there would be no advantage in doing so as "the United Kingdom already has a fishery zone extending to a maximum of 200 nautical miles and . . . rights over our continental shelf (which extends well beyond 200 miles) are inherent and do not have to be proclaimed."[153] The United States, on the other hand, does claim an EEZ.

Rights of coastal States within the EEZ

The coastal State does not enjoy complete sovereignty within the EEZ but only sovereign rights "for the purpose of exploring and exploiting, conserving and managing the natural resources, whether living or non-living, of the seabed and subsoil and the superjacent waters . . ." and jurisdiction, *inter alia*, with regard to: "(i) the establishments and use of artificial islands, installations and structures; (ii) marine scientific research; (iii) the protection and preservation of the marine environment."[154]

The coastal State is responsible for determining both "the allowable catch of the living resources in its exclusive economic zone"[155] and "its capacity to harvest the living resources of the EEZ."[156] The coastal State's task is to conserve resources within the EEZ and to this end is charged with adopting measures which will:

> "maintain or restore populations of harvested species at levels which can produce the maximum sustainable yield,

---

[150] *ibid.* at 23.
[151] The Icelandic government implemented its intention to extend Iceland's exclusive fishing zone to 50 miles by the Resolution of the Althing of February 15, 1972 and Regulations of July 14. See Lay, Churchill and Nordquist, *New Directions in the Law of the Sea*, Vol.1, pp.89–90.
[152] Above, n.149 at 29.
[153] *Hansard*, HL Vol.473, Col.46 (April 7, 1986).
[154] art.56.
[155] art.61(1).
[156] art.62(2).

as qualified by relevant environmental economic needs of coastal fishing communities and the special requirement of developing States . . ."[157]

Account must be taken of "the best scientific evidence available" with the coastal State co-operating, where appropriate, with the "competent international organisations, whether sub-regional, regional or global."[158]

The coastal State's most important task as far as foreign States are concerned is to decide, in respect of the EEZ's living resources, the surplus available over its own harvesting capacity.[159] That surplus, the Convention provides, is to be made available to other States either through agreements or other arrangements to certain criteria which the coastal State is, especially with regard to developing States, to take into account. Such criteria include the "significance of the living resources of the area to the economy of the coastal State and its other national interests", the interests of land-locked States and those States "with special geographical characteristics" and the interests of those States "whose nationals have habitually fished in the zone."[160] The final say remains, however, with the coastal State.

The coastal State is responsible for regulating fishing by foreign vessels within the EEZ[161] and is required to give due notice of conservation and management regulations[162] and to exercise control over foreign vessels granted access.[163] The Convention provides for co-operation in the event of stocks occurring within the EEZ of two or more coastal States.[164] The coastal State enjoys rights within the EEZ, but it is also charged with obligations. The coastal State is not the owner, but rather the guardian of the natural resources within its EEZ.

Rights and duties of other States

Other States enjoy the right of free navigation, overflight and the laying of submarine cables and pipelines in the EEZ, provided

---

[157] art.61(3).
[158] art.61(2).
[159] art.61(2).
[160] art.62(2); art.69; art.70; arts 69 and 70 do not apply to coastal States whose economy is overwhelmingly dependent on the exploitation of the living resources of its exclusive economic zone.
[161] art.62(4) gives a list of the measures, which the coastal State may take, e.g. licensing of fishermen.
[162] art.62(5).
[163] art.73.
[164] art.63(1); art.63(2); art.64.

they respect the rights and duties of the coastal State and comply with the laws and regulations of the latter.[165] The rights of foreign States are reinforced by the obligation on the coastal State to pay "due regard to the rights and duties of other States . . ."[166]

Delimitation of the EEZ between States with opposite or adjacent coasts

Article 74 of the 1982 Convention provides that the delimitation of the EEZ between States with opposite or adjacent coasts is to be effected "by agreement on the basis of international law as referred to in art.38 of the Statute of the International Court of Justice, in order to achieve an equitable solution." The *Jan Meyen* case affirmed the desirability for a common maritime boundary between the EEZ and the continental shelf. However Oda J., in his dissenting opinion, stated that because of the separate and independent legal regimes of the EEZ and the continental shelf, a common maritime boundary cannot be presumed.[167]

In the *Delimitation of the Maritime Boundary in the Gulf of Maine Area*,[168] the Chamber established to decide the delimitation of both the continental shelf and the fishery zone, submitted that the criteria to be employed should be those which, by their neutral character, were best suited for employment in a multi-purpose delimitation. In the case before it the Chamber utilised criteria especially derived from geography. Likewise the practical methods to be employed to give effect to the criteria should, the Chamber held, be "basically founded upon geography and be as suitable for the delimitation of the seabed and subsoil as to that of the superjacent waters and their living resources" and accordingly the Chamber concluded that "only geometrical methods" would be utilised. The Chamber denied that the parties' respective scale of fishing or petroleum exploitation could serve as an equitable criterion unless:

> ". . . unexpectedly, the overall result should appear radically inequitable as entailing disastrous repercussions on the subsistence and economic development of the population concerned."[169]

---

[165] art.58(1) and (3).
[166] art.56(2).
[167] I.C.J. Rep. 1993 p.34. See, also, *Delimitation of Maritime Areas between Canada and France (St Pierre and Miquelon)* 1992 31 I.L.M. 1145.
[168] I.C.J. Rep. (1984) at 246.
[169] *ibid.* at 342.

CONTINENTAL SHELF

"Continental shelf" is the geographical term used to describe the gently sloping ledge covered by shallow water projecting from the shoreline of many land masses before a steep descent to the ocean waters. Continental shelves vary considerably in width: off the west coast of the United States the shelf is less then five miles whereas the entire area under the water of the North Sea is continental shelf.

In accordance with the principle of the freedom of the high seas, all States equally enjoy the right to explore the seabed. Continental shelves are rich in oil reserves, and by the 1940s States possessed the technology to exploit such resources. Furthermore, economically, exploration had become a viable proposition.

President Truman's Proclamation of September 28, 1945, whereby the United States regarded:

> ". . . the natural resources of the subsoil and seabed of the continental shelf beneath the high seas but contiguous to the coasts of the United States as appertaining to the United States, subject to its jurisdiction and control,"

but that "the character as high seas of the waters above the continental shelf and the right to their free and unimpeded navigation are in no way affected",[170] precipitated numerous assertions of coastal States' rights over the continental shelf and marked the beginning of the change in the legal status of the continental shelf.

The claims, which followed in the wake of the Truman Proclamation, differed in nature. Some were restrained, some asserted exclusive sovereignty by the coast State while Argentina and El Salvador claimed not only the continental shelf but also the superjacent waters and the airspace above, whereas Chile and Peru claimed sovereignty over the seabed, subsoil and water around their coasts to a limit of 200 miles.[171] It was against the background of such claims that the International Law Commission addressed itself to the issue of the continental shelf.

Article 1 of the Geneva Convention on the Continental Shelf defines the continental shelf as referring:

> "(a) to the seabed and subsoil of the submarine area adjacent to the coast but outside the area of the territorial sea, to a depth of 200 metres or, beyond that limit, to

---

[170] 4 Whiteman 756.
[171] Chile and Peru possess no geographical continental shelf.

> where the depth of the superjacent waters admits of the exploitation of the natural resources of the said areas;
>
> (b) to the seabed and subsoil of similar submarine areas adjacent to the coasts of islands."

The 1958 definition emphasises exploitability contrary to the 1982 Convention, which is silent on exploitation.

Article 76 of the 1982 Convention defines the continental shelf as:

> "the seabed and subsoil of the submarine areas that extend beyond its territorial sea throughout the natural prolongation of its land territory to the outer edge of the continental margin,[172] or to a distance of 200 nautical miles from the baselines from which the breadth of the territorial sea is measured where the outer edge of the continental margin does not extend up to that distance."

The continental shelf extends to 200 nautical miles for all States, but retains an advantage for the geographically favoured. However, art.76(6) provides the continental shelf shall not exceed 350 nautical miles from territorial baselines, and art.76(7) provides the method of delimitation to be employed where the continental shelf exceeds 200 nautical miles.

Regarding a coastal State's rights over the continental shelf, the 1982 Convention essentially reproduces the provisions of the 1958 Convention. A coastal State's rights are not territorial sovereign rights but are, rather, functional rights for the purpose of exploring and exploiting the natural resources of the continental shelf.[173] The coastal State's rights are exclusive, and exploration and exploitation activities may not be undertaken without the consent of the coastal State. Natural resources are defined as the mineral and other non-living resources of the seabed and subsoil, together with living organisms belonging to sedentary species. The 1982 Convention provides that the coastal State has the exclusive right to authorise and regulate drilling on the continental shelf for all purposes.[174]

---

[172] i.e. the continental margin consists of the continental shelf, slope and rise that separate the landmass from the deep ocean floor (abyssal plain).
[173] art.2 of the 1958 Convention; art.77 of the 1982 Convention.
[174] art.81.

The coastal State's rights in the continental shelf do not affect the status of the superjacent waters as high seas or that of the airspace above those waters,[175] and States in exercising their rights on the continental shelf must not impede the laying or maintenance of submarine cables or pipelines and must not result in:

> "any unjustifiable interference with navigation, fishing or the conservation of the living resources of the sea, nor result in any interference with fundamental oceanographic or other scientific research carried out with the intention of open publication."[176]

A coastal State may construct artificial installations on the continental shelf and may establish safety zones around such installations to a maximum of 5,000 metres. Article 82 of the 1982 Convention further restricts the maximum limit of the continental shelf by providing for the payment of contributions in kind by coastal States in respect of the exploitation of the non-living resources when their continental shelf exceeds 200 nautical miles from the territorial baselines. Payments and contributions are to be made five years after production. Developing States that are net importers of a mineral resource produced from its continental shelf will be exempt from making such payments or contributions. The payments or contributions shall be made through the Authority (see below) which shall distribute to States who are parties to the Convention "on the basis of equitable sharing criteria, taking into account the interests and needs of developing States, particularly the least developed and land-locked among them."[177]

Delimitations of the continental shelf between States with opposite or adjacent coasts

Articles 6(1) and (2) of the 1958 Convention on the Continental Shelf provide formulae for delimiting the outer limit of the continental shelf between opposite and adjacent States. In both instances the boundary should be determined by agreement between the States concerned, in the absence of which the boundary for opposite coasts "is the median line, every point of which is equidistant from the nearest point of the baselines from which the breadth of the territorial sea of each State is measured." For

---

[175] art.3 of the 1958 Convention; art.78 of the 1982 Convention.
[176] art.5(1) of the 1958 Convention; art.246 of the 1982 Convention applies to research on the continental shelf and the EEZ.
[177] art.82.

adjacent coasts "the boundary shall be determined by application of the principle of equidistance from the nearest point of the baselines from which the breadth of the territorial sea of each State is measured." Both rules show a recognised exception, namely that neither the median line nor the principle of equidistance will apply if "another boundary is justified by special circumstances."

However, the Geneva Convention failed to provide any indication of what would constitute "special circumstances". The International Court of Justice in the *North Sea Continental Shelf* cases[178] provided that delimitation was to be "effected by agreement in accordance with equitable principles, and taking account of all the relevant circumstances."[179] Relevant circumstances identified by the Court were, *inter alia*, the general configuration of the coasts of the parties; so far as known or readily ascertainable, the physical and geological structure and the natural resources of the continental shelf areas involved; the element of a reasonable degree of proportionality, which a delimitation carried out in accordance with equitable principles ought to bring about between the extent of the continental shelf areas pertaining to the coastal State and the length of its coast measured in the general direction of the coastline, account being taken for this purpose of the effects, actual or prospective, of any other continental shelf delimitations between adjacent States in the same region.[180] Nevertheless, having identified the possible relevant circumstances, the Court concluded that there was:

> "no legal limit to the considerations which States may take account of for the purpose of making sure that they apply equitable procedures, and more often than not it is the balancing-up of all such considerations ... rather than reliance on one to exclusion of all others."[181]

and in the absence of any "imperative rules" recognised by international law for the delimitation of the continental shelf, resort could be made to "various principles or methods, as may be appropriate, or a combination of them, provided that, by the application of equitable principles, a reasonable result is arrived at."[182]

In the *Continental Shelf (Libyan Arab Jamahiriya v Malta)* case,[183] the parties agreed the delimitation of the continental shelf had to

[178] I.C.J. Rep. (1969), p.3.
[179] *ibid.* at 46.
[180] *ibid.* at 50–52.
[181] *ibid.* at 50.
[182] *ibid.* at 49.
[183] I.C.J. Rep. (1985), p.13.

be effected by the application of equitable principles in all the relevant circumstances in order to achieve an equitable result. Certain principles then identified by the Court were: there should be no question of refashioning geography; non-encroachment by one party on areas appertaining to the other; respect for all relevant circumstances; that equity did not necessarily imply equality nor could there be any question of distributive justice.[184] The Court also refuted the respective economic positions of the parties concerned should be taken into account but did acknowledge the existence of economic resource and security and defence interests might be given cognisance.[185]

Note that in the *Continental Shelf (Tunisia v Libya)* case economic and political factors were dismissed unless to do so would be "radically inequitable". See also *Gulf of Maine* case in which such factors were dismissed as "ineligible for consideration".[186]

In the *North Sea Continental Shelf* cases, the Court maintained the equidistance principle was not, in light of the special circumstances exception, a principle of international law but merely an application in appropriate situations of a more general rule. In the *English Channel Arbitration*,[187] the Arbitrators held that art.6 did not formulate the equidistance principle and "special circumstances" as two separate rules but rather as a combined equidistance–special circumstances rule.

Relevant circumstances were considered in the *Gulf of Maine* case.[188] The Chamber adopted the stance that the objective of a delimitation of an equitable maritime boundary should (unless the parties agree otherwise) be to attain "an equal division of areas where the maritime projections of the coasts of the States between which delimitation is to be effected converge and overlap."[189] Unless, that is, there were "special circumstances in the case which would make that criterion inequitable."[190] Both parties (the United States and Canada) made submissions as to what "relevant circumstances" should embrace. These included, *inter alia*, environmental (United States) and economic (Canada)

[184] *ibid.*

[185] *ibid.*

[186] Above, n.147 at 340. The Court acknowledged that they could be relevant to assessment of the equitable character of delimitation, first established on the basis of criteria borrowed from physical and political geography.

[187] 18 I.L.M. 397 (1979).

[188] Above, n.168 at 246, in which the Chamber was called to decide the "maritime boundary" as between the continental shelves and fishing zones of the two parties. The objective for the establishment of such a boundary was held to be that of attaining "an equitable result".

[189] Above, n.168 at 327.

[190] *ibid.*, at 301.

circumstances. In rejecting the arguments advanced, the Chamber stated that, under international law, the equitable criteria for delimitation were to be derived essentially from geographical factors.[191]

The Tribunal in the *Guinea/Guinea Bissau Arbitration* stated that, as it was concerned only with: "a contemporary evaluation, it would be neither just nor equitable to base a delimitation on the evaluation of data which changes in relation to factors that are sometimes uncertain"[192] and that its prime objective had been "to avoid that either Party, for one reason or another should see rights exercised opposite its coast or in the immediate vicinity thereof, which could prevent the exercise of its own rights to development or compromise its security".[193] In the *Continental Shelf (Tunisia v Libya)*, case the Court maintained "each continental shelf case in dispute should be considered and judged on its own merits, having regard to its peculiar circumstances."[194]

The International Court has, in other words, minimised the equidistance principle.[195] This is reflected in the 1982 Convention, which has abandoned the art.6 formulae and provides delimitation is to be "effected by agreement on the basis of international law, as referred to in art.38 of the Statute of the International Court of Justice, in order to achieve an equitable solution".[196] What the 1982 Convention envisaged was characterised in the *Gulf of Maine* case as being "singularly concise", but one which served "to open the door to continuation of the development effected in this field by international case law."[197] The way in which the Chamber arrived at a solution in the *Gulf of Maine* dispute probably best represents how delimitation disputes will be tackled under contemporary international law. The Chamber acknowledged that there was no "body of detailed rules" in customary

---

[191] *ibid.*, at 278.
[192] 25 I.L.M. 251 (1986) at 122.
[193] ibid. at para.124.
[194] I.C.J. Rep. (1982) p.18 at 92; see also Delimitation of the Maritime Boundary in the Gulf of Maine (Canada v United States of America), above, n.168 at 292 ". . . any agreement or other equivalent solution should involve the application of equitable criteria." The Chamber in this case did not apply the equidistance principle.
[195] The equidistance principle has been used in treaties between States. However, see also *Guinea/Guinea Bissau Arbitration*, above, n.147, in which the equidistance method was identified as "just one among many and that there is no obligation to use it or give it priority, even though it is recognised as having a certain intrinsic value because of its scientific value and the relative ease with which it can be applied" at para.102.
[196] art.83(1); art.74 articulates a similar formula for the delimitation of the EEZ between States with opposite or adjacent coasts.
[197] Above, n.168 at 252

international law, nor indeed under general international law, which would "provide a ready made set of rules" for the solution of delimitation rules, and that rather what had to be sought was "a better formulation of the fundamental norm … whose existence in the legal convictions not only of the Parties to the present dispute, but of all States, is apparent from an examination of the realities of international legal relations."[198] The fundamental norm in question was identified by the Chamber as meaning:

(a)   no maritime delimitation between States may be effected unilaterally by one of the affected States;

(b)   delimitation is to be sought and effected through agreement, following negotiation conducted in good faith with a genuine intention of achieving a positive result;

(c)   in the absence of agreement recourse should be made to a third party;

and in all instances delimitation is to be effected by:

(a)   the application of equitable criteria;

(b)   the use of practical methods capable of ensuring, with regard to the geographic configuration of the area and other relevant circumstances, an equitable result.

Subsequent to the foregoing the International Court of Justice upheld the principle of the equidistance line and acknolwedged it may be varied on the basis of special circumstances.[199] In the *Land and Maritime Boundary between Cameroon and Nigeria (Equitorial Guinea intervening)*,[200] the Court reiterated that equitable agreement must be reached. However the Court stressed equity does not represent a method of delimitation but rather an aim to be borne in mind when making the delimitation. The imprecise nature of equitable considerations was highlighted by the Permanent Court of Arbitration (Tribunal) in *Barbados/Trinidad and Tobago Maritime Delimitation*[201] where the Tribunal said the role of equity lay within, and not beyond, the law. The Tribunal gave cognisnace to relevant circumstances such as the coastline of the

---

[198] *ibid.*, at 299.
[199] *The Maritime Delimitation on Territorial Questions between Qatar and Bahrain* (Qatar v Bahrain) I.C.J. Rep. (2001) p.40.
[200] I.C.J. Rep. (2002), p303.
[201] April 11 2006, Arbitration Tribunal, Permanent Court of Arbitration.

parties and ajusted the provisional equidistance line in the light of these circumstances.

A Commission on the Limits of the Continental Shelf was established pursuant to art.76(8) of the 1982 Convention. This Commission is made up of 21 experts elected by the State parties. Since its inception the Commission has dealt with numerous submissions from various countries parties to the Convention. The deadline for submissions to the Commission was May 13, 2009.[202] Article 298 of the 1982 Convention provides that States may opt to exclude delimitation disputes from procedures involving a binding decision and may refer them instead to "compulsory" conciliation.

DEEP SEABED

The deep seabed and its subsoil are rich in mineral resources, particularly in manganese nodules. The extraction of these resources is close to becoming a reality (albeit still an expensive process).

To whom should the resources belong? Should they belong to those relatively few States which, because of a technological and capital advantage, are able to finance deep-sea mining or should the resources of the ocean bed belong to all States and should the benefits derived be distributed among the international community generally? If the answer is the latter, then what conditions should apply?

The United States, for example, regards deep-sea mining as a freedom of the high seas, whereas developing and technologically disadvantaged States in particular have adopted the view that the deep seabed should be designated an "area" which is the "common heritage of mankind" and the natural resources of which should not be liable to appropriation by any State. The years preceding the sessions of UNCLOS witnessed the emergence of two groups—one representing developing States, calling for an international body to conduct all exploitation in the deep seabed and the second, that of the developed States maintaining that deep-sea activity should be undertaken by States and/or national companies subject to a registration and licensing system. Both groups did however agree on the need to avoid a "free-for-

---

[202] Decision of the Eleventh Meeting of the State Parties May 2001 UNSPLOS/72. However owing to the workload of the Commission and the (in)ability of States, in particular developing States, to meet this deadline it was intimated that it would be sufficient if by the deadline States had submitted preliminary information indicative of the outer limits of the Continental Shelf beyond 200 nautical miles, the status of preparation of their submission and the intended date of their complete submission, Decision of the Eighteenth Meeting of the States Parties June 2008, UN SPLOS/183.

all". Accordingly, the General Assembly Declaration of Principles Concerning the Sea Bed and the Ocean Floor and the Subsoil Thereof, Beyond the Limits of National Jurisdiction 1970[203] provided that the area and its resources "are the common heritage of mankind" and that no State or person, natural or juridical, could "claim, exercise or acquire rights with respect to the area or its resources incompatible with the international regime to be established . . ."[204]

The regime articulated in the 1982 Convention represents a compromise between the demands of the developed and the developing States.

Under the 1982 Convention all deep seabed exploration and exploitation is to be carried out and controlled by an International Seabed Authority.[205] The General Assembly decided in the 1994 Agreement relating to Part XI of the 1982 Convention to fund, for an initial interim period, the International Seabed Authority from the regular budget of the United Nations.[206]

International Seabed Authority[207]

The organs of the International Seabed Authority are the Assembly,[208] the Council and the Secretariat. The Assembly, with a representative from each Member State, is the supreme policy-making organ, adopting decisions by a two-thirds majority. The Council is made up of 36 Member States elected by the Assembly representing various special interest groups, such as the largest investors in sea mining, land-locked nations and potential producers. The executive organ of the Authority is the Council, which will take decisions, depending on the subject, by two-thirds majority, three-quarters majority or consensus. The Secretariat is responsible for conducting the activities of the Authority.

The Convention also provides for the compulsory settlement of deep-seabed disputes, either by judicial settlement (by reference to the International Tribunal for the Law of the Sea) or by commercial

---

[203] GA Resolution 2749 (XXV) December 17, 1970. 10 I.L.M. 230 (1970).
[204] ibid. arts 1 and 3.
[205] art.153.
[206] Details of the funding arrangements are established in s.1 of the Annex to the 1994 Agreement (para.14) as well as in decisions of the 5th Committee of the General Assembly (A/C. 5/48/90). The long-term objective is that the Authority will fund itself once it has sufficient funds from the proceeds of mining.
[207] arts 156–188.
[208] The Assembly of the Authority was inaugurated by the UN Secretary General in Kingston, Jamaica on November 16, 1994 and held its first session on February 27 to March 17, 1995.

arbitration. Pursuant to art.283 of the Convention in the event of a dispute arising the parties concerned are to advance "expeditiously to an exchange of views regarding its settlement by negotiation or other peaceful means." Article 284 provides the options for parties to invoke conciliation procedures by way of establishing a conciliation commission which in turn will produce a non-binding report. In the event of a failure to reach settlement the compulsory procedures prescribed in Part XV of the Convention s.2 apply.

INTERNATIONAL TRIBUNAL FOR THE LAW OF THE SEA

The International Tribunal[209] for the Law of the Sea was established under the Convention as an independent judicial body to hear disputes relating to the interpretation and application of the Convention.[210] The Tribunal sits in Hamburg, Germany and has 21 members. Members are independent and are elected from persons who have a high reputation for fairness and integrity and have a recognised competence in the law of the sea. Each State party may nominate up to two candidates. No two members of the Tribunal may be nationals of the same State and an equitable geographical distribution is sought. Members are elected for nine years and may be re-elected. Elections are staggered with one-third of members being elected every three years.[211] The Tribunal was granted observer status by the General Assembly of the United Nations on December 17, 1996.[212] The Tribunal's jurisdiction extends to all disputes submitted in accordance with the Convention and any other agreements which specifically confer jurisdiction on the Tribunal. Unless provided to the contrary the Tribunal's jurisdiction is mandatory in respect of the prompt release of vessels and crews,[213] provisional measures[214] and in certain circumstances the Tribunal may also give an advisory opinion. There are also some limitation on the Tribunal's jurisdiction, for instance disputes arising from a coastal State exercising its sovereign rights or jurisdiction in the EEZ.[215] The first case before the Tribunal was the *M/V Saiga (Saint Vincent and the Grenadines v Guinea)* case in which a decision was given on December 4, 1997,

[209] art.287 in accordance with Annex VI.
[210] art.288.
[211] In the absence of a national judge on the Tribunal a party to a dispute may chose an *Ad hoc* judge to participate in the settlement of the dispute. art.17
[212] Resolution A/RES/51/204 of December 17, 1996.
[213] art.292. See *Juno Trader* (Saint Vincent and the Grenadines v Guinea-Bissau), Prompt Release, December 18, 2004.
[214] art.290, pending the creation of an arbitral Tribunal (id para.5). Note provisional measures are legally binding.
[215] art.297 (1).

ordering the prompt release of the tanker *Saiga* and its crew from detention by Guinea. Judgement on the merits was given on July 1, 1999. It was held that Guinea had violated the rights of St Vincent and the Grenadines in arresting their tanker, and the Tribunal awarded compensation of $2,123,357. Fifteen cases have been referred to the Tribunal, including the dispute between Ireland and the United Kingdom as to whether the mixed oxide fuel (MOX) facility at Sellafield would have detrimental effects on the marine environment of the Irish Sea, as alleged by Ireland. An order for provisional measures was granted whereby both parties were required to co-operate, consult, exchange information and to monitor the risks involved.[216]

The Tribunal has, under its Statute, formed the following Chambers:

- Chamber of Summary Procedure;
- Chamber for Fisheries Disputes;
- Chamber for Marine Environmental Disputes;
- a special Chamber to deal with a case between Chile and the EC, namely the case Concerning the Conservation and Sustainable Exploitation of Swordfish Stocks in the South-Eastern Pacific Ocean.

Disputes relating to the activities in the International Seabed Area are brought before the Seabed Disputes Chamber of the Tribunal. Any party to a dispute within the competence of the Seabed Disputes Chamber may ask that an *ad hoc* chamber be constituted from three of the 11 judges who make up the Chamber. The Chamber is also competent to give advisory opinions.

The jurisdiction of the Tribunal is only compulsory with regard to disputes arising over deep seabed mining under Part XI of the Convention.[217]

CONCLUSION

The 1982 Convention reinforces many of the established customary and Convention laws, however it also gave the hallmark of law to the EEZ and articulates a legal regime applicable to the deep seabed and emphasises that the seas should be the "heritage of all mankind".

---

[216] Order December 18, 2001; decision can be found at: www.itlos.org/start2_en.html
[217] See Oda J. of the I.C.J., "Dispute Settlement Prospects in the Law of the Sea" (1995) 44 *I.C.L.Q.* 863.

8. STATE RESPONSIBILITY

State responsibility in international law refers to liability—that of one State to another for the non-observance of the obligations imposed by the international legal system. A State may incur liability for injury to the defendant State itself. This may be, for example, for a breach of a treaty obligation or for injury to the defendant State's nationals or their property.

State responsibility is a complex issue. The International Law Commission initiated a study of State responsibility in 1949, but its early efforts to produce a draft Convention proved inconclusive.[1] The Commission's work culminated in the adoption of the Draft Articles on the Responsibility of States for Internationally Wrongful Acts on August 2001 and General Assembly Resolution 56/83 recommended the text of the Draft Articles to governments.[2] These Articles "seek to formulate, by way of codification

---

[1] I.L.C. Drafts arts on State Responsibility, 1979, II Y.B.I.L.C., (Pt II), p.90; 1980, II Y.B.I.L.C., (Pt II), pp.14, 70; arts 1–32, 18 I.L.M. 1568 (1979); arts 33–35, 74 A.J.I.L. 962 (1980). Revised Draft Articles were adopted by the Commission in 1996 and were more detailed than the draft adopted in 1969.

[2] December 10, 2001. International Law Commission Commentary, Official Records of the G.A., 53rd session, Supplement No.10 (A/56/10 Ch.IV.E.1). The Articles and the Commentaries of the International Law Commission are

and progressive development, the basic rules of international law concerning the responsibility of States for internationally wrongful acts".[3] The emphasis is on the secondary rules of State responsibility, that is to say the general conditions under international law for a State to be considered responsible for wrongful actions or omissions and legal consequences which flow there from. The Articles do not attempt to define the content of international law obligations, breach of which gives rise to responsibility. This is the function of primary rules, whose codification would involve restating most of substantive international law, customary and conventional.

> "The Articles take the existence and content of the primary rules of international law as they are at the relevant time; they provide the framework for determining whether the consequent obligations of each State have been breached, and with what legal consequences for other States."[4]

The Articles are concerned only with the responsibility for internationally wrongful conduct. The Articles do not address instances of State responsibility arising from the injurious consequences of conduct which is not prohibited and may even be allowed under international law. The Articles are concerned only with State responsibility and do not address the issue of responsibility incurred by international organisations or other non-State entities.

The Articles are divided into four parts. Part One, the Internationally Wrongful Act of a State, sets out the requirements necessary for international responsibility to be incurred; Part Two, Content of the International Responsibility of a State, deals primarily with the legal consequences for the responsible State for any internationally wrongful acts, particularly regarding cessation and reparation; Part Three, the Implementation of the International Responsibility of a State; and Part Four deals with the general provisions applicable to the Articles as a whole.

The basic rule is spelt out in Draft art.1, namely "Every internationally wrongful act of a State entails the international responsibility of that State." This article is supplemented by Draft art.2, which provides:

---

contained in Crawford, J., *The International Law Commission's Articles on State Responsibility, Introduction, Text and Commentaries,* Cambridge University Press, 2002.

[3] *ibid.,* p.74, Commentaries 1.

[4] *ibid.,* p.75.

"There is an internationally wrongful act of a State when conduct consisting of an action or omission:

  (a) is attributable to the State under international law; and
  (b) constitutes a breach of an international obligation of the State."

Thus Draft art.2 specifies the conditions required to establish the existence of an internationally wrongful act of the State, i.e. the constituent elements of such an act.

Draft art.3 provides "the characterisation of an act of a State as internationally wrongful is governed by international law. Such characterisation is not affected by the characterisation of the same act as lawful by internal law".

Breaches of international obligations by States are dealt with in Draft art.12 ". . . when an act of the State is not in conformity with what is required of it by that obligation, regardless of its origin or character." However, "An act of State does not constitute a breach of an international obligation unless the State is bound by the obligation in question at the time the act occurs."[5]

However, a State will be deemed liable if implicated in the wrongful acts of another State: that is by assisting, controlling or coercing the activities of the "offending" State[6]. A State cannot relieve itself of responsibility by invoking either provisions or omissions of its domestic legislation.[7] In a federal State, such as Canada or the United States, the Federal Government is responsible on the international plane and will incur international liability for any actions or omissions of its constituent provinces/states which result in international injury. A federal government may not exonerate itself from responsibility by submitting that individual provinces/states are independent or autonomous.[8]

Recognised defence pleas, which may be utilised by a State to deny responsibility, are consent, self-defence, counter measures, force majeure, distress and necessity.[9]

---

[5] Draft art.13.
[6] Draft arts 16 and 17.
[7] *Free Zones of Upper Savoy and the District of Gex* P.C.I.J.Rep., ser.A/B. No.46 at 167 (1932), Draft art.3.
[8] E.g. Franco-Italian Conciliation Commission, *Heirs of Duc de Guise* (1951) 13 RIAA 161.
[9] See Draft arts 20–25; also note art.26, regarding compliance with peremptory norms.

NATURE OF LIABILITY

A notable absence from the 2001 Draft Articles is the distinction between international delict and international crimes, which were previously identified in Draft art.19.[10] The more generally framed Draft art.12 is designed to define what constitutes a breach of an international obligation.

The origin of an internationally unlawful act is, as noted above, irrelevant. The origin neither affects the characterisation of the act as unlawful nor does it affect the international responsibility of the State concerned.[11] The basic principle contained in Draft art.1 spells out a rule of customary international law; this rule was acknowledged in the case of *Chorzow Factory (Indemnity) (Merits)*,[12] when the Court maintained ". . . any breach of an engagement involves an obligation to make reparation."[13] See also Draft art.31 and below.

Is State responsibility absolute or must there be fault? In other words, is liability strict or must there be a degree of blameworthiness which can be attributed to the State? Must there be intention, recklessness, or negligence?

The customary international law rule on these questions is not clear. While evidence in the form of arbitral and judicial decisions can be found in support of both standpoints, conclusive evidence in support of either theory is absent. Fault liability appears to have received support in the *Home Missionary Society Claim*[14] and the *Corfu Channel (Merits)* case,[15] while the Claims Commission in the *Caire Claim*[16] supported absolute liability. State practice throws little light on the issue which is, anyway, essentially theoretical and one of largely academic interest. It is true that certain primary obligations may well require that fault be shown before there can be a breach of that obligation and ensuing state responsibility, for example, the 1948 Genocide Convention requires acts to be "committed with intent" in order to qualify as genocide. The proliferation of State organs and agencies has witnessed an increased application of strict liability. Fault liability has, because of the growth of State activities, become too complicated to apply in practice. However, note that Draft art.39 states "In the determination of reparation, account shall be taken of the contribution to the injury by wilful or negligent action or omission of the

---

[10] I.L.C. Draft Arts on State Responsibility, 1979, II Y.B.I.L.C. (Pt II).
[11] See Draft art.12, above.
[12] P.C.I.J. Rep., ser.A, No.17 (1928).
[13] *ibid.* at 29.
[14] 6 R.I.A.A. 42 (1920).
[15] I.C.J. Rep. 1949 p.4.
[16] 5 R.I.A.A. 516 (1929).

injured State or any person or entity in relation to whom reparation is sought." In the *La Grand* case, the I.C.J. recognised that the conduct of the claimant State could be pertinent in determining the extent of reparation due.[17]

Imputability

"Imputability" in the context of State responsibility means "attributable" and is dealt with in Ch.II of the Draft Articles, where Draft art.4 sets out the basic rule namely "the conduct of any State organ shall be considered an act of that State under international law, . . ." Draft art.5 deals with conduct of entities other than an organ of the State, but which is empowered to exercise elements of governmental authority and thereby "shall be considered an act of the State under international law, provided the person or entity is acting in that capacity in the particular instance". Draft art.6 deals with the special case where an organ of one State is placed at the disposal of another State and acts temporarily for the benefit of that State and under its authority. Draft art.7 makes it clear that the conduct of organs or entities empowered to exercise governmental authority is attributable to the State even if that conduct exceeded the authority of the organ or person concerned or was contrary to instructions. Draft arts 8–11 then deal with certain additional cases where conduct, not that of a State organ or entity, is nonetheless attributed to the State in international law. Draft art.8 deals with conduct carried out on the instructions of a State organ or under its direction or control. Draft art.9 deals with certain conduct involving the exercise of elements of governmental authority carried out in the absence of the official authorities and without any actual authority to do so. Draft art.10 concerns the special case of responsibility in defined circumstances for the conduct of insurrectional movements, namely when that insurrectional movement subsequently becomes the new government of the State or succeeds in establishing a new State. Draft art.11 deals with conduct not attributable to the State under one of the earlier Articles which is nonetheless adopted by the State, expressly or by conduct, as its own.[18]

A State is only responsible for acts or omissions which can be attributed to it as its own. What, for the purposes of State responsibility, constitutes the State?[19]

---

[17] *LaGrand (Germany v United States)* 40 I.L.M. 1069 (2001).

[18] See also the judgment in the *Nicaragua (Nicaragua v The United States) (Merits)* I.C.J. Rep. 1986 p.14 and also case IT-94–1, *Prosecutor v Tadic*, (1999) I.L.M., Vol.38, p.1518.

[19] "Without a fixed prescription for State authority, international law has to accept, by and large, the actual systems adopted by States, and the notion of

In international law a State is responsible for the actions of:

(a)   the government;

(b)   any political sub-division of the State;

(c)   any organ, agency official employee or other agent of its government or of any sub-division acting within the scope of their employment.

Imputability is a legal fiction assimilating the acts of those identified above to the State as if they were its own.

A State is not responsible for acts committed by one of its nationals (provided, that is, he is a private individual and is not, for example, a policeman) against a foreigner. The individual may, of course, be liable to prosecution in the municipal courts and indeed the government concerned may be held internationally liable if it fails to discharge its duty "of diligently prosecuting and properly punishing".[20] Thus a distinction can be made between direct responsibility—where acts of individuals are attributable to a State—and indirect responsibility—where a State breaches a primary obligation to control the conduct of individuals. Acts of private persons performed on their own initiative in an emergency, e.g. a natural disaster, are attributable to the State.[21] An individual can, however, now be held responsible for certain crimes under international law.[22]

A State cannot deny responsibility for an international wrong on the grounds that the act is, under its municipal law, *ultra vires*. As already noted, a State can be held liable for the conduct of an official, even when official competence has been exceeded, provided that is the official acted with apparent authority as a competent official or organ, and the powers or methods used were appropriate to this official authority.[23] For example, in 1993 the International Centre for Settlement of Investment Disputes rejected the argument submitted by Egypt that it was not responsible for the acts of certain high-ranking officials, as the officials

---

attribution thus consists primarily of a *renvoi* to the public institutions or organs in place in the different states": ILC, "Report of the ILC on the Work of its 25th Session" (May 7–May 13, 1973) UN Doc. A/CN.4/SER.A/1973/Add.1, 190, para.8.

[20] *Noyes Claim* 6 R.I.A.A. 308 at 311 (1933); see also the *Zafiro* case 6 R.I.A.A. 160 (1925).

[21] Draft art.8.

[22] See the Statutes of the ICTY, ICTR and ICC. (See further Chs 4 and 9).

[23] Draft art.7; Caire Claim, above n.15 and *Velasquez Rodirguez* case Inter -Am. C.t H.R., Series C, No.4 (1989), at para.170.

had not followed the correct procedures required under Egyptian law.[24] The Tribunal stated:

> "the principle of international law which the Tribunal is bound to apply is that which establishes the international responsibility of States when unauthorized or *ultra vires* acts of officials have been performed by State agents under cover of their official character. If such unauthorized or *ultra vires* acts could not be ascribed to the State, all State responsibility would be rendered illusory."[25]

In the *Youmans Claim*,[26] Mexico was held liable for the conduct of certain members of its militia who acted in defiance of orders and, instead of affording protection to a group of Americans, opened fire on the house where the latter were seeking refuge. The United States–Mexican General Claims Commission maintained that the Mexican Government was liable for the soldiers' unlawful acts, even though the soldiers had exceeded their powers.

A State is responsible for the acts of all its officials irrespective of their rank[27] and, as is illustrated by the *Rainbow Warrior* case,[28] that includes responsibility for the acts of its security services. However, as highlighted previously a State is not held liable for the activities of insurrectionaries,[29] but should the insurrectionaries be successful in their objective and become the subsequent government, they (as the legitimate government) will be held liable for any wrongful act committed during their struggle for power.[30] A state is not responsible for the acts of individuals who act as State organs when they act in a private capacity.[31] As per Draft art.13 a State will only be held responsible for an international obligation, which it was bound by at the time the act occurred. Draft art.13 reflects the general principle of intertemporal law.[32] Draft art.17 deals with derived responsibility and

---

[24] *Southern Pacific Properties (Middle East) Ltd v Arab Republic of Egypt* 32 I.L.M. 933.

[25] See art.20 of the ICTY and the ICTR. See further Chs 4 and 9 and art.30 of the Statute of the ICC.

[26] Draft art.7; *Caire Claim*, above, n.16.

[27] *Massey (US v Mexico)*, 4 R.I.A.A. 155 at 157 (1927).

[28] 26 I.L.M. 1346 (1987).

[29] *Sambaggio (Italy v Venezuela)*, 10 R.I.A.A. 499 at 513 (1903).

[30] Draft art.10. See *Short v Iran* (1987) 16 Iran–USCTR 76; *cf. Yeager v Iran* 17 Iran–USCTR 92.

[31] E.g. the *Bensleys case*: see ILC, "Report of the ILC on the Work of its 25th Session" (7 May–13 May 1973) UN Doc. A/CN.4/SER.A/1973/Add.1, 192, para 9.

[32] See statement of Judge Huber in the *Island of Palmas* case, R.I.A.A., Vol.II, p.829 [1949], at p.845.

namely the circumstances in which "... one State is responsible for the internationally wrongful act of another State ..."[33] The legal consequences of an internationally wrongful act are primarily twofold, namely the responsible State should cease from the wrongful conduct and secondly make full reparation for the injury as stated in Draft Arts 30 and 31. It should also be noted Draft art.41 provides that States are charged with co-operating to "... bring to an end through lawful means any serious breach within the meaning of Article 40."[34] Furthermore, "No State shall recognize as lawful a situation created by a breach within the meaning of Article 40, nor render aid or assistance in maintaining that situation."[35]

Erga omnes

While the foregoing is concerned with the obligation owed by one State to another, contemporary international law also recognises the concept of *erga omnes*—that is, obligations owed by every State to the international community as a whole. These obligations were identified by the International Court of Justice in the *Barcelona Traction* case[36] as deriving from "the outlawing of acts of aggression, and of genocide ..." and from "rules concerning the basic rights of the human person, including protection from slavery and racial discrimination."[37] Thus, by their nature, such obligations are the concern of all States and because of the importance of the rights involved all States have a legal interest in their protection. This decision prompted the International Law Commission to include Draft art.19, which distinguished between civil and criminal liability, but as noted previously this distinction was omitted in the 2001 version of the Draft Articles. What the Draft Articles recognise, discussed in the Commentary, is that there are:

---

[33] Liability will be incurred if: a) a State acts in the knowledge of the circumstances of the internationally wrongful act; and b) the act would be internationally wrongful if committed by that State.

[34] Draft art.41(1) also see discussion on *erga omnes*.

[35] Draft art.41(2). The obligations in Draft art.41(1) and (2) can be seen in operation in *The Legal Consequences of the Construction of a Wall in the Occupied Palestinian Territory* (Advisory Opinion) 2004, para.159.

[36] I.C.J. Rep. 1970 p.3.

[37] *ibid.* at p.32 at para. 34. see also *East Timor* (Portugal v Australia) case I.C.J. Rep. (1995) p.90; "Legality of the Threat or use of Nuclear Weapons" I.C.J. Rep. (1996) p.226; *Application of the Convention on the Prevention and Punishment of the Crime of Genocide (Preliminary Objections)*, I.C.J. Rep. (1996) p.595.

"... certain consequences flowing from the basic concepts of peremptory norms of general international law and obligations to the international community as a whole within the field of State responsibility. Whether or not peremptory norms of general international law and obligations to the international community as a whole are aspects of a single basic idea, there is at the very least substantial overlap between them. The examples which the International Court has given of obligations towards the international community as a whole all concern obligations which, it is generally accepted, arise under peremptory norms of general international law. Likewise the examples of peremptory norms given by the Commission in its commentary to what became article 53 of the Vienna Convention [i.e. the Vienna Convention on the Law of Treaties] involve obligations to the international community as a whole. But there is at least a difference in emphasis while peremptory norms of general international law focus on the scope and priority to be given to a certain number of fundamental obligations, the focus of obligations to the international community as a whole is essentially on the legal interest of all States in compliance— i.e., in terms of the present articles, in being entitled to invoke the responsibility of any State in breach. Consistently with the difference in their focus, it is appropriate to reflect the consequences of the two concepts in two distinct ways. First, serious breaches of obligations arising under peremptory norms of general international law can attract additional consequences, not only for the responsible State but for all other States. Secondly, all States are entitled to invoke responsibility for breaches of obligations to the international community as a whole."[38]

Draft art.40 defines the scope of the breaches covered by Ch.III and distinguishes "serious breaches of obligations under peremptory norms of general international law" from other types of breaches. The obligation breached must be derived from a peremptory norm and the breach must be serious. A breach of such an obligation is serious if it involves a gross or systematic failure by the responsible State to fulfil the obligation.[39] However, Draft art.40 does not provide any illustrative examples of peremptory norms.[40] Draft art.42 provides that the implementa-

---

[38] International Law Commission Commentaries, pp.244–245.
[39] art.40(2).
[40] See Ch.2 "Sources" for discussion of art.53 Vienna Convention on the Law of Treaties.

tion of State responsibility is the entitlement of "an injured State" and recognises a State may be responsible to a group of States including the injured State or to the international community as a whole. The latter is dealt with in Draft art.48.

Reparation

The State which has committed the internationally wrongful act is under an obligation to make full reparation for the injury caused. This is in line with the Permanent Court of International Justice decision in the *Chorzow Factory* case, namely "it is a principle of international law that the breach of an engagement involves an obligation to make reparation in an adequate form".[41] Reparation may be by way of diplomatic negotiation, which may produce an apology or an assurance that the offending breach of international law will not recur.

The object of reparation should be to wipe out, as far as possible "all the consequences of the illegal act and re-establish the situation which would, in all probability, have existed if that act had not been committed."[42] Reparation is designed to restore previous conditions and if this is not possible, to compensate for the injury itself.[43]

Reparation may be awarded through restitution in kind and if restitution is not possible, through:

> "payment of a sum corresponding to the value which a restitution in kind would bear; the award, if need be, of damages for loss sustained which would not be covered by restitution in kind or payment in place of it—such are the principles which should serve to determine the amount of compensation due for an act contrary to international law."[44]

Draft art.35 details two exceptions to the obligation to provide reparation: where it is materially impossible, and where it involves a burden out of all proportion to the benefit deriving from restitution instead of compensation. Restitution in kind

---

[41] *Chorzow Factory* case, Jurisdiction, 1927, P.C.I.J., Series A, No.9. However, note any conduct whereby the injured State has contributed to that injury will be taken into account, see Draft art.39.

[42] *Chorzow Factory (Indemnity) (Merits)* P.C.I.J.Rep., ser.A, No.17 (1928) at 47. See also Draft Arts 34 and 35.

[43] Draft art.36(1) expresses the primacy of restitution over compensation, as the latter will only apply to the extent that damage "is not made good by restitution".

[44] *ibid.*

is infrequent.[45] More frequently monetary compensation is awarded to cover the cost of the injury suffered.

The I.C.J. held in the *Case concerning the Gabcikovo-Nagyamaros Project:*

> "It is a well established rule of international law that an injured State is entitled to obtain compensation from the State which has committed an internationally wrongful act for the damage caused by it."[46]

In *Chorzow Factory (Indemnity)*,[47] the Permanent Court of International Justice held the rules of law governing reparation should be:

> "the rules of international law in force between the two States concerned, and not the law governing relations between the State which has committed a wrongful act and the individual who has suffered damage. Rights or interests of an individual the violation of which rights causes damage are always in a different plane to rights belonging to a State, which rights may also be infringed by the same act. The damage suffered by an individual is never therefore identical in kind with that which will be suffered by a State; it can only afford a convenient scale for the calculation of the reparation due to the State."[48]

Compensation is normally a matter of negotiation. There are no established principles for calculating the sum to be paid. In respect of material loss, the sum awarded is generally commensurate with the loss sustained and will take account of "loss of profits . . . as compared with other owners of similar property".[49] Draft art.36 provides that the compensation shall cover any financially assessable damage including loss of profits in so far as it is established. Draft art.36 deals only with financially assessable damage and Draft art.37 deals with non-material injury. However, while damages have been awarded for non-material loss international

[45] Restitution in kind was ordered in *Martini (Italy v Venezuela)* 2 R.I.A.A. 975, 1002 (1930), the *Temple* Case, I.C.J. Rep. 1962 p.6, and *Case concerning the Arrest Warrant of 11 April 2000 (Democratic Republic of Congo v Belgium)* 2002 I.C.J. Rep. 3, para.76.
[46] *Case concerning the Gabcikovo-Nagyamaros Project (Hungary v Slovakia)* 1997 I.C.J. Rep p.7, para.152.
[47] Above, n.42. See also Draft art.31 above, and for various forms of reparation. See Draft art.34 and Draft art.37 for reparation in the form of an apology.
[48] *ibid.* at 28.
[49] *Norwegian Shipowners Claim (Norway v U.S.)* 1 R.I.A.A. 307 at 338 (1922).

tribunals have been reluctant to grant exemplary or punitive damages:

> ". . . Counsel has failed to point us to any money award by an international arbitral tribunal where exemplary, punitive, or vindictive damages have been assessed against one sovereign nation in favor of another presenting a claim on behalf of its nationals."[50]

In the *Lusitania* case, the United States–Germany Mixed Claims Commission refused to award punitive damages. The Commission did not impose a penalty and only awarded reparation in respect of the injury suffered. However, in the *I'm Alone* case,[51] $25,000 was awarded against the United States as a "material amend in respect of the wrong suffered by Canada".

A State will be liable to another State if it, *inter alia*, breaches a treaty obligation, violates its territorial integrity, injures its diplomatic representatives, mistreats one of its nationals or causes injury to the property of one of its nationals.

TREATMENT OF ALIENS—THE TREATMENT OF NATIONALS OF OTHER STATES

If an individual allegedly sustains injury while in another State, redress may only be sought through the individual's State of nationality. (See nationality of claims rule below.) An individual cannot force a State to espouse a claim on his/her behalf. It is a matter of State discretion whether a claim is taken up and if a State does pursue a claim on behalf of an individual, it is not required to hand over any damages which may be received.[52] Nor can an individual prevent a State from exercising its rights of diplomatic protection if it (the State) feels its right to have its nationals treated properly has been violated:

> ". . . an alien . . . cannot deprive the government of his nation of its undoubted right of applying international remedies to violations of international law committed to his damage. Such government frequently has a larger interest in maintaining the principles of international law than in recovering

[50] *Lusitania (United States v Germany)* 7 R.I.A.A. 32 at 38–44 (1956), Parker J.
[51] *(Canada v United States)* 3 R.I.A.A. 1609 (1933/35); 29 A.J.I.L. 326 (1935).
[52] *Civilian War Claimants Association v The King* [1932] A.C. 14. *Cf.* Draft Article 19 Draft Articles on Diplomatic Protection 2006 proposes a "recommended practice" that the State exercising diplomatic protection "transfer to the injured person any compensation obtained for the injury from the responsible State subject to any reasonable deductions".

damage for one of its citizens in a particular case, and manifestly such citizen cannot by contract in this respect, tie the
hands of his Government."[53]

In other words, in espousing a claim on behalf of an individual, a
State is protecting a State right which must be respected, namely
that its nationals be treated in a particular manner. Once a State
has taken up a claim on behalf of an individual, the State enjoys
exclusive control over the handling and presentation of the
claim[54] which becomes one between two States:

> "it is true that the dispute was at first between a private per-
> son and a State . . . Subsequently, the Greek Government took
> up the case. The dispute then entered upon a new plane; it
> entered the domain of international law, and became a dis-
> pute between two States . . . Once a State has taken up a case
> on behalf of one of its subjects before an international tribunal,
> in the eyes of the latter the State is sole claimant."[55]

In 2006, the ILC adopted a set of Draft Articles on Diplomatic
Protection.[56] These Draft Articles represented both codification
and progressive development of existing customary international
law on diplomatic protection. Given the varied definitions of
diplomatic protection, the ILC opted for a rather strict defintion:

> "For the purposes of the present draft articles, diplomatic
> protection consists of the invocation by a State, through
> diplomatic action or other means of peaceful settlement, of
> the responsibility of another State for an injury caused by an
> internationally wrongful act of that State to a natural or legal
> person that is a national of the former State with a view to the
> implementation of such responsibility."[57]

Standard of treatment

A State is not required to admit foreign nationals. Immigration
control is a matter of national law although, e.g. in the European
Union, nationals of Member States may only be denied admission
to other Member States in specifically defined circumstances.

[53] *North American Dredging Co. (U.S./Mexican)* 4 R.I.A.A. 26 at 29 (1926).
[54] See e.g. *Administrative Decision No.V (U.S. v Germany)* 7 R.I.A.A. 119 (1924).
[55] *Mavrommatis Palestine Concessions* case, P.C.I.J.Rep., ser.A, No.2 (1924) at 12.
[56] ILC, "Report of the ILC on the work of its 58th Session" (May 1–June 9 and
July 3–August 11, 2006) (2006) UN Doc A/61/10, Ch.IV.
[57] Draft art.1, Draft Articles on Diplomatic Protection 2006.

Once non-nationals are admitted, if a State should then fail to treat them in a particular way the host State will be in breach of an international obligation. This was endorsed by the General Assembly in 1985, in the Declaration on the Human Rights of Individuals who are not Nationals of the Country in which They Live,[58] which articulates the fundamental human rights to be observed by the host State. Non-nationals are assured of certain rights, such as the right of equality within the judicial process and protection from torture, cruel or inhuman treatment they are, of course, required to observe the laws of the host State and to respect the host State's customs and traditions.

By what standard is the treatment to be gauged? There are two views, one representing that of developing "new" States and the other representing that of developed States.

The national treatment standard

Originally supported by Latin American countries during the nineteenth and early-twentieth centuries, this view is favoured today primarily by new and developing States. According to the national treatment standard, non-nationals are to be treated in the same way as nationals of the host State. Obviously, if applied consistently, this would be advantageous to non-nationals. However, international law does not regulate a State's treatment of non-nationals in all activities, for example non-nationals in the United Kingdom may not vote nor may they be admitted to public office.

The disadvantage of the national treatment standard is obvious. A State could subject a non-national to inhuman treatment and justify such treatment on the grounds that nationals could be similarly treated. Thus, international arbitration tribunals and developed western States have denied that a State can exonerate itself by pleading that nationals are treated in the same way in the event that the treatment of non-nationals falls short of the international minimum standard.[59]

International minimum standard

The international minimum standard is difficult to define. International law has not provided a definition, although an attempt at such was made in 1957 when the International Law Commission debated the Second Report on State Responsibility of its Special Rapporteur.[60] In the Report, an article which

---

[58] GA Res. 144 (XL), G.A.O.R., 49th Sess., Supp.53, p.253.
[59] Roberts Claim 4 R.I.A.A. 77 (1926). See also *Asian Agricultural Products Ltd* case (1990) 30 I.L.M. p.577.
[60] *Y.B.I.L.C.*, 1957, II, p.104.

embraced both the national minimum standard and the international minimum standard was proposed. States were to afford to a non-national the same treatment as that enjoyed by nationals but in no circumstances was such treatment "to be less than the 'fundamental human rights' recognized and defined in contemporary international instruments". However, the proposal was too far-reaching and since then the International Law Commission has concentrated its attention on the codification of general principles of responsibility.

To violate the international minimum standard, a State's treatment of foreign nationals must fall so short of established civilised behaviour "that every reasonable and impartial man would readily recognize its insufficiency".[61]

A State may incur responsibility if a non-national is physically ill-treated,[62] or if his/her property is damaged.[63] A State may also incur responsibility if a non-national suffers a maladministration of justice, for example is denied assistance of counsel[64] or denied adequate protection. Liability will only be incurred if the lack of protection has been either wilful or due to neglect.[65]

States are required to afford a higher degree of protection to internationally-protected persons[66] than to "ordinary" non-nationals.

Although international law is against the arbitrary and unjustified expulsion of non-nationals,[67] States do enjoy discretion to deport non-nationals if the presence of such non-nationals is a threat to the public interest. Article 12 of the EC Treaty[68] prohibits discrimination between the nationals of Member States on the grounds of nationality and arts 39–42 of the Treaty provide for the free movement of workers. Member States can deny the exercise of that right on the grounds of public health, public security and

---

[61] *Neer Claim* 4 R.I.A.A. 60 at 62 (1926).

[62] *Roberts Claim*, above, n.59; *Quintanilla Claim (Mexico v U.S.)* 4 R.I.A.A. 101 (1926).

[63] *Zafiro* case, above, n.20 Draft art.9, Harvard Draft Convention on the International Responsibility of States for Injuries to Aliens 1961, 55 *A.J.I.L.* 548 (1961).

[64] *Pope* case, 8 Whiteman 709.

[65] *Noyes Claim (US v Panama)*, above, n.20; *Janes Claim (U.S. v Mexico)* 4 R.I.A.A. 82 (1926).

[66] See the Convention on the Prevention and Punishment of Crimes Against Internationally Protected Persons including Diplomatic Agents 1973, 13 I.L.M. 42 (1974); Misc.19 (1975) Cmnd.6176.

[67] See art.3. 1955 European Convention on Establishment, 529 U.N.T.S. 141; U.K.T.S. 1 (1971) Cmnd.4573; Fourth Protocol of the European Convention of Human Rights 1963, Misc.6 (1964) Cmnd.2309; 58 *A.J.I.L.* 334 (1964).

[68] Consolidated version of the Treaty Establishing the European Community, O.J. 24.12.2002, C325/33.

public order. However, when deported the individuals concerned should be advised of the reasons for their deportation, save where to do so would be contrary to national security.[69]

Nationals

If a national of a State is expelled from another State, the State of nationality is obliged to receive the individual, unless he/she is willing to go to another State and that State is willing to admit him/her.

Refugees

International law does not require a State to admit asylum seekers,[70] nevertheless under the 1951 Convention Relating to the Status of Refugees[71] and the 1967 Protocol Relating to the Status of Refugees,[72] Contracting Parties undertake to accord refugees treatment no less favourable than that accorded to non-nationals generally and no individual may be expelled to territory "where his life or freedom would be questioned".[73] To fall within the ambit of the Refugee Convention, the individual must show a well-founded fear of persecution because of race, religion, nationality, membership of a particular social group or political opinion, and is outside the country of nationality and is unable or unwilling to invoke the protection of that country.[74] The Office of the United Nations High Commissioner for Refugees (UNHCR) was created in December 1950 and has responsibility for providing international protection to refugees and also to finding long-term solutions to the displacement of refugees.[75] Of particular contemporary concern to UNHCR is the displacement of civilians in their own country of origin. Globally it is estimated there are some

---

[69] Regulation No.72/194 EEC Council Directive of May 18, 1972, [1972] O.J. L121/32 (May 26, 1972).

[70] It was significant that art.14 of the United Nations Declaration of Human Rights was omitted from further international instruments. However see the European Charter of Fundamental Rights OJ 2000 C 3641.

[71] 189 U.N.T.S. 150; 39 (1954) Cmnd.9171.

[72] 606 U.N.T.S. 267; U.K.T.S. 15 (1969) Cmnd. 3906; 6 I.L.M. 78 (1967); 63 A.J.I.L. 385 (1969). Currently two-thirds of the international community have ratified either or both the Convention and the Protocol.

[73] See art.33 of the Refugee Convention.

[74] art.1A(2) of the Convention Relating to the Status of Refugees 1951.

[75] See 87 A.J.I.L. 157 (1993). The Cairo Declaration was adopted by consensus at the I.L.A. Conference in Cairo, April 20–26, 1992. See also Statute of the Office of the United Nations High Commissioner for Refugees, GA Res 5/428, annex, G.A.O.R. 5th Sess., Supp.20 p.46, UN Doc A/1775 (1950) adopted December 1950. The office came into existence on January 1, 1951.

26 million internally displaced persons. There are no specific international instruments affording them protection, however, the United Nations has produced a booklet called Guiding Principles on Internal Displacement, which contains 30 pointers for governments. It is not legally binding, however the UNHCR notes the booklet is increasingly accepted by States.

The 1993 Vienna Declaration reaffirmed the right of an individual to seek asylum from persecution in other countries and the right to be able to return home. The granting of refugee status is a matter for individual States subject to art.33(1) of the 1951 Convention.[76] The 1951 Convention was introduced to deal with a specific problem arising in Europe in the wake of the Second World War; regional organisations have promulgated refinements of the 1951 definition, for example as by the Organisation of American States,[77] the Organisation of African Unity[78] and the European Union. The European Union adopted a Joint Position on March 4, 1996, relating to the implementation of the Convention criteria for refugee status and subsequent developments have included a common asylum procedure and a uniform status valid throughout the union for persons granted asylum.[79]

International Refugee Law is not static and continues to evolve, and now addresses issues such as gender-related persecution, unaccompanied minors and the scope and meaning of "particular social group".[80]

---

[76] See art.32(1). art.32(1) will not apply if the "individual is reasonably suspected of being a security risk or having been finally convicted of a particular serious crime, constitutes a danger to the Community"—art.33(2).

[77] Definition of Refugee Status (Cartagena Declaration) OAS/SER.I/ V/II.66, doc.10, rev.1, pp.190–193, adopted by 10 Latin American states in 1986

[78] (OAU) Convention Governing the Specific Aspects of Refugee Problems in Africa, UNTS.14, 691 entered into force June 20, 1974.

[79] Communication for the Commission to the Council and the European Parliament COM (2002) 755 Final. See also Council Directive On Minimum Standards on Procedures in Member States for Granting and Withdrawing Refugee Status, 2005/85 and Council Directive, On Minimum Standards for the Qualification and Status of Third Country Nationals or Stateless Persons as Refugees or as Persons Who Otherwise Need International Protection and the Content of the Protection Granted,2004/83 27 April 2004. Other measure which have been introduced in furtherance of a common asylum policy include Council Regulation 275/2000 (Eurodac System Regulation), Council Directive 2001/55/EC (Temporary Protection Directive), Commission Regulation 343/2003/EC (Member State responsible for asylum application) Council Directive 2003/9/EC (Minimum standards for the reception of asylum seekers), Council Regulation 343/2003/EC (Dublin II Regulation). See further G. Clayton, *Textbook on Immigration and Asylum Law*, 3rd edn 2008, Oxford University Press.

Expropriation of the property of non-nationals

Expropriation is the compulsory taking of private property by the State. Initially the definition of property was said to include "all moveable and immovable property, whether tangible or intangible, including industrial, literary and artistic property, as well as rights and interests in any property"[81] but not, however, rights derived from contracts. Nevertheless, the jurisprudence of the United States–Iran Claims Tribunal has extended the definition to include contractual rights.[82]

Expropriation extends beyond the actual physical taking of property to include any action, which unreasonably interferes with "the use, enjoyment or disposal of property . . .".[83] The application of taxation and regulatory measures designed specifically to deny the effective use of private property may be referred to as "creeping", "constructive" or indirect expropriation.[84]

Expropriation, particularly in the post-colonial period, became an important issue in international law. Possibly more than any other issue, expropriation highlighted the opposing views of the capitalist developed countries, the socialist States and the "new" developing States. Capitalist developed countries require a guarantee of protection and security before investing abroad, while the latter (that is, socialist and developing States) are reluctant to allow too much foreign investment for fear of undermining control of their own resources. Both developed and developing States recognise that every State has a legitimate right to expropriate property, but while the developed States of the western tradition maintain that expropriation is only legitimate if it complies with an international minimum standard and if, in particular, it is accompanied by effective compensation, developing "new" States deny this.

The position of the capitalist developed States is represented in General Assembly Resolution 1803 on Permanent Sovereignty over Natural Resources.[85] The Resolution recognises the right of peoples and nations "to permanent sovereignty over their natural wealth and resources . . ."[86]

Paragraph 4 of the Resolution, which is regarded as reinforcing customary international law, provides:

---

[80] Further examination of these topics is outwith the scope of this text.
[81] Draft art.10(7), 1961 Harvard Draft Convention, above, n.63.
[82] See e.g. *Starrett Housing Corp. v Iran (Interlocutory Award)* 4 Iran-USCTR 122; 23 I.L.M. 1090 (1984); *Amoco International Finance Corp. v Iran* 15 Iran-USCTR 189; 82 A.J.I.L. 358 (1986).
[83] Draft art.10(3)(a), 1961 Harvard Draft Convention, above, n.63.
[84] See the *Starrett* case, above, n.82.
[85] (1962) G.A.O.R., 17th Session, Supp.17, p.15.

> "[N]ationalization, expropriation or requisitioning shall be
> based on grounds or reasons of public utility, security or the
> national interest which are recognized as overriding purely
> individual or private interests, both domestic and foreign. In
> such cases the owner shall be paid appropriate compensation
> in accordance with the rules in force in the State taking such
> measures in the exercise of its sovereignty and in accordance
> with international law."

In other words, in order to be valid, expropriation should be for
public purposes, should not be discriminatory (not specified but
implied in para.4) and should be accompanied by compensation
assessed in accordance with the rules in force in the appropriate
State *and* international law.

Public purpose

The requirement that nationalisation should be for a public purpose for it to be valid under international law was identified in
the *Certain German Interests in Polish Upper Silesia* case[87] and in
Amoco International Financial Corp. v Iran.[88] The concept of a "public purpose" whereby expropriation is lawful remains undefined
and consequently States enjoy considerable discretion in its application. In the *BP* case of 1974,[89] the British challenged Libyan
nationalisation measures on the grounds that, *inter alia*, they were
not motivated by considerations of a political nature related to the
international well-being of the taking State. In that case, the arbitrator confirmed the measures in question violated international
law, as they were made for purely extraneous political reasons.[90]
However, three years later in the *Liamco* case,[91] the arbitrator dismissed the independent public purpose requirement on the
grounds "it is the general opinion in international law that the
public utility principle is not a necessary requisite for the legality
of a nationalisation."[92] In practice, public purpose has not been
predominant in international claims, and where it has featured
it has been of secondary importance. Public purpose is a broad
concept which is not readily susceptible to objective examination.

---

[86] *ibid.*
[87] P.C.I.J. Rep., ser.A, No.7, (1929), p.22.
[88] Above, n.82.
[89] 53 I.L.R. 297 (1974).
[90] *ibid.* at 329.
[91] 20 I.L.M. 1 (1981).

Discrimination

Nationalisation,[93] which discriminates against foreigners, foreigners of a particular nationality and particular foreigners, has been regarded by developed States as being contrary to international law.[94] Discrimination is difficult to prove. There may, for example, be no comparable enterprises owned either by local nationals of other countries. Like public purpose, arguments inferring discrimination have not predominated when expropriation has been challenged, and in the *Amoco* case,[95] although acknowledged as being prohibited, an element of discrimination may be tolerated in certain circumstances, e.g. being reasonably related to the public purpose.[96]

Compensation

What has been decisive has been whether or not compensation has been paid and whether, if paid, it complies with the standard prescribed by international law. To comply with international law as represented by western developed States compensation must be "prompt, adequate and effective".[97] These terms have been used in many bilateral commercial treaties. The expression "appropriate compensation" was adopted in Resolution 1803 and has been subsequently endorsed as reflecting the standard demanded under customary international law in the *Texaco* case[98] and the *Aminoil* case.[99] "Appropriate compensation" is, according to the Tribunal in the latter case, to be assessed in the light of the circumstances peculiar to the particular case. Compensation has traditionally been considered as involving payment equivalent to the full value of the property taken, possibly with a margin allowed for future loss of profits. Payment should be made in a readily convertible currency (that is, the recipient should be in a position to use and benefit from the compensation) either before

---

[92] *ibid*. 58–59.
[93] Nationalisation is used synonymously with expropriation and requisitioning.
[94] See UK's objections in the *Anglo–Iranian Oil Co.* case I.C.J. Rep. (Pleadings) 1951 at 81; also in the *BP* case, above, n.89; US's argument in the *Liamco* case, above, n.91, also arbitrator's findings in that case.
[95] Above, n.82.
[96] *ibid*. at para.145.
[97] See e.g. Statement of US Secretary of State, Hull, in letter to Mexican Government, Harris, p.568 and *Anglo–Iranian Oil Co.* case, above, n.94 at 105
[98] 53 I.L.R. 389 (1977); 17 I.L.M. 1 (1978).
[99] *Kuwait v American Independent Oil Co.* 21 I.L.M. 976 (1982). More recently, in *Southern Pacific Properties (Middle East) Ltd v Arab Republic of Egypt* 32 I.L.M. 933 (1993), the International Centre for Settlement of Disputes held "fair" compen-

or at the time of the takeover. Deferred payment will only be
allowed if the amount to be paid is fixed promptly and provision
is made for the payment of interest.

This traditional approach has been challenged and, to some
extent, rejected by developing countries. The position of these
States is reflected particularly in art.2(c) of the 1974 Charter of
Economic Rights and Duties of States,[100] which provides "appropriate compensation should be paid by the State adopting such
measures, taking into account its relevant laws and regulations
and all circumstances, that the State considers pertinent." Article
2(c) further provides that in the event of a dispute arising over
compensation it should be decided, unless otherwise mutually
agreed, by the domestic law of the nationalising State. However,
note that the 1974 Charter has, as yet, been denied the status of
customary international law.[101]

In the *Amco Indonesia* case,[102] it was stated that compensation
should be awarded for the loss suffered (*damnum emergens*) and
expected profits (*lucrum cessans*).

It is important to distinguish between expropriation which is
lawful and unlawful. The distinction was highlighted in the
Amoco case as being necessary "since the rules applicable to the
compensation to be paid by the expropriating State differ according to the legal characterisation of the taking".[103] In accordance
with the established rules of State responsibility, unlawful expropriation should merit full restitution in kind or, alternatively, the
equivalent pecuniary value and in some instances, a payment for
loss or expected loss of profits. On the other hand, lawful expropriation would only warrant compensation reflecting the value of
the property taken at the time of takeover. However, a by-product
of the collapse of the former communist powers was that of
removing considerable ideological opposition to the payment of
compensation.[104]

Settlement of disputes

The increasing uncertainty regarding the customary international
law of expropriation has prompted bilateral treaties between
developed and developing States guaranteeing compensation in

---

sation was the standard that should be applied when assessing compensation
in a lawful expropriation.

[100] GA Res.3281 (XXIV) 14 I.L.M. 251 (1975); see also GA Res.3171 (XXVIII) 1973,
68 A.J.I.L. 381 (1974); GA Res.3201 (S-VI) Declaration on the Establishment of a
New International Economic Order 1974, 13 I.L.M. 765 (1974).
[101] See Arbitrator's finding in the *Texaco* case, above, n.98.
[102] *Amco Asia Corporation v The Republic of Indonesia* 24 I.L.M. 1022 (1985).

the event of expropriation. The United States and other developed western capital-exporting countries also operate insurance schemes for nationals engaged in foreign investment.

Frequently, disputes will be resolved by a compromise settlement, whether settlement is by straightforward negotiation between the parties or by a "lump-sum settlement" agreement. "Lump-sum settlement" agreements have found increasing favour since the late 1940s, e.g. United Kingdom–USSR Agreement on the Settlement of Mutual Financial and Property Claims. Under "lump-sum settlements", the expropriating State agrees to pay the investor State a "lump sum" in respect of all subsisting claims by nationals of the investor State. The investor State is then responsible, normally via a national claims commission (e.g. in the United Kingdom the Foreign Compensation Commission and in the United States the Foreign Claims Settlement Commission of the United States) for adjudicating upon and settling, in accordance with international law, individual claims.

In 1981, an international tribunal was established at The Hague to settle the claims of US nationals against Iran and the claims of Iranian nationals against the United States.[105]

In August 1991, the United Nations established a compensation fund to settle war claims against Iraq arising from the hostilities in the Gulf. The UN Claims Commission gave its first decision in 1996.[106]

In 1965, the Convention on the Settlement of Investment Disputes between States and Nationals of Other States[107] established the International Centre for the Settlement of Investment Disputes in Washington, DC. The Convention, through the Centre, provides for parties who agree procedures for the settlement of disputes between Contracting Parties and companies of the nationality of a Contracting Party. The procedures established by way of the International Centre for the Settlement of Investments Disputes (ICSID) have been endorsed by States as an appropriate mechanism for the settlement of investment disputes. This is reflected in the provisions of an increasing number of Bilateral Investment Agreements (BIAs).

---

[103] *Amoco International Finance Corp. v Iran*, above, n.95 at 246.

[104] See O'Brien, p.385.

[105] The Tribunal was set up under the Claims Settlement Declaration made on January 19, 1981 by the Governments of Iran and the US-see 20 I.L.M. 230 (1981).

[106] 30 I.L.M. 846 (1996), see also p.292. For further information on the UN Compensation Commission see: www.uncc.ch.

[107] U.K.T.S. 25 (1967) Cmnd.3255; 575 U.N.T.S. 159; 4 I.L.M. 532 (1965).

Breach of contract

Contracts between a State and a non-national as a rule are governed by the national law of the former and consequently seldom involve international law. A State will only therefore incur liability if it denies the foreigner concerned access to an effective domestic forum for adjudication of the alleged dispute.

A contract between a State and a non-national, however, can be "internationalised". A contract may be "internationalised" if a State legislates to abolish or repudiate its contractual obligations. The State can, by its unilateral action, place itself on a different level than the other party to the contract. In the *Norwegian Loans* Case,[108] such was the alleged effect of Norwegian legislation on the contract between Norway and French bondholders.[109] Others maintain the insertion of a clause that a concession agreement is to be governed not by the law of the State party to the agreement, but e.g. by "general principles of the law of nations" or "principles of the law of the concessionary State not inconsistent with international law", removes the contract from the municipal plane and "internationalises" it. One view, for example, is such a clause transforms the agreement into an international agreement and breaches of contract into breaches of international law.[110] Developing States in particular refute such arguments and do not accept such clauses as valid, as they deny a State its sovereign right to control its natural resources. Accordingly, the norm is that a contract between a State and a foreigner will be governed by the municipal law of the State concerned.

The Calvo Clause

The Calvo Clause, which was named after an Argentinian jurist and statesman, was frequently included in agreements between Latin American States and foreigners. Under the Calvo Clause, foreigners accepted in advance that, in the event of a dispute, they would not attempt to invoke the assistance of their national State. The Calvo Clause purported to deny a State its right of exercising diplomatic protection on behalf of one of its nationals. The validity of the Calvo Clause has been refuted by international tribunals, which have maintained that an individual is not competent to fetter his/her State in such a way, and the right of diplomatic protection and its exercise belong exclusively to the

---

[108] I.C.J. Rep. 1957 p.9.
[109] The Court did not decide on the merits of the case, but individual judges considered the internationalisation of the contract; Read J. at 87–88; Lauterpacht J. at 38.

State of nationality.[111] The requirements to exhaust local remedies still exist.[112]

Nationality of claims rule

Nationality is important in the context of State responsibility. A State may only espouse a claim against another State on behalf of one of its nationals. Draft art.3 of the Draft Articles on Diplomatic Protection 2006 provides that the State entitled to exercise diplomatic protection is the State of nationality. International law lays down no definition of nationality, as the granting of nationality is exclusively a matter of domestic law.[113] A State is free to determine for itself who are to be deemed its nationals.[114] In spite of this *prima facie* unfettered discretion, a State may have its grant of nationality challenged when it attempts to raise a claim against another State. A State's right to afford diplomatic protection may be challenged on the grounds that the link between it and its alleged national is only tenuous and not genuine. In the absence of such a link, a claimant State will be prohibited from proceeding with an international claim. The need for there to be an obvious genuine link between the claimant State and the individual concerned was emphasised in the *Nottebohm* case. In that case, Liechtenstein attempted to exercise diplomatic protection, on behalf of Nottebohm, against Guatemala. Nottebohm had become a naturalised Liechtenstein citizen after only a few weeks' residence in that State and Guatemala challenged Liechtenstein's right to espouse a claim on his behalf. The I.C.J. maintained:

" . . . a State cannot claim that the rules it has thus laid down are entitled to recognition by another State unless it has acted in conformity with this general aim of making the legal bond of nationality accord with the individual's genuine connection with the State . . ."[115]

[110] See e.g. Arbitrator in *Texaco* case, above, n.98.
[111] *North American Dredging Co. Claim* (1926), above, n.53 at 29.
[112] See below, p.222.
[113] Nationality may be acquired in a variety of ways but the two most common ways of attaining nationality are: (i) by descent from parents (*jus sanguinis*); or (ii) by birth in the territory of the State (*jus soli*). Draft art.4. Draft Articles on Diplomatic Protection 2006 states that nationality is acquired "in accordance with the law of that State, by birth, descent, naturalization, succession of States or in any other manner, not inconsistent with international law."
[114] art.1 of the 1930 Hague Convention on Certain Questions Relating to the Conflict of Nationality Laws, 179 L.N.T.S. 89; U.K.T.S. 33 (1937) Cmd.5553.
[115] *Nottebohm* case (*Second Phase*), I.C.J. Rep. 1955 p.4 at 23.

The I.C.J. characterised nationality as:

> "a legal bond having as its basis a social fact of attachment, a genuine connection of existence, interests and sentiments, together with the existence of reciprocal rights and duties. It may be said to constitute the juridical expression of the fact that the individual upon whom it is conferred, either directly by the law or as the result of an act of the authorities, is in fact more closely connected with the population of the State conferring nationality than with that of any other State."[116]

The *Nottebohm* case, endorses not only must an individual possess the claimant State's nationality, but that the nationality must be effective. The *Nottebohm* judgment extended the concept of "genuine connection", which previously had been utilised to resolve problems of dual nationality,[117] to the issue of diplomatic protection generally.

The general rule is a State will only espouse a claim on behalf of an individual if the latter is a national at the time when the injury occurs and at the time when the claim is presented.[118]

In respect of an individual possessing dual nationality, the traditional view is that a claim by one national State against another national State will not be entertained. The United Kingdom has conceded, however, that it may take up a claim against the State of nationality if the other State of nationality has treated the claimant as a UK national.[119]

In respect of claims against a third State on behalf of an individual with dual nationality, it is not altogether clear which of the national States has the right to espouse the claim. In the *Merge Claim*,[120] it was suggested only the State with which the individual had the closest connection could espouse a claim on his behalf, whereas in the *Salem* case[121] it was suggested that both States could do so and the Iran–United States Claims Tribunal spoke in terms of "dominant and effective nationality" as a basis

---

[116] *ibid.*

[117] See *Canevaro* case (Italy v Peru) 11 R.I.A.A. 397; 6 A.J.I.L. 746 (1912) Translation.

[118] See e.g. Rule I of the Rules Regarding International Claims issued by the British Foreign and Commonwealth Office 1985, (1998) 37 *I.C.L.Q.* 1006. See also Draft art.5, Draft Articles on Diplomatic Protection 2006.

[119] Rule III, *ibid.* See also Draft art.7 *ibid.*, which provides for a claim against one State by another in respect an individual who is a national of both states, where that individual is "predominantly" the national of the claimant state both at the time of injury and at the date the claim is presented.

[120] 22 I.L.R. 443.

[121] (Egypt v U.S.) 2 R.I.A.A. 1161 (1932).

for exercising jurisdiction.[122] The British attitude is that although the government of the day may take up a claim on behalf of an individual possessing dual nationality, it prefers to do so jointly with the other national State.[123] The Draft Articles on Diplomatic Protection provide that one State or two or more States jointly may exercise diplomatic protection in respect a dual national against a third State.[124]

The absence of nationality, that is statelessness, means that a State which inflicts injury against a stateless person cannot be held internationally responsible nor is any State competent to intervene on such a person's behalf.[125] An element of progressive development in the Draft Articles on Diplomatic Protection relates to stateless persons and refugees. Draft art.8 provides that States *may* exercise diplomatic protection in respect of stateless persons and refugees who, at the date of injury and the date of presentation of claim, are "lawfully and habitually resident in that State".[126]

"Genuine link" is not limited to individuals. Accordingly, "ships have the nationality of the State whose flag they are entitled to fly. There must exist a genuine link between the State and the ship."[127]

Companies and shareholders

Which State may espouse a claim on behalf of a corporation? A company has traditionally been regarded as having the nationality of "the State under the laws of which it is incorporated and in whose territory it has its registered office".[128] However, these are not the only two criteria whereby a link between a company and a State may be evidenced. For example:

> "it has been the practice of some States to give a company incorporated under their law diplomatic protection solely when it has its seat (*siège social*) or management or centre of control in their territory, or when a majority or a substantial

---

[122] Iran–United States No.A/18 (1984) 5 Iran-U.S.C.T.R. 251.

[123] Rule III, above, n.118. See also Draft Articles on Diplomatic Protection arts 5 and 6.

[124] *ibid.*, Draft art.6.

[125] *Dickson Car Wheel Company case (US v Mexico)* (1931) 4 R.I.A.A. 669, but note ILC Draft Articles on Diplomatic Protection, Draft art.7.

[126] Emphasis added.

[127] art.5 of the Geneva Convention on the High Seas 1958—see above and art.91 of the 1982 Law of the Sea Convention. See also Chicago Convention 1944, arts 12 and 18.

[128] *Barcelona Traction, Light and Power Co.* case, I.C.J. Rep. 1970 p.3 at 42.

proportion of the shares has been owned by nationals of the State concerned."[129]

The I.C.J. concluded in the *Barcelona Traction* case, with respect to "the diplomatic protection of corporate entities, no absolute test of the 'genuine connection' has found general acceptance".[130] In the *Barcelona Traction* case, the I.C.J. was confronted with the question of whether Belgium could intervene on behalf of Belgian nationals and shareholders in a company, Barcelona Traction, which was incorporated in Canada and where it maintained its registered office. The losses sustained had been as a result of measures taken by Spain, the country in which the company operated. Canada initially intervened, but subsequently withdrew and did not proceed with a claim. The Court upheld Spain's objection to Belgian intervention on the grounds that Canada's failure to act did not increase Belgium's right. According to the I.C.J.'s judgment, the State whose nationality a company possesses, even if it operates in a foreign country and is controlled by foreign shareholders, has the right to make the claim on its behalf. It was the company which had suffered the injury, but the company was not defunct and, therefore, whether or not to espouse a claim on behalf of the company remained within Canada's discretion. Regarding shareholders, the general rule is that a State may not pursue a claim on behalf of nationals who suffer injury as a consequence of a measure taken against foreign companies in which they own shares. The I.C.J. in the *Barcelona Traction* case concluded that to recognise diplomatic protection on behalf of shareholders would result in confusion, as the shares of international companies are "widely scattered and frequently change hands".[131] The I.C.J. did admit one exception to the general rule, namely if the company ceased to exist. In such circumstances, the I.C.J. recognised that the State of the shareholders' nationality could initiate a claim on behalf of the shareholders in respect of losses sustained by them as a result of the injury to the company.[132] The I.C.J.'s judgment failed to acknowledge that a State in which a company is incorporated may have little interest in pursuing a claim on its behalf. A company may be incorporated in a particular State as a matter of convenience. In that event, the State whose nationals are shareholders may indeed have considerable interest in espousing a claim.

---

[129] *ibid.*
[130] *ibid.*
[131] *ibid.* at 49.
[132] *ibid.* at 41.

In the *Case Concerning Ahmadou Sadio Diallo (Republic of Guinea v Democratic Republic of the Congo)*[133] the I.C.J. was again faced with the issue of the substitution of the State of nationality of the Company with the State of nationality of its shareholders. The Court concluded the "substitution doctrine" is not a rule of customary international law.[134] The Court did however, leave open the possibility that a more limited rule of substitution exists, allowing substitution where incorporation in the State of wrongdoing was a precondition to doing business there.[135]

The United Kingdom Rules Regarding International Claims[136] provide that where a UK national has an interest as a shareholder or otherwise in a company incorporated in another State and the company is injured by a third State, a claim will normally only be espoused by Britain in conjunction with the State in which the company is incorporated. Independent intervention will only take place exceptionally when the company concerned has ceased to exist.[137] If a State in which a company is incorporated injures the company and a UK national is a shareholder, the British Government may intervene to protect the interests of the UK national.[138] There are, therefore, two exceptions in UK practice to the Court's denial of any right to intervene on behalf of shareholders. In instances where capital in a foreign company is owned in various proportions by shareholders of several nationalities including British nationals, Britain will seldom intervene, unless those states whose nationals hold most of the capital support its representations. Draft art.44(a) of the Draft Articles provides "The responsibility of a State may not be invoked if: (a) The claim is not brought in accordance with any applicable rule relating to the nationality of claims." It also reflects an established rule of Customary International Law, namely that of exhaustion of local remedies.[139]

Draft art.9 of the Draft Articles on Diplomatic Protection states:

"For the purposes of diplomatic protection of a corporation, the State of nationality means the State under whose law the corporation was incorporated. However, when the corpora-

---

[133] *(Preliminary Objections)*, I.C.J. 2007, judgment of May 24, 2007, http://www.icj-cij.org/docket/files/103/13856.pdf?PHPSESSID=def87be91a3dfcceea7a20f1c2e5dc40
[134] *ibid.*, para.89.
[135] *Ibid.*, para.93.
[136] Above, n.112, Rule V.
[137] *ibid.*
[138] *ibid.*, Rule VI.
[139] I.L.C. Drafts Articles on State Responsibility, 1979, II *Y.B.I.L.C.*, Draft art.44(b). See also I.L.C. Draft Articles on Diplomatic Protection Draft arts 8, 9 and 10.

tion is controlled by nationals of another State or States and has no substantial business activities in the State of incorporation, and the seat of management and the financial control of the corporation are both located in another State, that State shall be regarded as the State of nationality."

As with nationality of natural persons, a State's entitlement to exercise diplomatic protection is subject to the rule of continuous nationality.[140] The Draft Articles also provide a general rule that States shall not be entitled to exercise diplomatic protection on behalf of shareholders. However, Draft art.11 provides two exceptions; first, as in the *Barcelona Traction* case, where "the corporation has ceased to exist according to the law of the State of incorporation for a reason unrelated to the injury",[141] and second, where "the corporation had, at the date of injury, the nationality of the State alleged to be responsible or causing the injury, and incorporation in that State was required as a precondition for doing business there".[142]

Exhaustion of local remedies

It is an established rule of customary international law that before diplomatic protection is afforded, or before recourse may be made to international arbitral or judicial processes, local remedies must be exhausted. The *raison d'être* of the rule is:

(a) to allow the State concerned the opportunity to afford redress within its own legal system for the alleged wrong;

(b) to reduce the number of possible international claims; and

(c) respect for the sovereignty of States.

"Local remedies" means:

"not only reference to the courts and tribunals, but also the use of the procedural facilities which municipal law makes available to litigants before such courts and tribunals. It is the

[140] Draft art.10 Draft Articles on Diplomatic Protection 2006.
[141] *ibid.*, Draft art.11(a).
[142] *ibid.*, Draft art.11(b).

whole system of legal protection, as provided by municipal law . . .".[143]

An individual must, therefore, employ "all administrative, arbitral or judicial remedies".[144] Only effective remedies which could affect the final outcome of the case need be exhausted.[145] The exhaustion of local remedies has been strictly applied, but local remedies need not be exhausted if it is evident that there is no justice to exhaust, or where it is apparent that any attempt to seek redress would be thwarted.[146] If it is apparent a UK national, in exhausting municipal remedies, has encountered prejudice or obstruction and accordingly a denial of justice, the British Government may intervene in order to seek redress on his behalf.[147] The exhaustion of local remedies is not required when the alleged wrong is a direct injury by one State against another State. The requirement to exhaust local remedies may be dispensed with by treaty, but this must be explicitly stated and not merely implied. This position generally reflects that adopted by the Draft Articles on Diplomatic Protection.[148]

STATE RESPONSIBILITY FOR THE ENVIRONMENT

Since the early 1970s, there has been increasing concern for the environment and a realisation that protection, to be effective, must be based on international co-operation. "States shall co-operate in a spirit of global partnership to conserve, protect and restore the health and integrity of the Earth's eco system."[149] The international community now focuses on preventative measures rather than on the traditional approach whereby responsibility was attributed to the State deemed to have caused the harm. The expansion of international/regional environmental norms is reflected in the focus environmental law now receives within the increasing number of academic programmes.

---

[143] *Ambatielos Arbitration* (Greece v U.K.) 12 R.I.A.A. 83 (1956); 23 I.L.R. 306 (1956).
[144] See Draft art.19, 1961 Harvard Draft Convention on International Responsibility of States for Injuries to Aliens.
[145] *Finnish Ships Arbitration* 3 R.I.A.A. 1479 (1934); *cf. El Oro Mining and Railway Co.* case (Great Britain v Mexico) 5 R.I.A.A. 191 (1931); *Interhandel* case *(Preliminary Objections)* I.C.J. Rep. 1959 6 at 26–29.
[146] *Robert E. Brown* case 6 R.I.A.A. 120, 129 (1923). See also Rule VII, above, n.118.
[147] Rule VIII, above, n.118.
[148] Draft art.14, Draft Articles on Diplomatic Protection. See further Draft art.15 for an comprehensive list of situations in which local remedies do not need to be exhausted.
[149] Principle 7 Rio Declaration (see below n.152).

The regulation of the international environment has increased dramatically in the last 40 years, and the preventative approach is reflected in a plethora of arrangements both at an international and regional level (see below). The UN in 1972 established UNEP (United Nations Environment Programme) to implement the Action Programme adopted at the Stockholm Conference that year on the Human Environment. This international "legislative" activity has been accompanied by regional developments. Initially, the international community tackled responsibility for the environment by way of customary international law and imposed certain restrictions on the enjoyment of a State's recognised right "in accordance with the Charter of the United Nations and the principles of international law, ... to exploit their own natural resources pursuant to their own environmental policies".[150] The responsibility incumbent on States under customary international law is expressed in Principle 21 as being "to ensure that activities within their jurisdiction or control do not cause damage to the environment of other States or of areas beyond the limits of national jurisdiction"[151] It is currently reiterated in Principle 2 of the Rio Declaration.[152] Article 30 of the Charter of Economic Rights and Duties of States also provides:

> "The protection, preservation and enhancement of the environment for the present and future generations is the responsibility of all States. All States shall endeavour to establish their own environmental and developmental policies in conformity with such responsibility ... All States have the responsibility to ensure that activities within their jurisdiction or control do not cause damage to the environment of other States or of areas beyond the limits of national jurisdiction. All States should co-operate in evolving international norms and regulations in the field of the environment."[153]

Article 24 of the African Charter on Human and Peoples' Rights (the Banjul Charter) 1981 heralds as a right of all people "a general satisfactory environment favourable to their development".

---

[150] Declaration on the Human Environment (Stockholm, 1972) 11 I.L.M. 1416 (1972), Principle 21.

[151] *ibid.*

[152] The Rio Declaration on the Environment was adopted on June 14, 1992, at the UN Conference on Environment and Development, Rio de Janeiro, June 3–14, 1992. It was attended by 176 States; see 31 I.L.M. 814 (1992).

[153] It may be recalled that the status of the Charter under international law is not fully established.

The extent and scope of a State's responsibility under customary international law was illustrated in two cases involving the US and Canada, namely the *Trail Smelter Arbitration*[154] and *Gut Dam Arbitration*.[155]

The *Trail Smelter Arbitration* related to damage caused in the State of Washington by sulphur dioxide emitted since 1925 from a smelter plant at Trail on the Columbian River, ten miles from the US/Canadian border on the Canadian side.

In the Tribunal's final decision in 1941, a general principle of international law was recognised, namely "a State owes at all times a duty to protect other States against injurious acts by individuals from within its jurisdiction".[156] The Tribunal concluded from decisions of the US Supreme Court relating to disputes between Member States of the Union and there existed in US law and international law a principle that:

> "[N]o State has the right to use or permit the use of its territory in such a manner as to cause injury by fumes in or to the territory of another or the properties or persons therein, when the cause is of serious consequences and the injury is established by clear and convincing evidence."

The Gut Dam, on the border between the US and Canada, raised the water levels of Lake Ontario between 1947 and 1952 and resulted in considerable damage being sustained to properties on the lakeshore. On the re-establishment of an International Arbitral Tribunal, Canada agreed to pay compensation in respect of the damage caused to the property of US citizens.

Similarly in the *Corfu Channel* case[157] it was maintained that incumbent on every State is the duty "not to allow knowingly its territory to be used for acts contrary to the rights of other States".[158]

Principle 22 of the Stockholm Declaration emphasised State co-operation in the further development of international law on liability and compensation for the victims of pollution and extra-territorial damage, while Principle 24 called upon States to act in a co-operative spirit for the protection and improvement of the

---

[154] 3 R.I.A.A. 1905.
[155] 8 I.L.M. 118 (1969).
[156] 3 R.I.A.A. 1905, at 1963.
[157] I.C.J. Rep. 1949 p.4.
[158] *ibid.* at 22. See also the I.C.J. acknowledgment a State's territorial sovereignty is restricted by obligations towards the environment. This is now part of the corpus of international law relating to the environment, as was stated in the *Nuclear Weapons* case, per Weeramantry J. See also the separate opinion of Weeramantry J. in the *Nagymaros* case.

international environment. The requirement to co-operate is a
recurring theme in contemporary international agreements.[159]

In 1992, the UN convened a Conference on Environment and
Development (UNCED) in Rio de Janeiro in response to the
growing recognition that environmental problems should be
addressed at an international level. The Conference endorsed the
concept of sustainable development[160] and introduced a number
of general principles in its Declaration on Environment and
Development (the Rio Declaration) in particular the obligation on
States to take precautionary measures (Principle 15), the polluter
pays principle (Principle 16) and environmental impact assessment (Principle 17). The Declaration also imposes obligations
upon States to notify emergencies and engage in consultation
where there is a risk of transboundary pollution. The Conference
also adopted a Programme of Action (Agenda 21), a Convention
on Biological Diversity, a Convention on Climate Change and a
Statement of Principles on Forests. Agenda 21, although not a
legally binding instrument, is regarded as a comprehensive plan
of action for the international community and combines environmental and development concerns in 40 chapters. A Commission
on Sustainable Development was created in 1992 to monitor
progress concerning the implementation of Agenda 21.[161] A
review of the progress made in the implementation of what was
agreed at Rio in 1992 was the focus of the World Summit on
Sustainable Development, held in Johannesburg, South Africa,
between August 26 and September 4, 2002. The preparatory
process for the Johannesburg summit was encouraged by the
General Assembly to "ensure a balance between economic development, social development and environmental protection as
these are interdependent and mutually reinforcing components
of sustainable development."[162] It will be some time before the
principles enunciated in the Rio Declaration and Agenda 21 are

---

[159] e.g. art.5 of the 1979 Long-Range Transboundary Air Pollution Convention;
and Vienna Convention on Early Notification of a Nuclear Accident 1986—see
below.
[160] Sustainable development can be described simply as meeting the needs of
present generations without compromising the ability of future generations
to do the same. See, the Bruntland Report of the World Commission on
Environment and Development (WCED) 1987, titled *Our Common Future*. With
the population of the earth set to double in the next 50 years, sustainable development is regarded as vital to the survival of the planet. See Ch.39 of Agenda
21 generally.
[161] UN GA Res. 47/191, December 22, 1992. Based on Ch.38 of Agenda 21 on
International Institutional Arrangements.
[162] General Assembly ten-year review of progress achieved in the implementation
of the outcome of the UN Conference on Environment and Development,
A/RES/55/199, December 20, 2000, point 4.

fully implemented. International environmental law is, however, no longer confined to the adoption of measures to regulate States' behaviour. Instead, it is increasingly concerned with implementation, environmental impact assessment and the development of effective dispute resolution techniques. The recognition by the international community of the link between the environment and development has already produced a substantial body of law and is one of the fastest-growing areas of international law in contemporary society.

In addition to the issues identified at the Rio Conference as priorities for the international community, other problem areas of concern include, *inter alia*, desertification, transboundary air pollution, global warming/depletion of the ozone layer, the transfer and disposal of hazardous waste and control of nuclear activities. Special conditions and environmental problems which some Third World countries face have been recognised by the United Nations in a Convention to Combat Desertification in those Countries Experiencing Serious Drought and/or Desertification, particularly in Africa.[163] The purpose of the Convention is to identify the factors contributing to desertification, the practical measures necessary to it and the mitigation of the effects of drought through international co-operation and partnership agreements. The problem of drought has far-reaching repercussions for economic growth, social development and poverty eradication.[164]

The 1979 Convention on Long-Range Transboundary Air Pollution and the subsequent Protocols[165] tackle the problem of transboundary air pollution and Contracting Parties agree to "endeavour to limit and, as far as possible, gradually reduce and prevent air pollution including long-range transboundary air pollution". The Convention defines transboundary air pollution as that which originates:

> "within the area under the national jurisdiction of one State and which has adverse effects in the area under the jurisdiction of another State at such a distance that it is not generally possible to distinguish the contribution of individual emission sources or groups of sources."

The Convention does not address the issue of liability for pollu-

---

[163] 33 I.L.M. 1328 (1994). Entered into force December 26, 1996.
[164] See Ch.12 of Agenda 21 generally.
[165] All eight Protocols are in force. The last entering into force on May 17, 2005, for further information on the Protocols, see http://www.unece.org/env/lrtap/status/lrtap_s.htm.

tion across State frontiers, but rather emphasises research and the exchange of information.[166]

The Protocols have extended the Convention in a variety of ways for example the 1985 Protocol required Contracting Parties to reduce, by 1993 at the latest, sulphur emissions by at least 30 per cent, while the 1988 Protocol required a reduction, by the end of 1994, in the annual emission of nitrate oxides or their transboundary fluxes to a minimum of the 1987 level. The 1994 Protocol establishes an implementation committee to "review the implementation of the present protocol and compliance by the parties with their obligations"[167] as well as requiring further reduction of sulphur emissions. The 1999 Protocol is designed to abate acidification, eutrophication and ground-level ozone.

In a further effort to minimise transboundary pollution, the UN adopted a Convention on Environmental Impact Assessment in 1991.[168] The obligation incumbent on Contracting Parties is to "either individually or jointly, take all appropriate and effective measures to prevent, reduce and control significant adverse transboundary environmental impact from proposed activities".[169]

Throughout the 1980s, the issue of global warming and the depletion of the ozone layer was widely recognised by governments and individuals alike as requiring urgent attention. The need to protect the ozone layer precipitated an international response, which culminated in the 1985 Vienna Convention for the Protection of the Ozone Layer,[170] the 1987 Montreal Protocol on Substances that Deplete the Ozone Layer,[171] and the 1989 Helsinki Declaration on the Protection of the Ozone Layer.[172] The 1985 Vienna Convention entered into force in 1988 and essentially provides for co-operation, scientific research and the exchange of information, while the 1987 Protocol, as amended in 1990, entered into force in 1990 and stipulates maximum consumption levels of chlorofluorocarbons and imposes a freeze on the use of halons.

---

[166] 18 I.L.M. 1442 (1979).

[167] art.7.

[168] 30 I.L.M. 800 (1991).

[169] *ibid.*, art.2.1. There have been two amendments to the Convention (2001 and 2004) which once in force will extend the potential membership (to States other then members of the UN Economic Commission for Europe, (2001)) as well as extending the scope of activities (2004).

[170] 26 I.L.M. 1516 (1987).

[171] *ibid.* at 1541. The 1987 Montreal Protocol was amended at the Fourth Meeting of the Parties to the Protocol at Copenhagen in 1992. Besides shortening the deadlines for already scheduled substances, the adjustments also provided for new rules on other substances. See UN: Montreal Protocol on Substances that Deplete the Ozone Layer—Adjustments and Amendments, Copenhagen, November 23–25, 1992 32 I.L.M. 874 (1993).

[172] 28 I.L.M. 1335 (1989).

However, the 1989 Helsinki Declaration required a phasing out of CFCs by the year 2000 and, as soon as practical, other ozone-harming materials. The most notable international measures regarding global warming are the Hague Declaration on the Environment 1989,[173] calling for the establishment of an international body exclusively dedicated to the consideration of such issues, and the Framework Convention on Climate Change 1992.[174] The primary objective of the Framework Convention was to stabilise greenhouse gas concentrations in the atmosphere while recognising some climate change was inevitable. Although the Framework Convention did not impose binding provisions on the reduction of emissions, States are required to adopt national measures to limit the emission of greenhouse gases. These measures are then to be reviewed at an international Conference by all parties.[175] The Kyoto Protocol to the Convention was adopted on December 10, 1997, amended by the Marrakesh Accords and Declaration in 2001[176] and entered into force on February 16, 2005. Under the Kyoto Protocol, developed States are required to limit or reduce their greenhouse gas emissions according to legally-binding, individual targets which differ for developed and developing countries. The UN Convention on Biological Diversity was negotiated under the auspices of UNCED[177] and was designed to protect the planet's biodiversity by promoting its sustainable use (art.2). The Convention imposes a number of obligations upon States, including national monitoring of biological diversity, national *in situ* and *ex situ* conservation measures, environmental impact assessments and national reports, from countries concerned, on the steps they have taken to implement the Convention. It prescribes a 2010 target for the "significant reduction of the current rate of biodiversity loss at the global, regional and national level as a contribution to poverty alleviation and to the benefit of all life on earth".[178]

A number of international measures regulate the transfer and dumping of hazardous waste,[179] e.g. the 1989 Basle Convention on the Control of Transboundary Movements of Hazardous Wastes

[173] *ibid.* 1308 (1989).
[174] The Convention was signed by 155 States and entered into force on March 24, 1994. It was the first international environmental agreement to be negotiated by almost all of the international community. 31 I.L.M. 849 (1992).
[175] art.7 of the Convention establishes the Conference of the Parties as the body responsible for monitoring the implementation of the Convention and of taking any necessary decisions to ensure implementation is effected.
[176] FCCC/CP/2001/13, January 21, 2002.
[177] 31 I.L.M. 818 (1992) entered into force on December 29, 1993.
[178] http://www.biodiv.org/2010–target/default.asp.
[179] For those relating to the protection of the marine environment, see Ch.7 above.

and Their Disposal[180] controls and in certain circumstances pro-
hibits the transfer of such material between Contracting Parties. A
Protocol to the Basle Convention was adopted on December 10,
1999, namely the Basle Protocol on Liability and Compensation for
Damage Resulting from Transboundary Movements of Hazardous
Waste and Their Disposal.[181]

In 1992, the UN adopted a Convention on the Transboundary
Effects of Industrial Accidents.[182] The Convention applies to the
prevention of and response to industrial accidents capable of
causing transboundary effects, including the effects of such accidents caused by natural disasters. An industrial accident is
defined as an event resulting from an uncontrolled development
in the course of any activity involving hazardous substances
(art.1(a)) either in an installation (art.1(a)(i)) or during transportation (art.1(a)(ii)). The Convention also sought to promote international co-operation concerning mutual assistance, research and
development, exchange of information and exchange of technology in the area of industrial accidents. It does not apply to, *inter
alia*, nuclear accidents or oil spillages.[183]

International watercourses and their use, the protection of
ecosystems and the marine environment[184] were the subject of
Draft Articles[185] produced by the International Law Commission
in 1994. These Draft Articles culminated in the 1997[186] Convention
on the Law of Non-navigational Uses of International
Watercourses. A Convention on the Protection and Use of
Transboundary Watercourses and Lakes was adopted in 1992
under the auspices of the UN Economic Commission for
Europe.[187] The 1992 Convention codifies regional rules concerning the protection and use of watercourses and contributes to the
progressive development of the law relating to the conservation
and restoration of ecosystems and pollution control, e.g. the polluter pays principle. The International Law Commission, on
August 5, 2008, adopted draft articles for an international framework convention on transboundary aquifers. The Draft Articles
emphasise the principle of equitable and reasonable utilisation as
well as the obligation not to cause significant harm. It further

---

[180] 28 I.L.M. 649 (1989).
[181] This Protocol is not yet in force and will enter into force on the ratification of
20 parties.
[182] Adopted March 17, 1992, in Helsinki, 31 I.L.M. 1330 (1992).
[183] See art.2 generally.
[184] See Pts II and IV of the Draft Articles.
[185] For a commentary of these Draft Articles, see Reports of the Commission in II
Yearbook of the I.L.C. (1993) and (1994).
[186] Approved by a General Assembly Resolution, GA Res.51/229, May 21, (1997).
[187] 31 I.L.M. (1992) 1312.

emphasises the need to cooperate. The International Law
Commission has recommended that a General Assembly
Resolution be adopted in support of the Draft Articles and that a
negotiating conference should possibly be considered.

Nuclear weapons and the environment

Fears of radioactive fall-out prompted the 1963 Treaty Banning
Nuclear Weapons Tests in Outer Space and Under Water.[188]
Article 1(1)(b) of the Treaty forbids testing "in any . . . environment if such explosion causes radioactive debris to be present
outside the territorial limits of the State under whose jurisdiction
or control such explosion is conducted".[189]

Australia in the *Nuclear Tests* cases[190] advanced the argument
that there existed a rule of customary international law prohibiting atmospheric nuclear testing and the prohibition was
expressed in absolute terms, thus constituting an obligation *erga
omnes*—an obligation owed to the international community as a
whole and not just to one State.[191] The I.C.J. declared, in 1996, that
the threat or use of nuclear weapons is "contrary to the rules of
international law applicable in armed conflict"[192] and there is
now a customary obligation upon States to negotiate in good faith
for nuclear disarmament.[193]

The 1986 Chernobyl incident highlighted the inadequacies of
the international nuclear safety regime and brought an almost
immediate international response in the form of the Vienna
Convention on Early Notification of a Nuclear Accident[194] and the
Convention on Assistance in the Case of a Nuclear Accident or
Radiological Emergency.[195]

The Convention on Nuclear Safety was opened for signature by
the General Conference of the International Atomic Energy
Agency (IAEA) in Vienna, 1994.[196] The Convention does not

---

[188] 480 U.N.T.S. 43; U.K.T.S. 3 (1964) Cmnd.2245.
[189] Discussed further in Ch.7. See also Ch.11—The Use of Force.
[190] I.C.J. Rep. 1973, Pleadings, at 333–336.
[191] The I.C.J., on the basis of France's undertakings to refrain from any further
testing, declined to give a ruling on the claims presented—see I.C.J. Rep. 1974
253.
[192] 35 I.L.M. 809 (1996). This was in response to a request from the GA. The I.C.J.
in 1993 was asked by WHO to give an advisory opinion concerning the legality of the use of nuclear weapons in armed conflict on the grounds that the
request as submitted by WHO "did not relate to a question within the scope of
[the] activities of that Organisation."
[193] ibid. See Declaration of President Bedjaoui. See also Ch.11 for further discussions on nuclear weapons.
[194] 25 I.L.M. 1370 (1986).
[195] *Ibid,*. at 1377.

establish an internationally binding regime and was originally intended as a framework Convention introducing a system of accountability whereby States are required to take appropriate measures in order to implement their obligations under the Convention. Responsibility for nuclear safety rests with the State having jurisdiction over a nuclear installation, e.g. a nuclear power plant.

The conduct of hostilities does not relieve States of their responsibilities to the environment. The 1977 Convention on the Prohibition of Military or Any Other Hostile Use of Environmental Modification Techniques[197] and Protocol 1 of the 1980 Conventional Weapons Treaty[198] prohibits modes of warfare having a severe and long-term effect on the environment and requires respect to be shown for the natural environment and its protection from severe widespread and lasting damage. In 1993, the UN adopted a Convention on the Applicability of the Development, Production, Stockpiling and Use of Chemical Weapons and on their Destruction, the purpose of the Convention being to prohibit and eliminate all chemical weapons[199] and para.39.6(a) of Agenda 21 also highlights this issue by calling on States to adopt measures which address the problem of large-scale destruction of the environment during international armed conflict.[200] The Prohibition of the Use, Stockpiling, Production and Transfer of Anti-personnel Mines and Their Destruction was adopted in Ottawa 1997.

International liability for the injurious consequences of acts not prohibited by international law

Akin to responsibility, but not identical to it, is the possible liability of States for the injurious consequences of acts which are not prohibited by international law. The essence of the distinction between responsibility and liability is that the prerequisite to the former is an act breaching international law, while the latter is concerned with harmful effects of an activity which is not per se a violation of international law. The International Law Commission has had this matter on its agenda since 1978 and much of its work has been focused on such liability for harm to the environment. At the 53rd Session, 2001, the International Law Commission adopted Draft Articles on the Prevention of

---

[196] 33 I.L.M. 1514 (1994).
[197] 16 I.L.M. 88 (1977).
[198] 19 I.L.M. 1529 (1980).
[199] Adopted in Paris, January 13, 1993, 32 I.L.M. 800 (1993).
[200] UN GA Res.47/191, December 22, 1992.

Transboundary Harm from Hazardous Activities. The activities to which the Articles apply are those "not prohibited by international law which involve a risk of causing significant transboundary harm through their physical consequences."[201] These Articles only apply to instances where there is risk of significant harm arising in the territory of a State other than the State in which the activity is undertaken. The Commentaries to the Draft Articles provide valuable insight into the interpretation of the terms used within the Convention, e.g. the Commentary highlights:

> ". . . that the element of 'risk' is concerned with future possibilities and thereby implies some element of assessment or appreciation of risk. The notion of risk is thus to be taken objectively as denoting an appreciation of possible harm resulting from an activity which a properly informed observer had or ought to have had."[202]

States remain reluctant to pursue claims against other States for environmental damage despite there being a solid legal basis for such an action, e.g. the Chernobyl incident in 1986. International Conventions that have sought to address this issue have tended to focus on liability for oil pollution.

International environmental law continues to be a changing paradigm. The Stockholm Conference drew the world's attention to the environment and the Rio Summit recognised that contemporary environmental problems stem from underdevelopment, hence the attention now given to the concept of "sustainable development". The concept of "sustainable development" is one which is increasingly interwoven in discussions of human rights and the term is frequently being debated within corporate social responsibility.[203] This shift in approach is evident from recent international Conventions and other legal instruments. The international community has also recognised the particular problems that developing countries face when adopting international standards for regulation of the environment, and some Third World countries have received preferential treatment in international Conventions.

---

[201] Draft art.1.
[202] Commentaries to the Draft Articles on Prevention of Transboundary Harm from Hazardous Activities, p.385, Report of the International Law Commission on the work of its fifty-third session, Official Records of the General Assembly, 56th session, Supplement No.10 (A/56/10), Ch.V.E.2.
[203] HM Government Securing the Future, the UK Government Sustainable Development Strategy, March 7, 2005, Cm.6467.

International environmental issues are now recognised as requiring international co-operation seeking prevention. This is necessary if the human environment of succeeding generations is to be at least no worse than that which currently exists.

9. HUMAN RIGHTS

WHAT ARE HUMAN RIGHTS?

"All human rights are universal, indivisible and inter-dependent and interrelated."[1]

Human rights are difficult to define, notwithstanding that the term is used extensively and frequently. Generally, human rights are regarded as those fundamental and inalienable rights which are essential for life as a human being. There is, however, an absence of consensus as to what these rights are, and frequently it is easier to identify what it is human rights are intended to achieve rather than what they are, i.e. protection of the individual from an abuse of state authority. Human rights have escaped a universally acceptable definition, presenting a problem to international regulation. Human rights more than any other issue highlight the distinction between universalism and cultural relativism. Universalism reflects the position endorsed by the UN World Conference on Human Rights in June 1993 (The Vienna

---

[1] Pt I, para.5 of the Vienna Declaration and Programme of Action, adopted following the UN World Conference on Human Rights, Vienna, June 1993.

Conference). The relativist theory maintains human rights differ from State to State fashioned by a State's values, cultural and religious traditions. Adherents to the relativist theory frequently criticise international human rights instruments as simply rein-forcing western concepts and values in the guise of universal rights. At its simplest, the difference between the universality approach and that of the relativist is the emphasis on the individual. The emphasis in universalism is on the individual, whereas relativists place the emphasis on the State. Relativists accept the rights pertaining to individuals but emphasise that individuals are defined in terms of their relations with others and as a part of society. As with all theories there are varying degrees of obser-vance. At its strictest cultural relativists maintain human rights are inapplicable to non-western societies whereas others accept human rights are universal but that differences in society should be reflected within international human rights instruments. The debate between universalism and cultural relativism has increased in intensity with the development of human rights and the "chipping away" at State sovereignty and domestic jurisdiction.

Cultural diversity is not denied and universalism and cultural diversity are not mutually exclusive. The 1993 Vienna Conference concluded:

> "While the significance of national and regional particulari-ties and various historical, cultural and religious back-grounds must be borne in mind, it is the duty of States, regardless, of their political, economic and cultural systems, to promote and protect all human rights and fundamental freedoms."

An international instrument which highlights sensitivity to cul-tural diversity is the UN Convention on the Rights of the Child.[2] Article 20 para.3 identifies Kafala, in Islamic law, as an alterna-tive care system along side foster care and adoption, thereby acknowledging that adoption is not recognised within every society.

Traditionally human rights have been sub-divided into three classifications: "first, second and third generation" rights. According to this classification "first generation" rights are those which may be characterised as civil and political rights; eco-nomic, social and cultural rights, as "second generation" and group rights as "third generation" or "solidarity" human rights.

---

[2] 1989 28 I.L.M. 1448.

The distinguishing feature of the latter being the particular focus on collective rights as opposed to the emphasis on individual rights of the first and second generation classifications. The right to development and the right to self-determination are two principal examples of "third generation" rights. However, the right to peace and the right to a healthy environment are often also included in this category. The Vienna Conference affirmed the right to development as a fundamental human right. This was endorsed by the then UN Secretary-General, Boutros Boutros Ghali, who pledged his personal commitment in his "Agenda for Development",[3] which has since been reaffirmed in the Millennium Development Goals.[4] The concept of "third generation" rights originated in the 1970s and remains controversial, with the primary protagonists being the developing States. The definition and enforcement of third generation rights has given rise to considerable academic debate[5] with, for example, a denial of such rights as human rights to their acceptance as a subcategory of human rights. The classification of human rights by generations is highly contested as it perpetrates a difference between rights, which should be avoided. For instance, the classification of rights even as political, civil, economic, social and cultural has prompted debate, and a recurring theme has been the normative relationship between the various suggested categories of rights as to whether both categories merit characterisation as rights proper. One view is that civil and political rights alone merit the term human rights, whereas social, economic and cultural rights are only aspirations. An alternative argument is that social, economic and cultural rights are rights proper as they alone are vehicles of social change, whereas civil and political rights only maintain the *status quo*. A further distinction frequently made is that civil and political rights only require a State to abstain from doing something whereas economic, social and cultural rights demand positive action. However, if a right is a

---

[3] Report of the Secretary General A/48/935, May 6, 1995. In response to the Secretary General's Agenda, the General Assembly adopted a resolution, which created an *ad hoc* open-ended working group with the specific purpose of "elaborating further an action-oriented comprehensive agenda for development." A/Res/49/126, January 20, 1995.

[4] The Millennium Development Goals were drawn up in 2000 as a result of world leaders committing their nations to a new global partnership to reduce extreme poverty and setting out a series of time-bound targets—with a deadline of 2015. See Millennium Development Goals Programme Report 2008, found at: http://www.un.org/millenniumgoals/2008highlevel/pdf/newsroom/mdg%20reports/MDG_Report_2008_ENGLISH.pdf.

[5] See Harris for further discussion of the position of Sieghart and Crawford, p.770–772.

right it remains a right, irrespective of how it is to be achieved.
Such a distinction further fails to recognise that all rights involve
a cost/responsibility. It is erroneous to argue that civil and political rights do not involve a cost whereas economic, social and cultural rights do. For instance, the abolition of the death penalty is
an example in point. Not only is there the cost of maintaining
high security prisons, there is also the cost of educating prison
personnel. Notwithstanding the foregoing, any distinction
between civil and political rights and economic, social and cultural rights is at odds with the position of the Committee on
Economic Social and Cultural Rights and in particular General
Comment No.2, where it is stated ". . . efforts to promote one set
of rights should also take full account of the other. The United
Nations agencies involved in the promotion of economic, social
and cultural rights should do their utmost to ensure that their
activities are fully consistent with the enjoyment of civil and
political rights."[6] In other words, the civil and political rights and
economic, social and cultural rights are indivisible and interdependent. However, it is true that different conditions prevail and
different priorities in respect of human rights are inevitable—
inevitable because the world's resources are not perfectly distributed. States have and will have different priorities. Societies at
different stages in their development will emphasise the realisation of certain rights as being more important than others.
However, in light of this certain rights still remain core, inherent
in all human beings because of their humanity and transcending
all boundaries—geographical, historical, cultural, religious, political and economic. These core rights would be those from which
no derogation is allowed even in times of public emergency.[7]

However the term "human rights" is defined, the issue of
human rights is high on many agendas, there is an increasing
plethora of international instruments guaranteeing wide-ranging
rights and the provisions of these instruments have ramifications
far beyond the political arena. The challenges posed by globalisation for the promotion and protection of human rights were
assumed as general goals for the United Nations in the last
decade of the twentieth century. Former Secretary-General, Kofi
Annan, in his Millennium Report[8] called for the international
community to adopt as global challenges the distribution of the
benefits of globalisation and the organisation of the opportunities

---

[6] February 2, 1990, para.6. See HRI/GEN/1/Rev.7 (ESC) May 12, 2004.
[7] It is suggested these core rights can be identified in art.4 para.2 of the
    International Covenant on Civil and Political Rights, see below.
[8] "We the Peoples: The role of the UN In the 21st Century" UN Doc. A/54/2000,
    March 27, 2000.

it offers to the service of the individual.[9] This brings on to the international stage actors other than States and international organisations with the responsibility for the protection of human rights. Such actors include financial and economic institutions, the private sector and civil society.[10] Human rights are now firmly established in the vocabulary of international business, with an increasing number of businesses being called upon to demonstrate corporate social accountability.

This is not to say that businesses have become altruistic and are now invested with philanthropy. The truth lies in greater availability and transparency of corporation documents, a greater accessibility of shareholders who can be, and frequently are, the target of pressure groups, and intense media exposure. Expansion in the marketplace demands global competitiveness, of which social accountability is a critical dimension.[11]

In addition to definition, a major contributing difficulty has been that many States regard human rights as falling within domestic jurisdiction and, therefore, not a matter to be tackled by international law. In other words, treatment of one's own nationals should not, according to those States, be the focus of external review. The international law position is that severe violations of human rights can no longer fall within the exclusive jurisdiction of States.[12] There is an acknowledgment that under international human rights there are four principal duties on States, *viz* to respect, protect, promote and fulfil human rights. Respecting rights requires that a State does not breach human rights either through actions or omissions and that the State addresses any harm if a violation does occur. The promotion of rights involves raising awareness so as to inform, publicise and create a human rights culture. Fulfilling rights refers to the provision of resources so as to facilitate the realisation of rights, frequently this may be done progressively. Protection is now frequently interpreted so as to protect individuals within a State's jurisdiction from human rights breaches perpetrated by non-State actors. However, for the State to incur responsibility there must be evidence of some act or omission by the State demonstrating failure to exercise due diligence in fulfilling the duty to protect.

---

[9] *ibid.*

[10] *ibid.*, p.46 or see Resolution of the Human Rights Commission Globalisation and its Consequences for the Effective Enjoyment of Human Rights 2002/28, April 22, 2002.

[11] See guidelines for Cooperation between the United Nations and the Business Community, issued by the Secretary-General of the UN, July 17, 2000.

[12] See e.g. discussion of art.2(7) at p.319.

Human rights law is a subject of contemporary international law and the efforts to regulate human rights at an international level only gained momentum after World War II. It should be noted that human rights is not a static concept, as was highlighted by the European Court of Human Rights in the decision of *Selmouni*, regarding the characterisation of treatment as torture, which previously would have escaped such a label.[13] The importance of human rights on the political agenda is reflected in State practice, e.g. the Foreign and Commonwealth Office of the UK Government has, since 1998, published an annual report.

Rights of the individual recognised by international law

Pre-1945

Minority groups, that is those people of a different race, religion or language from the majority group within a State, came to be guaranteed certain rights, such as equality of treatment, by way of minority treaties, e.g. those concluded in Albania, Finland and Poland. Nevertheless, minority treaties were not renewed after the Second World War. Freedom from slavery has been recognised under customary international law since 1815 and was in international Conventions, such as the 1926 Slavery Convention[14] and the 1956 Supplementary Convention on the Abolition of Slavery, the Slave Trade and Institutions and Practices Similar to Slavery.[15] Trafficking women and children was similarly prohibited by Convention,[16] but with the exception of such isolated *ad hoc* intervention, there was no attempt to regulate human rights at an international level until after 1945. Prior to the Second World War, minority groups and foreign nationals were in a privileged position *vis-à-vis* majority groups and nationals of the host State. They were recognised as deserving at least a minimum standard of treatment, whereas such a guarantee was not afforded to the host State's nationals.

Post-1945

The signing of the United Nations Charter marked the formal realisation that human rights as a matter for international concern. One of the purposes for which the United Nations was founded was "to achieve international co-operation . . . in promoting and

---

[13] *Selmouni v France*, European Court of Human Rights, 25803/94, July 28, 1999.
[14] 60 L.N.T.S. 253; U.K.T.S. 16 (1927) Cmd.2910.
[15] 266 U.N.T.S. 3; U.K.T.S. 59 (1957) Cmnd.257.
[16] e.g. International Convention for the Suppression of Traffic in Women and Children, 60 U.N.T.S. 416; U.K.T.S. 26 (1923) Cmd.1986; the 1947 Protocol 53 U.N.T.S. 13.

encouraging respect for human rights and for fundamental freedoms for all without distinction as to race, sex, language or religion,"[17] Articles 55 and 56 charge the United Nations and Member States with achieving, *inter alia*, "universal respect for, and observance of, human rights and fundamental freedoms for all without distinction as to race, sex, language and religion." The language of the Charter is vague and although Members pledged themselves to the realisation of human rights, they were not required to do so within a particular time period. The UN Charter acknowledges certain benefits which individuals should enjoy, however it does not confer rights upon them.[18]

The protection of human rights in contemporary international law, including the conferring of rights and the provision of the machinery whereby rights, if infringed, may be enforced has been tackled at both an international and regional level. (This chapter deals only with international efforts.)

UNITED NATIONS

One of the initial resolutions adopted by the UN General Assembly was the Universal Declaration of Human Rights,[19] adopted on December 10, 1948. The Declaration spells out a series of political, civil, economic, social and cultural rights. As a resolution it is not, of course, legally binding. It was never intended to be, but rather, in the words of the United States representative to the General Assembly and Chairman of the United Nations Commission on Human Rights during the drafting of the Declaration, Mrs Eleanor Roosevelt, was to act as a "common standard of achievement for all peoples of all nations." The Declaration has been tacitly accepted by all Member States and has served as the blueprint for the constitutions of many newly-independent States. It is arguable that many, if not all, the rights and freedoms enunciated in the Charter have become accepted as customary international law. One right that is not is the right contained in art.14, namely the right to seek and to enjoy in other countries asylum from persecution.[20] The rights spelt out in the Universal Declaration are diverse and include, *inter alia*, the right to life, liberty and security of the person; freedom from slavery or

---

[17] art.1(3) of the UN Charter.
[18] See *Sei Fujii v California* (1952) 19 I.L.R. 312; and *Filartiga v Pena-Irala* 630 F (2d) 876 (1980); 19 I.L.M. 966 (1980).
[19] GA Res.217 (III), G.A.O.R., 3rd Session, Pt I, Resolutions, p.71. December 10 is celebrated annually as Human Rights Day.
[20] However, States are under an obligation not to return an individual to a country in which the individual's life or freedom would be threatened. See art.33 of the UN 1951 Convention Relating to the Status of Refugees.

servitude; freedom from torture or cruel, inhuman or degrading treatment or punishment; recognition as a person before the law; the right to nationality; the right to own property; freedom of thought, conscience and religion; the right to participate in government; the right to social security; the right to work and the right to education. The rights and freedoms are to be enjoyed without "distinction of any kind, such as race, color, sex, language, religion, political or other opinion, national or social origin, property, birth or other status"[21] and are only to be curtailed by:

> "such limitations as are determined by law solely for the purposes of securing due recognition and respect for the rights and freedoms of others and of meeting the just requirements of morality, public order and the general welfare in a democratic society."[22]

The rights and freedoms set out in the Universal Declaration have been articulated more precisely in two separate international Covenants; the Covenant on Civil and Political Rights 1966,[23] which entered into force in March 1976; and the Covenant on Economic, Social and Cultural Rights 1966,[24] which entered into force in January 1976.[25] Moreover, a General Assembly Resolution was adopted in 1985 regarding the human rights of individuals who are not nationals of the country in which they live.[26]

Under the Covenant on Civil and Political Rights, Contracting Parties undertake "to respect and to ensure to all individuals within its territory and subject to its jurisdiction the rights recognised in the present Covenant".[27] Whereas the Covenant on Economic, Social and Cultural Rights requires a Contracting Party "to take steps . . . to the maximum of its available resources, with a view to achieving progressively the full realisation of the rights recognised in the present Covenant."[28]

An initial difference between the two Covenants is the obligations assumed by a State under the Covenant on Civil and Political Rights where the rights are required to be implemented immediately upon ratification of the Covenant by a State, while

---

[21] art.2.
[22] art.29(2).
[23] U.K.T.S. 6 (1977) Cmnd.6702; 6 I.L.M. 368 (1967).
[24] U.K.T.S. 6 (1977) Cmnd.6702; 6 I.L.M. 360 (1967).
[25] The UK is a party to both.
[26] GA Res.144 (XL), G.A.O.R., 49th Session, Supp.53, p.253; see also p.205 above.
[27] ICCPR art.2(1).
[28] ICESCR art.2(1).

the Covenant on Economic, Social and Cultural Rights provides that the realisation of the rights it recognises may be achieved progressively. However, note the view of the Committee on Economic, Social and Cultural Rights in General Comment No.3:[29]

> "The concept of progressive realization constitutes a recognition of the fact that full realization of all economic, social and cultural rights will generally not be able to be achieved in a short period of time. In this sense the obligation differs significantly from that contained in article 2 of the International Covenant on Civil and Political Rights which embodies an immediate obligation to respect and ensure all of the relevant rights. Nevertheless, the fact that realization over time, or in other words progressively, is foreseen under the Covenant should not be misinterpreted as depriving the obligation of all meaningful content. It is on the one hand a necessary flexibility device, reflecting the realities of the real world and the difficulties involved for any country in ensuring full realisation of economic, social and cultural rights. On the other hand, the phrase must be read in the light of the overall objective, indeed the *raison d'être*, of the Covenant, which is to establish clear obligations for States parties in respect of the full realisation of the rights in question. It thus imposes an obligation to move as expeditiously and effectively as possible towards that goal. Moreover, any deliberately retrogressive measures in that regard would require the most careful consideration and would need to be fully justified by reference to the totality of the rights provided for in the Covenant and in the context of the full use of the maximum available resources."

The three UN instruments mentioned above: the Universal Declaration of Human Rights, the Covenant on Civil and Political Rights and the Covenant on Economic, Social and Cultural Rights, constitute what is referred to as the International Bill of Rights. These instruments have been complemented by other Conventions that aim to protect specific rights of groups of people, as will be seen below.

Even if these sets of rights appear to have developed independently of each other, human rights remain indivisible. The 1993 Vienna Conference, convened to further the protection and

---

[29] The nature of States parties' obligations (art.2, para.1): 14/12/90. CESCR General Comment 3.

promotion of human rights in the international community,[30] and established that "all human rights are universal, indivisible, interdependent and interrelated."

This Conference provided an opportunity for an extensive analysis of the international human rights system and the machinery used to afford such protection. The Vienna Conference culminated in a Declaration on Human Rights and the adoption of an Action Programme,[31] which identified particularly vulnerable groups of individuals as being women, minorities, children, refugees, indigenous people, prisoners and persons with disabilities. The Action Programme emphasised the need for frequent review and appraisal of the measures taken by the international community to ensure the rights of these groups are adequately protected.[32] The Vienna Declaration and the Programme of Action were reviewed in 1998.[33] The conclusion reached was that implementation of human rights throughout the world remains inconsistent. Nonetheless, the end of apartheid in South Africa and the emergence of governments in Central and Eastern Europe symbolise advances made towards "making human rights a reality".[34] On the other hand, national laws are still in force and legislation still adopted which "discriminate against women, fails to recognise economic, social and cultural rights and does not adequately protect individuals in proceedings".[35] Challenges to human rights realisation have continued to arise particularly in the wake of "9/11" and post-conflict situations. However, these are being addressed by way of such instruments as Resolution 1325[36] whereby the UN Security Council unanimously adopted the first resolution specifically to address the impact of war on women, and women's contributions to conflict resolution and sustainable peace.

---

[30] The conference marked the 45th anniversary of the Declaration of Human Rights. See 32 I.L.M. 1661 (1993).

[31] Adopted by the Conference on June 25, 1993 by 171 representatives.

[32] For the relevant international instruments protecting the rights set out in the Vienna Declaration, see below, p.254.

[33] Pt II(F), para.100.

[34] Note by the UN Secretary-General, September 11, 1998 on presenting the Report of the UN High Commissioner for Human Rights, to the General Assembly.

[35] Vienna Declaration and Programme of Action, A/CONF.157/23, 12 July 1993, art.5.

[36] S/Res.1325 (2000).

Rights protected by the ICCPR and ICESCR

The rights protected by the Covenant on Civil and Political Rights include the right to life, to liberty and security, to equality before the courts, to peaceful assembly, to marry and found a family and to vote; whereas the freedoms articulated include those of association and, of thought, conscience and religion. The Covenant explicitly prohibits torture, cruel, inhuman or degrading treatment or punishment,[37] slavery, servitude and forced or compulsory labour.

The exercise of a right may be subject to restriction, but these limitations must be provided by law and must be necessary to protect national security, public order, public health or morals, or the rights and freedoms of others, for example art.12(3), which concerns limitations on freedom of movement and residence within a country and the right to leave a country. Derogation is allowed in times of public emergency, e.g., in 1989, the United Kingdom intimated a notice of derogation with respect to Northern Ireland and the detention of suspects. This derogation in respect of art.9(3) was withdrawn in 2001 but was replaced by a notice of derogation from art.9(1) precipitated by the "terrorist threat" following September 11, 2001. Accordingly the United Kingdom promulgated the Anti-Terrorism, Crime and Security Act 2001 to meet the public emergency perceived as existing within the meaning of art.4(1) of the Covenant.[38] Article 4(1) provides for derogation in times of public emergency "which threatens the life of the nation and the existence of which is officially proclaimed." At such times, parties to the Covenant may take "measures derogating from their obligations . . . to the extent strictly required by the exigencies of the situation, provided that such measures are not inconsistent with their obligations under international law and do not involve discrimination solely on the ground of race, colour, sex, language, religion or social origin." Article 4(2) prohibits derogation in respect of arts 6, 7, 8 (paras 1 and 2), 11, 15, 16 and 18. The Human Rights Committee in General Comment No.29, States of Emergency (art.4) para.6:[39]

---

[37] This guarantee is supplemented by the UN Convention Against Torture and Other Cruel, Inhuman or Degrading Treatment or Punishment (New York, February 4, 1985) Misc.12 (1985) Cmnd.9593; 23 I.L.M. 1027 (1984); for amended text 24 I.L.M. 535 (1985).

[38] Note decision of House of Lords in (*A (FC) and Others*), (2005) UKHL 71, that detaining suspected foreign terrorists without charge or trial was incompatible with art.5 of the ECHR and the UK could not derogate from art.5.

[39] CCPR/C/21/Rev.1/Add.11, August 31, 2001.

"The fact that some of the provisions of the Covenant have been listed in article 4 (paragraph 2), as not being subject to derogation does not mean that other articles in the Covenant may be subjected to derogations at will, even where a threat to the life of the nation exists. The legal obligation to narrow down all derogations to those strictly required by the exigencies of the situation establishes both for States parties and for the Committee a duty to conduct a careful analysis under each article of the Covenant based on an objective assessment of the actual situation."

However the qualification of a Covenant provision as a non-derogable one does not mean that no limitations or restrictions would ever be justified, e.g. as in art.18(3).[40]

In 1989, the Second Optional Protocol to the Covenant Aiming at the Abolition of the Death Penalty[41] was adopted and entered into force in July 1991 on receipt of the 10th ratification.[42]

The Covenant on Economic, Social and Cultural Rights guarantees those rights originally spelt out in arts 22–27 of the Universal Declaration, for example the right to work, to just and favourable conditions of work and rights to medical and social services and social security. Article 4 of the Covenant provides that these rights are subject "only to such limitations as are determined by law only in so far as this may be compatible with the nature of these rights and solely for the purpose of promoting the general welfare in a democratic society."

Both Covenants recognise the right of all peoples to self-determination and the right to "freely dispose of their natural wealth and resources." These provisions do not appear in the Universal Declaration.

Implementation machinery

The Covenants establish the following implementation mechanisms:

- *Reporting system*—common to both Covenants.

- *Inter-State complaint*—art.41 of the Covenant on Civil and Political Rights.

---

[40] *ibid.*, para.7.
[41] For the First Optional Protocol, see below, p.250.
[42] The UK became a party to the Second Optional Protocol on December 10, 1999.

- *Individual communication to the Committee of Human Rights*—(First) Optional Protocol to the Covenant on Civil and Political Rights

Reporting system. A reporting system as a medium for enforcing the rights guaranteed is common to both Covenants, and States are required to submit periodic reports. Regarding the Covenant on Civil and Political Rights, States are required:

> "to submit periodic reports on the measures they have adopted which give effect to the rights recognised herein and on the progress made in the enjoyment of those rights: (a) within one year of the entry into force of the present Covenant for the State parties concerned."[43]

Article 40 is the only compulsory supervisory system to which States submit on ratifying the Covenant.

The Human Rights Committee is a body of 18 individuals elected by the Contracting Parties, but who sit as individuals, not as government representatives. The Committee's task is to study the reports received and transmit a report and "such general comments as it may consider appropriate to the States Parties." Additional information may be requested from the State by the Committee and will be provided either by a State representative who will be present at the Committee's discussions or at a later date by the government concerned. The reporting system is essentially a means of providing information which may provide the basis for the Committee to issue such "general comments, as it may deem appropriate."[44] These comments have concerned, *inter alia*, freedom of speech, freedom from torture as guaranteed by the Covenant[45] and the interpretation of discrimination for the purposes of the Covenant. Although for the most part non-controversial, the Committee, in the Second General Comment on the right to life as guaranteed by art.6, stated that nuclear weapons, their production, testing, possession and deployment should not only be prohibited but should be "recognised as crimes against humanity." General Comments have been of considerable importance in augmenting the jurisprudence evolving in respect of the Covenant and in particular elaborating upon the

---

[43] art.40.
[44] art.40(4).
[45] arts 19 and 7, respectively. As of 2009 there have been 31 General Comments, which can be found at www.ohchr.org.

views of the Committee issued in accordance with the Optional Protocol procedure.

However, the Committee has noted that few States have submitted reports on time.[46] Most States have submitted reports with delays ranging from a few months to several years. Indeed some States parties are still in default, despite repeated reminders by the Committee. Therefore the Committee has adopted new rules including, *inter alia*, para.4(b)(i):

> "When the State party has not presented a report, the Committee may, at its discretion, notify the State party of the date on which the Committee proposes to examine the measures taken by the State party to implement the rights guaranteed under the Covenant: (i) If the State party is represented by a delegation, the Committee will, in presence of the delegation, proceed with the examination on the date assigned; States submit subsequent reports whenever required to do so by the Commission-currently every five years."

State parties to the Covenant on Economic, Social and Cultural Rights are also required to submit reports:

> "in stages, in accordance with a programme to be established by the Economic and Social Council within one year of the entry into force of the present Covenant after consultation with the States Parties and the specialised agencies concerned."[47]

Reports are submitted not to the independent Human Rights Committee, but rather to the Committee on Economic, Social and Cultural Rights (the Committee) formally established in 1985 by ECOSOC. The Committee is composed of 18 independent experts in the field of human rights. The main task of the Committee is to examine the reports submitted by States in accordance with art.16 of the Covenant. Reports are examined with a view to ensuring that States are adopting suitable measures to implement the rights set out in the Covenant. Originally States reported in "stages" in respect of the rights contained within the Covenant,

---

[46] General Comment No.30: Reporting Obligations of States parties under art.40 of the Covenant: 18/09/2002. CCPR/C/21/Rev.2/Add.12, General Comment No.30. (General Comments). Guidelines for reporting were issued by the Committee in General Comment No.02: Reporting guidelines: 28/07/81. CCPR General Comment No.2. (General Comments).

[47] art.17.

however, as of 1988 this was amended with the effect that States had to report on all rights within the confines of one report. Regrettably, many States fail to submit reports, or when submitted they are long overdue.[48] The Committee makes concluding observations in which a State's performance will be praised and/or criticised. The Committee also submits an annual report to the ECOSOC Council. The Committee has also issued 19 General Comments on topics ranging from the nature of States Parties' obligations, to the right to water.

Inter-State complaint—art.41, Covenant on Civil and Political Rights. Article 41 is not compulsory for States. Acceptance by a State is independent to its ratification of the Covenant. Article 41 provides for optional inter-State petitions. A State may accept the right of other States to bring before the Human Rights Committee a claim alleging a violation of the Convention. The initiation of the art.41 procedure is dependent upon:

(a) the condition of reciprocity—both States, the one alleging the violation and the alleged offender, must have accepted art.41; and

(b) the exhaustion of local remedies.

Under the art.41 procedure the Human Rights Committee (HRC) shall make its good offices available to the States, and within 12 months will submit a report indicating the facts and solution reached. In the absence of a solution, the HRC's report will be confined to the facts accompanied by the submissions of the two parties. In the event of no solution being reached the HRC may, with the prior consent of the States concerned, appoint an *ad hoc* Conciliation Commission.[49] If the Conciliation Commission is used, but a solution is not achieved, the Conciliation Commission produces a report which is not binding but in which the Conciliation Commission may indicate "its views on the possibilities of an amicable settlement."[50] Compared to its European Convention counterpart,[51] art.41 lacks teeth. There is no provision for reference to a judicial body or for the taking of a decision in accordance with judicial procedures. Conciliation remains the primary aim.

---

[48] In November 2008 the Committee issued new reporting guidelines which take account of the harmonised guidelines on reporting under international human rights treaties, (HRI/GEN/2/Rev.5).

[49] art.42.

[50] art.42(7)(c).

[51] art.33.

Article 41 entered into force on March 28, 1979 but has not yet been utilised.

Individual communications to the HRC-(First) Optional Protocol to the Covenant on Civil and Political Rights.[52] Under the First Optional Protocol to the Covenant on Civil and Political Rights,[53] the HRC is competent to receive and consider communications from individuals who claim to be victims of a violation by a State Party to the Covenant, provided the latter is a party to the Optional Protocol.[54]

A communication must:

- not be anonymous;

- concern an alleged violation of one of the rights provided for in the Covenant;

- not relate to a matter which is under consideration in any other international forum (this provision is designed to prevent the simultaneous consideration of petitions by the HRC and, i.e. the European Commission of the Council of Europe); and

- all domestic remedies must have been exhausted, unless the application of such remedies is unreasonably prolonged.[55]

The Optional Protocol makes no provision for reference to a Court nor does the HRC perform a conciliatory role. The HRC's function is simply to receive applications, examine them and subsequently "forward its views to the State Party concerned and the individual" on whether the Covenant has been breached. The HRC considers applications in private, there are no oral hearings and the HRC's views, which are not binding, are published as annexes to its annual report.[56] Many of the applications initially considered by the HRC were against Uruguay (e.g. the *Weinberger* case)[57] but alleged breaches have also been considered, *inter alia*,

---

[52] U.K.T.S. 6 (1977) Cmnd.6702; 6 I.L.M. 383 (1967); 61 A.J.I.L. 870 (1967).
[53] art.1 of the 1966 Covenant; the Committee is also competent under art.5 of the Second Optional Protocol (1990).
[54] See: http://www.unhchr.ch/html/menu2/8/stat2.htm.
[55] arts 3 and 5.
[56] See General Comment No 33 For the Obligations of States Parties under the Optional Protocol to the International Covenant on Civil and Political Rights, CCPR/C/GC/33, November 5, 2008.
[57] Report of the Human Rights Committee, G.A.O.R., 36th Session, Supp.40, p.114.

by the HRC, regarding Canada, Mauritius, Finland, Spain and Australia.

In the *Lovelace* case,[58] a provision of Canada's Indian Act, denying an Indian woman from returning to her native Indian reserve on the break up of her marriage to a non-Indian, was held to be in violation of art.27 of the Covenant.

In the *Mauritian Women* case,[59] Mauritian legislation placing Mauritian women married to foreign husbands, but not Mauritian men married to foreign women, at risk of deportation was found to be contrary to arts 2(1), 3 and 26 in relation to arts 17(1) and 23(1) of the Covenant. As for compliance, Uruguay made little consistent effort, whereas Canada and Mauritius amended their "offending" legislation. In an effort to tackle the problem of non-adherence to the HRC's views a Special Rapporteur for the Follow up "on views" has been appointed.

The Optional Protocol entered into force in March 1976, and has been adopted by more than 100 parties but neither the United Kingdom nor the United States has accepted the Optional Protocol.

The Economic, Social and Cultural Committee, following protracted consideration, adopted an Optional Protocol to the Covenant on Economic, Social and Cultural Rights on December 10, 2008. The Optional Protocol provides that communications may be submitted by, or on behalf of, individuals or groups of individuals under the jurisdiction of a State party claiming there has been a breach to their rights as protected by the Covenant. The principle of reciprocity and the need to exhaust local remedies remain applicable.

The UN machinery provides for other general implementation mechanisms common to all human rights. The main UN implementation body is the Human Rights Council[60] established by General Assembly Resolution 60/251, March 15, 2006. The Council comprises representatives from 47 Member States, chosen by secret vote by the majority of members of the General Assembly. It depends directly on the Assembly. The first members of the Council were elected in September 2008. The Council was created to overcome some of the problems of its predecessor, the Commission on Human Rights, mainly that of its partiality and potential polarisation. The Commission on Human Rights was made up of 53 state representatives, which on occasion included representatives of States accused of gross human rights violations. These members, allegedly, made use of their seat on the

---

[58] 1981 Report of the Human Rights Committee, p.166.
[59] *ibid.*, p.134.
[60] The Human Rights Council replaces the Commission on Human Rights which had been established by ECOSOC in 1946.

Commission avoid international sanction of their government's policies. Council members are elected on the basis of their knowledge, experience, independence, impartiality, personal integrity and objectivity.

The Sub-commission on the Promotion and Protection of Human Rights[61] has also been substituted by a new Advisory Council to the Human Rights Council. It is composed of 18 independent experts and its mandate is to advise the Council and develop studies and investigations in specific topics but does not enjoy the competence to adopt resolutions or decisions.

The Council has a very broad mandate. In general, it fulfils a double function of promotion and protection of human rights through the promotion of universal respect for human rights and drawing attention to situations in which human rights are violated. These situations include severe and systematic violations, and the promulgation of recommendations. The Council will do this through a series of special public procedures, a confidential complaints procedure and a universal periodic review.

Together with the Human Rights Council, an important body within the United Nations rights protection system is the High Commissioner for Human Rights. This post was created by the General Assembly in 1993 to promote and protect civil, cultural, economic, political and social rights.[62] The first UN High Commissioner for Human Rights was Mr Jose Ayala-Lasso, the Ecuadorian Ambassador to the United Nations at the time. The current Commissioner is Navanethem Pillay of South Africa who was appointed in 2008. The Office of the High Commissioner for Human Rights provides the personnel, logistical and research assistance to support the Human Rights Council's mechanism of protection.

THE SPECIAL PROCEDURES

These procedures were established by the Commission on Human Rights in 1967. They consist of the Council addressing specific country situations where human rights are grossly and systematically being violated or involve the consideration of thematic issues. These procedures are heterogeneous and all are public. These can be created with the consent of the State concerned but such consent is not mandatory. Thematic issues

---

[61] The Sub-Commission was the main subsidiary body of the Commission on Human Rights and was previously known as the Sub-Commission on Prevention of Discrimination and Protection of Minorities. The name change was made in 1999.

[62] A/Res.48/141 adopted December 20, 1993.

include: enforced or involuntary disappearances; arbitrary detention; right to education; right to food; sale of children, child prostitution and pornography; situation of human rights and fundamental freedoms of indigenous populations, etc., whilst country mandates focus on countries or territories such as Burundi, Cambodia, Haiti, Myanmar, North Korea, Palestinian Occupied Territories, Somalia and Sudan. Special procedures involve either an individual or a working group. An individual will assume the name of "Special Rapporteur", "Special Representative of the Secretary-General", "Representative of the Secretary-General" or "Independent Expert". Working groups are usually composed of five members, one representing each geographical region. Individuals involved in this procedure have to be independent and impartial. Their mandate normally consists of the examination, monitoring, advice and public reporting on human rights situations in the specific countries or issue in question. They can also carry out country visits.

The complaints procedure

This mechanism provides for the consideration by the Human Rights Council of situations of consistent patterns of gross human rights abuses. This procedure is confidential and relies on the cooperation of the State (the object of the claim) and on the victim having exhausted all domestic remedies. The claims will be studied by two working groups: first by the Working Group on Communications and then by the Working Group on Situations.

This mechanism substitutes the previous individual complaints procedure of the Commission on Human Rights, established in ECOSOC Resolution 1503 (XLVIII), May 27, of individual complaints. This procedure allowed the Commission on Human Rights to deal with individual communications of human rights violations by considering them as part of a wider pattern of gross violations in one country or region. This procedure was very limited and had been criticised for its lack of efficiency.

Universal Periodic review

This procedure is new not having been within the mandate of the Commission on Human Rights. It consists of a review of the human rights records of all 192 UN Member States once every four years. This system is based on the cooperation of those States which are to report to the Council and indicate the actions they are taking to improve the human rights situation in their countries in order to fulfil their human rights obligations.

OTHER UNITED NATIONS CONVENTIONS
GUARANTEEING PARTICULAR HUMAN RIGHTS

A number of International Conventions guaranteeing specific human rights have been concluded under the auspices of the United Nations. Such Conventions include the 1948 Genocide Convention,[63] 1966 Convention on the Elimination of All Forms of Racial Discrimination,[64] 1973 Convention on the Suppression and Punishment of the Crime of Apartheid,[65] 1979 Convention on the Elimination of All Forms of Discrimination Against Women,[66] 1984 Convention Against Torture and Other Cruel, Inhuman or Degrading Treatment or Punishment,[67] 1989 Convention on the Rights of the Child, supplemented by two additional protocols, namely the Optional Protocol to the Convention of the Rights of the Child on the involvement of Children in Armed Conflict (GA Resolution A/RES/54/263, May 25, 2000 which came into force on February 12, 2002) and the Optional Protocol to the Convention on the Rights of the Child Concerning the Sale of Children, Child Prostitution and Child Pornography (GA Resolution A/RES/54/263, 25 May 2000 which came into force on January 18, 2002), the 1990 Convention on the Protection of the Rights of All Migrant Workers and Members of Their Families,[68] the 2006 Convention on the Rights of People with Disabilities and the 2006 Convention for the Protection of All Persons from Enforced Disappearance. Of the three foregoing Conventions only the 2006 Convention for the Protection of All Persons from Enforced Disappearance is not yet in force. Enforcement is primarily by the submission of reports from Contracting Parties to a relevant Committee, however, under the Convention against Torture and Other Cruel, Inhuman or Degrading Treatment or Punishment, there is provision for inter-State and individual petition, subject to the State concerned accepting the competence of the Committee in this respect.

An Optional Protocol to the UN Convention against Torture and Other Cruel, Inhuman or Degrading Treatment or Punishment, General Assembly Resolution 57/199, was adopted in December 2002 and entered into force on June 22, 2006 following receipt of the twentieth ratification. The Optional Protocol comprises a "two pillar" visiting mechanism to places of detention whereby an expert international visiting body, a Sub-Committee to the UN

---

[63] U.K.T.S. 58 (1970) Cmnd.4421; 79 U.N.T.S. 277; see also Chs 4 and 6, above.
[64] U.K.T.S. 77 (1969) Cmnd.4108; 60 U.N.T.S. 195.
[65] 13 I.L.M. 50 (1974).
[66] Misc.1 (1982) Cmnd.8444; 19 I.L.M. 33 (1980).
[67] Misc.12 (1985) Cmnd.9593; 23 I.L.M. 1027 (1984); 24 I.L.M. 535 (1985).
[68] 28 I.L.M. 1448 (1989).

Committee against Torture Sub-Committee, funded by the UN, is competent to conduct periodic visits to all State Parties and maintain a contact with both the State Party and the national visiting body.

States that ratify the Optional Protocol must establish or maintain a national visiting body to visit places of detention. The intention is for international and national bodies to work together.

There is now also an Optional Protocol to the Convention on the Elimination of All Forms of Discrimination against Women, which provides for individual petition against a consenting Contracting Party.[69]

Of particular note is the enforcement procedure of the Convention on the Elimination of All Forms of Racial Discrimination, which provides for an optional system of individual petition whereby an individual, or group of individuals, can lodge a complaint within the Convention (art.14). Forty-five States have made declarations recognising the competence of the Committee to receive such complaints. This can only occur if the alleged offending State has accepted the optional individual complaint procedure. The right of individual petition was employed successfully in *Yilmaz-Dogan v Netherlands*.[70] There is a compulsory inter-State complaint procedure, but this has never been utilised. The Committee on the Elimination of All Forms of Racial Discrimination, a body of 18 independent experts, is central to the enforcement of the Convention. It receives reports from Contracting Parties and forwards them to the General Assembly suggestions and general recommendations as it sees fit. Article 22 of the Convention provides for compulsory reference to the International Court of Justice in the event of any "dispute between two or more States Parties with respect to the interpretation or application of this Convention unless the disputants agree to another mode of settlement." This represents an interesting attempt at strengthening international enforcement. However,

---

[69] art.2. The Protocol entered into force December 22, 2000. GA RES. A/54/4. For a decision of the Committee on the Elimination of Discrimination against Women, declaring a communication inadmissible under the Optional Protocol to the Convention on the Elimination of All Forms of Discrimination against Women, see *Communication No. 1/2003, Ms B-J v Germany* (Decision adopted on July 14, 2004, 31st session), In *Ms A.T. v Hungary*, No.2/2003. Hungary was found not to have exercised due diligence in affording protection against violence perpetrated by a non-state actor. This was endorsement of the Committee's General Recommendation No.19 statement that States could be responsible for private acts through a failure to act with due dilegence, to prevent, investigate, punish and provide compensation.

[70] C.E.R.D. Report, G.A.O.R., 43rd Session, Supp.18, p.59 (1988).

the lodging by States of reservations to this provision undermines its potential.

A State which is a party to two or more instruments on human rights may be required to submit a number of reports, and this has prompted the suggestion that there should be a standardisation of reports, to the effect that such States could refer to documents already supplied, thereby preventing a duplication of information in the preparation of reports. The Vienna Conference identified a number of fundamental human rights which the Conference felt required international attention, some of which are briefly considered here. For instance, the elimination of racism and discrimination was highlighted as a priority for the international community.[71] The Vienna Conference also endorsed the appointment by the Commission on Human Rights of a Special Rapporteur to consider contemporary forms of racism, racial discrimination, xenophobia and related intolerance.[72]

Moreover, women were identified at the Vienna Conference as a group particularly vulnerable in the international community. The Conference confirmed the full and equal participation of women in political, civil, economic, social and cultural life at national, regional and international levels and eradication of all forms of discrimination on grounds of sex was an important objective.[73] The Declaration coincided with a Declaration on the Elimination of Violence Against Women, which recognised violence against women because of their gender as a specific problem[74] and urged States to ratify the 1979 Convention on the Elimination of Discrimination,[75] while leaving implementation of the objectives to States. The Fourth UN Conference on Women, held in Beijing in September 1995, looked specifically at areas of particular concern to the advancement of women and adopted a Platform of Action to tackle these issues.[76] The Platform of Action "is an agenda for women's empowerment"[77] and includes actions to eradicate poverty, eliminate violence and inequality in education, promote women's human rights and ensure access to relevant health care.[78] In June 2000, Beijing Plus Five was discussed in a special session of the General Assembly, and at the end of the

[71] The World Conference on Racism, held in South Africa in September 2001, culminated in the Durban Declaration and Programme of Action.
[72] The UN Commission on Human Rights adopted Res.1993/20, February 26, 1993 at its 49th session when Mr Dossou was appointed Special Rapporteur.
[73] Pt I, para.18 of the Declaration.
[74] Adopted by GA Res.48/104, February 23, 1994.
[75] See below, at n.66.
[76] A/CONF.177/20, October 17, 1995; 35 I.L.M. 401 (1996).
[77] Ch.1, Mission Statement.
[78] See Ch.IV, paras 45–285, which contain the Strategic Objectives and Actions.

session a political declaration was adopted, by consensus, confirming the political will to implement the Beijing Declaration and Platform for Action.

The United Nations adopted a Draft Declaration on the Rights of Indigenous Peoples in 1994,[79] which was submitted to the Commission on Human Rights in 1995 for further consideration.[80] The Declaration is unprecedented in its recognition of group rights of indigenous peoples. The United Nations declared 1994–2004 as the International Decade of the World's Indigenous People.

OTHER SYSTEMS OF PROTECTION OF HUMAN RIGHTS

The international protection of human rights does not lie exclusively with the United Nations. Regional bodies have promulgated regional instruments, among the most notable being the European Convention on Human Rights and Fundamental Freedoms (ECHR) and the American Convention on Human Rights.[81] Both Conventions have sophisticated enforcement mechanisms, and an extensive jurisprudence now exists from the European Court of Human Rights and the Inter-American Court of Human Rights respectively. Other regional Conventions include the Banjul Charter on Human and Peoples Rights, adopted by the Organisation of African Unity (OAU), which came into force in 1986 and the Arab Charter on Human Rights adopted in 1994, revised in January 2004 and entered into force on March 15, 2008.

In addition to the ECHR, the Council of Europe has adopted the European Social Charter 1961 and its successor, a revised European Social Charter, in 1996.[82] Other European instruments include the European Convention for the Prevention of Torture and the Human Dimension of the Final Act of the Conference on Security and Cooperation in Europe 1975 (the Helsinki

---

[79] Res.1994/45 adopted August 26, 1994 by the UN Sub-Commission on Prevention of Discrimination and Protection of Minorities, 46th Session, 1994. See 34 I.L.M. 541 (1995).

[80] The Human Rights Commission had on its agenda at the 53rd session in Geneva from March 10 to April 18, 1997 a report of the Secretary General on the possible establishment of a permanent forum for indigenous people within the UN. This was established and held its first meeting on May 13, 2002.

[81] ECHR—213 U.N.T.S. 221; U.K.T.S. (1953) Cmd.8969 and ACHR—O.A.S. Treaty Series No.36, 1144 U.N.T.S. 123 reprinted in Basic Documents Pertaining to Human Rights in the Inter-American System, OEA/Ser.L.V/II.82 doc.6 rev.1 at 25 (1992).

[82] (1965) UKTS., Cmnd. 2643; 529 UNTS 89 and ETS 163. The 1996 revised European Social Charter entered into force in 1999 and will eventually replace the 1961 Charter.

Declaration)[83] also has a human dimension. Human Rights also feature on the agenda of other bodies, for example the Red Cross and certain of the specialised agencies of the United Nations, i.e. the International Labour Organisation.

HUMAN RIGHTS AND INTERNATIONAL CRIMINAL LAW

In 1937, the League of Nations initiated a Convention for the Prevention and Punishment of Terrorism[84] and a Convention for the Creation of an International Criminal Court,[85] however the former received only one ratification, while the latter received none.

In the 1990s, televised reports of war camps, rape, genocide and the practice of ethnic cleansing in what was then Yugoslavia, shocked the international community, and led to the creation of an *ad hoc* International Tribunal under Ch.VII of the UN Charter to punish the alleged perpetrators of such crimes. The International Tribunal for the Prosecution of Persons Responsible for Serious Violations of International Humanitarian Law Committed in the Territory of the Former Yugoslavia (the ICTY) was established by UN Security Council Resolution 827 on May 23, 1993 for the sole purpose of:

> "prosecuting persons responsible for serious violations of international humanitarian law committed in the territory of the former Yugoslavia between 1st January, 1991 and a date to be determined by the Security Council upon the restoration of peace."[86]

The Tribunal was designed to establish a judicial process aimed at preventing the continuation of crimes against humanity and to contribute towards the restoration and maintenance of peace and security in the region.

The Tribunal has jurisdiction under its Statute to prosecute individuals responsible for grave breaches of the Geneva Conventions of 1949, violations of the laws or customs of war, genocide[87] and crimes against humanity.[88] The Tribunal differs

---

[83] 1975 14 I.L.M. 1292. See the concluding document of Vienna (1989), the Copenhagen document (1990) and the Charter of Paris for a New Europe (1991).
[84] 7 Hudson 862.
[85] Hudson 878. For a synopsis of events precipitating the crisis see, Marc Weller, "The International Response to the Dissolution of the Socialist Federal Republic of Yugoslavia" 86 *A.J.I.L.* 568.
[86] S.C.Res.827, UN SCOR, 48th Year, 3217th mtg at 1, reprinted in 32 I.L.M. 1203 (1993).
[87] arts 3 and 4 of ICTY Statute.
[88] *ibid.*, art.5 see also arts 2, 3, 4 and 5 of the Genocide Convention.

from its predecessor (Nuremberg) in that it may also hear cases of crimes perpetrated in the course of inter-State war and internal strife, whereas Nuremberg could only deal with crimes committed in international armed conflict. It is the first time the Security Council has created an international tribunal using Ch. VII powers and can therefore be said to be a truly international entity.[89]

The Statue of the Tribunal[90] embodies the most detailed rules and procedures ever drafted for an international criminal tribunal.[91] The rules reflect international human rights standards, particularly those enshrined in the International Covenant on Civil and Political Rights, e.g. art.21(a) which deals with the accused's right to be present at his trial, and art.25, which provides the accused with a right of appeal.

Eleven judges were elected by the General Assembly in September 1993 and took office on November 17, 1993.[92] Article 16 makes provision for a prosecutor who is charged with:

> "the investigation and prosecution of persons responsible for serious violations of international humanitarian law committed in the territory of the former Yugoslavia since January 1, 1991. Arts 23 and 24 confer sentencing powers on the Judges who must make their decision public along with a reasoned opinion. Convicted persons may be imprisoned but there is no death sentence."[93]

The Tribunal issued its first indictment and warrant for arrest against a former commander of the Susica camp in the Republic of Bosnia–Herzegovina, Dragan Nikolic, in November 1994. It also requested the deferral by the Federal Courts of Germany of criminal proceedings against Dusko Tadic, emphasising the international community's desire to create a truly international entity. Article 9(2) of the Statue provides that the ICTY shall have primacy over national courts. This applies to situations where the Tribunal requests national Courts to transfer the accused and the investigation to its jurisdiction. Jurisdiction is otherwise concurrent with national Courts.

---

[89] The Nuremberg Tribunal was established in very different circumstances when there was no government in power.

[90] Adopted by Security Council Res.827, May 25, 1993, reproduced in 32 I.L.M. 1192 (1993).

[91] Rules and Procedure and Evidence, adopted pursuant to Art.15 of the Statute of the Tribunal, which came into force, March 14, 1994; 33 I.L.M. 484 (1994). They have been amended on several occasions since, e.g. see 35 I.L.M. 1342 (1996).

[92] art.12. Judges are assigned to chambers for a period of one year, after which they will rotate.

[93] art.24.

The work of the Tribunal has been greatly impeded by a number of shortcomings, in particular unsatisfactory funding arrangements.[94] Problems have also arisen concerning the apprehension of alleged war criminals and the enforcement of international arrest warrants.[95] The ICTY passed its first sentence in December 1996, sentencing a Croatian soldier in the Bosnian Serb army to 10 years in prison for his part in the slaughter of Muslims in the UN "safe-haven" of Srebrenica, and Tadic was sentenced on July 14, 1997 to 20 years' imprisonment. One of the most wanted, Slobodan Milosevic, the former president of Serbia, was apprehended and handed over to the Tribunal in June 2001. His trial began in February 2002. However, the trial ended after his sudden death in March 2006. Another high-profile case is that of Radovan Karadzic, the former Bosnian Serb leader, who after 13 years of evading capture was apprehended and handed over to the ICTY in July 2008.

The events precipitating the creation of the International Tribunal for the Prosecution of Persons Responsible for Genocide and Other Serious Violations of International Humanitarian Law Committed in the Territory of Rwanda and Rwandan citizens responsible for genocide and other such violations committed in the territory of neighbouring states, between January 1, 1994 and December 31, 1994, (ICTR) were, according to one Report, "a pre-planned execution of severe human right violations, including systematic, widespread and flagrant breaches of international humanitarian law, large-scale crimes against humanity and genocide."[96] The estimated death toll in the 1994 massacre was approximately one million people.

The ICTR was established on November 8, 1994 by UNSC Resolution 955.[97] Despite efforts to extend the Statute of the ICTY to cover crimes perpetrated in the territory of Rwanda and maintain a single Tribunal to cover both Yugoslavia and Rwanda, the Rwandan government objected due to pressure from the Rwandan people to be seen to punish the perpetrators of genocide in the territory of Rwanda itself.[98] The ICTR does, however,

---

[94] This is no longer the case in respect to Yugoslavia, as the following figures reinforce—1993, $276,000; cf. 2002–03, $223,169,800.

[95] Those convicted of genocide and crimes against humanity include the Rwandan former Prime Minister and Head of Interim Government in 1994, Jean Kamboda.

[96] Preliminary Report of the Independent Commission of Experts established in accordance with Security Council Res.935 (2994) UN Doc.S/1994/1125 of October 4, 1994, para.42.

[97] S.C.Res.955, UN SCOR, 49th year, 3453rd mtg at 1. UN Doc.S/RES/955 (1994).

[98] It was eventually decided to establish the Tribunal in Arusha in the United Republic of Tanzania.

share the same chief prosecutor and appeals chamber as the ICTY. The first prosecutor was Louise Arbour of Canada, who has been succeeded by Carla del Ponte of Switzerland.

A third *ad hoc* international criminal court was established by the UN with the creation of a Special Court for Sierra Leone. This Special Court is distinctive from the ICTY and the ICTR in that it is a treaty-based Court established by agreement between the UN and Sierra Leone. The Special Court is composed of international judges and Sierra Leonean judges, prosecutors and staff, which is why it is called a "hybrid court". The subject matter of this Special Court's jurisdiction includes certain crimes under Sierra Leone's own law, but unlike the ICTY and the ICTR the Special Court does not have jurisdiction over genocide. This was because there was no evidence the mass killing in Sierra Leone was perpetrated against an identifiable national, ethnic, racial or religious group with the intention of annihilation of the group as such as required by the 1948 Genocide Convention. The agreement between Sierra Leone and the UN, which was signed in January 2002, provided the Court jurisdiction to prosecute persons who bear the greatest responsibility for serious violations of international humanitarian law and Sierra Leonean law committed in the territory of Sierra Leone since November 30, 1996.[99] In the first two years, the prosecutor of the Special Court indicted thirteen people from all sides involved in the conflict. Nine of those indicted had been arrested and transferred to the custody of the Special Court and were awaiting trial. Two had not been arrested but had surrendered to the Special Court.

The General Assembly of the UN adopted on May 13, 2002 a Resolution approving the proposal of an agreement between the UN and Cambodia on the prosecutions of crimes committed between 1975 and 1979 in Cambodia.[100] The Tribunal is an extraordinary chamber, part of the current Cambodian judiciary system and composed of Cambodian and foreign legal experts, with Cambodians in the majority. The Cambodian parliament ratified the agreement on October 4, 2004 and although the approval of Cambodia's Senate and Head of State is seen as being a mere formality, agreement has still to be reached on the funding of the Tribunal.

The practice of hybrid tribunals or similar mechanisms have been used in other scenarios, such as the East Timor Special Panels for Serious Crimes, established by the UN Transitional

---

[99] The Statute of the Special Court was annexed to the agreement and on March 7, 2002, Sierra Leone enacted the Special Court Agreement 2002, Ratification Act, 2002 to implement the Statute.

[100] (A/Res./57/228B).

Administration in June 2000, to deal with crimes against humanity, war crimes and other atrocities; and the special panels created
by the UN Mission in Kosovo in 2000 or Bosnia's War Crimes
Chambers, also composed of national and international judges,
prosecutors and other staff.

Notwithstanding the criticisms, the establishment of these
Tribunals was undoubtedly a significant step towards the
establishment of a permanent international criminal tribunal
and endorsed willingness among UNSC members to cooperate in apprehending and prosecuting alleged perpetrators of
international crime.

A permanent International Criminal Court

The experience of both the ICTY and the ICTR heightened calls
for the creation of a permanent Criminal Court.[101] The General
Assembly adopted a resolution on January 16, 1997, which confirmed its commitment to establish an International Criminal
Court (the ICC). The General Assembly renewed the mandate of
the Preparatory Committee[102] and decided to convene a diplomatic conference of plenipotentiaries in Italy in 1998 with the task
of finalising and adopting a Convention on the establishment of
a permanent International Criminal Court.[103]

The Permanent International Criminal Court.

The Convention,[104] once finalised and opened for signature,
received the requisite number of ratifications for entry into force
on July 1, 2002.[105] The establishment of the Court is regarded as
making good a deficiency in the international legal system. It will
also remove the need for *ad hoc* tribunals such as ICTY and ICTR
and guard against what has been referred to as "tribunal fatigue".

---

[101] See the Draft Statute for an International Criminal Court, in the Report of the
International Law Commission on Its Forty-sixth Session, UN G.A.O.R., 49th
Sess., Supp.No.10 at 43, UN Doc.A/49/10 (1994). See 33 I.L.M. 253 (1994). The
ILC had also been asked in the context of its work on the Draft Code of Crimes
Against the Peace and Security of Mankind to address the question of a per-
manent International Criminal Court. GA Res.48/31 UN G.A.O.R., 48th Sess.,
Supp.No.49, at 328, UN Doc.A/48/49 (1993).

[102] The Preparatory Committee was established by GA Res.50/46, December 11,
1995 with the specific task of preparing the text of an international Convention
for a permanent International Criminal Court.

[103] 51st session, UN GA Res.A/Res/51/207, January 16, 1997.

[104] The Rome Statute of the International Criminal Court General Assembly
Resolution ICC-ASP/2/Res.3, September 12, 2003.

[105] The UK is a Contracting Party. The US, in April 2002, withdrew notwithstanding the Clinton administration's acceptance as reflected in its signing the
Convention in October, 2000.

Delays are characteristic of any *ad hoc* system, but expeditious procedures are essential in criminal law. Otherwise memories fade and as a consequence, evidence is difficult to obtain. The Court is established in The Hague, the Netherlands. The Court is constituted of 18 judges elected for a nine-year term. The jurisdiction of the Court is set out in art.5.1 and is "genocide", crimes against humanity, war crimes and crimes of aggression. The various terms are defined in art.6 (genocide), art.7 (crimes against humanity), and art.8 (war crimes) and crimes of aggression.[106] The Court has jurisdiction in respect of crimes which occur after July 1, 2002.[107] The Court is currently dealing with cases of abuses in four countries: the Democratic Republic of Congo, Sudan, Uganda and the Central African Republic. The first case to be heard in the Court is that of Thomas Lubanga, the former leader of the Congolese militia, Union of Congolese Patriots (UPC), who is charged with the recruitment of child soldiers to actively participate in combat.

The establishment of the Court is evidence that the international community recognises that there is a role for a permanent international legal regime. To be effective, this demands the recognition that certain crimes are of international concern and arguably are more effectively dealt within an international forum. However, as highlighted, "No provision . . . relating to individual criminal responsibility shall affect the responsibility of States under international law."[108]

CONCLUSION

Human rights in the twenty-first century have to be seen in the international global context. The facts are not palatable and certainly do not suggest a world which respects human rights. The task confronting the international community is to work together to achieve a world in which there is mutual respect for all individuals as individuals and an absence of arbitrary discrimination. International human rights instruments in themselves will not prove the ultimate panacea but they do highlight awareness, which hopefully, with the passage of time, will cascade to all levels of society and will provide, at the very least, a minimum standard which will become the norm for all rather than the exception.

---

[106] The Court shall exercise jurisdiction over the crime of aggression once a provision is adopted in accordance with arts 121 and 123, defining the crime and setting out the conditions under which the Court shall exercise jurisdiction with respect to this crime. Such a provision shall be consistent with the relevant provisions of the Charter of the UN.

[107] For the jurisdiction of the Court, see Ch.6.

[108] art.25.4 of the Statute.

10. THE LAW OF TREATIES

The importance of treaties has already been acknowledged. Treaties are increasingly utilised to regulate relations between international persons, and the expansion in the content of international law is reflected in the diversity of subject matter regulated by treaty.

Treaty law is, for the most part, non-controversial. As the international law of contract, it is essentially "lawyers' law". What is a treaty? How is a treaty concluded? How is a treaty to be interpreted?

The law relating to these questions must be considered against the backcloth of the 1969 Vienna Convention on the Law of Treaties.[1] The Convention, which entered into force in January 1980, was the culmination of work by the International Law Commission spanning some 20 years. The Convention represents a codification of existing customary international law, see the *Fisheries Jurisdiction* case,[2] though some of the provisions reflect progressive development, e.g. art.53.

The Convention does not have retroactive effect. However,

---

[1] U.K.T.S. 58 (1980) Cmnd.7964; 8 I.L.M. 679 (1969); *A.J.I.L.* 875 (1969).
[2] I.C.J. Rep. 1973 p.3 at 14.

because the Convention spells out established rules, it may be applied to agreements which pre-date it, for example as in the League of Nations Mandate in the *Namibia (South West Africa)* case,[3] and in the *Beagle Channel Arbitration*,[4] where the Convention's rules were applied to the 1881 Argentina/Chile Treaty.[5]

A Convention on the Law of Treaties Between States and International Organisations or Between International Organisations was adopted on March 21, 1986,[6] but has yet to enter into force.[7]

DEFINITION OF A TREATY

"Treaty" is the generic term used to embrace convention, agreement, arrangement, protocol, and exchange of notes.[8] International law does not distinguish between agreements identified as treaties and other agreements. The name accorded to an agreement is not in itself important and is of no legal effect.[9]

A treaty for the purposes of the Convention means "an international agreement concluded between States in written form and governed by international law . . ."[10]

The Convention is concerned only with written agreements. But can States enter into oral agreements?

Treaties invariably are in written form. It cannot be stated unequivocally, however, that an oral agreement has no legal significance as oral statements have been held to have binding effect.

In 1919, the Danish Government informed the Norwegian Government, through the Danish representative in Norway, that Denmark would not raise any objection at the Paris Peace

[3] I.C.J. Rep. 1971 p.16 at 47.
[4] 17 I.L.M. 632 at 645 (1978).
[5] See also U.S. Department of State letter to the U.S. President (1971) 5 Exec. Doc. L 92nd Cong. 1st Sess. 1.
[6] Misc. 11 (1987) Cm.244; 25 I.L.M. 543 (1986).
[7] The Convention's provisions closely parallel those of the 1969 Convention.
[8] For definitions of key terms used in the United Nations Treaty Collection, including "treaty", "convention", "charter", etc, see http://untreaty.un.org/English/guide.asp#treaties.
[9] Within a national system "treaty" may have a specialised meaning, e.g. in the US.
[10] art.2(1)(a). Note the comments of the I.C.J. in the *Maritime Delimitations and Territorial Questions* case (Qatar v Bahrain) 1994 I.C.J. Rep. p.112 with respect to what may constitute an international agreement at pp.121–122. Particular caution should be taken in respect of agreements termed memorandum of understanding. A memorandum of understanding is a less formal agreement see the *International Law Commission Yearbook* 188 para.2. For further discussion of Memorandum of Understanding see A. Aust, *Modern Treaty Law and Practice*, (2007) pp.26–46.

Conference to the Norwegian claim over Spitzbergen, if Norway would not challenge Danish claims of sovereignty over Greenland. The then Norwegian Foreign Minister, M. Ihlen, subsequently reported to his Danish counterpart "the Norwegian Government would not make any difficulty." Denmark argued before the Permanent Court of International Justice in the Legal Status of Eastern Greenland[11] that Norway had, by the "Ihlen Declaration", recognised Danish sovereignty. The Court denied the "Ihlen Declaration" constituted recognition of Danish sovereignty, but nevertheless maintained that Norway had assumed a legally-binding obligation to refrain from contesting Danish sovereignty over Greenland. The Permanent Court did not, nevertheless, characterise the "Ihlen Declaration" as an oral agreement, nor did it define the circumstances, if any, in which a unilateral statement could be binding. The Court rather emphasised the contemporaneous acceptance by Denmark of the Norwegian claims over Spitzbergen.

The International Court of Justice was confronted with the legal nature of unilateral declarations in the *Nuclear Tests* cases,[12] in which Australia and New Zealand sought a decision from the Court against France, that the latter's testing of nuclear weapons in the atmosphere of the South Pacific was contrary to international law. The Court found that the series of public statements made by France announcing she would refrain from further testing was sufficient to commit her and negate Australian and New Zealand objections. The legal consequences flowing from the new Serbian authorities' statement of June 15, 2005 were discussed by the I.C.J. in the *Case Concerning the Application of the Convention on the Prevention and Punishment of the Crime of Genocide* (Bosnia and Herzegovina v Serbia and Montenegro)[13]. The I.C.J. concluded that the statement was of a political nature and it was clearly not intended to have legal effect. Accordingly the Court maintained that the statement did not constitute an admission of Serbian responsibility for the massacres in Srebrenica.[14] The issue of unilateral declarations of States capable of creating legal obligations has been addressed by the International Law Commission and

---

[11] P.C.I.J. Rep. ser.A/B, No.53 (1933).
[12] I.C.J. Rep. 1974 253, 457. See also comments of the I.C.J. in *the Frontier Dispute case* (Burkina Faso v Mali) I.C.J. Rep. 1986, p.554, in which the Court stated that unilateral statements could only bind a State where it was apparent the State intended to be bound, i.e. only in exceptional circumstances.
[13] Judgement of February 27, 2007.
[14] *ibid.* at para 378 p.135 see, however, dissenting opinion of Judge Al-Khasawneh at p.16 paras 57–8.

culminated with the adoption of Ten Guiding Principles in 2006.[15] The principles acknowledge that declarations publicly made, orally or in writing and manifesting the will to be bound may have the effect of creating legal obligations and when the conditions for this are met, the binding character of such declarations is based on good faith; States concerned may then take them into consideration and rely on them, such States are entitled to require that such obligations be respected. The legal effect of such delarations is to be determined with reference to the factual circumstances in which they were made and will only bind the State internationally if it is made by an authority vested with the power to do so.

Not all written agreements necessarily establish binding relations. The Charter of Paris for a New Europe, adopted at the Conference on Security and Co-operation in Europe,[16] is such an instance and is rather soft law.[17]

Article 102 of the UN Charter provides for registration[18] with the Secretariat of the United Nations of every treaty and international agreement entered into by any Member State. Only treaties or international agreements so registered, can be invoked before any organ of the United Nations. Registration provides tangible evidence that the agreement is to be regarded as a treaty and that is the intention of the parties concerned. For example, the Charter of Paris for a New Europe[19] provides that the Charter is "not eligible for registration under art.102 of the Charter of the United Nations . . ." Nonetheless, non-registration or late registration does not affect the binding nature of the agreement between the parties concerned.[20]

If the Vienna Convention is to apply to an international agreement, that agreement must be in written form, reflect the intention of the parties to be bound and must be governed by international law.[21]

---

[15] Text adopted by the International Law Commission at its 58th session in 2006 and submitted to the General Assembly as a part of the Commission's report covering the work of that session (A/61/10). For the report see the *Yearbook of the International Law Commission* 2006, Vol.11, Pt 2.
[16] 30 I.L.M. 190 (1991).
[17] See Ch.2.
[18] Approximately 40,000 treaties have been registered.
[19] Above, n.16.
[20] *Maritime Delimitation and Territorial Questions case* at 122, above, n.10.
[21] Treaties may be employed as a vehicle for the expression of soft law.

TREATY-MAKING COMPETENCE

National law

States enjoy discretion as to the allocation of treaty-making competences and the constitutional arrangements for the ratification of treaties. These arrangements vary widely. However, a State may not plead a breach of its constitutional provisions relating to treaty-making competence so as to invalidate an agreement, unless such a breach was manifest and "objectively evident to any State conducting itself in the matter in accordance with normal practice and in good faith."[22]

International law

A State representative may conclude a treaty on behalf of a State if: (a) he possesses full powers; or (b) if it can be deduced he enjoys full powers from the practice of the States concerned or from other circumstances.

"Full powers" refers to the document:

> "emanating from the competent authority of a State designating a person or persons, to represent the State for negotiating, adopting or authenticating the text of a treaty, for expressing the consent of the State to be bound by a treaty, or for accomplishing any other act with respect to a treaty."[23]

Heads of State, governments and foreign affairs ministers are regarded as possessing by virtue of their office "full powers".[24]

An act relating to the conclusion of a treaty performed by a person who cannot be considered as enjoying "full powers" and thereby authorised to represent a State for that purpose is without legal effect, unless afterwards confirmed by that State.[25]

Adoption and confirmation of the text of a treaty

The text of a treaty may be adopted by the consent of all States participating in the drafting, by the majority vote of two-thirds of States present and voting, or by a different procedure if the two-thirds majority so agree.[26]

[22] art.46.
[23] art.2(1)(c).
[24] In *Qatar v Bahrain*, above, n.10 at 121–122, the Court denied the claim of Bahrain's Foreign Minister that he had no authority under Bahrain's constitution to conclude a treaty as the existence of a valid treaty had to be determined objectively.
[25] art.8.
[26] art.9.

Expression of consent

A State may indicate its consent to be bound by a treaty in a variety of ways, e.g. signature, signature *ad referendum*, ratification and accession.

Simple signature may be sufficient to bind parties, but frequently signature *ad referendum* is employed, that is signature subject to later ratification. Although lacking legal effect, *ad referendum* implies political approval and a moral obligation to seek ratification. Ratification in international law refers to the subsequent formal confirmation (subsequent to signature) by a State that it is bound by a treaty. Ratification is employed most frequently by those States (e.g. the United States) which are required to initiate some parliamentary process to gain approval for the State being bound by the international agreement in question. Between signature and ratification, a State is under an obligation to refrain from acts which would defeat the object and purpose of the treaty.[27]

Accession

A State may, by acceding to a treaty, express its consent to be bound by the terms of the treaty, that is a non-signatory State may subsequently become a party under a procedure provided by the treaty concerned. The term "adhesion" may also be encountered. Adhesion is distinct from accession in that it refers to a State's acceptance of either only certain aspects of the treaty or certain principles contained within it.

Reservations

Treaties may be likened to legislation, but unlike national law, where legislative measures apply uniformly to all, international law allows a State to become a party to a treaty while opting out from the application of certain provisions.

Article 2(1)(d) of the Vienna Convention defines a reservation as a:

---

[27] art.18(a). See for example the United States statement that it did not intend to become party to the ICC Statute: the US "has no legal obligations arising from its signature on December 31, 2000. The United States requests that its intention not to become a party. be reflected in the depositary's status lists relating to this treaty (US Dept. of State Press Statement, May 6, 2002)". See also *R v O* (Court of Appeal) (Criminal Division) September 2, 2008 *Times Law Reports* October 2, 2008 where it was held that the United Kingdom was obliged by Article 18 of the Vienna Convention on the Law of Treaties to refrain from acts which would defeat the purpose of the Trafficking Convention (Convention on Action against Trafficking in Human Beings (Council of Europe Treaty Series 197).

"unilateral statement, however phrased or named, made by
a State, when signing, ratifying, accepting, approving or
acceding to a treaty, whereby it purports to exclude or to
modify the legal effect of certain provisions of the treaty in
their application to that State."

A reservation is distinct from an "interpretative declaration" in
that the latter is simply a statement by a party to the treaty as to
the position it adopts concerning some aspect of the treaty.
However, it is only a reservation which allows a State to derogate
from an application of the treaty.[28]

Reservations only apply in respect of multipartite treaties. They
cannot apply with regard to bipartite treaties, as the rejection of a
proposed provision constitutes the refusal of an offer made and
therefore demands a renegotiation of the proposed term.[29]

Traditionally, it was maintained that a reservation could only
be inserted if all contracting parties to the treaty consented. In the
absence of unanimous agreement, the reservation was null and
void. However, with the increase in the number of States and the
simultaneous growth in the complexity of treaty subject matter,
obtaining the consent of States became increasingly difficult.
What was required, if States were not to reject treaties completely
which contained a particular provision to which they took exception, was a more flexible approach to reservations. The Advisory
Opinion requested in respect of the *Reservations to the Convention
on Genocide* case[30] heralded the necessary change in approach.

The Court expressed the view that a State making a reservation
to which one or more but not all parties to the Convention had
raised an objection could be regarded as a party to the
Convention provided (emphasis added) the reservation was compatible with the object and purpose of the Convention. As to the
effect of a reservation between the reserving State and: (i) those
objecting; and (ii) those accepting the reservation, the Court's
response was:

---

[28] For further discussion, see D. McRae 49 *B.Y.I.L.* 155 (1978) and the case of *Belilos
v Switzerland* E.C.H.R., Series A, No.132, Judgment of April 20, 1988. See also
Loizidou v Turkey (Preliminary Objections) E.C.H.R. Series A Number 301 (1995).
See also the general comments of the UN Human Rights Committee on the
effect of reservations made to the International Covenant on Civil and Political
Rights and the Optional Protocols, General Comment 24/52, November 2, 1994,
34 I.L.M. 1995, 839, 840; International Law Commission—Preliminary
Conclusions on Reservations to Normative Multi-lateral Treaties including
Human Rights Treaties, 1997, Report of the I.L.C. on its 49th Session,
A/52/10,pp.126–7.

[29] For distinction between bipartite and multipartite see Ch.2 p.20.

[30] I.C.J. Rep. 1951 15. Note that the Genocide Convention does not contain a
reservation clause.

"(a) that if a party to the Convention objects to a reservation which it considers to be incompatible with the object and purpose of the Convention, it can in fact consider that the reserving State is not a party to the Convention;

(b) that if, on the other hand, a party accepts the reservation as being compatible with the object and purpose of the Convention, it can in fact consider that the reserving State is a party to the Convention."[31]

The Court's opinion introduced the test of compatibility. This test, which is applied by States themselves, is a matter of subjective interpretation. The Court's opinion marked a sharp contrast to the previous approach, namely one of unity and a minimising of deviance from treaty provisions. This opinion opened up the possibility of different legal relationships existing between parties to the same agreement.

The Vienna Convention allows reservations unless:

"(a) the reservation is prohibited by treaty;" for example Art.64 of the European Convention on Human Rights prohibits "reservations of a general character";[32]

"(b) the treaty provides that only specified reservations, which do not include the reservation in question, may be made; or

"(c) in cases not falling under sub-paragraphs (a) and (b), the reservation is incompatible with the object and purpose of the treaty."[33]

Incompatibility with the object and purpose of the treaty can relate either to substantive provisions of the treaty, or to the nature and spirit of the treaty. For a case involving the "object and purpose" issue, see the *Restrictions to the Death Penalty* case.[34] A Convention may provide a mechanism for deciding whether a

---

[31] *ibid.* at 29–30.

[32] See *Belilos v Switzerland*, above, n.28 in which the Swiss reservation was declared invalid because, inter alia, it was "couched in terms that are too vague or broad for it to be possible to determine their exact scope or meaning", thus it was a "reservation of a general character".

[33] art.19. In the *Effect of Reservations Case*, 22 I.L.M. (1983), it was stated that art.75 of the American Convention on Human Rights 1969 had impliedly incorporated art.19(c) and thus allowed reservations which were not "incompatible with the object and purpose of the treaty." art.75 provides the American Convention on Human Rights "shall be subject to reservations only in conformity with" the Vienna Convention on the Law of Treaties.

[34] 23 I.L.M. 320 (1983).

provision is compatible or not, e.g. the UN Convention on the Elimination of all Forms of Racial Discrimination 1966 deems a reservation to be incompatible if at least two-thirds of Contracting Parties object.[35]

Acceptance of and objection to reservations

A reservation which is expressly authorised by a treaty does not demand the subsequent approval of other Contracting Parties unless required by the treaty.

If, however, it is apparent from the limited number of States concerned and from the object and purpose of the treaty "the application of the treaty in its entirety between all the parties is an essential condition of the consent of each one to be bound by the treaty", then any reservation must be accepted by all the parties.

In respect of a treaty which is the constituent instrument of an international organisation, a reservation, unless it is otherwise provided, must be accepted by the competent organ of the relevant organisation.

The general rules to be followed in other cases are:

"(a)   acceptance by another contracting State of a reservation constitutes the reserving State a party to the treaty in relation to that other State if or when the treaty is in force for those States;

(b)   an objection by another contracting State to a reservation does not preclude the entry into force of the treaty as between the objecting and reserving States unless a contrary intention is definitely expressed by the objecting State;

(c)   an act expressing a State's consent to be bound by the treaty and containing a reservation is effective as soon as at least one other contracting State has accepted the reservation."[36]

If a State does not object to a reservation: (a) within 12 months of having been informed of the reservation; or (b) within 12 months of having expressed consent to be bound by the treaty—depending on which is later—that State will be deemed to have expressed its consent to be bound by the treaty.[37]

---

[35] art.20 of the International Convention on the Elimination of All Forms of Racial Discrimination 1966, U.K.T.S. 77 (1969) Cmnd.4108.

[36] art.20(4).

[37] art.20(5).

Legal effects of reservations and of objections to reservations

The effect of a reservation established with regard to another party is that it:

> "(a) modifies for the reserving State in its relations with that other party the provisions of the treaty to which the reservation relates to the extent of the reservation; and
>
> (b) modifies those provisions to the same extent for that other party in its relations with the reserving State."[38]

If a State objects to a reservation, but does not oppose the entry into force of the treaty between itself and the reserving State, the provisions to which the reservation relates do not apply between the two States to the extent of the reservation. The provisions of the treaty for the other Contracting Parties are not modified by the reservation.[39] The effect of art.21(3) is illustrated by the Arbitration Tribunal's decision in the *English Channel Arbitration*:[40]

> "the combined effect of the French reservations and their rejection by the United Kingdom is neither to render Art.6 [that is, Art.6 of the 1958 Geneva Convention on the Continental Shelf] inapplicable *in toto*, as the French Republic contends, nor to render it applicable *in toto*, as the United Kingdom primarily contends. It is to render the Article inapplicable as between the two countries to the extent of the reservations."[41]

The effect in practice is that a multipartite agreement becomes fragmented. States will be parties to the same agreement, but in effect one agreement will exist between some Contracting Parties while another agreement will exist between other parties. In other words, under the umbrella of one multipartite Convention, several separate agreements may evolve. The overall purpose of the reservation system is to induce as many States as possible to adhere to a multipartite agreement.

---

[38] e.g. Libya's reservation to the Vienna Convention on Diplomatic Relations, whereby the diplomatic bag could be intercepted in suspicious circumstances, would by the operation of the principle of reciprocity have entitled the UK to exercise the same right; see Libyan People's Bureau Incident.

[39] art.21(3).

[40] 18 I.L.M. 397 (1979).

[41] *ibid.* at 341.

A reservation and an objection to a reservation must be expressed in writing but may be withdrawn at any time, unless otherwise provided for in the treaty. The withdrawal of a reservation becomes operative only when the State(s) concerned receive notice of the withdrawal. Similarly, the withdrawal of an objection to a reservation only has effect when received by the reserving State.[42] An express acceptance of a reservation must also be formulated in writing. The International Law Commission is currently preparing a Guide to the Practice on Reservations to Treaties. This Guide will be supplementary to the provisions on reservations contained in the Vienna Convention.[43] At its sixtieth session in 2008 the International Law Commission adopted 23 draft guidelines dealing with the formulation and withdrawal of acceptances and objections as well as the procedure for acceptance of reservations together with commentaries.[44] The International Law Commission also considered the thirteenth report of the Special Rapporteur on Reservations to Treaties.[45]

Entry into force

A treaty enters into force in such a manner and upon such a date as it (the treaty) may provide, or as the negotiating States may agree.[46] A multipartite treaty normally comes into force following receipt of a stipulated number of ratifications or accessions, e.g. the Vienna Convention provided for its own entry into force "on the thirtieth day following the date of deposit of the thirty-fifth instrument of ratification or accession."[47] Once the required number of ratifications have been received, a treaty will normally provide how soon after receipt of consent an agreement enters into force at the international level for the States concerned. For example, the 1982 Law of the Sea Convention entered into force one year after the 60th ratification, namely on November 16, 1994 whereas the Rome Statute, establishing the Permanent International Criminal Court, entered into force on July 1, 2002, 60 days after the 60th State became a party to the Statute.

---

[42] See *Democratic Republic of the Congo v Rwanda* I.C.J. Rep. 2006, paras 41–42.

[43] For text of Guidelines see International Law Commission's Annual Reports, G.A.O.R., A/50/10 to A/58/10.

[44] International Law Commission, Report on the work of its sixtieth session, (May 5 to June 6 and July 7 to August 8, 2008), G.A.O.R., 62nd Session, Supplement No.10 (A/63/10). The draft guidelines may be found in the International Law Commission's 2008 Annual Report found at Ch.VI, pp.136–248.

[45] A. Pellet, on Reactions to Interpretative Declarations. Official Records of the General Assembly, 49th Session, Supplement No.10 (A/49/10), para.382.

[46] art.16.

[47] art.84(1).

OBSERVANCE AND APPLICATION OF TREATIES[48]

States are charged with performing and fulfilling their treaty obligations, which are binding in good faith—*pacta sunt servanda* is the maxim which expresses this basic canon of treaty observance. As a rule, treaties do not have retroactive effect. If they are to have such effect, this will be expressly stated. Unless otherwise provided, a treaty applies to all the territory of a Contracting Party. The Vienna Convention did not address itself to the question of dependencies, but an agreement may spell out the dependencies to which it is to apply. If silent, e.g. under US law, an agreement will be held as applying to all dependencies of the United States. Parties to a multipartite treaty may agree to conclude a new treaty and accordingly negate any preceding agreement.

If all States consent then no problem arises, however there may be parties to the old treaty which do not accede to the new agreement. The relationship between two such States will be governed by the treaty to which both States are parties (that is, the former).[49]

TREATY INTERPRETATION

How is a treaty to be interpreted? There are three main approaches in international law to treaty interpretation:

(a) the "objective" approach—interpretation in accordance with the ordinary use of the words of the treaty;[50]

(b) the "subjective" approach—interpretation in accordance with the intention of the parties to the treaty; and

(c) the "teleological" approach—interpretation in accordance with the treaty's aims and objectives.

Although characterised as distinct, the three approaches are in practice not mutually exclusive. Credence may be given to the principles found in the three approaches, as is reflected in the international jurisprudence which has emerged.

The Vienna Convention adopts an integrated approach to interpretation, but nevertheless gives emphasis to the ordinary-meaning approach. Article 31 of the Convention sets out the general rule of interpretation as being:

---

[48] art.26.
[49] art.30(4)(b).
[50] As reflected in the I.C.J.'s statement in Competence of the General Assembly for the Admission of a State to the United Nations, I.C.J. Rep. 1950, p.4 at 8.

"A treaty shall be interpreted in good faith in accordance with the ordinary meaning to be given to the terms of the treaty in their context and in the light of its object and purpose."

Article 31 allows the use of the teleological approach, but only to shed light on the ordinary meaning of the words of the treaty provisions.[51] It may be invoked as an ancillary aid in interpretation and not as an independent approach of interpretation. A special meaning may be given to a term if it is evident that is what the relevant parties intended. "Context" includes the text of the treaty, the preamble, any annexes and also:

"(a) any agreement relating to the treaty which was made between all the parties in connection with the conclusion of the treaty;

(b) any instrument which was made by one or more parties in connection with the conclusion of the treaty and accepted by the other parties as an instrument related to the treaty."[52]

In addition, account may be taken of:

"(a) any subsequent agreement between the parties regarding the interpretation of the treaty or the application of its provisions;

(b) any subsequent practice in the application of the treaty which establishes the agreement of the parties regarding its interpretation;

(c) any relevant rules of international law applicable in the relations between the parties."[53]

If giving the ordinary meaning in the terms of the treaty would lead to an ambiguous or obscure meaning, or would produce a manifestly absurd and unreasonable approach, supplementary means of interpretation may be invoked.[54] Supplementary includes "the

---

[51] The I.C.J. recognised the provisions of art.31 as customary international law in *Territorial Dispute (Libya v Chad)* I.C.J. Rep. 1994 p.6; see also the *Kisikili/Sedudu Island (Botswana v Namibia)* case 1999 I.C.J. Rep. 1045.

[52] art.31(2).

[53] art.31(3).

[54] The I.C.J. has rejected supplementary evidence when the text of the treaty is clear, see the *Maritime Delimitation and Territorial Questions* case above, n.10.

preparatory work of the treaty and the circumstances of its conclusion."[55]

Preparatory work—*travaux préparatoires*—is not defined in the Vienna Convention, but the term, it is accepted, refers to records documenting the treaty's drafting and includes the records of negotiations between the participating drafting States. A treaty is to be interpreted in the context of the circumstances prevailing at the time the treaty was concluded.[56] However account may be taken of "the present day state of scientific knolwedge, as reflected in the documentary material submitted to it by the parties."[57]

In certain cases, the opinion of expert bodies may also be utilised. "Circumstances" of its "conclusion" refer not only to contemporary circumstances but also to the historical context against which the treaty was concluded, e.g. *Anglo-Iranian Oil Co.* case.[58]

Interpretation of treaties authenticated in two or more languages

A text is equally authoritative in each language, unless the agreement provides and the parties agree that, in the case of divergence, a particular text shall prevail. One text may be designated as authoritative while other versions may only be recognised as having the status of "official texts" (that is, a text signed by the negotiating States, but not adopted as authoritative). In the event of any doubt as to the meaning between texts, the more limited interpretation and the one which will least restrict a State's sovereignty is preferred.

THIRD STATES

Pacta tertiis nec nocent nec prosunt—a treaty does not create either obligations or rights for a third State without its consent. This rule of customary international law is spelt out in art.34 of the Vienna Convention. This does not preclude a provision contained in a treaty from becoming law for a non-party when the provision has crystallised into international law. The non-party is bound, not by the treaty, but rather by customary international law.[59] Article 34 contains the general rule, however there are exceptions, and

---

[55] art.32.
[56] See *Cameroon v Nigeria*, I.C.J. Rep., 2002, p.303.
[57] *Botswana/ Namibia*, I.C.J. Rep., 1999, p.1045 at 1060.
[58] I.C.J. Rep. 1952 p.3 at 105.
[59] art.38. See also *North Sea Continental Shelf Case*, I.C.J. Rep. 1969, 3. Cf. *Military and Para Military Activities in and Against Nicaragua (Merits)*, I.C.J. Rep. 1986, p.14.

special territorial arrangements may produce obligations which third parties are obliged to respect (e.g. in the case of the Aaland Islands). Article 2(6) of the UN Charter provides:

> "the Organisation shall ensure that States which are not Members of the United Nations act in accordance with these Principles so far as may be necessary for the maintenance of international peace and security."

Article 2(6) is regarded as being customary international law, and any State acting contrary to art.2(6) would be violating customary international law.

A treaty can produce obligations for a third State "if the parties to the treaty intend the provisions to be the means of establishing the obligation and the third State expressly accepts that obligation in writing."[60] A third State may derive rights from a treaty, e.g. those guaranteeing freedom of passage through the Suez and Kiel Canals, if that is the intention of the parties to the treaty and the assent of the third State has been secured. In contrast, however, to the assent of States on which an obligation is incumbent, the assent of a benefiting State "shall be presumed so long as the contrary is not indicated, unless the treaty otherwise provides."[61]

AMENDMENT AND MODIFICATION

Both amendment and modification relate to a revision of treaty terms by parties. Amendment is the more formal process involving at least, *prima facie*, all parties to the treaty, whereas modification is a "private arrangement" between particular parties and in respect of particular provisions.

Amendment

In a bipartite treaty the amendment process is straightforward but in a multipartite treaty the agreement of all States to a proposed amendment may be difficult to secure. Article 40 lays down the procedure which, if not provided for by the treaty, should be followed. Article 40 allows for amendment by fewer than all Contracting Parties to the original treaty by permitting amendment between those parties in agreement after (emphasis added) all States have been given the opportunity to participate in considering amendment proposals. An amending agreement does not bind a State which, although a party to the original treaty, fails to become a party to the amending agreement.

---

[60] art.35.
[61] art.36(1).

Modification

Article 41 allows two or more parties to a multipartite treaty to conclude a modifying agreement between themselves, provided the possibility of modification is recognised by the treaty, is not prohibited by the treaty, does not affect the rights of other parties, nor relates to "a provision, derogation which is incompatible with the effective execution of the object and purpose of the treaty as a whole."[62]

VALIDITY OF TREATIES

The Vienna Convention stipulates five grounds on which the validity of an agreement may be challenged. The Convention is exhaustive as regards the grounds which may be raised. A State may not invoke other grounds of invalidity. The five grounds are:

(a) non-compliance with national law requirements;

(b) error;

(c) fraud and corruption;

(d) coercion;

(e) *jus cogens.*

Non-compliance with national law requirements

See above at p.208.

Error

Error is of limited significance and its role has been markedly less than that of error in the municipal law of contract. Error may only be invoked by a State if "the error relates to a fact or situation which was assumed by that State to exist at the time when the treaty was concluded and formed an essential basis of its consent to be bound by the treaty."[63]

Error has been invoked almost exclusively in respect of boundary questions. A State which contributed by its behaviour to the error, or should have known of a possible error, cannot relieve itself subsequently of its treaty obligations.[64] An error in the wording of the treaty is not a ground for invalidating the treaty. Such an error must be corrected in accordance with art.79 of the Convention and most frequently by a quite informal procedure.

---

[62] art.41(1)(b)(ii).
[63] art.48(1).
[64] art.48(2); see also the *Temple case*, I.C.J. Rep. 1962 p.6 at 26.

Fraud and corruption

Fraud and corruption, like error, are of little significance. Article 49 provides that a treaty may be invalidated "if a State has been induced to conclude a treaty by the fraudulent conduct of another negotiating State, . . ." Article 50 provides a treaty may be invalidated if a State's consent to a treaty "has been procured through the corruption of its representative directly or indirectly by another negotiating State, . . ." "Corrupts", "fraudulent conduct" and "corruption" are not defined in the Convention or by international jurisprudence.

Coercion

A treaty will be of no legal effect (emphasis added) if a State's consent "has been procured by the coercion of its representative through acts or threats directed against him . . ."[65] The use of coercion against a State's representative is rare, especially as art.51 is concerned with coercion of the representative's person, rather than with coercion by way of a threat of action against his State.

Acceptance of a treaty through coercion, and the threat of coercion against a State "in violation of the principles of international law embodied in the Charter of the United Nations", renders a treaty void.[66] Article 52 reflects modern international law's prohibition on the use of force. The Vienna Convention refers explicitly to the use of force as contained in art.2(4) of the Charter of the United Nations and does not extend to political and economic coercion.[67] For further discussion on the interpretation of force see Ch.11 pp.289 *et seq.*

Jus cogens

Jus cogens refers to peremptory norms of international law. A peremptory norm is defined, for the purposes of the Convention, as one which is "accepted and recognised by the international community of States as a whole", and from which "no derogation is permitted and which can be modified only by a subsequent norm of general international law having the same character."[68]

---

[65] art.51.
[66] art.52.
[67] However see acknowledgement of moral and political pressures in *Fisheries Jurisdiction Case*, I.C.J. Rep., 1973, p.3. Where it was noted "there are moral and political pressures which cannot be proved by the so-called "documentary evidence", but which are in fact indisputably real and which have, given rise to treaties and conventions claimed to be freely concluded and subjected to the principle of *pacta sunt servanda*." at 47.
[68] art.53.

Any treaty which conflicts at the time of its conclusion with such a norm will be void. Should a new peremptory norm of general international law develop, any existing treaty which is contrary to that norm becomes void and terminates.[69]

The Vienna Convention acknowledges that there are certain rules of international law which enjoy a superior status and as such cannot be affected by treaty. The Vienna Convention does not identify peremptory norms and, as already highlighted, such norms must not only be accepted by the international community, but must also be accepted as being of peremptory force.[70] It is now accepted that the prohibition on genocide, slavery, torture, the use of force and the right to self-determination all fall within the classification of *jus cogens*. However, given the developing nature of international law, the current list of rules regarded as *jus cogens* is not exhaustive.

TERMINATION OF A TREATY

A treaty may be terminated as provided for by the treaty or by the consent of the parties. Material breach by one of the parties may also terminate or suspend a treaty, as may a supervening impossibility or a substantial change in circumstances.

Termination by treaty provision or consent

A treaty may provide for termination. A treaty which is silent regarding termination may not be denounced unless it is apparent that the parties intended to admit the possibility of denunciation or withdrawal, or where such a right may be implied by the nature of the treaty.[71] Two or three parties to a multipartite treaty may at any time conclude an agreement suspending the operation of certain provisions temporarily between them, provided the treaty allows it, it does not restrict the rights of other parties and it is not incompatible with the object and purpose of the treaty.[72] It is common for a treaty either to be for a fixed term, e.g. the treaty establishing the European Coal and Steel Community had a term of 50 years and ended in July 2002, or to provide that a party may withdraw after giving a certain period of notice. If all parties to a treaty conclude a later treaty relating to the same subject matter, the original treaty will be considered terminated. Similarly, this will be the case where it appears the matter should be governed by the later treaty, or where the provisions of the

[69] art.64.
[70] For further discussion thereof, see Ch.2.
[71] art.56.
[72] art.58(1).

later treaty "are so far incompatible with those of the earlier one that the two treaties are not capable of being applied at the same time."[73]

Material breach

A mere breach of a treaty provision is not sufficient to terminate a treaty. Article 60(3) of the Vienna Convention defines a material breach as one constituting either:

"(a) a repudiation of the treaty not sanctioned by the present Convention; or

(b) the violation of a provision essential to the accomplishment of the object or purpose of the treaty."

In a bipartite treaty, material breach may be invoked by the "innocent" party to terminate the treaty or suspend its operation in whole or in part. Material breach of a multipartite treaty allows the "innocent" parties to suspend, by unanimous agreement, the operation of the treaty, in whole or in part, or to terminate it either: "(i) in the relations between themselves and the defaulting State, or (ii) as between all the parties."

The party particularly affected by the breach may invoke the breach as reason for suspending the operation of the treaty in whole or in part in relations between itself and the defaulting State. Any party other than the defaulting State may invoke the breach so as to suspend the operation of the treaty in whole or in part with respect to itself, if the treaty is of such a character a material breach of its provisions by one party radically changes the position of every party with respect to the further performance of its obligations under the treaty. Neither the definition of material breach nor the consequences of such a breach apply to:

"provisions relating to the protection of the human person contained in treaties of a humanitarian character, in particular to provisions prohibiting any form of reprisals against persons protected by such treaties."[74]

The 1949 Geneva Red Cross Conventions are instances of such treaties. Article 46 of Convention I states "Reprisals against the wounded, sick, personnel, buildings, or equipment protected by the Convention are prohibited."[75]

[73] art.59(1).
[74] art.60(5).
[75] See below, Ch.11.

The breach by one party of its obligation under a humanitarian or human rights Convention does not entitle other parties to either terminate or suspend their own obligations arising from the Convention. As to whether there has been a breach each party may decide for itself, except where the treaty provides a procedure for that purpose.

Supervening impossibility of performance

Article 61 of the Vienna Convention, which provides for termination of a treaty on the grounds of a supervening impossibility of performance, was designed to cover such relatively rare happenings as the "submergence of an island, the drying up of a river or the destruction of a dam or hydroelectric installation indispensable for the execution of a treaty."[76] Performance may become impossible because a party ceases to exist as a State (for the position when this occurs see "State Succession", below). If the impossibility is temporary, it may be invoked only as a ground for suspending the operation of the treaty. A party may not invoke impossibility of performance if that party has been responsible for making performance impossible.

Fundamental change of circumstances

The doctrine of *rebus sic stantibus* may be invoked to terminate a treaty. The operation of this doctrine, which literally means "things remaining as they are", rests on the assumption that a treaty may be denounced if circumstances change profoundly from those prevailing at the time of the treaty's conclusion. In the *Fisheries Jurisdiction* case,[77] Iceland challenged the Court's jurisdiction to hear the dispute between Iceland, Britain and Germany on the grounds that there had been a fundamental change of circumstances since the conclusion of the 1961 Exchange of Notes. These Notes contained, *inter alia*, a compromissory clause providing for reference to the International Court of Justice. Iceland alleged that there had been a fundamental change of circumstances as a consequence of changes in fishing techniques. The Court identified the changes of circumstances which would be recognised as fundamental or vital as those "which imperil the existence or vital development of one of the parties."[78]

---

[76] *Y.B.I.L.C.* 1966, II, p.256.
[77] *Fisheries Jurisdiction* case (Jurisdiction), I.C.J. Rep. 1973 p.3.
[78] *ibid.* at 19.

The Court held, however:

> "the apprehended dangers for the vital interests of Iceland, resulting from changes in fishing techniques, cannot constitute a fundamental change with respect to the lapse or subsistence of the compromissory clause establishing the Court's jurisdiction,"[79]

and for a change of circumstances to justify termination of a treaty, there would have to be:

> "a radical transformation of the extent of the obligations still to be performed. The change must have increased the burden of the obligations to be executed to the extent of rendering the performance something essentially different from that originally undertaken."[80]

The changed circumstances doctrine will only be invoked successfully when it applies to circumstances which were not contemplated by the parties when the treaty was concluded. In the Fisheries Jurisdiction case, the Court maintained that not only had the jurisdictional obligation not been radically transformed, it had remained precisely as it was in 1961. The compromissory clause indeed anticipated a dispute such as the one that had arisen. Similarly in the *Danube Dam* case,[81] the Court held that the prevailing political conditions were not sufficiently related to the object and purpose of the Treaty so as to constitute an essential basis of the consent of the parties. Thus, although changed, it did not radically alter the extent of the objectives to be performed; the same was also held to be true of the economic system in force at the time the said treaty was concluded in 1977. The Court also denied that advances in the law of environment were completely unforeseen. *Rebus sic stantibus* may not be invoked in respect of a boundary settlement or by a State which has caused the fundamental change.

Severance of diplomatic or consular relations

The severance of diplomatic or consular relations between parties to a treaty does not affect legal relations between the parties,

---

[79] *ibid.* at 20.
[80] *ibid.* at 21.
[81] *Gabcikovo-Nagymaros Project (Hungary v Slovakia)* (1997) I.C.J. Rep. p.7; 38 I.L.M. 162. See also for application of art.61.

except in so far as the existence of diplomatic or consular relations is vital for the treaty's application.[82]

Termination of an agreement normally applies to the treaty as a whole, unless the treaty provides otherwise. This is the norm reflected in art.44. Exception is admitted if the ground for termination relates to particular clauses which can be separated from the rest of the treaty. These clauses may be terminated if their acceptance was not an essential basis of the consent of the other parties to be bound, and if continued performance of the remainder of the treaty would not be unjust. A party, a victim of fraud or corruption, has the option of invalidating the agreement as a whole or in part. Such an option is not available in respect of the use or threat of force or violation of *jus cogens*.

A State loses its right to initiate a claim for invalidating, terminating, withdrawing from or suspending the operation of a treaty if, subsequent to becoming aware of the fact, it has expressly agreed the treaty is valid, or, by its conduct, it can be said to have acquiesced in the validity of the treaty.[83]

CONSEQUENCES OF INVALIDITY, TERMINATION OR SUSPENSION

A treaty which is established as invalid is void. The provisions of a void treaty have no legal force. If, however, acts have been performed in reliance upon such a treaty:

"(a) each party may require any other party to establish as far as possible in their mutual relations the position that would have existed if the acts had not been performed;

(b) acts performed in good faith before the invalidity was invoked are not rendered unlawful by reason only of the invalidity of the treaty."[84]

The above does not apply "with respect to the party to which the fraud, the act of corruption or the coercion is imputable."[85]

Termination of a treaty unless otherwise provided releases the parties concerned from any future obligations, but does not affect any right, obligation or legal situation of the parties created through the execution of the treaty prior to its termination. If a treaty is declared void under art.53 (conflict with a peremptory norm) the parties are charged with eliminating as far as possible

---

[82] art.63.
[83] art.45.
[84] art.69(2).
[85] art.69(3).

the consequences of any act performed in reliance on the offending provision, and with bringing their mutual relations into conformity with the peremptory norm of general international law. If art.64 is invoked to terminate a treaty, the parties are released from any further obligation to perform the treaty, but the rights, obligations and legal situation of the parties created prior to the treaty's termination are not affected, provided "those rights, obligations or situations may thereafter be maintained only to the extent that their maintenance is not itself in conflict with the new peremptory norm of general international law."[86]

Suspension has, for the period of suspension, a similar effect to termination. During the period of suspension, parties are to refrain from acts which would be likely to obstruct the resumption of the treaty's operation.

Parties to the Vienna Convention are called to seek a peaceful solution to disputes relating to the validity of treaties. This general rule is reinforced by art.66, which provides that if a solution is not achieved on the lapse of 12 months, the parties shall submit to the International Court of Justice, to arbitration or to the consultation procedure provided for in the Convention's Annex.

STATE SUCCESSION

What happens to a State's treaty obligations when it is replaced by another State on the international plane? In 1978, the International Law Commission produced the Vienna Convention on the Succession of States in Respect of Treaties.[87] The Convention reflects predominantly the views of the "newer" States and, as such, represents progressive development rather than a codification of existing law. Essentially, the "clean-slate" view is favoured with respect to successor States. That is, a State is not to be tied by the obligations of its predecessor. The obligations maintained by a State's predecessor by way of multipartite or bipartite agreements are not automatically incumbent on a State. A State has the option of assuming the multipartite treaties of its predecessor, nevertheless, it is not required to do so. The continuance of a bipartite treaty depends upon agreement, either express or implied, between the parties, that is the succeeding State and the other Contracting State.

There is, however, an exception to this general rule. It does not apply in respect of treaties establishing boundaries, territorial regimes and to those imposing restrictions on a territory for the

---

[86] art.71(2).
[87] Misc.1 (1980) Cmnd.7760; 72 *A.J.I.L.* 971 (1978); 1978 I.L.M. p.1488. The Convention entered into force on November 6, 1996.

benefit of another State. To apply the clean-slate principle in such instances would prove too disruptive. Accordingly a successor State is bound by treaties of that type to which its predecessor has been a party. In the event of States uniting or separating, the Convention stipulates that treaties continue in force for the territory concerned unless the parties have agreed otherwise, or the result would be inconsistent with the object and purpose of the treaty and would radically change the conditions for its operation.[88] State property, archives and debts are dealt with in the 1983 Vienna Convention on Succession of States in Respect of Property, Archives and Debts.[89]

Under art.11 of the German Unification Treaty,[90] West and East Germany took the position that international treaties of the Federal German Republic would remain in effect, and rights and obligations arising therefrom would also apply in the former German Democratic Republic. Under art.12, international treaties of the German Democratic Republic were to be reviewed with the Contracting States as to their applicability, modification or termination, with due regard to the aspects of pacta sunt servanda, the interests of the Contracting States and the contractual obligations of West Germany and the European Communities.

The transfer of Hong Kong to China in 1997 presented a unique situation in international treaty law, namely the continued application of Hong Kong's treaty obligations. Arrangements for the application of multilateral and bilateral international agreements after the transfer of the government of Hong Kong to China on June 30, 1997 were established in the 1984 Sino–British Joint Declaration on the Question of Hong Kong. The Declaration provides the Hong Kong Special Administrative Region (HKSAR) with a high degree of autonomy, able to conclude international agreements with States, regions and relevant international organisations in a number of areas, using the name "Hong Kong China".[91] Hong Kong therefore continues to have some treaty-making competence in the international legal system, independently of the Chinese relationship.

Notwithstanding the position of newer States, there is increasing argument in favour of treaties relating to human rights,

---

[88] State succession raises issues other than those raised by succession to treaties, but these are outside the subject matter of this text.

[89] UN Doc. A/Conf. 117/14 (1983) 12 I.L.M. 306.

[90] FRG: GDR: Treaty on the Establishment of German Unity, at Berlin, August 31, 1990, entered into force on September 29, 1991; 30 I.L.M. 457 (1991).

[91] Foreign and Commonwealth Office, London. Paper on the Application after June 30, 1997 of Multilateral and Bilateral International Agreements, Hong Kong Department, April 1996, para.26 of the Joint Declaration.

binding the successor States. In the *Case Concerning the Application of the Convention on the Prevention and Punishment of the Cirme of Genocide*[92] Judges Weeramanatry and Shaahbuddeen expressed the view that there is States succession to Conventions such as the Genocide Convention. Judge Shaahbuddeen was of the view this was demanded if the Genocide Convention was to fulfil its object and purpose. The views of both Judges resonante with the views of the UN Human Rights Committee as expressed in General Comment (No.26). Namely "once the people are accorded the protection of the rights under the Covenant, such protection devolves with territory and continues to belong to them, notwithstanding change in government of the State Party, including dismemberment in more than one state or state succession or any subsequent action of the State Party designed to divest them of their rights guaranteed by the Covenant."[93] Although the International Court of Justice did not specifically address the continued application of human rights treaties the issue is one of contemporary importance. Of course new States are bound by any customary human rights provisions that have been established.

---

[92] *Bosnia and Herzegovina v Yugoslavia* (Preliminary Objections) I.C.J. Rep. 1996, p.595.

[93] Human Rights Committee General Comment 26 (61), UN Doc. A/53/40, Annex VII, December 8, 1997, para.4.

11. THE USE OF FORCE

The use of force (that is, *jus ad bellum*—the right to wage war)[1] is prohibited by international law. The UN Charter requires Member States to settle disputes among themselves by peaceful means, and to refrain in their international relations with each other from either the threat of or the use of force.[2] The serious breach of an international obligation of essential importance for the maintenance of international peace and security has been characterised by the International Law Commission in its Draft Articles on Responsibility of States[3] for Internationally Wrongful Acts.[4] Contemporary international law may prohibit the use of force, but international law cannot prevent the use of force any more than national criminal law can prevent murder. International law consequently aims to regulate the use of force, and there is accordingly an accepted distinction between the legitimate and illegitimate use of force. Nevertheless, prohibition

---

[1] *Jus ad bellum* is to be distinguished from *jus in bello* relating to the conduct of hostilities—discussed below, p.320.
[2] UN Charter, arts 2(3) and 2(4).
[3] See Ch.8 above.
[4] Draft art.40.

on the use of force remains the general rule with the exceptions admitted by international law clearly defined. This, however, has not always been the case.

THE LAW BEFORE 1945

In earliest history, a "just war" was regarded as a legitimate use of force. St Augustine (AD 354–430) articulated the "just war" as one designed to avenge injuries which had been sustained and which "the nation or city against which warlike action is to be directed has neglected either to punish wrongs committed by its own citizens or to restore what has been unjustly taken by it." The "just war" was founded in theological doctrine but, with the breakdown of the Church's authority, power was assumed by the sovereign nation State, and the right to use force was recognised as an inherent right of every independent sovereign State. International law placed no restraints on the use of force; factors other than legal considerations affected a State's decision to resort to force and the use of force was regarded as a legitimate action for all States to adopt.

The unprecedented devastation of the First World War prompted States to establish an international forum in which it was hoped States would discuss their problems rather than resort to force. Consequently, the League of Nations was founded. The Covenant of the League of Nations, signed in 1919, did not prohibit war, but rather placed limitations upon the use of force. In the event of a dispute which was potentially disruptive, Member States agreed under the Covenant to submit the dispute to arbitration, judicial settlement or to inquiry by the Council of the League. War was not to be resorted to until three months after the award by the arbitrator, the judicial decision, or the Council's report. In this way the Covenant provided a "cooling-off" period for protagonists. Members also agreed not to go to war with fellow Members of the League who complied with either an arbitral award, judicial decision or with a unanimous report of the Council. The Covenant required Member States "to respect and preserve as against external aggression the territorial integrity and political independence of all Members of the League."[5] In 1928, the international community was successful in agreeing to a comprehensive ban on war as an instrument of national policy. Sixty-three States signed the General Treaty for the Renunciation of War (also known as the Kellogg–Briand Pact or the Pact of Paris),[6] in which parties agreed to seek a peaceful solution to all

---

[5] art.10 of the Covenant, U.K.T.S. 4 (1919) Cmd.153.
[6] U.K.T.S. 29 (1929) Cmd.3410; 94 L.N.T.S. 57; 22 *A.J.I.L.* Supp.171.

disputes arising between them. Nevertheless, the right of self-defence still existed. The Treaty, although it has never been terminated, has been superseded by art.2(4) of the United Nations (UN) Charter. Treaties, however, cannot prevent wars, and the Second World War broke out in 1939, only 11 years after the signing of the Renunciation Treaty.

THE LAW AS OF 1945

Article 2(3) of the UN Charter requires all Member States "to settle their international disputes by peaceful means in such a manner that international peace and security, and justice are not endangered". While art.2(4) demands that all Member States:

> "shall refrain in their international relations from the threat or use of force against the territorial integrity or political independence of any state, or in any manner inconsistent with the purposes of the United Nations."

Article 2(4), as a provision of the UN Charter, is addressed to all Members of the United Nations; however, the prohibition on the use of force as contained in art.2(4) is firmly established as a principle of customary international law, which has attained the character of *jus cogens*, and as such is addressed to all members of the international community.[7]

Extent of the prohibition contained in Article 2(4)

Article 2(4) prohibits the use of force. It is not concerned only with the outlawing of war: art.2(4) does not distinguish between war and the use of force falling short of war, e.g. reprisals.[8]

Article 2(4) thus embraces all threats of and acts of violence without distinction. The article specifically refers to the threat or use of force "against the territorial integrity or political independence of any State ...". Can force be used to enforce a right when force is not employed against territorial integrity or political independence? Can force be used to protect human rights? Article 2(4) should be read as a whole within the context of the UN Charter. Force contrary to "the purposes of the United

---

[7] Endorsed by the International Court of Justice in the case *Concerning Military and Paramilitary Activities in and against Nicaragua (Merits)* I.C.J. Rep. 1986 p.14 at 100.

[8] A declaration of war is seldom made by State parties to hostilities. "War" is a technical term. Acknowledgment of war produces consequences under international law, e.g. role of neutral States and the application of national law, e.g. regarding the status of non-nationals. For reprisals see below p.307.

Nations" is also prohibited. The purposes of the UN are spelt out in art.1 of the Charter. The purposes include respect for the principle of equal rights and self-determination and respect for human rights, but nevertheless the overriding purpose of the UN remains:

> "[T]o maintain international peace and security, and to that end: to take effective collective measures for the prevention and removal of threats to the peace, and for the suppression of acts of aggression or other breaches of the peace, and to bring about by peaceful means, and in conformity with the principles of justice and international law, adjustment or settlement of international disputes or situations which might lead to a breach of the peace; . . ."[9]

The emphasis is on the maintenance of peace and security and on resolving both potential and actual conflict by peaceful means.

Article 2(4) has been supplemented by the 1970 General Assembly Declaration on Principles of International Law Concerning Friendly Relations and Co-operation among States in Accordance with the Charter of the United Nations (the 1970 Declaration).[10] The Resolution is not legally binding on Members, however it is regarded as representing the consensus of the international community on the legal interpretation to be given to the principles enunciated in the UN Charter. This Declaration adds flesh to the prohibition on the use of force. It provides, *inter alia*:

> "A war of aggression constitutes a crime against the peace for which there is responsibility under international law. Every State has the duty to refrain from the threat or use of force to violate the existing international boundaries of another State or as a means of solving international disputes, including territorial disputes and problems concerning frontiers of States. States have a duty to refrain from acts of reprisal involving the use of force. Every State has the duty to refrain from any forcible action, which deprives peoples of realising equal rights and self-determination.
>
> Every State has the duty to refrain from organising or encouraging the organisation of irregular forces or armed

---

[9] UN Charter, art.1.1.

[10] G.A. Res.2625 (XXV), October 24, 1970—see also Resolution on the Definition of Aggression 1974, G.A. Res. 3314 (XXIX); 69 *A.J.I.L.* 480 (1975) and The Declaration on the Enhancement of the Effectiveness of the Principle of Refraining from the Threat or Use of Force in International Relations 1987, G.A. Res.42/22, G.A.O.R., 42nd Sess., Supp., 49, p.287 (1987).

bands, including mercenaries, for incursion into the territory of another State.

Every State has the duty to refrain from organising, instigating, assisting or participating in acts of civil strife or terrorist acts in another State or acquiescing in organised activities within its territory, directed towards the commission of such acts, when the acts involve a threat or use of force.

The territory of a State shall not be the object of military occupation resulting from the use of force. The territory of a State shall not be the object of acquisition by another State resulting from the threat or use of force. No territorial acquisition resulting from the threat or use of force shall be recognised as legal."

The international community's response to the September 11, 2001 terrorist attacks is reflected in Security Council Resolution 1373,[11] which calls upon all States, *inter alia*:

"to prevent and suppress the financing of terrorist attacks; refrain from providing any form of support, active or passive, to entities or persons involved in terrorist acts, including by suppressing recruitment of members of terrorist groups and eliminating supplies of weapons to terrorists."[12]

States were also called upon to engage in greater co-operation *vis-à-vis* the Convention for the Suppression of the Financing of Terrorism, 1999.[13]

To put it simply, any threat or use of force by a State, other than in accordance with the exceptions provided for under the UN Charter, is contrary to, and prohibited by, contemporary international law.

Does Article 2(4) only prohibit use of armed force?

Force does not necessarily have to refer to armed force. Force can be economic and/or political. Does art.2(4) confine itself to

---

[11] 28 September, 2001. Resolution 1373 was adopted under Ch.VII of the UN Charter and is distinct from previous enforcement Resolutions in calling for sanctions against terrorism and terrorist groups without identifying a particular State or particular situation. See also General Assembly Res.A/Res./56/88 (on the report of the Sixth Committee (A/56/593)) and Security Council Resolution 1368 (2001).

[12] 1(a) and 2(a).

[13] *ibid.* 3(d).

prohibiting only the use of armed force or are other categories of force similarly prohibited?

The preamble of the UN Charter and art.51 (on a State's inherent right of self-defence, considered below) specifically mentions "armed force". The 1970 Declaration in the section on the principle of non-intervention, on the other hand, is inconclusive. It emphasises the duty of States to refrain, in their international relations, from military, political, economic or any other form of coercion. However in the section regarding the use of force, force is not qualified. The imprecision of definition reflects the dichotomy which existed essentially between developed and developing States. The latter would have interpreted force to encompass economic and political force,[14] while the former maintained it was only armed force which was outlawed. Although, the former group of States did concede that economic and political pressure might constitute illegal intervention. Economic coercion, although prohibited in the 1970 Declaration's section on non-intervention, remains undefined and in the *Nicaragua* case, the I.C.J. denied that American economic sanctions against Nicaragua constituted "a breach of the customary-law principle of non-intervention."[15]

As far as art.2(4) and the legal regime envisaged by the UN Charter are concerned, the prohibition is one aimed at outlawing armed force and "gunboat diplomacy" in relations between States.

Exceptions to the prohibition on the threat or use of force

The use of force only remains legitimate under international law in particularly well-defined circumstances:

- in self-defence either individual or collective—in accordance with art.51 of the UN Charter;

- collective measures taken under the auspices of the UN; and

- if authorised by a competent organ of the UN.

Self-defence

Customary international law recognised a State's right of self-defence, but the extent of that right was ill-defined. It was only as

---

[14] See also para.4(e) of the 1974 Declaration on the Establishment of a New International Economic Order, 13 I.L.M. 715 (1974).
[15] Above, n.7, at 126.

States imposed restrictions on the employment of force that the need to articulate the concept of self-defence in international law became more acute.

Under customary international law, the use of force had to be justified if States were at peace. The use of force by one State against another with which it was not at war was, *prima facie*, unlawful. The circumstances which allowed the exercise of self-defence were articulated in the now famous communication of the US Secretary of State Webster to the British Government following the Caroline incident.[16]

The *Caroline* was a vessel which operated from US territory supplying rebel insurrectionaries in Canada. A British force destroyed the *Caroline* and two US citizens were killed. A British subject, Mcleod, was charged with murder and arson.

In his letter, Secretary Webster emphasised the success of the British government's defence was dependent on the British government establishing that such action was justified on grounds of "a necessity of self-defence and preservation" It had to be demonstrated that the need for self-defence was "instant, overwhelming, leaving no choice of means, and no moment for deliberation." It was also necessary for Britain to show that the Canadian authorities had done nothing "unreasonable or excessive; since the act, justified by the necessity of self-defence, must be limited by that necessity, and kept clearly within it."

To summarise, the exercise of force in self-defence was justified under customary international law provided the need for it was:

(a) instant;

(b) overwhelming;

(c) immediate; and

(d) there was no viable alternative action which could be taken.

The *Caroline* incident also affirmed the extent of force used in self-defence should be commensurate with the violation against which the self-defence is being used, that is to say proportionate.[17] These criteria have come to be described as "the Webster formula", and still apply today as is confirmed by the *Nicaragua*

---

[16] 29 B.F.S.P. 1137–1138; 30 B.F.S.P. 195–196.

[17] e.g. the intervention by Israel into Lebanon in 2006 was criticised by members of the Security Council for being disproportionate in nature, see Verbatim Record, Security Council 5489th meeting, UN Doc S/PV.5489.

case[18] and *Oil Platforms (Merits)* case,[19] and the *Legality of the Threat or Use of Nuclear Weapons, Advisory Opinion.*[20]

Article 51, United Nations Charter. Article 51 of the UN Charter acknowledges the right of self-defence as an inherent right of every State:

> "Nothing in the present Charter shall impair the inherent right of individual or collective self-defence if an armed attack occurs against a Member of the United Nations, until the Security Council has taken measures necessary to maintain international peace and security. Measures taken by Members in the exercise of this right of self-defence shall be immediately reported to the Security Council and shall not in any way affect the authority and responsibility of the Security Council under the present Charter to take at any time such action as it deems necessary in order to maintain or restore international peace and security."

Self-defence is permissible if an armed attack has taken place and art.51 confines itself to self-defence only in this situation. When does such an attack occur? What constitutes an armed attack?

> "There now appears to be general agreement on the nature of the acts which can be treated as constituting armed attacks. In particular, it may be considered to be agreed that an armed attack must be understood as including not merely action by regular armed forces across an international border, but also 'the sending by or on behalf of a State of armed bands, groups, irregulars or mercenaries, which carry out armed force against another State of such gravity as to amount to' (inter alia) an actual armed attack conducted by regular forces, 'or its substantial involvement therein . . .' The Court sees no reason to deny, that in customary law, the prohibition of armed attacks may apply to the sending by a State of armed bands to the territory of another State, if such an operation, because of its scale and effects, would have been classified as an armed attack rather than as a mere frontier incident had it been carried out by regular armed forces. But the Court does not believe that the concept of 'armed attack' includes not only acts by armed bands where such acts occur

---

[18] Above no.7, para.194.
[19] *Iran v United States* I.C.J. Rep. 2003 p.161, para 43 and 73–77.
[20] I.C.J. Rep. 1996, p.226, para.41.

on a significant scale but also assistance to rebels in the form of the provision of weapons or logistical or other support. Such assistance may be regarded as a threat or use of force, or amount to intervention in the internal or external affairs of other States."[21]

Can only States commit armed attacks? This issue has contemporary relevance given the increasing power of non-State actors, such as terrorist organisations. Article 51 does not identify the perpetrator of an armed attack, and the Article's *travaux préparatoirs* do not provide any guidance in this respect. Traditionally, art.51 has been interpreted as requiring a State to commit an armed attack. State practice to the contrary is limited,[22] however academic literature reflects a possible move away from the traditional interpretation.[23] To date, the I.C.J. appears to take the view that self-defence may only be inter-State in nature,[24] however, the Court is far from unanimous on this point.[25]

Can a State resort to force in anticipation of an armed attack? Anticipatory self-defence is excluded from art.51. Does that mean it is prohibited? The right of self-defence, which art.51 acknowledges as "inherent", exists under customary international law—that is, independently of art.51. Does, therefore, the right of anticipatory self-defence exist under customary international law?

States do employ force in anticipation of an alleged armed attack, for example Israel's strike on the United Arab Republic in June 1967. The justification for anticipatory self-defence can be reconciled with the obligation on UN Member States to refrain

---

[21] Above, n.7 at 103–104.
[22] For a discussion of state practice see Ruys and Verhoeven, "Attacks by Private Actors and the Right of Self Defence", (2005) 10(3) *Journal of Conflict and Security Law* 289, 292–298. One such example is Columbia's use of force against FARC in Ecuador throughout 2008, see http://www.asil.org/insights080822.cfm.
[23] e.g. see Wedgewood, "Responding to Terrorism: The Strikes Against Bin Laden", (1999) 24 *Yale Journal of International Law* 559, 563–564; Dinstein, *War, Aggression and Self Defence*, 4th edn, (Cambridge University Press, Cambridge 2005), 204.
[24] *Case Concerning Armed Activities on the Territory of the Congo* (Democratic Republic of the Congo v Uganda), Judgment of the 19 December 2005, available at http://www.icj-cij.org/docket/files/116/10455.pdf, para.146.
[25] See the Separate Opinions of Judge Simma (paras 4–16) and Judge Kooijmans (para.29), *ibid*. See also the Separate Opinions of Judge Higgins (para.33), Judge Kooijmans (paras 35–36) and Judge Buergenthal (paras 4–6) in *Legal Consequences of the Construction of a Wall in the Occupied Palestinian Territories, Advisory Opinion* (July 9, 2004), I.C.J. Rep. 2004, p.136.

from either "the threat or use of force". States which are threatened with the use of force may take appropriate anticipatory measures to repel such a threat, however such measures can only be justified if:

(a)   a state is the target of hostile activities of another State;

(b)   the threatened State has exhausted all alternative means of protection;

(c)   the danger is imminent;

(d)   the defensive measures are proportionate to the pending danger.

States enjoy the right of self-defence in the event of an armed attack under art.51 of the UN Charter. Under customary international law they also enjoy the right to use force in circumstances falling short of an armed attack—the I.C.J. did not feel it necessary to address the issue of anticipatory self-defence in the *Nicaragua* case. The existence of such a right was reaffirmed in the wake of the terrorist attack of September 11, 2001. Security Council Resolution 1368 and Security Council Resolution 1373 both recognise and reaffirm the inherent right of individual and collective self-defence as recognised by the Charter of the UN.[26]

However, whatever rights States enjoy with respect to the use of force, they are at all times required by the UN Charter and customary international law to settle their disputes by peaceful means.

Use of force to protect nationals abroad. What if a State's nationals or property are harmed abroad? Does that State have a right to intervene to defend its nationals when its territory has not been the object of an armed attack?

The Anglo–French invasion of Suez (1956), the Israeli raid on Entebbe Airport (1976), the abortive US rescue mission of the hostages in Iran (1980) and the US intervention in both Grenada (1983) and Panama (1989), are instances of force being used by the intervening State to protect its nationals. The legitimacy of intervention to afford such protection is not firmly established in international law. Such intervention can be reconciled with the

---

[26] See the US National Security Strategy (2002) 41 I.L.M. 1478, adopted in September 2002, for an unequivocal assertion that "for centuries, international law recognized that nations need not suffer an attack before they can lawfully take action to defend themselves against forces that present an imminent danger of attack" and for "the need to adapt the concept of imminent threat to the capabilities and objectives of today's adversaries."

doctrine of self-defence if the basic concept underlying diplomatic protection is stretched, so that an imminent threat of danger to nationals abroad may be regarded as an imminent threat to the national State itself. In other words, by invoking a legal fiction, intervention on behalf of the State's nationals can be reconciled with self-defence.

Non-fulfilment by the host State of its international duty to safeguard, to at least a minimum international standard, the interests of non-nationals, may lend support to intervention by the State of nationality. Thus, in the Security Council debate held in July 1976 on the Entebbe incident, an Israeli representative maintained Uganda had "violated a basic tenet of international law in failing to protect foreign nationals on its territory."[27]

Intervention to protect nationals is open to obvious abuse, particularly as it involves a subjective interpretation by a State of when nationals are in danger. Even if protective intervention is accepted, it must be recognised as the exception rather than the norm, not least because it involves violations of another State's territorial integrity and sovereignty. Protective intervention is more likely to be accepted by the international community if the danger to the rescuing State's nationals can be shown to be overwhelming. A successful mission, although it may not be legally condoned, is more likely to be accepted as expedient than one which fails. For example, compare the Entebbe raid with the US abortive mission to rescue the American hostages in Iran. As with self-defence the force used in such circumstances must be proportionate to the danger.

Intervention in civil wars. Civil wars are not prohibited by international law. Article 2(4) prohibits the use of force in respect of international relations only. International law does, however, have something to say on participation by other States. The general rule is one of non-intervention. The General Assembly's Declaration on the Inadmissibility of Intervention in the Domestic Affairs of States and the Protection of their Independence and Sovereignty prohibits any State from intervening:

> "directly or indirectly, for any reason whatever, in the internal or external affairs of any other State . . . no State shall organise, assist, foment, finance, incite or tolerate subversive, terrorist or armed activities directed towards the violent overthrow of the regime of another State, or interfere in civil strife in another State."

---

[27] See 15 I.L.M. 1228 (1976).

The prohibitions enunciated in the 1965 Declaration on the Inadmissibility of Intervention in Domestic Affairs of State[28] were reaffirmed in the 1970 Declaration on Principles of International Law.

States may, for a variety of political reasons, intervene to support the rebels, or alternatively to support the established authorities. Policy rather than law will determine a State's decision to intervene. Non-intervention is undoubtedly the best policy. The danger of intervention by a State in support of one party is that it may attract counter-intervention by another State in support of the other side and, consequently, an internal matter may escalate into an international war.[29]

Classical humanitarian intervention.

Humanitarian intervention is distinct from protective intervention in that it involves intervention to protect another State's nationals (or a group of nationals) and possibly those of the territorial State. The intervening State is, in other words, not protecting its own right. Although it may be contended that, at least *prima facie*, the intervening State is playing a more objective role than when intervening to protect its own nationals, humanitarian intervention is equally open to abuse. The intervening State may ostensibly intervene to promote an altruistic interest, but in reality, political motives and an anxiety to secure for itself some long-term benefit may prompt intervention.

Protagonists of humanitarian intervention support its use for the prevention of serious violations of basic human rights, normally the right to life, or instances of torture.

Contemporary humanitarian intervention.

The demise of the Cold War transferred the spotlight to the increasing number of internal conflicts which unfortunately remain a feature of the contemporary global community. Media images of human suffering in Sudan, Sierra Leone, Sri Lanka and Lebanon have heightened public awareness of the humanitarian dimension of civil war. Humanitarian intervention remains at odds with art.2(4) of the UN Charter and as yet the position in contemporary international law is not to recognise such an exception.[30] However, notwithstanding the foregoing, in certain cir-

---

[28] General Assembly Res. 2131 (XX).

[29] The threat to peace and security in a particular region may be such that the most appropriate response is through the UN, e.g. Sierra Leone.

[30] See UK Foreign Office Policy Document No.148 (U.K.M.I.L.) 1986. See also Harris, p.947.

cumstances a particular situation has demanded at least tacit acceptance of intervention, e.g. the NATO military intervention in Kosovo (Operation Allied Force) 1999 prompted by the repression of the ethnic Albanian population within Kosovo.[31]

"Operation provide comfort"—Northern Iraq

The first crisis in which intervention could be characterised as humanitarian was the relief operation in Northern Iraq following the Gulf War in 1990–1991. Reports of the deaths of over 1,000 Kurdish refugees a day fleeing Iraqi troops[32] and a growing concern in international political circles that this was largely a man-made disaster prompted the UN Security Council to pass Resolution 688 (1991).[33] The Resolution condemned the repression of the Iraqi civilian population and insisted that Iraq allow immediate access by international humanitarian organisations to those in need of assistance. Resolution 688 triggered a response from the US, the UK and France to set up "safe-havens" in Northern Iraq to protect the Kurdish people. Responsibility for protecting these safe-havens was subsequently assumed by the UN. The creation of "no-fly zones" was also the initiative of the US and the UK. Operation Provide Comfort was not based on Resolution 688 nor was it sanctioned by the UN Security Council, nor was it condemned by the Security Council, but was founded rather "in exercise of the customary international law principle of humanitarian intervention."[34] Subsequent events demonstrated that the humanitarian crisis in Northern Iraq was not an isolated incident.

The former Yugoslavia

Humanitarian considerations initially played little part in the conflict which broke out in Yugoslavia.[35] UN Member States ini-

---

[31] Security Council Resolution 1199, September 23, 1998. The NATO intervention was challenged by FRY (Federal Republic of Yugoslavia) in the *Legality of Use of Force* cases brought before the I.C.J. against NATO Member States, see for example *Legality of the Use of Force case (Yugoslavia v US et al) Provisional Measures*, June 2, 1999, I.C.J. Rep. 1999, p.916.

[32] *The New York Times*, April 10, 1991, A1, col.4.

[33] UN SC Res.688, 30 I.L.M. 858 (1991).

[34] Response of Foreign and Commonwealth Office (FCO) Legal Councilor to House of Commons Foreign Affairs Committee 1992, (Parliamentary Papers 1992–1993, HC, Paper 235– iii, pp.85, 92) see Harris, pp.950–951.

[35] For a comprehensive analysis of events leading to the dissolution of Yugoslavia, see Marc Weller, "The International Response to the Dissolution of the Social Federal Republic of Yugoslavia" *A.J.I.L.* 1992 at 569. Documents regarding the conflict can be found in 31 I.L.M. 1421 (1992).

tially saw the crisis as an internal matter which fell within art.2(7) of the Charter,[36] and were reluctant to authorise the use of military force to provide humanitarian aid. As the crisis escalated, however, with reports of war camps, rape and ethnic cleansing across Bosnia-Herzegovina, humanitarian issues dominated Security Council resolutions and various other international statements.[37] The international response nevertheless fell short of a full-scale military action under Ch.VII, leading many to conclude that, far from establishing a legal basis for humanitarian intervention, the crisis affirmed the inviolability of the principles of sovereignty and non-interference regardless of the human suffering concerned. The UN Interim Administrative Mission in Kosovo (UNMIK)[38] was established with the aim of providing interim administrative help. UNMIK was initially made up of more than 4,500 international police, however during 2008 UNMIK's role was progressively assumed by the European Union's Rule of Law Mission (EULEX). EULEX will police Kosovo under the authority of the UN.[39]

"Operation restore hope in Somalia"

In 1992, a two-year drought and the overthrow of the government contributed to Somalia's descent into anarchy. The international response to what was described as the greatest human emergency in the world placed particular emphasis on humanitarian considerations and has been characterised as an instance of a successful humanitarian intervention. Humanitarian aid was distributed quickly by US soldiers, under the authority of UN Resolutions,[40] to starving civilians caught up in a bitter civil war. It soon became apparent that military action was required to ensure safe delivery of humanitarian supplies, many of which had been confiscated by the warring factions. UN Security Council Resolution 794 authorised Member States to use "all necessary means to establish as soon as possible a secure environment for humanitarian relief operations in Somalia" and was the first UN Resolution under

---

[36] Recognition of Croatia as an independent State with international borders transformed the crisis from an internal conflict to one of international concern. Croatia, Bosnia–Herzegovina, Slovenia, Macedonia and the Federal Republic of Yugoslavia have all since been admitted to the UN.

[37] UNPROFOR's mission from the outset, e.g. was "to ensure the security and functioning of Sarajevo airport and the delivery of humanitarian assistance." UNSC Res.764, July 13, 1992. UNPROFOR ceased to exist in March 1995.

[38] S.C. Res.1244 1999, June 10, 1999.

[39] For further information on UNMIK see www.unmikonline.org/index.html.

[40] It is arguable whether Somalia was a sovereign State in the absence of a viable government. Security Council Res. 794, 47 UN SCOR at 63, U.N. Doc. S/RES/794 (1992).

Ch.VII to explicitly authorise intervention in a sovereign State without a request from the host government. Public opinion at home prompted the US to withdraw its troops rather than become involved in protracted fighting with Somali rebels. The Somalia crisis, although a successful humanitarian intervention because of the swift response of the international community in mobilising a force, also highlights the dangers of sending an international force into a civil war without a clear mandate.[41]

Responsibility to Protect

In 2000, the International Commission on Intervention and State Sovereignty (ICISS), an independent international body, was established by the Canadian Government, with the aim of building "broader understanding of the problem of reconciling intervention for human protection purposes and [State] sovereignty".[42] In particular, it attempted to move towards "global political consensus"[43] on the issue of how to deal with humanitarian intervention. In December 2001, the ICISS elaborated the doctrine of responsibility to protect.[44] The ICISS identified three elements to responsibility: to prevent conflict and other crises that put populations at risk; to react to situations of compelling human need; and to rebuild, particularly after a military intervention.

In 2004, the UN Secretary-General appointed a High-Level Panel on Threats, Challenges and Change, to assess current threats to international peace and security; evaluate how these threats have been dealt with; and make recommendations to strengthen the UN collective security system. The Report of the High-Level Panel endorsed "the emerging norm that there is a collective international responsibility to protect . . .".[45] The doctrine of responsibility to protect was endorsed by the General Assembly at the 2005 World Summit,[46] reaffirmed by the

---

[41] The UN was condemned in the former Yugoslavia by the Serbian government for appearing to side with the Muslim population, and yet was heavily criticised by the international community for its failure to allow Muslims to arm themselves against the might of the Serbian army.

[42] Report of the International Commission on Intervention and State Sovereignty, "The Responsibility to Protect", December 2001, available at http://www.iciss.ca/report2-en.asp, para.1.7.

[43] *ibid.*

[44] *ibid.*

[45] Report of the High-Level Panel on Threats, Challenges and Change, "A more secure world: our shared responsibility", available at: http://www.un.org/secureworld/report.pdf, para 203. See also paras 201–202.

[46] "2005 World Summit Outcome Document", UN Doc. A/60/L.1, paras 138–139, available at: http://www.who.int/hiv/universalaccess2010/worldsummit.pdf.

Security Council[47] and subsequently reiterated in the Secretary General's report of January 2009.[48] A number of States support the doctrine of responsibility to protect, including the UK and Canada, however its recognition as a rule of international law remains uncertain.

Conclusion

The international community has demonstrated its willingness to use humanitarian concerns as a basis for intervention into what are essentially civil-war conflicts. The alleviation of human suffering appears to be taking precedence over the principle of State sovereignty, and there is evidence of a shift in the international community's position regarding humanitarian intervention. However, what is required are accepted principles setting out the circumstances in which such international intervention would be lawful. The UK, with a view to establishing such a framework, produced Guidelines on Humanitarian Intervention.[49] It is important to note that these guidelines refer only to collective action and it is specifically stated "no individual country can reserve to itself the right to act on behalf of the international community". These guidelines further highlight that armed force should only be used as a last resort, immediate responsibility for ending the violence is that of the State in which it occurs, there should be convincing evidence of extreme humanitarian distress on a large scale requiring urgent relief and there should be no practical alternative to the use of force and any use of force or force used must be proportionate to achieving the humanitarian purpose, should be carried out in accordance with international law and must be likely to achieve its objectives. Acceptance of such Guidelines would avoid inconsistency in the international response to humanitarian crises.

Collective self-defence. The right of collective self-defence is recognised by art.51. Collective self-defence is something of a misnomer, as it refers to the right of each State to use force in defence of another State. The force is therefore employed on behalf of another State.

Collective self-defence refers, strictly speaking, to collective defence rather than self-defence. Article 51 is the legal basis of collective agreements such as the NATO Alliance, in which an attack

---

[47] Security Council Res. 1674, UN Doc. S/RES/1674 (2006), Operative Paragraph 4; Security Council Res. 1706, UN Doc. S/RES/1706 (2006), Preamble, para.2.
[48] The Report to the General Assembly 63rd session, January 12, 2009 A/63/670.
[49] (2000) 71 *B.Y.I.L.* 646.

on one member is treated as an attack on all. Under art.5 of the North Atlantic Treaty,[50] the Contracting Parties:

> "agree that an armed attack against one or more of them in Europe or North America shall be considered an attack against them all; and consequently they agree that, if such an armed attack occurs, each of them, in exercise of the right of individual or collective self-defence recognized by Article 51 of the Charter of the United Nations, will assist the Party or Parties so attacked, by taking forthwith, individually, and in concert with the other Parties, such action as it deems necessary, including the use of armed force, to restore and maintain the security of the North Atlantic area."

The bombing of Yugoslavian territory under the auspices of NATO (as previously mentioned) resulted in the legality of the use of such force being raised, by Yugoslavia, in the I.C.J. Proceedings were raised against the relevant Member States: Belgium, Canada, France, Germany, Italy, the Netherlands, Portugal, Spain, the United Kingdom and the United States. The I.C.J. in 1999 rejected the request for provisional measures in all cases and removed from its list the cases against Spain and the United States. The I.C.J. concluded on December 15, 2004 that it did not have jurisdiction to hear the merits in respect of the remaining cases.[51]

All measures adopted by Member States in self-defence must be reported to the Security Council, and the use of force in individual or collective self-defence should only be employed until the Security Council has taken appropriate measures to maintain international peace and security. The right of collective self-defence was recognised by the I.C.J. in the *Nicaragua* case as existing under customary international law, but its legitimate exercise depended on: (a) a declaration by the alleged victim that it had been attacked; and (b) a request by that State for assistance.[52] In the same case, the I.C.J. held that intervention by a third State could only be regarded as lawful ". . . when the wrongful act provoking the response was an armed attack."[53] The armed response

---

[50] U.K.T.S. 56 (1949) Cmd.7789; U.N.T.S. 243. The eastern European countries, Poland, the Czech Republic and Hungary were admitted into NATO in July 1997. Further enlargement of NATO occurred in March 2004 when another seven eastern European countries joined.

[51] See I.C.J. web page, under contentious cases: www.icj-cij.org/docket/index.php?pl-3&p.2=3.

[52] *Nicaragua* case, above, n.7 at 110.

[53] *ibid.*

(Operation Desert Storm) to liberate Kuwait was the exercise by that State of its legal right to collective self-defence.[54]

Regional arrangements. The right of States to make regional arrangements to deal with matters of international peace and security is protected by the UN Charter and, in particular, by art.52.

Article 52(1) provides:

> "Nothing in the present Charter precludes the existence of regional arrangements or agencies for dealing with such matters relating to the maintenance of international peace and security as are appropriate for regional action, provided that such arrangements or agencies and their activities are consistent with the Purposes and Principles of the United Nations."

Article 52(2), however, charges members of regional organisations with making "every effort to achieve pacific settlement of local disputes through such regional arrangements or by such regional agencies before referring them to the Security Council." Action taken *via* regional organisations will only be legitimate if it is consistent with the purposes and principles of the UN Charter, and does not amount to "enforcement action", unless this has been authorised by the Security Council. The Security Council must, under art.54, be kept fully informed at all times "of activities undertaken or in contemplation under regional arrangements or by regional agencies for the maintenance of international peace and security."

The Organisation of Eastern Caribbean States' peacekeeping mission, which with the support of Barbados, Jamaica and the US, landed in Grenada on October 25, 1983, is an instance of action being taken under the auspices of a regional organisation. Arguments supporting the legality of the invasion are founded, *inter alia*, on its legitimacy as a regional peacekeeping mission under art.52 of the UN Charter, especially as it was prompted by

---

[54] Commentators have maintained that the first "Gulf War" was a collective self-defence operation legitimised by the Security Council and that it would be wrong to call it a UN collective security operation. See Dr Max Hilaire, "Use of Force Against Iraq: Collective Security or Collective Self-Defence Under the United Nations Charter and Customary International Law?" I.L.R., April/June 1993, No.2 and Eugene Rostow, "Until What/Enforcement Action or Collective Self-Defence?" 85 *A.J.I.L.* 510 (1991). See also UN S.C. Res.661 (1990) in which the Security Council recognised for the first time that collective self-defence applied, even when the assisting State had not been attacked and there is no special treaty arrangement to provide help. UN Doc.S/Res./661, August 6, 1990.

the breakdown of government authority and a response to a request by the Governor General, Sir Paul Scoon.[55]

The legitimacy of the 1962 US quarantine imposed in respect of vessels destined for Cuba is purported to be based on art.52, namely through the authorisation of the Organisation of American States.

Regional organisations can play a vital role in the maintenance of international peace and security. For example, in the former Yugoslavia, there was evidence of an increasing utilisation of regional agencies. UN Security Council Resolution 787 authorised States "acting nationally or through regional agencies" to use appropriate measures to enforce the UN economic sanctions against Serbia and Montenegro. NATO also played a significant part and was specifically charged with the task of enforcing the no-fly zone over Bosnia in support of UN Security Council Resolution 816. The delegation of powers from the UN force in Bosnia at the time (UNPROFOR) to NATO troops (IFOR), although not strictly an authorisation to a regional organisation under art.53, was nevertheless evidence of the Council's willingness to delegate the maintenance of international peace and security to a regional organisation.[56]

The conflict in Liberia was a further example of the increased systematic cooperation between the United Nations and a regional organisation. The UN Security Council gave its support to the regional organisation, the Economic Community of West African States, known as ECOWAS, in March 1993, by imposing a "general and complete embargo on all deliveries of weapons and military equipment to Liberia until the Security Council decides otherwise."[57]

Reprisals. Reprisals (now more commonly referred to as countermeasures) are acts which in themselves are illegal under international law, and are adopted by a State in response to its

---

[55] For some of the arguments for and against the lawfulness of the Grenada invasion, see 78 *A.J.I.L.* 131–175 (1984); see also W. C. Gilmore, *The Grenada Intervention* (Mansell, 1984).

[56] NATO is specifically mentioned in the Annexes to the Resolution. It has been suggested that NATO was utilised in Bosnia only because the Security Council was prevented from taking unanimous action due to the reluctance of Russia to authorise force against one of its traditional allies.

[57] See the Report of the Secretary-General on the Question of Liberia, UN Doc. S/25402 (1993) for the background to this war. See also UN S.C. Res.788 (1992) November 19, 1992 and UN SC Res.866 (1993) September 22, 1993 which established the UN Observer Mission in Liberia (UNOMIL). Following a peace agreement on September 19, 2003 the UN Mission in Liberia (UNMIL) was established by a Security Council Res. 1509 (2003).

having been the victim of an unlawful act by another State. They were defined in the *Naulilaa* case[58] as:

> "acts of self-help by the injured State, acts in retaliation for acts contrary to international law on the part of the offending State, which have remained unredressed after a demand for amends. In consequence of such measures, the observance of this or that rule of international law is temporarily suspended in the relations between the two States. They are limited by considerations of humanity and the rules of good faith, applicable in the relations between States. They are illegal unless they are based upon a previous act contrary to international law. They seek to impose on the offending State reparation for the offence, the return to legality and the avoidance of new offences."[59]

Reprisals involving armed force have now to comply with the contemporary international law on the use of force if they are not to be contrary to international law. The Declaration on Principles of International Law Concerning Friendly Relations and Co-operation Among States in Accordance with the Charter of the UN[60] expressly prohibits reprisals and provides that States "have a duty to refrain from acts of reprisal involving the use of force."[61]

Retorsions. Retorsions are distinct from reprisals/countermeasures in they are acts which in themselves, although unfriendly, are not unlawful. They are a lawful means of expressing displeasure at the conduct of another State, e.g. the severance of diplomatic relations or foreign aid.

Collective measures through the UN

Under the UN Charter the primary responsibility for peacekeeping lies with the Security Council.[62] Member States agree, under art.25, to accept and carry out the decisions of the Security Council. The Security Council can act either under Ch.VI or Ch.VII of the Charter.

---

[58] 2 R.I.A.A. 1012 (1928).
[59] *ibid.* at 1026. See also *Air Services Agreement* case 18 R.I.A.A. 416.
[60] GA Res.2635 (XXV), October 24, 1970.
[61] See the International Law Commission's Draft Articles on Responsibility of States for Internationally Wrongful Acts, 2001, Ch.2, art.49 to art.52, which deal with the taking of counter-measures against another State.
[62] art.24.

Under Ch.VI arts 33–38, the Security Council can make recommendations with the objective of achieving a peaceful settlement to disputes.

Chapter VII arts 39–51 deals with the enforcement measures which the Security Council can adopt. Under art.39, the Security Council is authorised to determine "the existence of any threat to the peace, breach of the peace, or act of aggression . . .".

What constitutes aggression? A General Assembly Resolution adopted in 1974[63] defined aggression as "the use of force by a State against the sovereignty, territorial integrity, or political independence of another State, or in any other manner inconsistent with the Charter of the United Nations . . ." Examples of acts that would be identified as aggression include the invasion or armed attack by one State against the territory of another State; the blockade of the ports or coasts of a State by the armed forces of another State and the sending by or on behalf of a State of armed bands, groups, irregulars or mercenaries, to employ armed force against another State.[64]

Following an affirmative decision under art.39, the Security Council can make recommendations or decide what measures are to be taken in accordance with the Charter to maintain international peace and security. In practice, the Security Council seldom discusses the issue of whether it possesses jurisdiction under art.39, and consequently, upon which aspect (that is, "threat to the peace" or "breach of the peace") it is basing its action is not identified. "Threat to the peace", which should be read as international peace, has been interpreted extensively and has evolved to encompass situations which previously would have been designated "internal" and thereby protected by art.2(7) of the UN Charter. "Threat to the peace" was applied in the Middle East conflict (1948), in respect of Southern Rhodesia (1966), Somalia (1992), Liberia (1992), Rwanda (1994) and in respect of Sudan (regarding the situation in Darfur) (2004). "Threat to the peace" was also employed by the Security Council to the Libyan government's failure to demonstrate "by concrete actions its renunciation of terrorism."[65]

---

[63] GA Res.3314 (XXIX) above, n.10, note there is a distinction between a "war of aggression" which is characterised as a crime against international peace and "aggression" which gives rise to international responsibility, art.5(2). See also ILC Draft Code of Crimes Against the Peace and Security of Mankind 1996, art.16, which deals with the individual responsibility for the crime of aggression, Report of the ILC, A/51/10, 1996, p.9. ILC Draft Code can be found at www.un.org/law/ilc/texts/dcode.htm

[64] *ibid.* art.3.

[65] S.C. Res.748 (1992). Libya subsequently denounced terrorism in December 2003.

A "breach of the peace" has only been specifically identified in four cases: Korea (1950), the Falklands (1982), Iran–Iraq (1987) and in the invasion of Kuwait by Iraq (1990–91), which was characterised as an act breaching "international peace and security".[66] Article 40 provides that the Security Council may call upon the parties concerned to comply with such provisional measures as it deems necessary or desirable. For example the Security Council could call for a cease-fire. The enforcement action which the Security Council may consider necessary may be either:

(i)   measures not involving the use of force (art.41); or

(ii)   armed force (art.42).

(i) Acting under art.41, the Security Council may call upon Members of the UN to employ economic sanctions or diplomatic sanctions against a "defaulting" State. The economic sanctions imposed against Iraq, following the invasion of Kuwait by Iraq, represent the most comprehensive action of the UN under art.41.[67]

Resolution 661,[68] prompted by Iraq's failure to withdraw from Kuwait, called upon Member States to abstain from the importation of all commodities and products originating in Iraq or Kuwait and the exportation to those States of all products, save those "supplies intended strictly for medical purposes, and, in humanitarian circumstances, foodstuffs". Supervision of Resolution 661 was entrusted to a Committee established by the Security Council and, under Resolution 666,[69] that Committee

---

[66] S.C. Res.660, (1990) adopted August 2, 1990 by 14–0 (Yemen abstained), 29 I.L.M. 1325 (1990).

[67] Sanctions against South Africa and Southern Rhodesia (British colony which became independent Zimbabwe in 1979) were also based on art.41. Recent examples of sanctions are the arms embargo imposed against Rwanda in 1994, UK Order SI 1994/1637, and the international economic sanctions against Serbia, UN S.C. Res.757 September 30, 1992. The sanctions against Serbia were tightened further in UN S.C. Res.1993 820. A significant aspect of these measures was the prohibition on the provision of services, both financial and non-financial to any person or body for the purposes of business in Serbia and Montenegro, the only exceptions being telecommunications, postal services, certain legal services and services whose supply may be necessary for humanitarian purposes on a case by case basis by the UN Sanctions Committee. Sanctions against the Federal Republic of Yugoslavia were lifted by Security Council Resolution 1074 (1996). In 1998, arm sanctions were re-imposed owing to the situation in Kosovo, Security Council Resolution 1160 (1998) however these were lifted in 2001, Security Council Res.1367 (2001).

[68] (1990) adopted by 13–0 (Cuba and Yemen abstained) August 6, 1990; 29 I.L.M. 1325 (1990).

[69] (1990) adopted September 13, 1990, *ibid.* at 1330.

was charged with overviewing the supply of foodstuffs designated as falling within the humanitarian exception. Such supervision was undertaken in co-operation with humanitarian
agencies such as the International Committee of the Red Cross.
Resolution 665[70] called upon those Member States with maritime
forces in the region "to use such measures commensurate with
the specific circumstances to halt all inward and outward maritime shipping in order to . . . inspect and verify their cargoes and
destinations." This was for the purpose of enforcing the sanctions. Subsequently, Iraq's continued presence in Kuwait led to
stricter measures, namely the requirement that all States deny
clearance (that is, permission to take off from, or fly over) to
cargo-carrying aircraft bound for either Iraq or Kuwait.[71] The
sanctions remained in force after the cease-fire[72] and continued in
force, though mitigated to some extent by the "Oil for Food
Programme".[73] The lifting of economic sanctions against Iraq was
approved by the Security Council in May 2003.[74]

Resolution 748, adopted on March 31, 1992, requiring Libya to
comply with Resolution 731 (namely to co-operate in determining
responsibility for the activities which culminated at Lockerbie),
was also adopted under Ch.VII, as was the mandatory arms
embargo established against Yugoslavia by Security Council
Resolution 713 in September 1991, and also Security Council
Resolution 1373 (2001) in relation to the September 11 attacks of
2001.

(ii) If the Security Council considers that art.41 measures would
be, or have proved inadequate, it may take such action by air, sea
or land forces as may be necessary to maintain or restore international peace and security. Such action may include demonstra-
tions, blockades and other operations by air, sea, or land forces of
Members of the UN.

Article 42 is supplemented by art.43, according to which States
undertake to provide, under special agreements with the
Security Council, armed forces assistance and facilities, including rights of passage, to the extent necessary for maintaining
peace and security.

The force which operated in Korea in 1950 was designated a
UN force, but whether it was one in the true sense remains doubtful. The Security Council Resolutions calling upon Members to

---

[70] (1990) adopted August 25, 1990, above, n.68 at 1329.
[71] Res.1990 670 adopted September 25, 1990, above, n.68 at 1334.
[72] S.C. Res.687 (1991), which set out the terms of a permanent cease-fire.
[73] S.C. Res.986 (1995), the 'Oil for Food Programme' was further modified in S.C.
Res.1284 (1999), S.C. Res.1409 (2002) and S.C. Res.1472 (2003).
[74] S.C. Res.1483, May 22, 2003.

assist the UN in securing the withdrawal of the North Korean forces, to furnish "such assistance to the Republic of Korea as may be necessary to repel the armed attack and to restore international peace and security in the area", and authorising the use of the UN flag, were adopted through the fortuitous absence of the Soviet Union representative in the Security Council.[75] Control over the forces, which were provided by 16 States, was maintained throughout by the US, and indeed the troops were provided pursuant to agreements made by the US and the countries involved.

Operation Desert Storm, whereby a coalition of States supplied armed forces to enforce a series of UN Resolutions[76] is an instance of a legitimate use of force authorised by the UN. Iraq protested that force could only be sanctioned by the Security Council in accordance with arts 42 and 43 of the UN Charter. However the Security Council in this instance acted under art.42 and authorised States to use force with States being required to keep the Security Council regularly informed. Alternatively it has been argued that Security Council Resolution 678 was of little legal significance and in effect the action of the coalition States was one of collective self-defence being exercised in respect of Kuwait.

During, and subsequent to, the invasion of Iraq in 2003 a debate has raged as to the legality of the use of force. The case for intervention was put forward as being the non-compliance of Iraq with Security Council Resolution 687 paras 8–13 regarding the destruction of weapons of mass destruction and co-operation with the UN Monitoring Verification and Inspection Commission[77] (UNMOVIC) and the International Atomic Energy Agency (IAEA). In Security Council Resolution 1441, adopted December 20, 2002, Iraq was afforded "a final opportunity to comply with its disarmament obligations under relevant resolutions of the Council" and was warned it would face "serious consequences as a result of its continued violations of its obligations." Attempts to secure a second Security Council Resolution proved abortive and British and American forces (with the support of Spain, Australia, Denmark and Poland)

---

[75] The Soviet Union representative was absent in protest at the seating of the Nationalist Chinese delegation.

[76] S.C. Res.660 (1990) condemning the invasion of Kuwait by Iraq and calling for immediate withdrawal; S.C. Res.662 (1990) denying any legal validity to Iraq's assertion of annexation of Kuwait and S.C. Res.678 (1990) prescribing a time-frame for Iraq to meet demands of previous Resolutions and withdraw from Kuwait.

[77] Established by S.C. Res.1284 (1999) as successor organisation to UN Special Commission (UNSCOM).

undertook military action on March 20, 2003.[78] Essentially the basis for the use of force against Iraq was premised on Iraq's failure to comply with UN Security Council Resolutions.

Under the UN Charter, the General Assembly may discuss any questions relating to the maintenance of international peace and security, provided the matter is not before the Security Council.[79] The Security Council can make decisions, however the General Assembly can only make recommendations. Under the UN Charter, the role envisaged for the General Assembly was a less active one than that given to the Security Council. During the cold war era the Security Council was, through the use of the veto, rendered less effective and this led to a more active role than originally anticipated being assumed by the General Assembly.

It is generally accepted that the current membership of the Security Council does not accurately reflect the balance of economic power within the international community but rather still reflects, essentially, the global power structure of 1945. A UN-appointed high-level panel on "Threats, Challenges and Change" proposed two models for the enlargement of the Security Council, in December 2004;[80] in both models the Security Council would be increased to 24 Members. In one model there would be an additional six permanent seats with no veto and three new two-year termed elected seats. The alternative proposal creates a new category of eight semi-permanent seats renewable every four years and one new two-year non-renewable seat. However, neither the panel nor Kofi Annan's Report "Enlarging Freedom" express any preference and the issue has been placed on the General Assembly's agenda for 2005. The panel felt the existing Five Permanent Members should keep their seats and their veto.

The UN Secretary-General

The UN Secretary-General has an increasingly important role to play in the maintenance of international peace and security. On January 31, 1992, at a Security Council meeting, the former Secretary-General Dr Boutros Boutros Ghali, was invited to "prepare" "his analysis and recommendations on ways of strengthening and making more efficient within the framework and

---

[78] A comprehensive treatment of the legal argument for and against the invasion of Iraq is outwith the remit of this text. For the British case for war see "Iraq: Legal Basis for the Use of Force", United Kingdom Foreign and Commonwealth Office Memorandum, March 17, 2003; (2002) 52 *I.C.L.Q.* 812. The US, while relying primarily on a similar argument, did invoke the right of pre-emptive self-defence.
[79] arts 11 and 12.
[80] The panel was made up of 16 veteran diplomats and politicians under the chairmanship of the former Thai Prime Minister Anand Panyarachun.

provisions of the Charter, the capacity of the United Nations, for preventative diplomacy, for peacemaking and for peacekeeping".[81] The request from the Security Council reflected the growing need for the UN to adopt a more systematic and intrusive approach towards internal strife and aggression. The Secretary-General responded on June 17, 1992, by identifying important interconnected UN security functions in a Report entitled "An Agenda for Peace"[82] which included, *inter alia*:

- preventative diplomacy;

- peacemaking;

- peace building in its differing contexts;

- rebuilding institutions and infrastructures of nations divided by civil war and strife; and

- addressing the causes of conflict, for example economic deprivation, social injustice and political oppression.

The Secretary-General also called for the creation of permanent peace-enforcement units under art.43 of the UN Charter with the ability to respond to aggression immediately. These would be constituted by troops from all Member States and would be placed under the auspices of the Secretary-General. Deployment of these units would be on the basis of provisional measures in art.40 of the Charter. The UN Security Council endorsed the Report in principle, but have yet to adopt the recommendations.[83]

Dr Ghali's successor, Kofi Annan, was the first UN Secretary-General to be appointed from an African State,[84] and as a former Under-Secretary-General for peacekeeping, he was also the first to have worked his way through the ranks of the UN. Kofi Annan, during his term of office, focused on organisational reform within the UN as well as tackling the issues of AIDS, education, environmental issues, governance and human rights.[85] Kofi Annan was a driving force behind the adoption of

---

[81] UN Doc.S/23500.

[82] An Agenda for Peace: "Preventative Diplomacy, Peacemaking and Peacekeeping" June 17, 1992 31 I.L.M. 953 (1992) UN Doc.A/47/277,S/24111 (1992).

[83] To this date no UN Member State has signed an art.43 special agreement with the UN despite the fact the text of art.43 asks Member States to sign such agreements "as soon as possible".

[84] Ghana. In January 2007 the office of Secretary Genereal was assumed by Ban Ki-moon of the Republic of Korea.

[85] Kofi Annan's strategy had been designed to implement and achieve the UN Millennium Declaration—"Road Map towards the implementation of the Millennium Declaration". Report of the Secretary-General September 2001. (The General Assembly Res.53/202, December 1998, designated 55th Session of

the Millennium Declaration in 2000. World leaders have since reconfirmed their commitment to achieving the Millennium Development Goals by 2015 and this is supported by Secretary General Ban Ki-moon.

The veto. Every member of the Security Council has one vote.[86] Procedural issues, in order to be adopted, must receive the affirmative vote of nine members, while non-procedural matters require nine votes, including the concurring vote of the Five Permanent Members (China, France, the United Kingdom, the United States and, the Russian Federation). Absence and abstention are taken as concurrence.[87] The decision as to whether a matter is or is not procedural is itself a non-procedural issue, that is, the concurring vote of the Five Permanent Members is required.

The possibility of exercising a double veto is therefore open to a Permanent Member. If, because of the veto, the Security Council is unable to make any decisions, then the General Assembly, with residual authority for the maintenance of peace, can assume the responsibility which the Security Council is unable to discharge. The inability of the Security Council to take further action for the management of the Korean campaign (because of the return to his seat of the Soviet Union representative and his consequent use of the veto) led to the Uniting for Peace Resolution in November 1950.[88]

The Uniting for Peace Resolution provided that, in the event of the Security Council being unable, because of a lack of unanimity of the Permanent Members, to discharge its primary responsibility for the maintenance of international peace and security, the General Assembly could, where there appears to be a threat to the peace, breach of the peace or act of aggression:

"consider the matter immediately with a view to making appropriate recommendations to Members for collective

the General Assembly "The Millennium Assembly of the United Nations".) An integral part of the millennium assembly was the Millennium Summit, September 2000, and addressed the theme "The Role of the United Nations in the Twenty-First Century". See also Kofi Annan's Report "In Larger Freedom: Towards Development, Security and Human Rights for All", March 2005.

[86] art.27.
[87] In *Legal Consequences for States of the Continued Presence of South Africa in Namibia (South West Africa) Notwithstanding Security Council Resolution 276 (1970)* (Advisory Opinion) I.C.J. Rep., 1971, p.16, the I.C.J. found "abundant evidence" that rulings of the President of the Security Council and Members of the Security Council do not regard voluntary abstention by a Permanent Member as vetoing the adoption of a resolution.
[88] Res.377 (V), November 3, 1950; G.A.O.R., 5th Session, Supp.20, p.10.

measures, including in the case of a breach of the peace or act of aggression the use of armed force when necessary, to maintain or restore international peace and security."

If the General Assembly is not in session at the time, an emergency session may be called. An emergency session may be requested by the Security Council on the vote of any nine members, or by a majority of the members of the UN. The General Assembly has invoked the Uniting for Peace Resolution on a number of occasions, e.g. the Suez Question (1956), the Congo Question (1960), the Pakistan Civil War (Bangladesh) (1972), Afghanistan (1980), Namibia (1981) and alleged violations of the fourth Geneva Convention relating to the protection of civilian persons in times of war—Israel (1999). The Uniting for Peace Resolution was more effective in allowing issues to be discussed in the General Assembly, rather than as a means of preventing crises and preserving international peace and security. The demise of the cold war allowed the Security Council to act more frequently in the way envisaged by the UN Charter unhampered by the use of the veto. This has been reflected in the consequential overshadowing of the General Assembly.

Traditional peacekeeping forces. The UN Charter does not provide for those peacekeeping forces—e.g. forces which are designed to maintain peace rather than take enforcement action—which have made an important contribution in major crises. Peacekeeping forces, which consist of troops given voluntarily by UN Member States, must remain at all times impartial. They have been responsible for supervising a cease-fire, e.g. the UN Emergency Force (UNEF) in the Middle East in 1956. They have also been responsible for the UN Iran–Iraq Military Observer Group (UNIMOG), established in 1988; assisting a return to peace with the UN Force in the Congo (ONUC) in 1960, and the UN Protection Force in Yugoslavia (UNPROFOR) 1992, in patrolling a buffer zone. Peacekeeping forces also patrolled a buffer zone during the UN Iraq–Kuwait Observation Mission (UNIKOM) in 1991, supervising a withdrawal of occupying forces as did the UN Angola Verification Mission (UNAVEN) in 1989. They participated in the supervision of the attainment of independence, UN Transition Assistance Group (UNTAG established 1978, operational 1989) with respect to Namibia, the performance of basic civilian administrative functions (UNMIIC) in 1999 and a return to political stability (UNAMSIL) in 1999. In practice UN peacekeeping forces traditionally only operate in a territory as long as the host State consents. There have been over 60 peacekeeping operations since 1945.

The constitutionality of peacekeeping forces was affirmed in the *Certain Expenses of the United Nations* case.[89] The I.C.J. was requested by the General Assembly to give an Advisory Opinion on the legality of expenses levied on members for the purpose of financing the UN forces in the Middle East (UNEF) and the Congo (ONUC), following the refusal of a number of States, including the Soviet Union and France, to make their contributions. The I.C.J. held the expenses were legitimate as they were made for the fulfilment of a purpose of the UN.[90]

Regarding the respective roles of the Security Council and General Assembly in the maintenance of international peace and security, the I.C.J. emphasised that, while the Security Council enjoyed a primary responsibility, its responsibility was not exclusive. The I.C.J. did, however, acknowledge that only the Security Council could "require enforcement by coercive action against an aggressor."[91] In other words, the authorisation of enforcement measures involving the use of force is the prerogative of the Security Council. The General Assembly's competence is, in the light of the Court's opinion, limited to action which falls short of enforcement action *per se*. The General Assembly may not be competent to authorise enforcement measures which involve the use of force, but it can nevertheless recommend action when that does not involve "enforcement action" but rather the establishment of a peacekeeping force designed to maintain the peace.

Under the UN regime, although the Security Council is the organ exclusively competent to authorise the use of force, the General Assembly enjoys residual competence to recommend action falling short of coercive or enforcement action.

Peace-enforcement[92]

The situations with which UN peacekeeping operations have been asked to deal in recent years, e.g. that in the former Yugoslavia[93] and Somalia, highlight the complexity of the tasks

---

[89] I.C.J. Rep. 1962 p.151.

[90] *ibid*. at 172.

[91] *ibid*. at 163.

[92] This subject warrants greater attention than is permissible here. For further details, see generally Andrew Miller, "Universal Soldiers: A UN Army" *Georgetown Law Journal*, March 1993 at 773–828; W. M. Reisman "Peacemaking" (1993) 18 *Yale Journal of International Law* 415; Frederick L. Kirgis, "Security Council Resolution on Multinational Interim Forces in Haiti", ASIL Insight, March 2004 found at www.asil.org/insights/insigh128.htm and Alex J. Bellamy et al, *Understanding Peacekeeping* (Polity Press in association with Blackwell Publishing Ltd, Cambridge, 2004).

[93] The peacekeeping force (UNPROFOR) deployed in Bosnia-Herzegovina was the largest UN operation to date. The establishment of a UN Protection Force

confronting UN deployment forces. Both instances illustrate that the traditional remit given to UN peacekeeping forces is insufficient and new tasks demanded of UN peacekeepers conflict with their traditionally perceived image of mediators. This was probably most sharply illustrated in UNPROFOR, whose mandate was extended on an ad hoc basis in an effort to meet with particular needs as they emerged. However UNPROFOR was only authorised to use force as required in self-defence. The international community is now demanding that peacekeepers demarcate boundaries, disarm warring factions and deliver humanitarian aid with or without the consent of the parties to the conflict. As these are tasks which demand more powerful peacekeepers to enforce the peace, there is a growing body of opinion that the UN should concentrate efforts on creating a credible international enforcement mechanism under art.43, a provision of the Charter which, until recently, was stultified by the cold war powers.[94]

In "Agenda for Peace", Secretary-General Boutros Boutros Ghali recommended the deployment of "peace-enforcement units from Member States, which would be available on call and would consist of troops that have volunteered for such service",[95] the idea being that UN military forces would provide an effective means of deterring aggression and containing humanitarian crises.[96] In March 2000, Kofi Annan convened a high-level panel to undertake a review of the UN peace and security activities with a view to presenting a clear set of specific, concrete and practical recommendations. This panel produced a series of recommendations contained in what is known as the Brahimi Report.[97]

---

was approved by the Security Council in Res.743 (February 21, 1992) and full deployment was authorised by Res.749 (April 7, 1992). By April 1992, 8300 members of UNPROFOR were deployed and by July 23 of that year, almost all of the 14,000 members were in place. See above, n.37. UNPROFOR was replaced by an implementation force, the International Fellowship of Reconciliation (IFOR), made up of troops primarily from NATO countries in 1995, S.C.Res.1031 (1995).

[94] On April 30, 1947, the Military Staff Committee submitted a report to the SC, in which it set out principles for implementing a UN force under art.43. Although SC members provisionally adopted many of the Articles, the five permanent members failed to agree on many aspects of the composition and organisation of armed forces that would be committed under the agreement. See the Report from the Military Staff Committee to the President of the Security Council, Yearbook of the UN, 1945 at 403.

[95] Agenda for Peace doc, above, n.82.

[96] Note, jurisdictional immunity from the International Criminal Court (ICC) for personnel participating in situations authorised by the UN now exists. Exemption applies to personnel from countries that do not accept the jurisdiction of the ICC, e.g. the US. See S.C. Res.1422, July 12, 2002.

[97] A/55/305–S/2000/809, August 17, 2000, 39 I.L.M. 2000, p.1432.

Kofi Annan was receptive to these recommendations and a number were acted upon, e.g. Security Council Resolution 1353 (2001) On Strengthening Partnerships with Troop-Contributing States.

Domestic jurisdiction limitation. Article 2(7) of the UN Charter prohibits the UN from intervening in matters which are essentially within the jurisdiction of any State. This limitation does not apply in respect of Ch.VII enforcement action. Domestic jurisdiction has been interpreted restrictively and art.2(7) has not impeded the work of the UN.[98]

For instance, severe violations of human rights are no longer considered to be solely within a State's domestic jurisdiction and are therefore excluded from an application of art.2(7).[99] During Security Council debate concerning UN Resolution 688 (1991), it was declared that art.2(7) does not apply to matters which are not fundamentally domestic, such as human rights protection.[100] Intervention by the international community to prevent human suffering is, however, beset with conceptual difficulties. What constitutes human suffering? How widespread would it need to be before intervention would be triggered?

Certainly, the principles of State sovereignty and non-interference in internal affairs are no longer sacrosanct in a world where increased international telecommunications prevent governments from hiding behind the shield of the sovereign State.

Force authorised by a competent organ of the UN

A State may be authorised by the Security Council to use force, even in circumstances when the use of force would otherwise be illegal. This is the conclusion to be drawn from the Security Council Resolution 221 (1966), which called upon the UK:

> "to prevent by the use of force if necessary ... vessels reasonably believed to be carrying oil destined for Rhodesia, and ... to arrest and detain the tanker known as the Joanna V upon her departure from Beira in the event her oil cargo is discharged there."[101]

---

[98] For example, UN S.C. Res. 687, which was passed in the aftermath of the Gulf crisis, was considered particularly intrusive and authorised the destruction of Iraq's nuclear, chemical and biological weapons. See Lawrence D. Roberts, "United Nations Security Council Resolution 687 and Its Aftermath: The Implications for Domestic Authority and the Need for Legitimacy" [1993] 25, *International Law and Politics* 593.

[99] On human rights as an international concern beyond the domestic jurisdiction of States, see M. N. Shaw, International Law (6th ed., 2008), p.265.

[100] See UN Doc.S/PV 2982 at 58 (1991) (providing text of the Resolution debates).

[101] S.C.O.R., 21st year, Resolutions and Decisions, p.5; 5 I.L.M. 534 (1966).

Apparently, as art.42 authorises the Security Council to use force in circumstances where force would normally be illegal, the Security Council can authorise States to do likewise. Other instances where art.42 has been invoked in support of sanctions imposed under art.41 include Iraq (1990 and 1991), Former Yugoslavia (1992) and Haiti (1993 and 1994).

JUS IN BELLO

In the event of States turning from the procedures prescribed by international law for the settlement of their disputes by peaceful means, hostilities may occur. However, there still exists a legal regime which States are required to respect—*jus in bello*. These fall into two categories—those relating to the actual conduct of hostilities and those which afford a minimum protection to the individual (humanitarian law). The former are to be found principally in the Hague Conventions 1899 and 1907, and are referred to as "the Law of The Hague", while the Four Geneva Conventions 1949 ("Red Cross") and two Additional Protocols (adopted in 1977) comprise the latter, and are known as "The Law of Geneva". However, as noted by the I.C.J. the two "have become so closely interrelated that they are considered to have gradually formed one single complex system, known today as international humanitarian law."[102]

Conduct of armed conflict

Declarations of war are generally no longer heard. The UN Charter does not distinguish between war and other modes of armed force, nor do the Geneva Conventions or the 1977 Protocols, and the expression "armed conflict" is today frequently employed. However, a characterisation of the nature of the conflict may be important for neutral States and determining the status of aliens.

The promulgation of the Lieber Code[103] in 1863 by President Lincoln represent the first official statement on the laws relating to the conduct of hostilities. The Code, although originally adopted by the President for application during the American Civil War, continued to govern US practice for some 50 years, as well as influencing the conduct of other States. The Code served as a blueprint for the Brussels Conference when considering the law of land warfare. Although the Declaration emanating from

---

[102] *Advisory Opinion on the Legality of the Threat or Use of Nuclear Weapons* I.C.J. Rep. 1996, p.226.

[103] Called after its principal author, Professor Francis Lieber.

the Conference in 1874 was never ratified, its importance is evident in its contribution to the 1899 International Convention with respect to the Laws and Customs of War on Land[104] and the subsequent 1907 Convention Concerning the Laws and Customs of War on Land[105] and the regulations attached thereto. These constitute the core rules on the conduct of armed conflict in contemporary international law, and are recognised as customary international law.[106]

Essentially, the law restricts the manner of injuring the enemy by prohibiting unnecessary calculated suffering by the employment of arms, projectiles, or materials.

The Hague Conference of 1899 adopted two Conventions relating directly to the conduct of war and forbidden weapons,[107] a number of Declarations outlawing the discharge of projectiles and explosives from balloons, the use of asphyxiating gases and expanding bullets.

A further 13 Conventions were adopted at the 1907 Hague Conference. These related, *inter alia*, to the opening of hostilities, the rights and duties of neutral powers, the conversion of merchant ships into warships, the laying of automatic submarine contact mines and bombardments by naval forces in time of war.[108] The only Convention which was not ratified was the 12th, on the establishment of an International Prize Court.

In addition to the foregoing, subsequent attempts at international regulation include a Protocol (Geneva)[109] in 1925, forbidding the employment of asphyxiating, poisonous or other gases as well as bacteriological methods of warfare; a 1972 Convention,[110] prohibiting the development, production and stockpiling thereof; a 1980 Convention, prohibiting and restricting the use of certain conventional weapons deemed to be "Excessively Injurious or to have Indiscriminate Effects";[111] and a 1993 Convention on the Prohibition of the Development, Production, Stockpiling and Use of Chemical Weapons and On Their Destruction.[112] The Chemical Weapons Convention is the

---

[104] The Hague, July 29, 1899; T.S. 11 (1901); Cd.800.
[105] The Hague, October 18, 1907; T.S. 9 (1910); Cd.5030.
[106] For a more in-depth look at the laws of war see Ingrid Detter, *The Law of War* (2nd edn, Cambridge University Press, 2000) and for a synopsis of the laws of war, see, Jochnick and Normand, "The Legitimisation of Violence: A Critical History of the Laws of War" (1994) 35 *Harvard International Law Journal* 1.
[107] Hague Conventions I and II.
[108] Hague Conventions III, V, VII, VIII and IX.
[109] Geneva, June 17, 1925; T.S. 24 (1930) Cmd.3604.
[110] London, Moscow and Washington, April 10, 1972; T.S. 11 (1976) Cmnd.6397.
[111] Geneva, October 10, 1980; 19 I.L.M. 1523 (1980); Misc. 23 (1981) Cmnd.8370.
[112] January 13, 1993, 32 I.L.M. 800 (1993).

first disarmament agreement negotiated within a multilateral framework which provides for the elimination of chemical weapons under the control of an international agency.[113]

The effectiveness of the 1972 Biological and Toxin Weapons Convention[114] is severly restricted by the absence of monitoring compliance, and agreement as to what compliance mechanisms should be established.

International efforts have concentrated on tackling the devastating effects of landmines.[115] It is estimated that 25,000 people are maimed or killed by a landmine each year. Most are civilian women and children working and playing in fields. Some 100 million mines lie buried or hidden in over 62 countries and remain virtually undetectable because they contain no metal. The United Nations has estimated that present landmine areas would take 1,000 years to clear, which does not take into account areas currently being mined. An inter-governmental review conference was convened in May 1996 in Geneva, to amend the landmines Protocol to the 1980 UN Convention on Prohibition on the Use of Certain Conventional Weapons Which May Be Deemed to be Excessively Injurious or to Have Indiscriminate Effects, known more simply as the UN Inhumane Weapons Convention.[116]

Intergovernmental negotiations culminated in the 1997 Convention on the Prohibition on the Use, Stockpiling, Production and Transfer of Anti-Personnel (AP) Mines and on their Destruction (the Ottawa Convention). The Ottawa Convention prohibits the use of AP landmines and the gradual destruction of stockpiles and mines already in the ground. The Treaty entered into force on March 1, 1999. All types of conflict are covered, civil war and international; this is in recognition of the increasing use of land mines in civil wars (amendment to Protocol II of the 1980 Convention).[117]

---

[113] The Convention establishes a permanent agency, the Organisation for the Prohibition of Chemical Weapons, which will have its seat in The Hague.

[114] 1015 UNTS 163.

[115] In 1993, the UN GA unanimously adopted a resolution calling for a moratorium on the export of landmines A/Res/48/75K, November 1993. Other resolutions passed by the UN in 1993 were, *inter alia*—strengthening of UN assistance to mine clearance efforts (A/Res/48/7) and additional protection of children against the effects of mines (A/Res/48/157).

[116] UN Doc. A/Conf. 95/15. There are four Protocols to the Convention. Protocol II, which deals with Prohibitions or Restrictions on the Use of Mines, Booby Traps and Other Devices, was reviewed at the conference in 1996 and amended on May 3, 1996.

[117] The Organisation of American States (OAS) also adopted a resolution which provides for the establishment of a continent-wide zone free of all landmines at its 26th General Assembly in Panama City in June 1996. The resolution asks states to declare a moratorium on the production, use and transfer of all anti-

Similarly to the international effort to ban landmines, concern over the civilian suffering and casualties caused by cluster munitions, as well as the dangers presented by the large scale national stockpiling of cluster munitions for operational use, provided the impetus for the adoption of a treaty banning the use and stockpiling of cluster munitions. The Convention on Cluster Munitions[118] was adopted by 107 States, and requires each State Party to undertake never under any circumstances to:

"(a) Use cluster munitions;

(b) Develop, produce, otherwise acquire, stockpile, retain or transfer to anyone, directly or indirectly, cluster munitions;

(c) Assist, encourage, or induce anyone to engage in any activity prohibited to a State Party under this Convention".[119]

The Convention has, however, been opposed by a number of States that produce and stockpile cluster munitions, including the United States, China, Russia, India, Israel, Pakistan and Brazil. In particular, the United States has opined that the use of "smart" cluster munitions, with self-destruction capabilities, reduces the problems related to unexploded cluster munitions.

NUCLEAR WEAPONS

The control of nuclear weapons has been on the international agenda since the 1960s. The following is limited to identifying the principal instruments adopted.

Major agreements on nuclear weapons

Multilateral

Limited Test Ban Treaty (LTBT) 1963.[120] This treaty prohibits nuclear tests in the atmosphere, in outer space and underwater. Also prohibited is any such explosion by a State in any other

---

personnel mines and to ratify the 1980 UN Convention on Certain Conventional Weapons and the amended Protocol. It further provides for the opening of a register at the organisation's General Secretariat to record information on existing stocks and the mine-clearing situation.

[118] In Dublin inMay 2008.

[119] art.1 Convention on Cluster Munitions.

[120] 480 U.N.T.S. 43; U.K.T.S. 3 (1964) Cmnd.2245; 14 U.S.T. 1313.

environment if that would result in the presence of radioactive debris outside its territory.

Treaty on the Non Proliferation of Nuclear Weapons (Non Proliferation Treaty) 1968.[121] Under this treaty the "nuclear weapons parties" undertake not to transfer to any recipient nuclear weapons or devices, or to assist any "non-nuclear weapon State" to manufacture, acquire or control such weapons or devices. "Non-nuclear weapon parties" undertake corollary obligations.

Treaty for the Prohibition of Nuclear Weapons in Latin America 1967 and Additional Protocols I and II.[122] The treaty establishes Latin America as a deneutralised region. Protocol I requires States from outside the region to apply the treaty to territories within the region for whose international rules they are responsible and Protocol II requires States with nuclear weapons to respect the deneutralised status of the region.

Strategic Arms Limitation Talks (SALT I). The Strategic Arms Limitation Talks held between 1969 and 1972 produced a number of agreements, namely the 1971 Agreement on Measures to Reduce the Risk of Outbreak of Nuclear War (the Accidents Agreement); the 1971 Agreement on Measures to Improve the Direct Communications Link (the Hot-Line Upgrade Agreement) and the 1972 Treaty on the Limitation of Anti-Ballistic Missile Systems (ABM). The SALT II negotiations did not prove so fruitful as only one treaty was produced, the 1979 Treaty on the Limitation of Strategic Offensive Arms, and this was never ratified by the United States.

The 1980s witnessed the initiation of new talks—the Strategic Arms Reduction Talks (START) and Reduction of Intermediate-Range Nuclear Forces (INF). Treaties were signed, respectively, in July 1991 by Presidents Bush and Gorbachev (START I) and January 1993 by Presidents Bush and Yeltsin (START II). The emphasis is now more on reduction than elimination. On May 24, 2002, the US President, George W. Bush, and the Russian President, Vladimir Putin, signed a Nuclear Arms Reduction Treaty (the Moscow Treaty). The Treaty is designed to substantially reduce deployed, strategic, nuclear warhead arsenals by December 31, 2012. There is somewhat of an impasse, as although discussions have continued, progress on START III and START IV

---

[121] 729 U.N.T.S. 161; U.K.T.S. 88 (1970) Cmnd.4474; U.S.T. 483; 7 I.L.M. 809 (1968). Extended indefinitely in 1995.
[122] U.K.T.S. 54 (1970) Cmnd.4409; 6 I.L.M. 533–534 (1967).

remains negligible. A comprehensive Nuclear Test Ban Treaty was opened for signature in September 1996 after it received majority support in the General Assembly. The Treaty seeks to impose an international ban on all nuclear testing. However, a problem besetting its entry into force is the need for those States known to possess nuclear reactors to sign before the Treaty can become law.[123] The I.C.J. considered the legality of the use of nuclear weapons in 1996. In the *Advisory Opinion on the Legality of the Threat or Use of Weapons*, the I.C.J. expressed the view "[T]here is in neither customary nor conventional international law any specific authorisation of the threat or use of nuclear weapons."[124] The I.C.J. did not give a conclusive opinion on the use of nuclear weapons in self-defence but observed that the requirements of a lawful self-defence would have to be met, e.g. proportionality. Nor could the I.C.J. conclude definitively that the use or threat of nuclear weapons could legitimately be used in the extreme circumstances of self-defence if the very survival of the State were at stake. However, the I.C.J. found, unanimously, that an obligation did exist to negotiate, in good faith, and also bring to a conclusion those negotiations that would lead to nuclear disarmament under strict and effective international control.

HUMANITARIAN LAW

The first expression of protection for the individual involved in armed conflict was the 1864 Geneva Convention for the Amelioration of the Condition of the Wounded and Sick of Armed Forces in the Field.[125] However, contemporary humanitarian law is contained in the four 1949 Geneva Conventions and the two 1977 Additional Protocols,[126] which are now largely regarded as customary international law. Sick, wounded and shipwrecked military personnel are afforded protection by Conventions I and II. The third Convention sets out the minimum treatment to be afforded to prisoners of war. While the fourth articulates the protection of civilian persons (this represented an advance, in that earlier protection to civilians had been relatively limited, being contained in the Hague Regulations and customary international law). The Geneva Conventions originally applied only to all international armed-conflict situations, but this definition was extended in 1977 to include wars of "self-determination" (Protocol I) and victims of "non-international

---

[123] Annex 2; for full text, see 35 I.L.M. 1439 (1996).
[124] Re UN General Assembly Res. 49/75K. See 35 I.L.M. 809 (1996).
[125] Geneva, August 22, 1864; 129 C.T.S. 361; 55 B.F.S.P. 43.
[126] U.N.T.S. 31; U.K.T.S. 39 (1958) Cmnd.550; 16 I.L.M. 1391 (1977).

armed conflicts" (Protocol II). The latter builds on art.3, which is common to all four Conventions, and provides that certain minimum provisions apply in "armed conflict not of an international character."[127] Specifically excluded are instances of "internal disturbances and tensions, such as riots, isolated and sporadic acts of violence and other acts of a similar nature."[128]

Mention should also be made of the Convention for the Protection of Cultural Property in the event of Armed Conflict, adopted in 1954.[129] This Convention aims at protecting cultural objects and religious places, as well as objects designated vital to the survival of the civilian population—drinking-water supplies, foodstuffs, agricultural areas for production thereof and irrigation works (provided they are not used exclusively by the armed forces or in furtherance of military action).

Spies and mercenaries are denied the general protection which is enjoyed by either prisoners of war or combatants. Mercenaries are those who sell their fighting services for personal gain and their recruitment is deemed to be contrary to international law. See, for example, the Declaration on Principles of International Law Concerning Friendly Relations and Co-operation Among States in Accordance with the Charter of the United Nations 1970.

Contracting Parties to the four Geneva Conventions and the additional Protocols are under a duty "to respect and to ensure respect" for the provisions contained therein "in all circumstances." Article 8 of the International Criminal Court (ICC) Statute defines a grave breach of the Geneva Convention of "12 August 1949" as a war crime over which the ICC has jurisdiction. Committing rape, sexual slavery, enforced prostitution and forced pregnancy or any other forms of sexual violence is now also characterised as a grave breach of the Geneva Conventions.[130]

International Red Cross[131]

Any survey of humanitarian law would be incomplete without a mention of the International Red Cross. The International Red

---

[127] The I.C.J. decision in *Nicaragua (Merits)* I.C.J. Rep. 1986 p.3, at 114 regarding the application of Common art.3 as a "minimum yardstick" applicable in international armed conflicts. See also *Tadic* case no. I.T-94–1–AR 72 in which it was held art.3 of the ICTY Statute provided jurisdiction in respect of "violations of the laws or customs of war, regardless of whether they occurred within an internal or an international armed conflict."

[128] *ibid.*, art.1(2).

[129] The Hague, May 14, 1954; 249 U.N.T.S. 215; Misc.6 (1956) Cmd.9837.

[130] art.8(2)xxii.

[131] http://www.icrc.org.

Cross is made up of the International Red Cross Committee (ICRC), national Red Cross Societies and a co-ordinating body, the League of the Red Cross. The ICRC, which each of the Geneva Conventions recognise as "an impartial humanitarian body", has been responsible for developing much of substantive humanitarian law. Such work is evidenced in the international conference convened in Geneva in September 1993, specifically to discuss ways to protect war victims caught up in armed conflicts.[132] The Declaration adopted at the conference condemned, *inter alia*, violations of international humanitarian law and called for the establishment of an intergovernmental group of experts to "study practical means of promoting full respect for and compliance with that law …".[133] Another study conducted by the International Red Cross has identified "161 rules of customary international humanitarian law that offer legal protection for people affected by war".[134]

CONCLUSION

Force, save in the accepted exceptions acknowledged by international law, is prohibited by contemporary international law. However, a use of and resort to force is an all-too-frequent feature of the international scene. International law cannot prevent the use of force; it can only seek to regulate, and in the event of force being used provide a legal regime for its conduct. The use of force should be a last resort, as the employment of force is to turn from legal processes to an alternative, which is ultimately an untenable medium for the conduct of international relations.

---

[132] International Conference for the Protection of War Victims: Declaration for the Protection of War Victims 33 I.L.M. 297 (1994).

[133] *ibid.* at 302. The Vienna Declaration on Human Rights (1993) also confirmed: "effective international measures to guarantee and monitor the implementation of human rights standards should be taken in respect of people under foreign occupation, and effective legal protection against the violation of their human rights should be provided, in accordance with human rights norms and international law." 32 I.L.M. 1661 (1993) at para.3 for the text of the Declaration.

[134] See Jean-Marie Henckaerts, "Study on customary international humanitarian law: A contribution to the understanding and respect for the rule of law in armed conflict." (2005) 87 *International review of the Red Cross*, Number 857.

12. ARBITRATION AND JUDICIAL SETTLEMENT OF INTERNATIONAL DISPUTES

States are under an obligation to "settle their international disputes by peaceful means in such a manner that international peace and security, and justice, are not endangered".[1] However, States are reticent to submit disputes to independent, impartial adjudication and have been cautious about agreeing in advance to the compulsory jurisdiction of an independent judicial body. The majority of inter-State disputes—that is, "a disagreement on a point of law or fact, a conflict of legal views or of interests between two persons" (that is, international persons)[2]—are settled by direct negotiation. Negotiation is the primary vehicle for attaining settlement on the international scene, as peaceful co-

---

[1] art.2(3) of the UN Charter—also recognised as a rule of customary international law; see also art.33 of the UN Charter; 1970 Declaration on Principles of International Law Concerning Friendly Relations and Co-operation Amongst States (G.A. Res., 2625 (XXV)), 1982 Manila Declaration on the Peaceful Settlement of International Disputes (G.A. Res., 37/590), 21 I.L.M. 449 (1982).
[2] *Mavrommatis Palestine Concessions* case P.C.I.J. Ser.A, No.2 at 11–12 (1924).

existence and conciliation are regarded as being more important than the characterisation of one State as "guilty" and another as "innocent". The obligation to enter into negotiation was endorsed in the *North Sea Continental Shelf* cases,[3] when the International Court of Justice declared:

> ". . . parties are under an obligation to enter into negotiations with a view to arriving at an agreement . . . ; they are under an obligation so to conduct themselves that the negotiations are meaningful, which will not be the case when either of them insists upon its own position without contemplating any modification of it."[4]

However, negotiations

> "do not of necessity always presuppose a more or less lengthy series of notes and dispatches; it may suffice that a discussion has been commenced, and . . . a deadlock is reached, or if finally a point is reached at which one of the Parties definitely declares himself unable, or refuses, to give way."[5]

International agreements may require that negotiation be attempted before other settlement procedures are initiated. Negotiations as a rule are conducted through normal diplomatic channels involving only the parties to the dispute. These negotiations should be conducted in good faith.[6] Negotitations, in other words, must not be mere formalities.[7]

Other methods involving the participation of a third party, i.e. a State, a group of States or an individual, may be employed if the States party to the dispute consent. Such methods include good offices, conciliation, mediation and commissions of inquiry.[8]

Good offices

Good offices take place when a third party brings the disputing States to the negotiating table and suggests the general framework for producing a settlement.

---

[3] I.C.J. Rep. 1969 p.3.
[4] *ibid.* at para.85.
[5] Above, n.2 at 13.
[6] *Cameroon v Nigeria* I.C.J. Rep., 2002 p.303, para.244.
[7] *Lac Lanoux Arbitration*, 24 I.L.R., 101–119.
[8] All such methods are identified in art.33 of the UN Charter.

Mediation

Mediation likewise involves a third party, namely the mediator. The mediator may assume a more active role than the provider of good offices and may attempt to reconcile the positions and claims of the respective interested parties. Mediation has been employed in a number of instances, including the dispute between Chile and Argentina with regard to the Beagle Channel; in former Yugoslavia, leading ultimately to the conclusion of the Dayton/Paris agreement; and in respect of Kosovo. Suggestions of the third party do not have binding effect.

Conciliation

The task of a Conciliation Commission is to examine the claims of the parties and make proposals to the parties for a friendly solution. If agreement is not reached, the Commission produces a report containing observations, conclusions and recommendations. The Commission's findings or proposals are not binding upon the parties. Conciliation as a means of dispute settlement may be provided for by way of treaties, for example the 1969 Vienna Convention on the Law of Treaties and the 1982 Convention on the Law of the Sea. The dispute regarding the continental shelf between Iceland and Jan Meyen[9] is another instance of the conciliation procedure being employed.

Commission of Inquiry

The primary function of a Commission of Inquiry is to establish the facts pertaining to the dispute, for example by the hearing of witnesses or visiting the area where the alleged breach of international law is said to have occurred. Dispute settlement may also be initiated either in or by international organisations, for example as the Security Council of the United Nations did in 1982, when a fact-finding Commission was established following an attempted coup in the Seychelles. Specialised agencies of the United Nations, such as the International Labour Organisation (ILO)[10] and the International Civil Aviation Organisation (ICAO)[11] have also initiated inquiries. A Commission of Inquiry refers to a type of international tribunal introduced by the Hague Convention.[12]

---

[9] 20 I.L.M. 1981, 797.

[10] In respect of labour conventions.

[11] e.g. in respect of the shooting down of a South Korean aircraft over Soviet territory, KE007 Incident 1093.

[12] See the Hague Convention for the Pacific Settlement of Disputes (1899), arts 9–14; U.K.T.S. 9 (1901) Cd.798; see also the 1907 Hague Convention for the Pacific Settlement of Disputes 54 L.N.T.S. 435; U.K.T.S. 6 (1971) Cmnd.4575.

The common denominator reflected in all such dispute settlement methods is the consent of the parties involved. The success of these methods cannot be denied, however it is only by arbitration and judicial settlement that adjudication is carried out in accordance with legal principles and culminates in an award accepted as binding on the contesting parties.

ARBITRATION

The International Law Commission defined arbitration as "a procedure for the settlement of disputes between States by a binding award on the basis of law and as a result of an undertaking voluntarily accepted."[13]

The essential difference between arbitration and judicial settlement is that arbitration parties are more active in deciding, for instance, the law to be applied and the composition of the tribunal, whereas parties submitting to judicial settlement must accept an already constituted tribunal with its jurisdictional competence and procedure laid down in statute. Arbitration allows parties a degree of flexibility, which is denied to them in judicial settlement.

The idea of entrusting an impartial authority with finding a legally-based solution to international disputes is an old one, and examples of arbitration settlement were evident in ancient Greece, China and among Arabian tribes. However, the modern history of arbitration and the revitalisation of an interest in arbitration as a mode of settlement can be traced from the 1794 Jay Treaty between the United States and Great Britain. That Treaty provided for the establishment of three mixed Commissions to which both States nominated an equal number of members, presided over by an umpire. Although, strictly speaking, the Commissions were not organs of third party adjudication, they were intended to function to some extent as tribunals, e.g. the Commissions were to decide for themselves whether a claim fell within their jurisdictional competence. Throughout the nineteenth century, arbitration was frequently utilised, with each party to the dispute nominating two representatives to serve on the tribunal. In 1871, under the Treaty of Washington, whereby the United States and Britain agreed to submit to arbitration alleged breaches of neutrality by Britain during the American Civil War, it was provided that, while the United States and Britain were to nominate a member of the tribunal of five, so also were Brazil, Italy and Switzerland. The nomination and involvement of three independent States was an innovation and the Alabama Claims

---

[13] *Y.B.I.L.C.* 1953 11 at 202.

Arbitration[14] heralded an increasing utilisation of arbitration, as many treaties provided for recourse to arbitration in the event of a dispute.

The 1899 Convention for the Pacific Settlement of International Disputes,[15] adopted by the First Hague Peace Conference, marked a new era in arbitration settlement with the Convention providing for the creation of a Permanent Court of Arbitration. In 1907, following a Second Hague Conference, a further Convention was adopted revising its predecessor, but maintaining the Court.[16]

The Permanent Court of Arbitration, established in 1900, began functioning in 1902. It is still in existence, but it is neither a Court nor a permanent institution. It is rather a panel of some 300 persons (four nominated by each Contracting Party to the 1899 and 1907 Conventions) from whom States may select one or more arbitrators to constitute a tribunal for the settlement of a particular dispute. Only the Bureau of the Court, which acts as a registry, is permanent. What was established in 1899 was essentially a machinery to call tribunals into being. Since its inception, the Court has provided the mechanism for the hearing of over 40 cases, including some of considerable importance, e.g. the *Island of Palmas* case.[17]

Arbitration presupposes and depends upon the willingness of the States involved to submit to adjudication and their desire to reach a settlement. A State is not required to submit a dispute to arbitration, nevertheless consent is a prerequisite. Consent can be on an *ad hoc* basis, as in the *Canada/France Maritime Delimitation* case[18] and the *Guinea/Bissau Maritime Delimitation* case.[19] The identity of the arbitrators, the formulation of the question to be submitted to the tribunal, the rules of law to be applied and the time limit within which an award must be made must also be mutually agreed upon by the States concerned. Such issues are spelt out in a special agreement between the parties, known as the *Compromis*. The functioning of the Permanent Court therefore presupposes that the States not only have a desire to reach a

---

[14] Moore, 1 Int.Arb. 495 (1872).

[15] U.K.T.S. 9 (1901) Cd.798.

[16] U.K.T.S. 6 (1971) Cmnd.4575.

[17] 2 R.I.A.A. 829 (1928). An example of dispute settlement via the Permanent Court of Arbitration is that between Eritrea and the Yemen on questions of territorial sovereignty and delimitation of maritime boundaries; see Permanent Court of Arbitration (PCA): *Eritrea–Yemen Arbitration* (first stage: territorial sovereignty and scope of dispute) [October 9, 1998] 40 I.L.M. 900 (2001) and Permanent Court of Arbitration (PCA*): Eritrea–Yemen Arbitration* (second stage: maritime delimitation) [December 17, 1999] 40 I.L.M. 983 (2001).

[18] 31 I.L.M. 1145 (1992).

[19] 77 I.L.R. 636.

settlement, but they reach agreement on the issues which are the content of the *Compromis*.

Model rules on arbitration procedure, which were adopted by the 1899 Convention, were considerably revised in 1907. Arbitration agreements may refer to these, while others may refer to the General Act on the Pacific Settlement of International Disputes adopted under the auspices of the League of Nations in 1928 and revised by the United Nations in 1949.[20] "Model Rules on Arbitral procedures" were submitted by the International Law Commission to the General Assembly and adopted in 1958. Normally awards of arbitration tribunals are binding and will be provided for expressly in the *Compromis*.[21]

Compliance with the arbitration awards has been high. Rejection of an award has only occurred when the tribunal has allegedly exceeded its jurisdiction or has been guilty of a manifest procedural error.

The use of arbitration as a medium of dispute settlement declined, especially as disputes between States and treatment of aliens were increasingly solved by a "lump sum settlement agreement".[22] Nevertheless, arbitration has continued to be employed,[23] e.g. the Convention on the Settlement of Investment Disputes between States and Nationals of Other States 1965[24] makes available conciliation and arbitration procedures for the settlement of cases between Contracting Parties and companies of the nationality of a Contracting Party when both sides consent. See also the Iran/United States Claims Tribunal, established in 1981.[25] In 1996, the UN Compensation Commission (the UNCC) delivered its first decision concerning the corporate–governmental claims in the Iraq–Kuwait conflict. The UNCC specifically dealt with the costs to Kuwait of extinguishing the fires started by Iraqi troops in Kuwait's oilfields during the Gulf crisis.[26]

---

[20] 71 U.N.T.S. 101
[21] A dispute may be referred to arbitration for an advisory report, in which case the parties to the dispute will normally be charged with putting that report into effect.
[22] Discussed in Ch.8: State Responsibility.
[23] See, for instance, the decision of the Iran–US claims Tribunal: *Partial Award Containing Settlement Agreements on the Iranian Bank Claims Against the United States* and the International Court of Justice case *Concerning the Aerial Incident of July 3, 1988*–35 I.L.M. 553 (1996).
[24] U.K.T.S. 25 (1967) Cmnd.3255; 575 U.N.T.S. 159; 4 I.L.M. 532 (1965).
[25] 20 I.L.M. 223 (1981). For background information on these claims, see David Caron, "The Nature of the Iran–United States Claims Tribunal and the Evolving Structure of International Dispute" Resolution (1990) 84 *A.J.I.L.* 1990 104.
[26] The UNCC was established on April 3, 1991 by UN S.C. Res. 687 as a subsidiary organ of the UN SC, 30 I.L.M. 846 (1991).

Representatives from a third of the world's countries have sat on the UNCC's governing Council and all decisions have been adopted by consensus.[27]

Only with the establishment of a judicial organ by and through the League of Nations[28] was there created a permanent international judicial institution, that is, a Court in the real sense of the term, ready to function at any time. There was established an international tribunal of a corporate character before which a State could, by unilateral application, bring a dispute against another State calling upon it to appear before the Court, without the need for prior agreement to be reached on the composition of a tribunal and the questions to be submitted to it, provided, that is, the other State had accepted the jurisdiction of the Court.

The Permanent Court of International Justice (PCIJ) was the forerunner of the International Court of Justice.[29] The PCIJ sat for the first time at the Peace Palace in The Hague on February 15, 1922. The Court's activities were interrupted by the outbreak of the Second World War and the Court was dissolved in 1946 on the dissolution of the League of Nations.

THE INTERNATIONAL COURT OF JUSTICE

The International Court of Justice is the principal judicial organ of the United Nations and, as such, is an integral part of the organisation[30] with its Statute annexed to the UN Charter. Although favouring the creation of a new Court, the delegates at the San Francisco Conference wished to maintain continuity with the Permanent Court of International Justice and the Statute of the International Court is essentially that of its predecessor. The International Court adopted, without any substantial amendment, the Rules of Court of its predecessor.[31] At the last

---

[27] Kuwait was awarded $610,048,547 in December 1996.

[28] The Court was never an integral part of the League of Nations. There was close association between the two bodies, e.g. the League Council and Assembly elected the members of the Court and both the Council and the Assembly were competent to request an Advisory Opinion from the Court.

[29] Both Courts are frequently referred to as the World Court.

[30] art.92 of the UN Charter.

[31] The Rules of Court have since been substantially amended and the current version of the rules was adopted in 2000. However, the Court having looked at ways of improving its working methods and accelerating its procedures adopted Practice Directions in 2001. These Directions do not involve any alterations to the Rules of Court but are supplementary to the Rules and are to be employed by States appearing before it. This was an innovative step for the Court, designed to address the problem of a growing caseload within increasing budgetary constraints. Further measures to streamline procedures have been introduced by way of an amendment to art.45 para.1 regarding pleadings.

meeting of the Permanent Court it was decided to take the necessary steps to ensure the transfer of the archives and effects to the then new International Court of Justice. The judges of the Permanent Court resigned on January 31, 1946, and at the first meeting of the UN General Assembly the judges to the International Court were elected. The Permanent Court was formally dissolved in April 1946.

Composition of the International Court

The International Court is composed of 15 judges. The judges, of whom no two may be nationals of the same State, are elected by an absolute majority at separately and, in theory, simultaneously held meetings of the Security Council and the General Assembly. In practice, the frequent disagreement and political bargaining over the appointment of judges means the Security Council is aware of what the General Assembly is doing and *vice versa*. Candidates for election are nominated by the national groups in the Permanent Court of Arbitration or by specially constituted groups for those UN Members who are not represented in the Permanent Court of Arbitration. Persons eligible for election are those "of high moral character, who possess the qualifications required in their respective countries for appointment to the highest judicial offices, or are jurisconsults of recognised competence in international law."[32] Under the Court's Statute, judges are to be elected without regard to nationality and there is no entitlement on the part of any one State to membership. In practice, an equitable geographical distribution is sought and the five permanent members of the Security Council, save China, have always been represented.[33] Judges are appointed for a nine-year term and may be re-elected. To ensure continuity elections are staggered with five judges being elected every three years. A judge who is elected to fill a sudden vacancy holds office only for the remainder of his predecessor's term. The judges elect from amongst their number a President and Vice-president for three years and both may be re-elected.[34] The first woman judge was elected to the Court by the General Assembly and the Security Council in accordance with art.10 of the Court's Statute. Professor Rosalyn Higgins Q.C.

Any amendments to Practice Directions, once they have been adopted by the Court, are published on the Court's web site and its yearbook.

[32] art.2 of the I.C.J. Statute.

[33] China was not represented from 1967 to 1984, when no candidate was put forward. On November 7, 1984, Ni Zhangyu J. was elected.

[34] The current President is the Japanese Judge Hisashi Owada elected November 6, 2008. The Vice President is the Slovakian Judge Peter Tonka.

succeeded the previous UK judge, Sir Robert Jennings on July 12, 1995.[35]

A judge may only be dismissed from office when he/she is considered no longer fit to discharge his/her function and only then on the unanimous vote of the other judges. This has never happened. During his/her term in office, a judge may not perform any political or administrative function, nor may he/she act as counsel, agent, or advocate in any suit or participate in the decision of a case in which he has represented one of the parties involved. Nevertheless, a judge is not barred from sitting on the bench even if he/she has previously participated in an international forum when what is essentially the subject matter of the case was being discussed. For example in *Legal Consequences for States of the Continued Presence of South Africa in Namibia (South West Africa) Notwithstanding Security Council Resolution 276 (1970)*,[36] members of the bench, including the President, had been members of the Security Council when it had condemned South Africa's continued presence in Namibia. In spite of South African representations, the Court refused to withdraw those concerned.

A judge is not prohibited from sitting in a case in which the State of his/her nationality is a party. The Rules of Court do specify that if the President is a national of one of the parties to a case before the Court, then he/she will refrain from exercising his/her functions as President for that particular case. If a State to a dispute does not have a representing judge, an *ad hoc* (for that purpose only) judge may be appointed. If the bench includes no judge of the nationality of the parties involved, each of the parties may select an *ad hoc* judge. An *ad hoc* judge need not be of the same nationality as the nominating State. Cases which are conducted in either of the Court's two official languages, English and French,[37] are decided by a majority of the judges present. In the event of a split vote the President has the casting vote, which may be different from his/her initial vote. Dissenting judgments and separate opinions are published in full. Cases may be heard by either a full Court (a *quorum* of nine being sufficient) or by a Chamber of three or more judges constituted for handling a particular case or a particular category of case. The Court's Statute also makes provision for the establishment of Chambers.[38] In January 1982 the Court approved, for the first time, the creation

---

[35] She was re-elected on February 6, 2000. Judge Higgins served as President of the Court from 2006 until 2009. Judge Higgins' successor is Judge Christopher Greenwood.

[36] (Advisory Opinion) I.C.J. Rep. 1971 p.16.

[37] A Party may be authorised by the Court to use another language.

[38] art.34 of the I.C.J. Statute.

of a Chamber to deal specifically with the dispute between Canada and the United States over the Gulf of Maine area.[39] This procedure has been repeated in *Frontier Dispute* (Burkina Faso v Mali),[40] the *Land, Island and Maritime Frontier Dispute* (El Salvador v Honduras)[41] and the *Elettronica Sicula S.p.A. (ELSI)* (U.S. v Italy).[42] The Court has also created Chambers specifically to deal with environmental issues. On August 6, 1993, the Court established a Chamber for Environmental Matters pursuant to art.26(1) of the Statute. The agreement of all parties involved is required before a matter may be brought before the Chambers rather than the plenary court. The Chambers is constituted of seven judges, elected by secret ballot.

Jurisdiction of the court

The Court can hear contentious cases and deliver advisory opinions.

Contentious cases

Ratione personae (locus standi before the court). Only States have *locus standi* and may be party to a contentious case before the Court.[43] In the case concerning the *Application of the Convention on the Prevention and Punishment of the Crime of Genocide (Bosnia and Herzegovina v Yugoslavia Serbia and Montenegro)* (Indication of Provisional Measures in 1993),[44] the Court had to consider whether either State had *locus standi* in the action, as the Statehood of both countries was in dispute at that time. The Court ultimately decided that both were competent under art.35(2) of the Statute because they were parties to the Genocide Convention, which provides for a reference to the International Court of Justice on disputes arising from the Convention.

All members of the United Nations are *ipso facto* parties to the Court's Statute. A non-UN Member may become a party to the Court's Statute on conditions determined by the UN General Assembly pursuant to a Security Council recommendation. These conditions are: (i) an acceptance of the provisions of the Court's Statute; (ii) an agreement to accept and enforce the Court's judgments (that is, an acceptance of art.94, UN Charter); and (iii) an

---

[39] I.C.J. Rep. 1984 p.246.
[40] I.C.J. Rep. 1985 p.6. KJ Rep. 1986 p. 554.
[41] I.C.J. Rep. 1987 p.10.
[42] I.C.J. Rep. 1989 p.15.
[43] art.34 of the I.C.J. Statute.
[44] I.C.J. Rep. 1993 p.325.

undertaking to contribute to the Court's expenses as may be assessed by the General Assembly.[45]

Access to the Court may also be available to a State which is neither a member of the United Nations nor a party to the Court's Statute, if that State lodges a special declaration with the Court's registry accepting the obligations of the Court's Statute and art.94 of the UN Charter. A declaration may be either particular or general. A particular declaration accepts the Court's jurisdiction in respect of a particular dispute or disputes which have already arisen. A general declaration accepts the Court's jurisdiction in respect of all disputes, or of a particular class or classes of dispute(s) which have already arisen or which may arise in the future.

A State may be entitled to appear before the International Court of Justice, but no State, unless it has expressed its consent, is required to appear in proceedings before the Court. This was affirmed in the case *Concerning East Timor* (Portugal v Australia)[46] in which Portugal objected to a treaty between Australia and Indonesia. The Court was unable to exercise jurisdiction to adjudicate upon the dispute because Indonesia had not accepted the jurisdiction of the Court.[47] The Security Council can recommend, but only recommend, that disputing States refer to the Court.[48] Such a recommendation does not confer jurisdiction on the Court independently of the wishes of the parties to the dispute. A State must have agreed that the dispute, or the class of dispute, should be dealt with by the Court.

Acceptance of the Court's jurisdiction may be expressed in different ways.

Article 36(1). Article 36(1) of the Court's Statute provides that the Court has jurisdiction in all cases "which States in a dispute may agree to refer to it and all matters specially provided for in the Charter of the United Nations or in treaties and conventions in force." States need not express consent to the Court's jurisdiction in advance or in any particular form.[49] States may agree by special agreement (*"compromis"*) to submit an already existing

---

[45] States which have availed themselves of this are Switzerland and Nauru. Both are now members of the UN.

[46] 34 I.L.M. 1581 (1995).

[47] To do so would have meant the Court's deciding on whether or not the treaty between Indonesia and Australia was lawfully concluded. It was unable to do so given that Indonesia was not a party to the case. The Court thus reinforced the position it had taken previously in *Monetary Gold Removed from Rome in 1943*, I.C.J. Rep., 1954, p.32.

[48] art.36 of the UN Charter.

[49] *Corfu Channel* (Preliminary Objection) case I.C.J. Rep. 1948 p.15 at 27.

dispute to the Court and thereby recognise the Court's jurisdiction over that particular case. The Court may entertain the case once the special agreement has been lodged with the Court. Examples of cases which have come before the Court via a special agreement are the *Asylum case*,[50] *Minquiers and Ecrehos* case,[51] *Continental Shelf* (Tunisia v Libya) case,[52] *The Danube Dam* case[53] and *Kasikili/Sedudu island* (Botswana/Namibia).[54]

Forum prorogatum. Occasionally the Court has prorogated jurisdiction. This arises when at the initiation of proceedings only one State has expressly consented to the Court's jurisdiction for that particular dispute. However the other party, by its conduct, has inferred consent. The absence of express consent by one party has not acted as an obstacle to the Court being seised of the case, as consent can be implied. A letter from the Albanian Deputy Minister for Foreign Affairs was taken by the Court in the *Corfu Channel (Preliminary Objection)* case[55] as expressing Albania's consent, while consent to submit to the Court has been inferred through the acts of a State.[56] Jurisdiction may not be implied, however, from a consistent denial of the Court's jurisdiction.[57]

Prorogatum jurisdiction is rare, as States not wishing to submit to the Court's jurisdiction will refrain from behaviour from which consent could be deduced.

Attempts by one State to bring unilateral application proceedings against another State, when the former acknowledges that the latter has not recognised the Court's jurisdiction, have proved unsuccessful. The Applicant State, relying on the doctrine of *forum prorogatum*, invites a positive reaction from the Respondent State, that is a subsequent acceptance of the Court's jurisdiction.[58]

The Court's Rules, art.38(5) provides:

"where the applicant State proposes to found the jurisdiction of the Court upon a consent thereto yet to be given or manifested by the State against which such application is made, the application shall be transmitted to that State. It shall not

[50] I.C.J. Rep. 1950 p.266.
[51] I.C.J. Rep. 1953 p.47.
[52] I.C.J. Rep. 1982 p.18.
[53] *Gabcikovo-Nagymaros Project (Hungary v Slovakia)* (1997) I.C.J. 7; 38 I.L.M. 162.
[54] I.C.J. Rep. 1999 p.1045.
[55] Above, n.49.
[56] See e.g. "The Rights of Minorities in Polish Upper Silesia", P.C.I.J.Rep., ser.A, No.15 (1928); the *Monetary Gold* case, I.C.J. Rep. 1954 at 19.
[57] See *Anglo–Iranian Oil Co.* case I.C.J. Rep. 1952 93 at 114.
[58] e.g. *Treatment in Hungary of Aircraft of the U.S.A.* I.C.J. Rep. 1954 at 99, at 103; the *Antarctica* cases, I.C.J. Rep. 1956 p.12, at 15.

however be entered in the General List, nor any action be taken in the proceedings, unless and until the State against which such application is made consents to the Court's jurisdiction for the purpose of the case."[59]

Note also art.35(2) of the Rules provides the basis for the Court's jurisdiction should be specified in "as far as possible."

Jurisdiction is also conferred on the Court by treaties which States have negotiated. Many bipartite and multipartite treaties contain compromissory clauses providing for recourse to the Court in the event of a dispute.[60] Compromissory clauses are found in treaties which are of two types: (i) those designed specifically to promote the pacific settlement of disputes between two or more States and which frequently provide, not only for judicial settlement, but for the employment of conciliation and arbitration, e.g. Revised 1928 General Act for the Pacific Settlement of International Disputes 1949[61] and the European Convention for the Pacific Settlement of Disputes 1957;[62] and (ii) those on a particular subject which contain a provision for recourse to the Court in the event of a dispute arising over the interpretation or application of the treaty, e.g. the Convention for the Suppression of Unlawful Acts Against the Safety of Civil Aviation (the "Montreal Convention") 1971[63] and the UN Convention on the Law of the Sea 1982.[64] For an example of the Court establishing jurisdiction on such a basis, see the *Nicaragua* case.[65] Treaties with such compromising clauses are registered with the UN Secretariat, while

---

[59] See Liberia's application to the Court in a dispute with Sierra Leone concerning an international arrest warrant issued by the Special Court for Sierra Leone against the Liberian President (filed August 4, 2003). For an application of art.38 (5) see Criminal Proceedings in France Case Provisional Measures Order 17th June 2003 and the *Case of Certain Questions of Mutual Assistance in Mutual Matters* (Djibouti v France), judgement given 4th June 2008.

[60] e.g. *Territorial Dispute (Libya v Chad)* I.C.J. Rep. 1994 p.6 was referred to the Court under a jurisdictional clause in a bipartite treaty whereas the *Prevention of Genocide* case, above, n.44 was brought before the Court under the multipartite Genocide Convention.

[61] 71 U.N.T.S. 101.

[62] 320 U.N.T.S. 243; U.K.T.S. 10 (1961) Cmnd.1298.

[63] U.K.T.S. 10 (1974) Cmnd.5524; 10 I.L.M. 1151 (1971).

[64] 21 I.L.M. 1261 (1982).

[65] *Case Concerning Military and Paramilitary Activities in and against Nicaragua* I.C.J. Rep. 1984 p.392 at 429 in respect of the 1956 Treaty of Friendship, Commerce and Navigation. Libya's application to the Court in March 1992 was based on art.14(1) of the Montreal Convention, which provides for submission to the Court of a dispute between two or more Contracting Parties, which cannot be settled through negotiation. See *Questions of Interpretation and Application of the 1971 Montreal Convention Arising from the Aerial Incident at Lockerbie.* (Jurisdiction and admissibility) (1998) I.C.J. Rep. p.3.

the Yearbook of the International Court publishes the text of the compromissory clauses.[66]

Article 36(2)—The optional clause. States may accept the Court's jurisdiction by way of a declaration under art.36(2):

> "The States Parties to the present Statute may at any time declare that they recognize as compulsory *ipso facto* and without special agreement, in relation to any other State accepting the same obligation, the jurisdiction of the Court in all legal disputes concerning:
>
> (a)   the legal interpretation of a treaty;
> (b)   any question of international law;
> (c)   the existence of any fact which, if established, would constitute a breach of an international obligation;
> (d)   the nature or extent of the reparation to be made for the breach of an international obligation."

States are not required to make a declaration under art.36(2).[67] Declarations under art.36(2) are optional, but once the Court's jurisdiction has been accepted, reference to the Court is compulsory. Such declarations, being unilateral acts, obviate the need for agreement. The effectiveness of art.36(2) depends on the participation of many States. States have been reluctant to make declarations; 65 States have currently made a declaration under art.36(2). Declarations must be lodged with the UN Secretary-General and copies transmitted to parties to the Statute and the Registrar of the Court. States which have made a declaration accepting the Court's jurisdiction, in principle, possess the right to bring before the Court another State accepting the same obligation, while conversely it has by its declaration undertaken to appear before the Court should proceedings be initiated against it. The subject matter of the dispute must fall within the terms of the acceptance lodged by both parties, as the Court only has jurisdiction to the extent that the declarations coincide. Common ground is not always easy to find, as art.36(3) provides that declarations may be made "unconditionally or on condition of reciprocity on the part of several or certain States or for a certain

---

[66] art.37 of the I.C.J.'s Statute stipulates that in respect of compromissory clauses which conferred jurisdiction on the PCIJ, the I.C.J. is to be substituted, thus preventing such clauses from losing their effectiveness.

[67] In the *Jan Meyen* case (Denmark v Norway), Denmark invoked art.36(2), the first time compulsory jurisdiction has been exercised in a maritime delimitation case.

time." Reservations are found in most declarations and the Court's jurisdiction over a case is restricted to those disputes that States have not excluded from its jurisdiction.[68] If, for example, State A has accepted the compulsory jurisdiction of the Court as of April 2 and State B accepts the Court's jurisdiction but excludes all disputes relating to incidents arising before May 14, the Court will only have jurisdiction to hear a case arising after May 14. This would be the case regardless of which State was the applicant— that is, if State B in spite of its reservation attempted to bring before the Court a dispute relating to an incident on April 30, State A could rely on State B's reservation to prevent the Court being seised of the case. A reservation of this type is a reservation *ratione temporis*. In the case of *Military and Paramilitary Activities in and against Nicaragua*,[69] the Court held that Nicaragua (whose declaration contains no reservation) was entitled to invoke against the United States the six-month time *proviso*, contained in the latter's 1946 declaration, stating that the declaration could be terminated, but that termination would only be effective six months after notice of such intention had been intimated. The undertaking to give six months' notice formed an integral part of the declaration, and, accordingly, the 1984 notification providing for immediate effect could not "override the obligation of the United States to submit to the compulsory jurisdiction of the Court *vis-à-vis* Nicaragua."[70] In this context, the Court held that the most important question was whether the United States

> "was free to disregard the clause of six months' notice which, freely and by its own choice, it had appended to its 1946 Declaration. In doing so the United States entered into an obligation which is binding upon it *vis-à-vis* other States parties to the Optional-Clause system."[71]

The Court refuted the argument, advanced by the United States, that Nicaragua had not accepted the same obligation for the purposes of art.36(2)[72] and stated that the notion of reciprocity is one "concerned with the scope and substance of the commitments entered into, including reservations, . . .". Furthermore the Court

---

[68] Hence, the Court found it had no jurisdiction to adjudicate in the dispute between Spain and Canada, because the said dispute came within the terms of the reservation contained in para.2(d) of the Canadian Declaration of May 10, 1994—*Fisheries Jurisdiction* (Spain v Canada) I.C.J. Rep. 1998 p. 432.

[69] Above, n.64.

[70] *ibid.* at 421.

[71] *ibid.* at 419.

[72] The US argument was based on the undefined duration of the Nicaraguan Declaration.

stated that "reciprocity cannot be invoked to excuse departure from the terms of a State's own declaration, whatever its scope, limitations or conditions." The Court then reiterated the position it had adopted with respect to the effect of reciprocity in the *Interhandel* case:[73]

> "Reciprocity enables the State which has made the wider acceptance of the jurisdiction of the Court to rely upon the reservations to the acceptance laid down by the other party. There the effect of reciprocity ends."[74]

A State may, in other words, invoke a reservation to an acceptance which it has not expressed in its own declaration, but which the other party has expressed in its own declaration.[75]

Reservations most frequently exclude disputes for which another means of peaceful settlement is provided; which arose before a specific date or which relate to a situation prior to that date, normally the date of the State's initial declaration; which arose during or because of hostilities; which arise between certain States, e.g. as between Commonwealth countries;[76] which relate to matters falling within the domestic jurisdiction of the declaratory State, as determined by international law[77] or by the declaratory State itself as, e.g. expressed in United States' 1946 declaration.[78] Such automatic or self-judging reservations particularly undermine the idea of compulsory jurisdiction. It is possible for a government, relying upon such a reservation, to declare that a question in relation to the subject matter of the proceedings initiated against it falls within its national jurisdiction, and thereby seek to deprive the International Court of jurisdiction. Such a reservation was successfully invoked in the *Certain Norwegian Loans* case,[79] when the International Court of Justice discussed the French claim and allowed Norway to invoke, on the basis of reciprocity, the automatic/self-judging reservation contained in the French declaration.[80] Although the Court itself

---

[73] I.C.J. Rep 1959 p.6.
[74] ibid. at 23, quoted in the *Nicaragua* case at 419.
[75] See decision in *Norwegian Loans*, I.C.J. Rep. 1957 p.9; and judgment in *Interhandel* case, above, n.72.
[76] See the UK Declaration accepting the compulsory jurisdiction of the Court under art.36 (2) deposited July 5, 2004.
[77] e.g. as in Canadian Declaration 1985.
[78] US Declaration, August 26, 1946, 61 Stat.1218; 1 U.N.T.S. 9.
[79] Above, n.74.
[80] It was also invoked in the *Interhandel* case, but was not dealt with by the Court, as the case was dismissed on grounds of the non-exhaustion of local remedies; see also *Aerial Incident* of July 27, 1955, I.C.J. Rep. 1960 p.146. Note the American

has not pronounced on the validity of such reservations, judges in both the *Norwegian Loans* case (Lauterpacht and Guerrero JJ.) and the *Interhandel* case (Lauterpacht, Spender and Klaestad JJ.) have questioned their validity. The principal objection being that they are contrary to art.36(6) of the Court's Statute, which provides "in the event of a dispute as to whether the Court has jurisdiction, the matter shall be settled by the decision of the Court." The Court is also prohibited, as an organ of the United Nations, from intervening in matters "which are essentially within the jurisdiction of any State . . .".[81]

Declarations are generally made for a specific period, normally five years, with tacit renewal. Declarations can generally be terminated on notice, taking effect after a specified time or immediately and may also be subject to modification. Ideally, at least from the Court's standpoint, declarations should be for a definite period as a declaration which can be unilaterally terminated at any time, which provides a State, anticipating a dispute, with the opportunity of denying the Court jurisdiction.[82] Thus in 1954, Australia withdrew its existing declaration and issued a new one, excluding from the Court's jurisdiction any disputes relating to pearl fishing off the Australian coast, the possibility of Japan raising a dispute on such a matter under art.36(2) having prompted this move. The United Kingdom narrowed the scope of its declaration so as to exclude an application to the Court in its dispute with Saudi Arabia over the Buraimi Oasis (after the breakdown of the attempted arbitration).[83] A temporal reservation relating to the termination of acceptance cannot operate retroactively so as to deseise the Court's jurisdiction by reserving to themselves the right to remove on notice certain classes of disputes from the Court's competence. For example on April 6, 1984, the United States withdrew from the Court's jurisdiction "disputes with any Central American State or any dispute arising out of or related to events in Central America over a period of two years." The International Court found it had jurisdiction, as, *inter alia*, the United States could not validly derogate from the time-limit

statement in the *Nicaragua* case that the US did not intend to invoke such a reservation before the Court but that this did not prejudice its right to do so in any subsequent pleadings, proceedings or cases before the Court, above, n.64 at 422.

[81] art.2(7) of the UN Charter.

[82] See Separate Opinion of Jennings J. in the *Nicaragua* case, above, at 551 in which he considered the "most striking examples".

[83] *ibid.* on effect of Reservation 1(b) contained in UK's declaration excluding a dispute which has already been submitted to arbitration by agreement with any States which had not at the time of submission accepted the compulsory jurisdiction of the I.C.J.

proviso included in its 1946 declaration. Namely "this declaration shall remain in force for a period of five years and thereafter until the expiration of six months after notice may be given to terminate this declaration."[84] The UK Government, in its acceptance, reserves:

> "the right at any time, by means of notification addressed to the Secretary-General of the United Nations, and with effect as from the moment of such notification, either to add to, amend or withdraw any of the foregoing reservations, or any that may hereafter be added . . ."

There also exists what is known as a multilateral treaty reservation, the effect of which is to exclude disputes "arising under a multilateral treaty", and require that "all parties to the treaty affected by the decision "be parties to the case before the Court." The US 1946 Declaration accepting art.36(2) contained such a reservation which the United States invoked before the Court in an attempt to exclude the Court's jurisdiction in the *Nicaragua* case. The United States accordingly maintained that the Court would only enjoy jurisdiction if all treaty parties (that is, to those treaties being submitted to the Court by Nicaragua—including, *inter alia*, the UN Charter) affected by a prospective decision of the Court were also parties to the case.[85] The Court observed that all the "affected" treaty parties were not only free to invoke art.36(2) (all having made a declaration) but could avail themselves of the incidental procedures offered by the Court's Statute. The affected States were not left defenceless against any consequences that may have arisen out of adjudication by the Court, or their needing the protection of the multilateral reservation of the United States.[86] As to the question of which States may be affected by the decision, the Court concluded that this itself was not a jurisdictional problem and that this particular objection of the United States did not constitute an obstacle to the Court's exercise of jurisdiction.

Declarations must be valid at the time of application for proceedings to be initiated. However, the modification or expiry of a declaration once the Court has been validly seised of a case will not deny the Court jurisdiction.[87]

---

[84] The US on October 7, 1985 terminated its acceptance of the Court's jurisdiction under art.36(2), 24 I.L.M. 1742 (1985).
[85] The affected parties in this instance were El Salvador, Honduras and Costa Rica.
[86] Above, n.64 at 425.
[87] *Nottebohm (Preliminary Objection)*, I.C.J. Rep. 1953 p.111 at 122.

Article 36(5) of the Statute of the International Court of Justice provides that declarations made under the optional clause of the Statute of the Permanent Court of International Justice, and still in force, are "deemed, as between the parties to the present Statute, to be acceptances of the compulsory jurisdiction of the International Court of Justice for the period which they still have to run and in accordance with their terms." This provision's applicability was discussed at considerable length in the *Nicaragua* case,[88] as a consequence[89] of the United States' allegation that the International Court of Justice was not competent to hear the case brought by Nicaragua. As the latter had never become a party to the Statute of the Permanent Court of International Justice and, although Nicaragua had made a declaration in 1929 accepting the Court's jurisdiction, no instrument of ratification was received by the League of Nations in Geneva. Accordingly, the American argument was that Nicaragua could not and did not make an effective acceptance of the compulsory jurisdiction of the Permanent Court of Justice, and that the 1929 acceptance could not be said to be "still in force" for the purposes of art.36(2).[90] The Court responded by acknowledging that although Nicaragua's Declaration "had not acquired binding force prior to such effect as art.36(5), of the Statute of the Court of Justice might produce", the Declaration "could have done so." The Court continued by articulating the nature of the Nicaraguan's Declaration as having a "potential effect which could be maintained indefinitely" because of the fact that it had been made "unconditionally" and was valid for an unlimited period.[91]

The Court, on the basis of the potential effect argument was able to conclude:

> "Nicaragua's 1929 Declaration was valid at the moment when Nicaragua became a party to the Statute of the new Court; . . .".[92]

---

[88] Above, n.64 at 392.
[89] And considered here in some length because, in the Court's words, of the "novelty" of the problem.
[90] Above, n.64 at 400.
[91] The Court illustrated this point by stating that if the declaration had contained a time limitation provision of five years then the potential effect would have disappeared in 1934.
[92] Above, n.64 at 404. Nicaragua ratified the I.C.J. Statute in 1945 and the Court cited in favour of its conclusion official publications of the Court identifying Nicaragua as having made a declaration under art.36(2) by virtue of art.36(5), and the non-registration of any objection by any State to this being the position (pp.411–415). *cf.* the *Aerial Incident (Israel v Bulgaria)* I.C.J. Rep. 1959 p.127 where

Reservations apply only to the Court's jurisdiction under art.36(2). The Court may have jurisdiction over the subject matter in question by some other means, for example a treaty. The majority of cases come before the Court by means other than art.36(2). However, cases in which art.36(2) formed the basis of jurisdiction were the *Temple* case (1962),[93] *Military and Paramilitary Activities in and against Nicaragua*[94] and the arrest warrant of April 11, 2000 (DRC v Belgium).[95] The importance of art.36(2) lies in the fact it is the only provision which seeks to establish universal compulsory jurisdiction by an international legal body over disputes, which arise between States. The Court has highlighted a "fundamental distinction between the existence of the Court's jurisdiction over a dispute, and the compatibility with international law of the particular acts which are the subject of the dispute."[96] This has been held to be the position even with respect to obligations *erga omnes* or *jus cogen* norms. Jurisdiction remains dependent upon the agreement of the disputing States.[97]

Incidental jurisdiction. The Court may be called upon to exercise an incidental jurisdiction, that is, independently of the main proceedings, of preliminary objections; an application to intervene; and interim measures.

Preliminary objections. A party may challenge the Court's jurisdiction. The most common instance is that of preliminary objections raised by the respondent State in an attempt to prevent the Court from delivering a judgment on the merits. The filing of objections suspends the proceedings on the merits (and obviously delays any decision on the merits) and gives rise to independent proceedings pursuant to which the Court will either uphold or reject each objection. Preliminary objections must be raised and made within three months after the delivery of the memorial of the applicant State.

the issue was whether a declaration that was binding under the Permanent Court of International Justice could be transposed to the I.C.J. when the State making the declaration was neither present at the San Francisco Conference nor had become a Party to the I.C.J. Statute until long after the extinction of the PCIJ. The Court concluded that in these circumstances the Bulgarian declaration was not valid.

[93] Judgment on Preliminary Objections, I.C.J. Rep. 1961 p.17.
[94] Above, n.64.
[95] I.C.J. Rep. 2002 p.3.
[96] *Serbia and Montenegro v United Kingdom*, I.C.J. Rep., 2004, p.1307 at 1351.
[97] *Democratic Republic of the Congo v Rwanda*, I.C.J. Rep., 2006, p.632 and p.652.

Intervention. A State which is party to a convention, the construction of which is before the Court, but is not a party to the main proceedings, has the right to intervene.[98] Under art.62 of the Court's Statute, a State which considers that it has an interest of a legal nature which may be affected by the decision in the case may submit a request to the Court for permission to intervene. It is for the Court to decide upon such a request to intervene, e.g. in 1981 Malta's request to intervene in the case between *Tunisia v Libyan Arab Jamahiriya* was rejected by the Court. The Court considered that the interest invoked by Malta would not be affected by the decision in the case.[99] However, in 1990, Nicaragua was granted permission to intervene with respect to the *Land, Island and Maritime Frontier Dispute* between El Salvador and Honduras,[100] establishing new principles of intervention by third parties. In that case the purpose of intervention was identified as being that of protecting a State's "interest of a legal nature" that might be affected by a decision in an existing case already established between other States, the parties to the case, and not to enable a third State to "tack on a new case". "Interest of a legal nature" and its meaning was considered by the Court in *Sovereignty over Pulau Ligitan and Pulau Sipadan* (Indonesia v Malaysia) (Philippines intervening).[101] The Court in that case stated interest of a legal nature included the reasons constituting the necessary steps to the judgement as well as the dispositif or the operative paragraphs of the judgement. The State claiming it has the "interest of a legal nature" warranting intervention has to demonstrate convincingly that such is the case[102] and it is that State that has to discharge the burden of proof. The State has to show with a particular clarity the existence of the "interest of a legal nature" which it claims to have.[103]

Third parties are in any event protected by art.59 of the Statute, which states "the decision of the Court has no binding force except between the parties and in respect of that particular case." Provided the immediate dispute before the Court does not form the "very subject-matter" of a dispute involving an unrepresented State, the interests of a third State which is not a party to the case are protected by art.59. This was applied in the

---

[98] art.63 of the I.C.J. Statute.
[99] I.C.J. Rep. 1981 p.3.
[100] *Case Concerning Land, Island and Maritime Frontier Dispute (El Salvador v Honduras* (Nicaragua Intervention), I.C.J. Rep. 1992 p.92.
[101] I.C.J. Rep. 2002 p.625, para.82.
[102] *ibid.*, pp.117–118.
[103] *ibid.*, para.59.

Certain Phosphate Lands in Nauru (Nauru v Australia, Preliminary Objections) case.[104]

Interim measures. Article 41 of the Court's Statute provides that the Court "has the power to indicate, if it considers that circumstances so require, any provisional measures which ought to be taken to preserve the respective rights of either party." The Court can, on the basis of art.41, indicate interim measures of protection for the purpose of protecting "rights which are the subject of dispute in judicial proceedings."[105] If appropriate, the Court may then call upon the parties to refrain from any acts that might jeopardise the effectiveness of any decision, which the Court may make on the request. A request for interim protection is given priority and a decision is reached quickly. Not all requests are granted. The Court will indicate provisional measures if "there is urgency in the sense that action prejudicial to the rights of either party is likely to be taken before a final decision is given."[106] Interim orders may request parties not to take any action that may aggravate the tension between the parties or increase the difficulty of resolving the dispute, e.g. the *Case Concerning United States Diplomatic and Consular Staff in Tehran*.[107] Interim measures may be indicated to prevent "irreparable prejudice" to the rights which are in dispute, as in the *Nuclear Tests* cases[108] where the possible effect on Australian and New Zealand territory of radioactive fall-out as a consequence of the French tests, was considered irreparable.[109] The principal difficulty confronting the

---

[104] 1993, 32 I.L.M. 46.

[105] *Aegean Sea Continental Shelf* I.C.J. Rep. 1976 3 at 9; *Diplomatic and Consular Staff in Tehran* I.C.J. Rep. 1979 p.7 at 19. *cf. Passage Through the Great Belt* (Finland v Denmark) Provisional Measures, below, in which the Court was asked by Denmark to adjudicate not on whether there was a basis of jurisdiction but whether or not Finland possessed any rights which required protection.

[106] *Passage through the Great Belt* (Finland v Denmark) (Provisional Measures) I.C.J. Rep. 1991 12 at 17. Although the Court refused to indicate provisional measures the refusal was issued with an assurance to reach a decision on the merits with all possible expedition, *ibid.* at 20.

[107] Above, n.105.

[108] I.C.J. Rep. 1973 p.99, 135.

[109] Libya on March 3, 1992 requested that the Court indicate provisional measures in order "to preserve the rights of Libya." The Court found by 11 votes to 5 on April 14, 1992 that the circumstances of the case(s) did not warrant indicating provisional measures. In the *Application of the International Convention on the Elimination of All Forms of Racial Discrimination* (Georgia v Russian Federation) October 15, 2008 General List No. 140, the Court found interim measures were appropriate the Court was of the view such interim measures should be addressed to both parties to the dispute. The request for interim measures had initially come from Georgia. The Court noted in Request for Interpretation of the Judgment of 31 March, 2004 in the Case concerning *Avena and Other*

Court in respect of interim measures has been that of identifying the conditions in which measures should be indicated before the Court's jurisdiction has been established. Accordingly, the Court will be satisfied that there is, at least *prima facie*, a good basis for jurisdiction. Interim measures will only be indicated if the Court is of the opinion that it does not, manifestly, lack jurisdiction. However, such measures are only "indicated" and are not required or ordered. For instance, the Court declined to exercise certain aspects of its jurisdiction in the case of *Libya v UK* (the "Lockerbie" case) as the Security Council was seized of the dispute at that time and had adopted substantive measures under Chapter VII of the UN Charter.[110] Interim measures were, however, indicated in the *Prevention of Genocide* case, due to the gravity of the case.[111] Requests for interim measures have to date come only from an applicant State, though they may be requested by the respondent State or by a motion of the Court itself. The granting of interim measures is not a guarantee that the respondent State will comply, e.g. as in the Tehran Hostages Incident. The International Court of Justice has made it unequivocally clear that "orders on provisional measure under Article 41 have binding effect."[112] The Court continued that the Order issued on March 3, 1999 "was not a mere exhortation. It had been adopted pursuant to Article 41 of the Statute. This Order was consequently binding in character and created a legal obligation for the United States."[113] The Court in *LaGrand* interpreted art.41 of the I.C.J. Statute in the light of the Statute's object and purpose and noted the "preparatory work of the Statute does not preclude the conclusion that orders under Article 41 have binding force." Importantly, from the object and purpose of the Statute, the Court concluded:

Mexican Nationals (Mexico v United States of America) January 19, 2009, that the United States had breached the Order indicating provisional measures of July 16, 2008 in the case of Mr. Jose Ernesto Medellin Rojas who was executed August 5, 2008. In February 2009 Belgium instituted proceedings against Senegal regarding the latter's compliance with its obligation to prosecute the former President of Chad, Hissène Habré.

[110] The Court specifically declined to indicate interim measures of protection. See I.C.J. Rep. 1992 p.3. It also refused to order interim measures in the *Guinea-Bissau v Senegal* case in I.C.J. Rep. 1990 64.

[111] *Case Concerning the Application of the Convention on the Prevention and Punishment of Genocide* (Bosnia and Herzegovina v Yugoslavia Serbia and Montenegro) (Indication of Provisional Measures) 1993, above, n.44.

[112] *LaGrand* (Germany v United States) June 27, 2001 (2001) 40 I.L.M. 1069 at para.109.

[113] *Ibid.*, para.110.

"the power to indicate provisional measures entails that such measures should be binding, in as much as the power in question is based on the necessity, when the circumstances call for it, to safeguard, and to avoid prejudice too, the rights of the parties as determined by the final judgement of the Court. The contention that provisional measures indicated under Article 41 might not be binding would be contrary to the object and purpose of that Article."[114]

The law applied by the Court. The function of the International Court of Justice is "to decide in accordance with international law such disputes as are submitted to it"[115] and in furtherance of its task, the Court applies:

"(a) international conventions, whether general or particular, establishing rules expressly recognized by the contesting States;

(b) international custom, as evidence of a general practice accepted as law;

(c) the general principles of law recognized by civilized nations;

(d) subject to the provisions of art.59, judicial decisions and the teachings of the most highly qualified publicists of the various nations, as subsidiary means for the determination of rules of law."[116]

The Court may also decide a case *ex aequo et bono*—according to the principles of equity—should the parties agree thereto.[117]

The decision. A case may be brought to a conclusion in one of three ways:

(a) at any stage in the proceedings the parties concerned may inform the Court that they have reached a settlement. On receipt of this information, the Court will issue an Order for the removal of the case from its list— e.g. the *Border and Transborder Armed Actions* (Nicaragua v Honduras) case, May 11, 1992;

---

[114] *ibid.*, para.102.
[115] art.38(1) of the I.C.J. Statute
[116] See Ch.2 in which art.38 is fully discussed.
[117] This provision has never been applied.

(b) the applicant State may decide to withdraw and not proceed any further with the case. An Order for the case to be removed from the Court's list will then be made. If the Court is not sitting, the President will issue the Order;

(c) the Court delivers a judgment.

Effect of judgment. "The decision of the Court has no binding force except between the parties and in respect of that particular case."[118] In spite of the absence of *stare decisis* the Court does in fact have regard to previous decisions to substantiate its reasoning for arriving at a judgment. There would have to be good reason, e.g. the subsequent development of international law, for the Court to depart from an earlier decision if confronted with a similar case.

The Court's decision is binding, final and without appeal.[119] The Court will, however, interpret at the request of either party a judgment where there is uncertainty or disagreement as to the meaning and ambit of the Court's judgment[120]. A revision of the Court's judgment may be requested if there should come to light material of a decisive nature previously unknown to both the Court and the party requesting a revised judgment.[121] A revision of the judgment must be requested within six months of the new fact emerging and within 10 years of the delivery of the judgment.[122]

In 1985, the Tunisian Government requested a revision and interpretation of the judgment of February 24, 1982 in the *Continental Shelf (Tunisia v Libya)* case. This was the first time the

---

[118] art.69 of the I.C.J. Statute.

[119] A number of treaties provide that appeal may be made to the Court following a decision, e.g. from an organ of an international organisation—art.84 of the Convention on International Civil Aviation (the Chicago Convention) Cmd.8742 provides for appeal to the I.C.J. from decisions of the Council of the International Civil Aviation Association.

[120] Requests for interpretation of judgments may be denied, e.g. the I.C.J. on January 19, 2009 held that matters claimed by the United Mexican States to be in issue between the Parties, requiring an interpretation under Article 60 of the Statute were not matters that had been decided by the Court in its Judgment of 31 March 2004 in the case concerning *Avena and Other Mexican Nationals (Mexico v United States of America)* and as such could not give rise to the interpretation requested by the United Mexican States.

[121] art.61 of the I.C.J. Statute.

[122] For the Court's interpretation of art.61, see *Application for Revision of the Judgement of 11th July 1996 Concerning Application of the Genocide Convention (Preliminary Objections)*, I.C.J. Rep., 2003, p.7 and *the Application for Revision of the Judgement of 11th September 1992 Concerning the El Salvador/Honduras (Nicaragua Intervening)* case, I.C.J. Rep., 2003, p.392.

International Court had received a request to revise one of its judgments and only the second time it had been requested to interpret a judgment.[123] The Tunisian request was also the first combined request for a revision and an interpretation.

Compliance with the Court's decision. The majority of the Court's judgments have been complied with by the parties. There have been exceptions, for example Albania did not adhere to the Court's order to pay compensation to the United Kingdom for the damage inflicted on the latter's warships while passing through the Corfu Channel in 1946.[124] Iran also failed to comply with the Court's decision in the *Case Concerning United States Diplomatic and Consular Staff in Tehran*.[125] The issue of compliance is not one with which the Court itself is concerned. In the *Nuclear Test* case the court made its position clear and expressed the view "once the Court has found that a State has entered into a commitment concerning its future conduct it is not the Court's function to contemplate that it will not comply with it."[126]

Non-appearance however, presents a problem. There have been a number of cases particularly, in which the respondent State has failed to appear, absenting itself from either certain parts of the proceedings or from the entire case—as did the United States in the *Nicaragua* case.[127] The Court will proceed with the case if it is satisfied that it has jurisdiction and will eventually issue judgment, though it is likely to be disregarded by the respondent State, as in the *Fisheries Jurisdiction* case.[128]

Advisory opinions

In addition to its jurisdiction in contentious cases, the International Court of Justice is also competent to give an Advisory Opinion[129]

---

[123] The first application for an interpretation was in respect of the judgment given by the Court in the *Asylum* case, November 1950. The Court ruled unanimously on December 10, 1985 that the request for a revision of the 1982 judgment was inadmissible and that although the request for an interpretation was admissible the 1982 judgment should be implemented.

[124] *Corfu Channel* (Assessment of Compensation) I.C.J. Rep. 1949 p.244. Compensation was fully paid in 1996.

[125] I.C.J. Rep. 1980 p.3.

[126] I.C.J. Rep. 1974 p.477.

[127] *Nicaragua (Merits)* case, I.C.J. Rep. 1986 14. Note Security Resol. (UN Docs S/18250 (1986); 25 I.L.M. 1352–65 (1986) and GA Res. calling for "full and immediate compliance" with the Court's judgment. see also case *Concerning the Maritime Delimitation and Territorial Questions (Qatar v Bahrain)* I.C.J. Rep. 1995 p.6, in which Bahrain failed to appear, although it did indicate this in advance and submitted written pleadings.

[128] I.C.J. Rep. 1974 p.3.

[129] art.65 of the I.C.J. Statute.

on any legal question at the request of the General Assembly of the United Nations, the Security Council[130] and other bodies so authorised. States are excluded from seeking an Advisory Opinion, but they may participate in proceedings before the Court.[131] Advisory Opinions are not legally binding on the requesting body, though an international organisation may undertake to recognise such an Opinion as binding. As such, an Advisory Opinion is, in theory, a weaker statement of law than a judgment. In practice, however, Advisory Opinions have been accepted by the requesting body and any other party so affected.[132] Certain Advisory Opinions have undoubtedly contributed to the development of international law, e.g. the *Advisory Opinion on Reparation for Injuries Suffered in the Service of the United Nations 1949*[133] (legal personality of United Nations); *Advisory Opinion on Certain Expenses of the United Nations*[134] (legitimate expenses of the organisation); *Advisory Opinion on Western Sahara*[135] (decolonisation); the *Advisory Opinion on the Legality of the Threat or Use of Nuclear Weapons*,[136] which specifically dealt with the issue raised in UN General Assembly Resolution 49/75 K as to whether the threat or use of nuclear weapons is, in any circumstance, permitted under international law; and that given on July 9, 2004 on the *Legal Consequences of the Construction of a Wall in the Occupied Palestinian Territory*.[137] On the other hand, others have been concerned with more specific issues raised by the requesting body: *Applicability of Article VI, Section 22, of the Convention on the Privileges and Immunities of the United Nations*[138] (first request by the Economic and Social Council of the United Nations); and *Application for Review of Judgment No. 333 of the U.N*,[139] and *Difference Relating to Immunity from Legal Process of a Special Rapporteur of the Commission of Human Rights*.[140] In 2008 the General Assembly requested an Advisory Opinion on the *Unilateral Declaration of Independence by the Provisional Institutions*

---

[130] art.96 of the UN Charter.
[131] art.66 of the I.C.J. Statute.
[132] Note art.30 of the 1946 General Convention on the Privileges, Immunities of the United Nations, which provides if a difference arises between the UN and a member a request should be made for an Advisory Opinion by an organ of the UN and the Opinion rendered by the Court is to be accepted as decisive by the parties.
[133] I.C.J. Rep. 1949 p.174.
[134] I.C.J. Rep. 1962 p.151.
[135] I.C.J. Rep. 1975 p.12.
[136] 35 I.L.M. 809 (1996).
[137] I.C.J. Rep. 2004 p.136.
[138] I.C.J. Rep. 1989 p.177.
[139] I.C.J. Rep. 1987 p.18.
[140] I.C.J. Rep. 1999 p.62.

of Self Government of Kosovo and its compatability with international law.[141] The system of Advisory Opinions has been com-
paratively seldom employed, with the International Court of
Justice delivering fewer Opinions than the Permanent Court of
International Justice. It has been suggested that the reason for
the relatively low number of Advisory Opinions is because
the organisations eligible to seek such Opinions employ highly
qualified legal advisers.[142]

Role and future of the Court

The impact of the Court has been somewhat *ad hoc*. This is under-
standable given the Court has to wait until it is seised of a case or
requested to give an opinion. The Court, since 1946, has delivered
over 100 judgements in contentious cases, 25 Advisory Opinions
and currently has 16 cases pending.[143] To encourage States and, in
particular, developing States to seek a solution to their legal disputes through the Court is the declared purpose of the UN
Secretary-General's Trust Fund, established in 1989. The Trust
Fund makes available limited financial assistance to help defray
the cost involved in employing the Court procedures.

The Court's jurisdiction is restricted to legal disputes and
art.36(2) specifically limits the jurisdiction of the Court to "legal
disputes", but art.38(1) of the International Court of Justice's
Statute instructs the Court to "decide in accordance with international law such disputes as are submitted to it." However,
although the Court has acknowledged that there are limitations
on the exercise of its judicial function,[144] no dispute has ever been
rejected because it involved non-legal issues. The Court has maintained that to dismiss a case because the legal aspect is only one
element of a political dispute would be to impose a "far-reaching
and unwarranted restriction upon the role of the Court in the
peaceful settlement of international disputes."[145] The Court's
decision in finding jurisdiction in the *Nicaragua* case precipitated
the termination of the United States' acceptance of art.36(2), as
that decision represented "an over-reaching of the Court's limits,

---

[141] Resolution 63/3 (A/63/L.2) October 10, 2008; request lodged with the I.C.J.
October 17, 2008.
[142] O'Brien, J., *International Law*, p.667.
[143] The President of the Court advised the UN General Assembly that 2007–2008
had been the Court's most productive year in its history. The Court's case
load can be viewed at "General List" at: http://www.icj-cij.org/docket/
index.php?p1=3.
[144] *Northern Cameroons* case I.C.J. Rep. 1963 p.15 at 29.
[145] *Case Concerning United States Diplomatic and Consular Staff in Tehran* I.C.J. Rep.
1980 p.3 at 19 endorsed in the *Nicaragua (Jurisdiction)* case at 439–440.

a departure from its tradition of judicial restraint, and a risky venture into treacherous political waters."[146]

In international relations political and legal issues are intertwined, and it must be acknowledged that the decision to seek judicial settlement is itself often a political one. The Court refused to deliver an opinion in the *Eastern Carelia* case,[147] as the Permanent Court felt would be tantamount to giving a decision in a dispute. The only other occasion when the Court has refused to provide an Opinion when requested was in the *WHO Nuclear Weapons* case in which the Court found the question being put to the Court was one which did not fall within the competence of the WHO in that it concerned legality of the use of nuclear weapons rather than the effect of the use of nuclear weapons.

One question which has not yet been fully addressed but has certainly appeared in a dissenting opinion is that of the relationship between the Court and the Security Council, and the extent to which the Court may have competence to review the legality of Security Council Resolutions.[148] The I.C.J. does not have the competence of judicial review or appeal with regards to the Security Council's actions. However, the Security Council does not have unfettered jurisdiction but it remains as yet undecided as to the extent of the I.C.J.'s competence to make pronouncements on the extent or legality of Security Council actions.

However the Court, as a permanent institution, has served as a constant reminder to States that judicial channels do exist through which the peaceful settlement of international disputes may be sought. The Court's procedures and jurisdiction are known to the international community, and the growth in different mechanisms which States can employ to settle their disputes is testament to the impact of the Court. Nevertheless, the International Court of Justice is no longer the only player in the field and there has been a marked growth in the number of permanent and ad hoc international courts and tribunals. These bodies have been established to deal with disputes in specific

---

[146] Department of State File No.P85, 0009–2151, reproduced in 79 *A.J.I.L.* 441 (1985).

[147] P.C.I.J. Rep. ser.B, No.5 (1923).

[148] Dissenting opinion of Judge Weeramantry in case *Concerning Questions of Interpretation and Application of the Montreal Convention arising out of the Aerial incident at Lockerbie (Provisional Measures Libya v United Kingdom)* I.C.J. Rep. 1992 p.3. See also the case of *Kadi and Al Berakaat v Council of the EU and EC Commission*, Judgement of the Grand Chamber of the European Court, September 3, 2008, in which the European Court held that a community measure designed to give effect to a Security Council Resolution infringed the Appellant's fundamental rights, their right to an effective legal remedy and a right to property.

subject matter frequently limited geographically and temporally. For example, the European Court of Human Rights, the Inter American Court of Human Rights, the *ad hoc* criminal tribunals on Yugoslavia (ICTY) and Rwanda (ICTR), the Tribunal on the Law of Sea, the dispute settlement procedure within the World Trade Organisation (WTO) and the Permanent International Criminal Court. In the final analysis, the future role of judicial settlement does not lie with the Court but with the States. States must be willing to submit their disputes to independent adjudication and demonstrate a willingness to comply with the Court's decision.

13. CONCLUSION

International law is often disconcerting. Why? Essentially, because it is different from municipal law, but law students and trained lawyers are guilty of approaching international law with the prejudices of a lawyer trained to deal with a mature domestic legal system.

Law is most commonly associated with authoritative institutions possessing the competence to prescribe the necessary legal rights and duties for the community within which it operates or proscribe certain conduct. International law does not fit into such a mould. This to many, and particularly the legally trained, makes international law confusing in character and disappointing in outcome as it fails to meet their expectations. The rules of international law are not yet as readily identifiable and established as those of the domestic legal system. International law is all too frequently perceived of as intrusive, a constraining force seeking to protect and preserve State sovereignty rather than setting a common global standard, which is shared, respected and mutually supported. However some migration toward the latter is reflected in the mechanisms which have evolved and are now in place ensuring, e.g. that individuals may be held responsible under international law for actions perpetrated within a national context.

Article 38 of the Statute of the International Court of Justice is a direction to the Court on how disputes confronting the Court should be tackled. It is not an exhaustive statement on the sources of international law. An established source, international agreements (international law's nearest equivalent to legislation), provides for States to opt out by way of the mechanism of "reservations". The international legal system is essentially voluntary in character. It is not mandatory. International law is not imposed on States, but has evolved as States have come into greater contact with each other and have been confronted by problems of common concern including that of establishing the boundaries of State action. International law is an expression of the need for States to co-exist. The problems confronting the international community are complex. The search for a solution demands not only co-operation, but an acknowledgement of the inter-dependency of all participants within the global community. Such an acknowledgement is pre-requisite if effective solutions are to be realised.

The concept of international legal personality is not static, and any definition must be sufficiently flexible and open-ended to accommodate those new entities now participating on the international plane. The recognition of an entity as a State demonstrates that factors other than law, such as politics, play a role in interstate relations. Lawyers must therefore appreciate the influence of politics. Lawyers, however, are guilty of over-emphasising rules of law not least in interstate relations and frequently they fail to appreciate that States are influenced and motivated by politics, and that in international relations there is, as a norm, more than one course of action available. Lawyers, should avoid adopting a blinkered approach to international law. This is not to deny that international law is law but nevertheless demands adopting approaches other than the conventional stereotype and thinking 'outside the box'. It is important to be aware of the ways in which politicians may utilise and indeed manipulate international law, e.g. to identify and accomplish goals. Accordingly, international law may be described as the politicians' "box of tools".[1]

The absence of mandatory sanctions distinguishes international law from municipal law. This, however, should not be perceived as a fault or weakness in the international legal system, but rather a consequence of the intrinsically different character of international law. The overriding aim of international law is to achieve international peace and security, not through the characterisation of an alleged offending State as 'guilty', but through the promotion of conciliation. Hence, low-key negotiations are the

[1] R. Fisher, "International Law: A Toolbox for the Statesman" (1979) 9 *C.W.I.C.J.* 3.

principal channels initially utilised in efforts to settle international disputes.

All States are in theory equally sovereign, however States do not share common ideologies . The number of independent States increased markedly in the latter half of the twentieth century, and a noticeable effect of this was a questioning and challenging of some of the traditional established rules of international law. International law is not confined to regulating the relations of a homogeneous grouping of States, but rather is confronted with bringing within its ambit States which differ politically, economically, ideologically and socially from each other—a very heterogeneous group. The challenge facing contemporary international law is to accommodate and regulate the behaviour of not just States but other entities such as international organisations, non-governmental organisations and civil society groups, multinational corporations, armed and terrorist groups and even individuals.

The subject matter of international law is not exhaustively defined, and its boundaries are not firmly established. International law is still a relatively young and developing system, which now embraces subject matter that was traditionally considered exclusively domestic.

Why are the expectations of international law higher than the expectations of municipal law? Why is there an anticipation that international law can prevent all violations of international law— when it is accepted, for example domestic criminal law does not prevent all crimes and the existence of contract law does not prevent contracts from being broken? Lawyers and laymen seem to forget that municipal law is disregarded every day and yet they base their criticism and scepticism of international law on the fact that international law is breached. Such a stance forgets that international law in itself cannot exert influence independently, but only primarily through the organs of the State. Those who criticise international law the most vocally forget that international law functions very efficiently over a wide range of subject matter every day and that violations of international law occur, predominantly in politically sensitive issues. That is what makes them newsworthy and is responsible for them receiving extensive, high-profile media coverage. Violations of international law must be seen in perspective. A legal system rooted in the rule of law can accommodate a breach of law. Compliance with the international rule of law is distinct from compliance with international law.

If the optimum advantage of studying international law is to be achieved, preconceived notions of "law" must be disregarded. The newcomer to international law must refrain from attempting to fit international law into the character of municipal law. If not, international law will most definitely be regarded as deficient. Furthermore, a guard should be taken against having too high an expectation of the international legal system. International law can only be employed to the extent that States are willing to invoke international law: international law is dependent upon and not independent of States for its use and success. However, international actors should recognise they are required to conduct themselves within a legal, and not simply a political, framework.

What international law can do is mould behaviour; it can do this by being dynamic, adapting to, accommodating and responding to different conditions and sets of circumstances. International law is a system, but it may also be conceived of as a language—a language which will not necessarily solve all international problems but which will rather facilitate the resolution of the issues which confront and concern the contemporary global community—a language which will address the needs, the circumstances and expectations of all its members. The participating members of the international community need to speak to each other, that is accepted, but to do this there must be a medium of communication—a common language which in its vocabulary includes respect for the rule of law, democracy, justice, and above all the human dignity of all individuals, without distinction. The members of the international community speak in many languages, but there is one language which is readily translated— international law. What is required is an increasing fluency in international law so it may be employed to educate and shape the conduct of those responsible for the policies of States, and those other actors which now feature on the international stage. What must be fostered is the development within the international fora of a political culture which possesses a respect for the international rule of law and reflects the truism "that united, there is little we cannot do in a host of cooperative ventures. Divided, there is little we can do—for we dare not meet a powerful challenge at odds and split asunder".[2] This is essential if the role, present and potential, of international law in the contemporary global community is to be realised to its maximum and the vision of the Millennium Forum[3] is to be realised, namely:

---

[2] John F. Kennedy, Inaugural Address, January 20, 1961.
[3] Millennium Forum was organised and convened by Civil Society Organisations and held at the UN Headquarters New York, May 22–26, 2000. See also General Assembly Resolution A/Res/55/2, United Nations Millennium Declaration, September 18, 2000.

"a world that is human centered and genuinely democratic, where all human beings are full participants and determine their own destiny. In our vision we are one human family in all our diversity, living on one common homeland and sharing a just, sustainable and peaceful world, guided by the universal principles of democracy, equality, inclusion, voluntarism, non-discrimination and participation of all persons, men and women, young and old, regardless of race, faith, disability, sexual orientation, ethnicity or nationality. It is a world where peace and human security as envisaged in the principles of the Charter of the United Nations, replace armaments, violent conflict and wars. It is a world where everyone lives in a clean environment with a fair distribution of the earth's resources. Our vision includes a special role for the dynamism of young people and the experience of the elderly, and reaffirms the universality, indivisibility and interdependence of all human rights—civil, political, economic, social and cultural"

BIBLIOGRAPHY

General texts

Brownlie, I., *Basic Documents in International Law* (6th edn, Clarendon Press, Oxford, 2009).

Cassese, A., *International Law* (2nd edn, Oxford University Press, Oxford, 2005).

Evans, M., *International Law Documents* (8th edn, Blackstone Press, Oxford, 2007).

Harris, D.J., *International Law* (6th edn, Sweet & Maxwell, 2005).

Henkin, L., Pugh, R., Schachter, O. and Smit, H., *International Law: Cases & Materials* (2nd edn, Aspen Publishers, 2002).

McCorquodale, R. and Dixon, M., *Cases and Materials on International Law* (4th edn, Blackstone Press, 2003).

Merrils, J.G., *International Dispute Settlement* (4th edn, Cambridge University Press, Cambridge, 2005).

O'Brien, J., *International Law* (Cavendish Publishing, London, 2001).

Shaw, M.N., *International Law* (6th edn, Cambridge University Press, Cambridge, 2008).

Reference

Encyclopaedia of Public International Law (Max Planck Insitute for Comparative Public andInternational Law, 5 Vol. Consolidated edn).

Specialised texts

The list of texts identified below should not be treated as exhaustive.

Alston, P. (edn), *The United Nations and Human Rights: A Critical Appraisal* (Oxford University Press, Oxford, 1995).

Aust, A., *Modern Treaty Law in Practice* (2nd edn, Cambridge University Press, Cambridge, 2007).

Birnie, P.W. and Boyle, A., *International Law and the Environment* (3rd edn, Oxford University Press, Oxford, 2009).

Churchill, R. and Lowe, V., *The Law of the Sea* (3rd edn, Manchester University Press, Manchester, 1999).

Crawford, J., *The International Law Commission's Articles on State Responsibility* (Cambridge University Press, Cambridge, 2008).

Detter, I., *The Law of War* (2nd edn, Cambridge University Press, Cambridge, 2000).

Franck, T.M., *Recourse to Force; State Action Against Threats and Armed Attacks* (Hersch Lauterpacht Memorial Lectures) (Cambridge University Press, Cambridge, 2009).

Goodwin-Gill, G., *The Refugee in International Law* (3rd edn, Clarendon Press, Oxford, 2007).

Gray, C., *Judicial Remedies in International Law* (Clarendon Press, Oxford, 1990).

Gray, C., *International Law and the Use of Force* (3rd edn, Oxford University Press, Oxford, 2008).

Hargrove, J.L. and Henkin, L. (eds), *Human Rights: An Agenda for the Next Century* (Washington, 1994).

Higgins, R., Problems and Process, *International Law and How to Use It* (Clarendon Press, Oxford, 1994).

Kindred, H. et al., *International Law Chiefly as Interpreted and Applied in Canada* (7th edn, Emond Montgomery Publications Limited, Ontario, 2006).

Roberts, A. and Kingsbury, B. (eds), *United Nations, Divided World* (Clarendon Press, Oxford, 1995).

Schwebel, S.M., *Justice in International Law. Selected Writings of Judge Stephen M. Schwebel* (Cambridge University Press, Cambridge, 1994).

Steiner, H.J. and Alston, P., *International Human Rights in Context, Law, Politics and Morals* (3rd edn, Clarendon Press, Oxford, 2008).

Wallace, R.M.M., *International Human Rights, Text and Materials* (2nd edn, Sweet & Maxwell, London, 2001).

Journals

Journals featuring articles on general issues of contemporary international law

American Journal of International Law
America University Journal of International Law and Policy
Australian Yearbook of International Law
British Yearbook of International Law
Canadian Yearbook of International Law
Common Market Law Review
Cornell International Law Journal
Denver Journal of International Law and Policy
European Journal of International Law
Georgia Journal of International Comparative Law
German Yearbook of International Law
Harvard International Law Journal
International Comparative Law Quarterly
Melbourne Journal of International Law
Netherlands International Law Review
Recueil des Coeurs
Stanford Journal of International Law
Virginia Journal of International Law
Yale Journal of International Law

There are an increasing number of law journals which focus on specialised topics of international law in addition to those which provide a more general coverage. The following examples are particularly recommended:

Human rights

Human Rights Law Journal
Human Rights Quarterly
International Journal of Refugee Law

Use of force

International Affairs
International Peacekeeping
Journal of Armed Conflict
International Environmental Law
Colorado Journal of International Environmental Law and Policy
Harvard Environmental Law Review
Yearbook of International Environmental Law

USING THE INTERNET

International law is particularly well served by the Internet. There are an increasing number of world web sites, which a student of international law would be well advised to consult in order to keep abreast of developments in the contemporary international society.

The sites identified below are merely starting points for further research, and because of this the list has been kept to a minimum, rather than extended. The Kent University web page is a good starting point; as is the United Nations web page, see both below.

WORLD WEB SITES (N.B. SITE LOCATIONS ARE SUBJECT TO CHANGE).

International Court of Justice

www.icj-cij.org

US Supreme Court

supct.law.cornell.edu/supct

European Court of Human Rights

www.echr.coe.int.

United Nations

www.un.org
http://untreaty.un.org/

Human Rights

www.umn.edu/humanrts/index.html
www.ohchr.org

United Nations High Commissioner for Refugees

www.unhcr.ch/

International Red Cross

www.icrc.org/eng

U.K. Foreign and Commonwealth Office

www.fco.gov.uk/

Sources

http://untreaty.un.org/

Law of the Sea

www.un.org/Depts/los/index.html

General international law

www.asil.org
http://www.kent.ac.uk/lawlinks/
www.llrx.com/international_law.html
http://worldlii.org
http://amnesty.org/

Electronic Journals

www.ejil.org
http://stu.findlaw.com/journals/international.html

INDEX